WHY ARE THEY LEAVING US?

Recovering the Years Eaten by Locusts

PASCHAL NWAEZEAPU

LEONINE PUBLISHERS
Phoenix, Arizona, USA

Imprimatur: ✠ Most Reverend Alfred Adewale Martins
Archbishop of Lagos, Nigeria
24 December 2025

The Scripture citations used in this work are taken from the *Christian Community Bible: Catholic Pastoral Edition.*

Published by

Leonine Publishers LLC
Phoenix, Arizona, USA

ISBN-13: 978-1-942190-74-5

Library of Congress Control Number: 2024925558

Printed in the United States of America and the United Kingdom

10 9 8 7 6 5 4 3 2 1

Visit us online at www.leoninepublishers.com
For more information: info@leoninepublishers.com

CONTENTS

CHAPTER THREE

WHY ARE PEOPLE LEAVING US?

THE ACCUSATION THAT CATHOLICS DO NOT READ THE BIBLE

CHAPTER FOUR

WHY ARE PEOPLE LEAVING US?

CHAPTER FIVE

WHY ARE PEOPLE LEAVING US?

SOME ISSUES REVOLVING AROUND THE CLERGY

Chapter Six

WHY ARE THEY LEAVING US? IMPROPER FORMATION AND EMPOWERMENT OF THE LAITY

Chapter Seven

WHY ARE PEOPLE LEAVING US? OTHER REASONS

CHAPTER EIGHT

PROPER FORMATION OF FUTURE PRIESTS

CHAPTER NINE

CHAPTER ELEVEN

LEARNING FROM THE PAST AND MAKING NECESSARY CHANGES

CHAPTER TWELVE

REDISCOVERING THE PLACE OF THE HOLY SPIRIT AND THE CHARISMS

"I will repay you for the years
that the swarming locust has eaten…"
~ Joel 2:25

FOREWORD

by Michael J. Rayes, Ph.D. Cand.

Why do lay people leave our holy Catholic Church? This question is both complicated and simple. It is also heart-rending for those who understand the true nature of the church of God and why it is so important to remain within her structure. Msgr. Nwaezeapu has such an understanding. He also has an obvious zeal for souls. This work represents his energy and the work of his heart to analyze the problems of Catholic attrition and to implement a solution.

The problem of Catholic lay attrition is complex. Msgr. Nwaezeapu carefully navigates the facets of people leaving the Church when he discusses the true mission of the Church in the world and the unfortunate reality of the drift into Pentecostal churches. The author knows there is not one simple answer, but the solution must be multi-faceted. The true answer, as Msgr. Nwaezeapu makes clear, is the Holy Spirit, who gives life to the Church and will retain people if we surrender our hearts to Him.

The multi-faceted complexity of the problem also lies in the practical Mass experience people encounter each week. The laity need better formation, it is true; but Msgr. Nwaezeapu doesn't stop there. He also directly confronts the need for better priestly formation. He also discusses the need for spirit-filled music and the appalling lack of knowledge about the Bible and catechesis. Msgr. Nwaezeapu points out in his book the U.S. religious knowledge survey published on September 28, 2010, by the Pew Research Center. This survey revealed that Catholics in the United States scored lower than the Protestants (including Pentecostals), Mormons, Jews, the agnostics and even the atheists in religious knowledge of the Bible and Christianity. Clearly, more emphasis on the Bible is needed, as well as better catechesis, but Catholics in the pew truly need help making a movement of their free will (not merely the intellect) toward Christ.

While complex, the problem of Catholic lay attrition is also simple. The reality is that no one needs to leave the Catholic Church to find Jesus, or to experience spirit-filled worship. The Catholic Church throughout history goes all the way back to Christ. With better formation, an emphasis on the Holy Spirit and a new culture of evangelization, no one would leave. Rather, they would experience spiritual fulfilment in their own parish. As Msgr. Nwaezeapu wrote, "...we need to rediscover the place of the Holy Spirit in the life, mission, and activities of the Church as a matter of necessity and urgency."

Msgr. Nwaezeapu elaborates on what is needed when he discusses the need for a welcoming environment at the parish level. He also strongly exhorts building a new culture of discipleship and evangelization in our own Catholic Church. What is the foundation for such discipleship? The author provides a detailed analysis of the "great commission" verse (Mt 28:19-20) so we have a roadmap for our spiritual journey.

Publisher's Note

Msgr. Nwaezeapu came to us a few years ago with the idea for his book and he submitted the initial manuscript. There were a myriad of delays, which were beyond our control and certainly beyond the author's control! A synod in Rome in 2024 produced some very similar ideas to those of Msgr. Nwaezeapu. However, his ideas were original and his initial manuscript featured all the chapters herein. This was well before the synod and well before any discussion of the trend of young people finding their faith to faith and conversion.

Here then, at last, is Msgr. Nwaezeapu's grand work. Please join me in prayer and hope that his detailed analysis takes root and will bear much fruit.

Chapter One

THE MISSION OF THE CATHOLIC CHURCH IN THE WORLD

The Fall of Man and the Need for Salvation

God is self-sufficient, but he chose to create mankind out of love. Created in God's image and likeness (cf. Gen 1:26-27), man was made to be in a loving, intimate relationship with him. *The Penny Catechism* puts it thus, "God made me [man] to know him, to love him, to serve him and to be happy with him in this world and in the next." In other words, man was created for God's pleasure and can only find fulfillment or true happiness in a loving relationship with he who calls him to share in the fullness of his divine life.[1] Saint Augustine captured it so well when he wrote, "O God you made me for yourself and my heart is restless until it rests in you."[2]

The Fall of Man

Before the Fall, man existed in the state of original justice or holiness. At this point in time, man (Adam and Eve) did not merely know God intellectually as most people know him today. More importantly, they knew God experientially; they enjoyed a relationship with him. God himself is Eternal Life[3] and, in being in this loving relationship with him, man possessed eternal life. Conversely, eternal death would consist of total separation from God

[1] Cf. R. SCHROEDER, *What Is the Mission of the Church? A Guide for Catholics* (Maryknoll, New York: Orbis Books, 2008), p. 15.

[2] SAINT AUGUSTINE, *The Confessions,* 1:1-2, 2.5, 5.

[3] B. MASON, *Kerygma, A Proclamation of the Gospel of Jesus Christ–Leader's Manual* (Washington, DC: The Confraternity of Christian Doctrine, 2013), p. 10.

who is Eternal Life. By choosing to disobey God in search of the divinization which, unknown to him he already had, in view of the fact that he was made in the image and likeness of God, man broke his loving relationship with God and was separated from him. Although he continued to be the image of God after the separation, he lost the likeness of God and was doomed to eternal death.[4]

In this state of original sin, neither man nor the angels nor the blood of animals could save man. As Michael Dopp states, "sin against God is infinite offence against God and we can't make up for our sins."[5] But out of love, God himself took the step to save man and re-establish the right relationship of intimate love with God as contained in the promise to send a Saviour (cf. Gen 3:15; See Rom 5:6-8).[6] This was fulfilled by the sending of his Son, Jesus Christ. So, in coming into the world, Jesus was on a mission from the Father—a mission of salvation which entails the redemption of man from sin and its eternal consequence and showing men how to live the divine life of God as his adopted children.[7]

Jesus Christ and His Salvific Mission

Jesus was an intentional missionary. During his ministry on earth, he saw himself as the "Sent One" and his Father as the "Sender" (cf. Jn 20:21). According to his own testimony, the Father anointed him with his Spirit and sent him to proclaim the Good News to the poor (Lk 4:18-19). His ministry was characterized by three main things: preaching and teaching, serving, and witnessing to the kingdom and reign of God.[8] In the Sermon on the Mount and in many other ways, he proclaimed the kingdom of God, exposed its mysteries, and invited his hearers to repent

[4] CATECHISM OF THE CATHOLIC CHURCH (CCC) – SECOND EDITION, Vaticana: Libreria Editrice, 1992, n. 705; B. MASON, *Kerygma, A Proclamation of the Gospel of Jesus Christ…, op. cit.*

[5] M. DOPP, "Relit – The Heart of Evangelization," – A Ministry 23 DVD – Ministry 23, 2015. See Session 1 – The Great Story.

[6] Cf. R. SCHROEDER, *What Is the Mission of the Church…, op. cit.*, p. 1.

[7] Cf. *Ibid.*

[8] See *Ibid.*, pp. 15-16.

and come under the reign of God. His service to the kingdom was visible in his ministry of forgiveness, exorcism, and healing. His act of witness was clear in a simple and godly lifestyle, marked by love, sacrifice, holiness, obedience, total submission to the will of his Father and his plan to lead people into a new relationship with him and with one another.[9]

In all of this, he was totally committed to his mission. He revealed God's closeness to the people and his desire to save them from their sins and sufferings and from every form of evil that oppresses them.[10] His ministry was all-encompassing, extending beyond the Jews to the Samaritans and the Gentiles. Examples include his encounter with the Samaritan woman (cf. Jn 4) and his healing of the servant of the Roman centurion (Mt 8:5-13). His salvation was for all men and women of every race who come to believe in him (cf. Jn 3:16). This total commitment to his salvific mission culminated in his suffering, death, and ultimately his resurrection.[11] It was because of this total commitment to his salvific mission that Pope Paul VI stated that Jesus was the "first and greatest evangelizer."[12]

Mission of the Apostles and the Early Church

During his ministry, Jesus discipled some of his followers and sent them out on mission as an integral aspect of their formation or apprenticeship (see Lk 9:1-6; Mt 10:5-15). Before his ascension, he commissioned them to embark on extensive evangelizing and disciple-making activities all over the world. They were to convert and make all men and women everywhere his disciples and baptize them in the name of the Holy Trinity (cf. Mt 28:19-20; cf. Mk 16:15-18). This is called the Great Commission. The mission is beyond human power and intelligence; it involves collaboration between them and the Holy Spirit who is to be the Principal Agent and Leader of the mission. Although they were to evangelize the

---

[9] Cf. *Ibid.,* p. 16.

[10] Cf. *Ibid.,* p. 16.

[11] See *Ibid.*

[12] POPE PAUL VI, Apostolic Exhortation *Evangelii Nuntiandi* (EN) – On Evangelization in the Modern World, December 8, 1975, n. 7.

people, the work of conversion belonged to the Holy Spirit. Hence, he commanded them to wait and receive the Holy Spirit before setting out on their mission.

At Pentecost, Jesus sent the Holy Spirit upon them and their lives were significantly transformed. This life-changing encounter with the Holy Spirit was to bring about a personal conviction about Christ and his mission of salvation. Led by the Holy Spirit, they were to continue his mission in the world, which is also the mission of the Holy Spirit.[13] According to William Barclay, they "gallantly faced their task"[14] to take the Gospel to the world. At first, they restricted their evangelizing activities to Palestine. There they formed a community of believers that bore strong witness to Christ by their extraordinary lifestyle, their miracles, and their works of charity, and the number of disciples multiplied greatly (cf. Acts 2:42-47). But with the persecution that arose against them in Jerusalem, they turned to the Gentile world. They proclaimed the Gospel everywhere they went and converted many to Christ.

The conversion of Saint Paul, who was a fierce champion of Judaism and a stiff opponent of the Way, as Christianity was then known (cf. Acts 9:2), was a great boost to the mission of the Church. The Good News soon spread to different parts of the ancient world and many churches were established. The commitment of the infant Church to the mission of spreading the Gospel was so amazing that in a period of about thirty years, Christianity had reached the heart of the ancient world, Rome.[15] Some of the characteristics of the infant Church that made such a spread possible in such a short period of time include the fact that it was a highly Spirit-guided community. The leaders were men of the Spirit; the Spirit was the source of day-to-day courage and power. In fact, to put it in the exact words of William Barclay,

---

[13] Cf. CATECHISM OF THE CATHOLIC CHURCH (CCC) – Second Edition, Vaticana: Libreria Editrice, 1992, nos. 689-690. Here, the Catechism, promulgated by Pope John Paul II on December 8, 1992, states that, "In their joint mission, the Son and the Holy Spirit are distinct but inseparable."

[14] W. BARCLAY, *The Daily Study Bible – The Acts of the Apostles, Revised Edition* (Bangalore: The Theological Publications in India, 1976), p. 16.

[15] Cf. *Ibid.*, p. 5.

> The Spirit was the source of day to day courage and power. The disciples are to receive power when the Spirit comes (Acts 1:8); Peter's courage and eloquence before the Sanhedrin are the result of the activity of the Spirit (Acts 4:31); Paul's conquest of Elymas is the work of the Spirit (Acts 13:9). The Christian courage to meet the dangerous situation, the Christian power to cope with life more adequately, the Christian eloquence when eloquence is needed, the Christian joy which is independent of circumstances are all ascribed to the work of the Spirit.... In the first thirteen chapters of Acts there are more than forty references to the Holy Spirit; the early Church was a Spirit-filled Church and that was the source of its power.[16]

One of the symbols used for the Holy Spirit is water. The ancients knew the importance of water so well and often commented that without water there can be no life or without water nothing can grow. Applied to the Holy Spirit, it is easy to see that when he is not operative in a person or an organization, that person or organization cannot be spiritually alive or grow in divine life. Conversely, the presence and work of the Holy Spirit in us will always give life and bring about growth and fruitfulness. Another characteristic of the early Church was that it had a strong culture of mission. It was indeed a missionary Church. In everyday parlance, one may say mission was in the Church's DNA. Sharing the Gospel and witnessing to Christ were a culture, not an exception, and that was so because the early Church was a Spirit-filled and a Spirit-led Church. What becomes apparent here is that the success of the Church in the area of mission arises more from the action of the Holy Spirit than from human calculations and efforts, even though man still has a role to play.

The Catholic Church

With a population of about 1.2 billion people[17] out of the 7.7 billion population of the world in the most recent estimate by the

---

[16] *Ibid.,* pp. 19-20.

[17] See "World Population Clock: 7.8 Billion People (2020)" in www.worldometers.info/world-population, accessed June 21, 2020.

United Nations,[18] there is no doubt that the Catholic Church is the largest and most extensive Church in the world. Historically it is the oldest Church in the world. The general claim is that it is the only Church Jesus Christ himself founded. For example, while we cannot trace the Catholic Church to any human founder, it is a well-known fact that Martin Luther founded the Lutheran church in 1521; King Henry VIII founded Anglicanism, the Church of England, in 1534; John Knox founded the Presbyterian church in the 1560s; John Smyth founded the Baptist church in 1609; John and Charles Wesley founded the Methodist church in 1738; Ellen G. White and others officially founded the Seventh-day Adventist church in 1863, even though we can trace its root back to William Miller and the Millerite Movement of the 1830s to the 1840s; William Booth founded the Salvation Army in 1878.[19] The list here is certainly not exhaustive, for we have simply mentioned a few to clarify our position and it is worthwhile to note, however, that Pentecostalism arose in the early twentieth century.

Similarly, when we consider the fact that the line of apostolic succession in the Catholic Church has not been broken since the time of Saint Peter, the first Pope, the claim regarding the divine origin of the Church is perfectly in order. What further strengthens this truth is the historical fact that the Christian Church was one until the Reformation of the sixteenth century. The name "Catholic" itself means universal. Consistent with her age, the Catholic Church has the richest history among all the Churches—a history spanning over two thousand years. Thus we can talk of numerous positive contributions in the areas of Church art, university education, Western civilization, medicine, and others.

---

[18] See "How many Roman Catholics are there in the world?" in https://www.bbc.com/news/world-21443313, posted March 14, 2013. This information is according to the Vatican figures. Latin America accounts for about 40% although the biggest growth in recent times is coming from Africa.

[19] See "The Salvation Army," in en.wikipedia.org/wiki/The_Salvation_Army; See also "History of the Seventh-day Adventist" in en.wikipedia.org. Officially, Ellen G. White, James Springer White, Joseph Bates, and J. N. Andrews are often cited as the founders of the church.

Although many of the new-generation churches often claim to be "Bible-churches" and tend to see the Catholic Church as a "non-Bible church," the fact remains that the history of the Bible in its present form (with the Old and the New Testament books) would never be complete without the Catholic Church. She did not only determine the canon of the Bible with seventy-three books (forty-six Old Testament and twenty-seven New Testament books),[20] but also was a custodian of the Bible in history. The world is indebted to the Catholic Church for the preservation of the books of the Bible (the manuscripts) during the era of pagan emperors who persecuted Christians. For example, at a period when there were no typewriters or computers, and printing was not in existence, it took the Cenobite monks to copy the books of the Bible after Emperor Diocletian ordered the destruction of the sacred books of the Christians.

One of the central achievements of the Catholic Church is the faithful preservation and celebration of the sacraments, especially the Eucharist. One can rightly argue without any fear of contradiction that when it comes to sacramental life, no church can compare with the Catholic Church. Numerous spiritual benefits are available to the faithful in the celebration of the sacraments and the Holy Mass in particular. In the real sense, each of these sacraments is a vehicle of grace which should foster ongoing conversion and transformation in the life of the recipient, provided the individual has the necessary disposition for growth. As we know, the sacraments are not magic rites. After they are validly administered, they

[20] At some point in their history, the Jews revised their canon (the 46 Old Testament books) and eliminated seven of the books for various reasons, such as language of composition, place of composition, and time of composition. Even after that, some Jewish rabbis continued to accept those books. Until the Reformation, the Christians accepted and used the 73 books of the Bible (that is, the 46 Old Testament and the 27 New Testament books). After the Reformation, the reformers rejected the seven books which they now call *apocrypha,* but which we rightly call the Deutero-canonical books. Even Martin Luther almost rejected the Letter of Saint James because of the emphasis on "works" and not just "faith alone" as well as the Book of Revelation, which he thought to be unintelligible.

still require the cooperation of the recipient with the grace that is bestowed in order to produce the necessary fruit in his life.

The Mission of the Church in the World

During the Second Vatican Council held between 1962 and 1965, an entire document, *Gaudium et Spes*–On the Church in the Modern World, was dedicated to the mission of the Church in the world. Even after the Council, a great deal has been written about our mission as a Church. Our interest here is to discuss that mission. In doing so, we hope to draw the attention of the reader to the understanding of mission in the Church both before and after Vatican II.[21]

Mission in the Church Prior to Vatican II

Prior to Vatican II, "mission was defined geographically."[22] It was always from Western Europe, North America, and Australia to the rest of the world. Then, the motivation for mission was mainly twofold. The first was the salvation of the souls of individuals through the administration of the Sacrament of Baptism, while the second was the establishment of the Church in "mission lands."[23] Scripture states in Mark 16:16 that, "The one who believes in it [the Gospel] and is baptized will be saved; the one who refuses to believe is condemned." As Roger Schroeder observes, the understanding of this statement in a narrow sense by many missionaries motivated them to baptize as many people as possible.

This belief was reinforced by the statement that "there is no salvation outside the Church" often attributed to Cyprian of Carthage.[24] Saint Cyprian had described the "Church as a great ark

---

[21] To help the reader comprehend mission in the Church before and after Vatican II, I shall focus more on the work by Roger Schroeder in his book, *What Is the Mission of the Church?*

[22] R. SCHROEDER, *What Is the Mission of the Church*..., op. cit., p. 106.

[23] See *Ibid.*, p. 90.

[24] *Ibid.* The Church did not teach that there is no salvation outside the Church in the narrow sense. On the contrary, she believes in God's goodwill to save others who through no fault of theirs do not come to believe

or ship which holds sinners as well as saints and martyrs, yet is the only place where salvation could be found in a dying, pagan world."[25] In actual fact, the Church did not hold the view "there is no salvation outside the Church" in the narrow sense in which some tend to view it. On the contrary, *Lumen Gentium* states that those who have not yet received the Gospel are related in various ways to the people of God. God's plan of salvation includes the Jews and the Muslims who acknowledge the Creator, those who in shadows and images sincerely seek the unknown God, and those who through no fault of theirs do not know the Gospel of Christ or his Church, but sincerely seek God and, moved by grace, strive to carry out his will as it is known to them according to the dictates of conscience.[26] Nevertheless, as a result of the narrow understanding of Matthew 16:16, the emphasis of some missionaries was clearly on baptism in order to save as many souls as possible. A good example of such great figures in history that did a lot in this area was Saint Francis Xavier who baptized about 700,000 people.[27]

The second thing which motivated missionaries to do mission or engage in intensive missionary work outside the Western world in pre-Vatican II times was what Schroeder describes as the ethnocentric evaluation of the Western culture. In fact, the ethnocentric theology of the West portrayed their culture as Christian and as a superior culture to all other cultures in the world. According to him,

> The second motivation for mission, of establishing the visible Church was rooted in an ethnocentric evaluation of Western Culture as Christian and superior to other cultures. *Ethnocentric* (from the Greek word *ethnos,* "nation" or "people") refers to the almost universal human tendency to evaluate the world from a perspective centered on

---

in the Gospel.

[25] See A. SCHRECK, *The Compact History of the Catholic Church.* (Ann Arbor, Michigan: Servant Books, 1987), p. 22.

[26] SECOND VATICAN COUNCIL, *Lumen Gentium* (LG)–On the Dogmatic Constitution on the Church of the Second Vatican Council, November 21, 1964, n. 16.

[27] R. SCHROEDER, *What Is the Mission of the Church…, op. cit.,* p. 91.

> one's own cultural or national outlook. Even though there was great diversity in Christian history, Western Catholicism seems to have lost consciousness of that variety. From 1492 onward, many Western missionaries saw themselves as ambassadors of a higher Western Christian civilization.... This ethnocentric model of mission can also be called Christendom model, a vision of Christianity rooted in the ideals of medieval Christendom whereby only Christians were considered full members of society. But the truth is that no people or tribe can legitimately claim to be superior over others and no culture can truly claim to be fully Christian.[28]

Highlighting this same problem, the writer of the introduction to the *Christian Community Bible* maintains,

> In those days which may seem remote to us, the Churches of Europe already accumulated centuries of tradition; they had their culture, their own way of thinking about the faith and of living the Gospel. It was very difficult for people of that time to understand people of another culture and to pass the Gospel on to them in such a way that they could organize themselves into a Church suited to their own temperament and according to their own way of thinking. It is the main reason why the mission which the Church established in these distant places did not prosper and the Church became identified with European Christianity.[29]

The emphasis here is that the failure of the early missionaries to understand and recognize the local cultures and religions of the natives in the mission territories presented the faith with a major challenge. While in Africa they baptized many people, this did not mean that they succeeded in converting the depth of their hearts. In many parts of Asia, especially China and India, the story was no different as they could only convert the minorities except in

---

[28] *Ibid.*

[29] *Christian Community Bible: Catholic Pastoral Edition* (CCB). (Quezon City, Philippines: Claretian Publications, 2004), p. 22.

some parts of India and Vietnam. Similarly, in the Americas the Spaniards mostly destroyed the culture of the indigenous nations. Although these peoples did not resist the faith, the problem was that "under a thin layer of Catholic practices, the native people preserved their pagan beliefs. Most of them did not encounter Christ, nor did they convert to his message in a meaningful way."[30]

Nevertheless, these two elements we discussed above, the salvation of the souls of individuals through the administration of baptism and the ethnocentric evaluation of the Western culture, were the primary motivations for the wide-scale missions by some Western missionaries in other parts of the world in pre-Vatican II times. But as we shall see, a number of things changed with the coming of Vatican II.

The Kerygmatic Movement of the 1950s

The strong emphasis on evangelization in the Church today has a connection with the theology and activities of the kerygmatic movement which flourished in the 1950s. The movement was led by some great Australian theologians, especially Josef Jungmann and Johannes Hofinger, who sought the renewal of religious education in the Church. Their approach was clearly kerygmatic which explains the designations—the *kerygmatic movement* and *kerygmatic theologians.*

The major interest of the kerygmatic theologians was to lead people to a personal encounter with the Jesus of the Gospels. They considered such an encounter to be critical to authentic Christian living, verifiable in the imitation of Christ and the example of the early Christians in the Bible.[31] They placed a strong emphasis on the salvation message (the kerygma) over the former doctrinal approach as the way to achieve this.[32] Thus, they insisted on the need

[30] *Ibid.*

[31] See S. HAHN, *Evangelizing Catholics, A Mission Manual for the New Evangelization* (Huntington, Indiana: Our Sunday Visitor, Inc., 2014), p. 19.

[32] See "The Journey of Religious Education in Australia, The Kerygmatic Approach," in https://sites.google.com/site/reprofessionalresource/the-kerygmatic-approach, accessed 2020.

to address the salvific message (the Good News) directly to people because such simple, direct, and effective proclamation of the fundamental message of Christianity will put the hearers in direct contact with the Christ of the Gospel and get them to make a personal response to him and give their lives to him.[33]

In view of this, they challenged priests to lead the baptized to a more intimate encounter with Christ by exposing them to the living Word of God. Importantly, they wanted the Church to recover the new Testament kerygma preached by the Apostles, especially in the Acts of the Apostles, and make the Gospel more central in the area of teaching, preaching, and living, rather than just catechizing the faithful on the moral law or the saints.[34] Although they did not reject catechism, they favoured the kerygma as absolutely necessary to stimulate the awareness of young people and their understanding before any memorization of Catholic doctrines.[35]

Mission in the Second Vatican Council

The Second Vatican Council took place at the Vatican from 1962 to 1965. Although Pope John XXIII convened it in 1962, it was Pope Paul VI who concluded it, following the death of the former. Interestingly, the position and goals of the kerygmatic movement influenced some of the discussions at the Council. Their influence accounts for the changes we see both in the use of certain terms and the emphasis put on them. More specifically, the terms *Gospel* and *evangelization* came to receive greater attention in the documents of Vatican II. While Vatican I used the term *Gospel* only once, Vatican II mentioned it 157 times. Again, while the term denoting *evangelization* or the verb *to evangelize* was not mentioned in the former, Vatican II mentions *evangelization* 31 times and the verb *to evangelize* 18 times.[36]

These facts clearly indicate a significant shift of emphasis both in language and in the focus of the Church as far as her mission is

[33] See S. HAHN, *Evangelizing Catholics…*, *op. cit.*, p. 19.

[34] See *Ibid.*, p.18.

[35] See "The Journey of Religious Education in Australia, The Kerygmatic Approach…, *op. cit.*

[36] See S. HAHN, *Evangelizing Catholics…*, *op. cit.*, p. 19.

concerned.[37] Drawing from the writings of the kerygmatic movement and Vatican II, Pope Paul VI made evangelization a critical focus of his pontificate. Other popes after him followed suit in placing critical emphasis on mission as the nature and vocation of the Church, while calling upon all the faithful to participate in her evangelizing mission.

In general, the outcome of the Second Vatican Council brought about some significant changes in the Church. Here, there were three major shifts that defined the Church's new understanding of mission as a participation in the mission of God himself.[38] These are discussed below.

The first is the understanding of the Holy Trinity as the centre and origin of mission. The Trinity is the origin and the end of the Church and every Christian. Here, mission came to be redefined as God's mission that cannot be limited to any geographical boundaries defined by human beings as was the case in the past.[39] Mission begins with the Father who calls the entire humanity to the fullness of God's life both as individuals and as a gathered people. The mission of God breaks into human history in the incarnation and the mission of the Son. The same mission continues in the world through the Spirit.[40] Thus, in this understanding of mission, the Church, since it has its foundation in the Trinity, is to be in communion with God's triune life and its life and mission should be a visible sign and instrument of God's presence in all of creation.[41] If God as a "Sender" is missionary, then the Church is also by nature missionary. This insight led to an important shift in the Church's understanding and practice of mission. With this, the Church

---

[37] See *Ibid.,* p. 19.

[38] R. SCHROEDER, *What Is the Mission of the Church…, op. cit.,* p. 92.

[39] See *Ibid.,* pp. 106-107.

[40] Cf. VATICAN COUNCIL II, *Ad Gentes* (AG) – On the Missionary Activity of the Church, promulgated by Pope Paul VI on 7 December 1965, n. 4; See R. SCHROEDER, *What Is the Mission of the Church…, op. cit.,* p. 92.

[41] *Ibid.,* p. 93.

moves from "having missions" to "being missionary by nature"[42] or to "mission having the Church."

The second shift is the clarification of the Church's role. The primary image of the Church on earth from the various descriptions of the Church in *Lumen Gentium* is that of the Church as the pilgrim people of God.[43] Although the Church is holy,[44] the people of God are far from being a perfect society without any fault. This actually portrays the Church as a gathered people striving towards perfection or the reign of God. Nevertheless, the Church remains a universal sacrament of salvation[45] whose mission in the world is to proclaim and witness to the reign of God.[46]

The third shift is the clarification in understanding of other religions. The Church recognized the presence of God in other religions in a way that is known to God himself who offers all access to the riches of grace that come from the Paschal mystery of Christ's life, death, and resurrection.[47] Nevertheless, while Christians were to dialogue prudently and collaborate with the adherents of other religions,[48] the Council states that "salvation is for all, and Chris-

---

[42] R. SCHREITER, "Changes in Roman Catholic Church Attitudes toward Proselytism and Mission" in J. SCHERER–S. BEVANS, ed., *New Directions in Mission and Evangelization 2* (Mary Knoll, NY: Orbis Books), pp. 113–125. See p. 117. Cited also by R. SCHROEDER, *What Is the Mission of the Church…, op. cit.,* p. 93.

[43] When we speak of the Church beyond this earth it also includes the suffering and triumphant people of God.

[44] See A. SCHRECK, *The Compact History of the Catholic Church, op. cit.,* pp. 10-11. Oftentimes, we describe the Church as "holy." This is not to be understood in the sense of being a perfect Church. As Schreck explains, we need to note that "holy" literally means "set apart." In reality, the Church is made up of saints and sinners and yet it is holy, not because of its own perfection or merits, but because it is a gathered people whom God has set apart, consecrated, and chosen to receive his mercy.

[45] Cf. *LG* 1.

[46] Cf. *LG* 5; Cf. R. SCHROEDER, *What Is the Mission of the Church…, op. cit.,* p. 93.

[47] Cf. *GS* 22; See R. SCHROEDER, *What Is the Mission of the Church…, op. cit.,* p. 94.

[48] Cf. SECOND VATICAN COUNCIL, *Nostra Aetate*–In our Time, A

tians are to live and proclaim their faith."[49] Just as "the Church needs to acknowledge and esteem the seeds of the word in other religions,"[50] she must do so without losing sight of her own responsibility to proclaim, serve, and witness to the kingdom of God in the world.

Motivation for Mission and the Duty to Proclaim Christ

God created man out of love to be in communion with him. After the Fall, his desire that all men should be saved and come to the knowledge of the truth (cf. 1 Tim 2:4) was borne out of love. This same love moved him to send his only begotten Son to save the world (cf. Jn 3:16) and bring mankind into relationship and to the fullness of life with him. So, this unconditional love of God is the primary motivation for mission. In fact, it is what creates a mission for the Church and every Christian. Put differently, we can say that, just as God's love for us is the reason for his missionary action in the world, similarly, our own love for him and the salvation of his people should be the primary motive for mission in the Church and among all Christians. This participation in mission allows the Church and each of her members to flow with God's vision and plan for his world, to continue the mission of Jesus in the world and to cooperate with the missionary action of the Holy Spirit in every age.

Although the Church, as we said, acknowledges God's presence in other religions, this does not in any way free her from fulfilling her own mission to proclaim Christ. As Bevans and Schroeder assert, "mission is the basic and most urgent task of the Church… because to be Christian is to become part of God's life and God's vision for the world."[51] More importantly, Pope John Paul II reminds

---

Declaration on the Relation of the Church to Non-Christian Religions (NA); Promulgated by Pope Paul VI on 28 October 1965.

[49] See R. SCHROEDER, *What Is the Mission of the Church…, op. cit.*, p. 94.

[50] See *EN* 53; See R. SCHROEDER, *What Is the Mission of the Church…, op. cit.*, p. 103.

[51] S. BEVANS–R. SCHROEDER, *Constants in Context: A Theology of*

us that, "Christ is the one Saviour of all, the only one able to reveal God and lead to God."[52] Thus, this leaves the Church and the Christian with no option than to proclaim Christ to all. In fact, as "the Universal Sacrament of Salvation,"[53] the Church has this basic obligation to God and to man and cannot deprive mankind the opportunity of hearing the Gospel and meeting Christ. Put differently, *missionlessness* on the part of the Church or the Christian is not an option, but always a grave omission. Every man or woman has a right to hear the saving Gospel of Christ or to "the fullness of truth" in Christ, and this creates a duty for the Church and each of her members to forever be on mission everywhere.[54]

Sadly, there are several misconceptions about mission and who should go on mission among Catholics. In the past, it was believed that lay people only shared in the mission of the clergy. The implication was that they left mission to the ordained ministers. Up until now, this understanding of who should go on mission has not changed among the vast majority of Catholics. Most lay people do not understand that they, just as the clergy, share in the mission of Christ and his Church and are therefore, missionaries. This misconception probably arises from a wrong understanding of the "Church" as referring to the "hierarchy" or the "clergy" rather than the entire people of God. As such, they still consider the work of evangelization as the responsibility of the bishops, priests, and the deacons, even though many Church documents have clarified the issue.[55]

Mission for Today (Mary Knoll NY: Orbis Books, 2004), p. 303; Also cited in R. SCHROEDER, *What Is the Mission of the Church…, op. cit.,* p. 102.

[52] JOHN PAUL II, Encyclical *Redemptoris Missio* (RM) – On the Permanent Validity of the Church's Missionary Mandate, 7 December 1990, 5.

[53] *LG* 48.

[54] Cf. S. BEVANS – R. SCHROEDER, "Constants in Context…, *op. cit.,* p. 324; Also cited in R. SCHROEDER, *What Is the Mission of the Church…, op. cit.,* p. 103.

[55] Most of our lay people in Nigeria hardly read the documents of the Church. Besides the fact that most Nigerians do not have a reading culture, the problem is partly that of the ordained ministers who fail to study these documents with them.

According to the official teaching of the Church, the Church is the people of God and the mission of the Church belongs to all her baptized members. According to the Fathers of the Second Vatican Council in *Ad Gentes,* "the whole Church is missionary, and the work of evangelization is the basic duty of the people of God."[56] Pope Paul VI states that the mission of evangelization is a task for the whole Church and "the work of each member is important for the whole."[57] In like manner, Saint Pope John Paul II reminds every Catholic that "the missionary activity is a matter for all Christians, dioceses and parishes, Church institutions and associations."[58] In particular, lay people can no longer take the back seat as if they are not involved in mission. Their baptism is a basis for participation in the Church's mission.

In his writing, Pope Paul VI goes on to describe an essential role of the laity in mission. It is to permeate the world and temporal affairs and the family with the spirit of Christ and the light of his Gospel.[59] From all this, it is clear that the mission of evangelization is not exclusive to a chosen few in the Church. Rather, it is a shared responsibility for every Catholic everywhere. Put differently, if the Church (that is, the universal or local Church) is missionary by nature, then it can also be said that every baptized person or Catholic or association in the Church or the Christian family is also missionary by nature and has an important vocation to be forever on mission. On her own part, the Church has a serious responsibility to bring her members to a new level of consciousness regarding mission in general and their specific role in mission.

---

[56] *AG* 35.

[57] *EN* 15.

[58] *RM* 2.

[59] See *EN* 71.

Chapter Two

THE DRIFT OF CATHOLICS TO PENTECOSTAL CHURCHES

The Drift from the Catholic Church

Sometime in 1987, some high-ranking Church officials in a particular province met in one of the cities in Nigeria. During their interaction with the students of a major seminary, a young seminarian in his second-year philosophy raised a serious concern about the drift of Catholics to Pentecostal churches.[60] The response by one of the clerics was that people were not leaving the Church. On the contrary, more people were coming into the Catholic Church, implying that we were experiencing growth in numbers.

The Denials

In the last thirty years, Nigeria has witnessed a high-scale proliferation of churches. At the time of writing, the exact number of Pentecostal churches in Nigeria is not even known. What is clear is that they are in every nook and cranny of our major cities as well as our villages. Some of them are established and are almost everywhere, while others are small and appear to be restricted to certain areas or parts of the country. That is not even the primary issue here. Our major concern here is whether or not many of our Catholics are leaving the Church to join them and, if it is so, why are they leaving?

[60] The drift was quite noticeable then, although the situation was not exactly what it is today. But the significant thing here is that a young seminarian was able to see what the high-ranking clerics could not see or chose to deny. Perhaps, the situation would have been nipped in the bud and things would have been different today if the "right people" were able to see what he saw or did not deny what was seemingly obvious.

For a long time, many Catholics—lay, clergy, and the hierarchy—were in denial as to whether or not a significant number of the faithful were leaving the Church for the Pentecostal churches. But in spite of the denials, there is clear and strong evidence that we are losing people to them, which makes the statement that people are returning to the Catholic Church unrealistic. Even though it is true that some Catholics are returning and a few non-Catholics are joining us, the fact is that Matthew Warner's observation about the Church in the United States in his blog is equally applicable to the Church in Nigeria. According to him, "for every one person who joins the Church more than six are still drifting out the back door."[61]

A Glimpse of the Situation in America

A recent survey by Pew Research Center in the US shows that about half (52%) of Americans raised as Catholics have abandoned the Catholic faith or left the Church at one point or the other.[62] According to the survey by Public Religion Research Institution, the number of this group of "former Catholics" is about 15% of the American population. Most of those in this group are mainly in Protestant churches, other Christian denominations, even non-Christian denominations, or have given up religion altogether. Pew Research Center found that about 89% of those former Catholics do not have any intention of returning to Catholicism.[63]

---

[61] See M. WARNER, "Why the world doesn't take Catholicism seriously" in https://cgcatholic.org.au/my-family-my-faith/blog/why-the-world-doesn-t-take-catholicism-seriously/. Nevertheless, we should note that the figure cited for the Church in America is not exactly the same with Nigeria.

[62] See C. MURPHY, "Half of U.S. adults raised Catholic have left the church at some point" in https://www.pewresearch.org/fact-tank/2015/09/15/half-of-u-s-adults-raised-catholic-have-left-the-church-at-some-point/.

[63] See PEW RESEARCH CENTER, "America's Changing Religious Landscape," May 12, 2015, in https://www.pew forum.org/2015/05/12/americas-changing-religious-landscape/. See also ANTONIA BLUMBERG, Associate Religion Editor, The Huffington Post, posted 13/09/2015; Cf. S. WEDDEL, *Forming Intentional Disciples* (Huntington, Indiana: Our Sunday Visitor, Inc., 2012), p. 16.

Another report from Pew Research is that out of the Americans who were raised Catholic, only about 30% of them are still practising Catholics who go to Mass at least once a month. While another 38% still hold on to their Catholic identity in spite of not attending Mass. Again, the remaining 32% (almost one-third of all adults who were raised Catholic in the United States) have left the Church altogether and do not regard themselves as Catholic anymore.[64]

In general, the loss of members in the United States is not restricted to the Catholic Church alone. In fact, the fastest-growing religious demographic in the US is the "unaffiliated" who are also known as the "nones" and those who make up this group are from the different denominations.[65] Nevertheless, the reality on the ground is that the Catholic Church is one of the worst hit by this phenomenon. While about 10% of Catholic adults in the US left the Church, only about 2.6% (which is only a quarter of that number) entered the Church. In comparison, 11% of adult Protestants left Protestantism while about 8.4% joined them. The "unaffiliated" gained about 12.7% while about 3.9% left them.[66]

As Weddell reveals, the only religious groups in the US that matched the growth rate of the "unaffiliated" is non-denominational Evangelicals.[67] The most important reason cited by former Catholics who left to join the Protestants, especially the Evangelicals, is that their "spiritual needs were not being met" in the Catholic Church.[68] What is generally clear from all this is that the Catholic Church in the US is losing members rather than gaining members, a situation that is certainly not heart-warming and which true and faithful shepherds need to address as a matter of urgency.

---

[64] See PEW RESEARCH CENTER, "U.S. Religious Landscape Survey: Religious Beliefs and Practices," June 1, 2008, https://www.pewresearch.org/religion/2008/06/01/u-s-religious-landscape-survey-religious-beliefs-and-practices/. Also cited in S. WEDELL, *Forming Intentional Disciples,* (Huntington, Indiana: Our Sunday Visitor, Inc., 2012), p. 24.

[65] *Ibid.,* p. 19.

[66] *Ibid.,* p. 26.

[67] *Ibid.,* pp. 26-27.

[68] *Ibid.,* p. 29.

The Situation in Nigeria and the Denial of Reality

Although in Nigeria, there are no studies or clear statistics in this area, the truth is that the spread of Pentecostalism in the last thirty years has been phenomenal and the victims have been the traditional churches. What is more worrisome is that we still do not have an answer to this reality as a Church. The fact that we, as a Church, have not carried out an official investigation to find out why we are losing our members to them, and then devise a well-thought-out strategy to address and reverse the trend and forestall any future occurrence, is a reflection of a poor attitude towards mission within the Church. Speaking with particular reference to the administration of the Sacrament of Penance, Pope John Paul II writes,

> Moreover, all priests with faculties to administer the Sacrament of Penance are always to show themselves wholeheartedly disposed to administer it whenever the faithful make a reasonable request. An unwillingness to welcome the wounded sheep, and even to go out to them in order to bring them back into the fold, would be a sad sign of a lack of pastoral sensibility in those who, by priestly Ordination, must reflect the image of the Good Shepherd.[69]

No doubt, one can confidently apply the above to our poor attitude to the issue of Catholics who are leaving the Church either to join other Churches or because they no longer believe in God or the Church. In fact, the unwillingness to go after them in order to bring them back to the fold is always "a sad sign of a lack of pastoral sensibility" among the clergy and lay leaders, and it does not reflect the image of Christ the Good Shepherd who was always willing to go out in search of the lost sheep.

While some of us may be living in denial because our Churches are full on Sundays, we should not ignore the experiences of some churches in other parts of the world as regards the drift of Catholics to Pentecostal churches, whether the Evangelicals or charismatics.

---

[69] Cf. SAINT POPE JOHN PAUL II, Apostolic letter in the form of Motu Proprio *Mesiricordia Dei* (MD) – On Certain Aspects of the Celebration of the Sacrament of Penance, April 7, 2002, n. 1.

In the 1910s, the three countries with the largest Catholic population were in Europe. Italy had 99.9%, Spain 99.9%, and France 98.4%.[70] But now, we have Brazil, Mexico, and the United States in the top three positions.[71] Today, less than 10% of Catholics go to church in France. Even Brazil, which used to have a Catholic population of 95.6% in 1910, has witnessed a decline, whereas Pentecostalism has risen from 0.9 to about 30%.[72] The experience is the same in sub-Sahara African countries. This situation suggests that we are either not evangelizing vigorously or we are not doing what we are doing well, or the Pentecostals are doing what they are doing better or, perhaps, some other reasons or a combination of factors are responsible.

Negative Consequence of Denial: Denial Does Not Change Reality

In general, such denials are not helpful and do not change reality. They often arise from a number of factors. These include ignorance of reality, insincerity, sheer insecurity, the inability to take responsibility for one's actions or omissions, pride or the fear of acknowledging one's failure, the unwillingness to step out of one's comfort-zone and do the needful to correct a bad situation, or a combination of these and other factors. But what is absolutely clear is that denial is a wrong approach to a problem and a foolish one for that matter. This is because truth will always manifest itself no matter how long we try to cover it up or deny it. Consistent denials only leave us in a state of coma and delusion and allow a bad situation to fester and get worse over time. This makes solutions even more complex and difficult in every sense as we see in the case of a curable or manageable disease, which has deteriorated to a level

[70] PEW RESEARCH CENTER, "Brazil Catholic Population is 65%," February 13, 2013. See https://www.pewresearch.org/religion/2013/02/13/the-global-catholic-population/.

[71] S. HAHN, "Evangelizing Catholics: The Bible, the Eucharist, and the New Evangelization." CD by LightHouse Catholic Media.

[72] Cf. PEW RESEARCH CENTER, "Brazil Catholic Population is 65%..., *op. cit.*

where it is incurable or extremely difficult and more expensive to manage due to a long period of denial.

No matter how we look at it, the initial denial of the fact that many Catholics were drifting to Pentecostal churches, especially in the early 1980s, has not helped the Catholic Church in Nigeria. Psychologists claim that when a person acknowledges a problem that is real, the problem is half-resolved. If we admit that we are losing members, the most-likely thing will be to begin a search for meaningful solutions. But if we continue to deny the existence of a problem that is there, then we do nothing. This was exactly the case with us in the early days of the growth of Pentecostalism in Nigeria. We did little or nothing to tackle it, because we lived in denial. The outcome of that denial, omission, and inaction on our part is the proliferation of Pentecostal churches in Nigeria and the drift of some of our faithful to these churches.

Today, the proliferation and growth of Pentecostal churches is obvious even to the "blind." It is so real that it would be a delusion to deny it. Indeed, they have come of age and have a strong presence, voice, and influence in society. Besides their physical expansion, they are all over the television and their teaching and style are impacting both positively and negatively on a good number of Nigerians, including Catholics. More importantly, we have been forced to come to terms with the obvious fact that, not only are we losing members to the Pentecostals, but that the new reality now constitutes a threat to us as a Church and challenges us to renew our zeal for mission, to rethink our methods, and to adjust our approach to things in some areas.

Even now that our eyes are open to this reality and the threat it poses to us, the problem is that we have not taken any bold step to reverse it. In fact, it seems that some of us are neither interested nor bothered about the situation. Even for those who are concerned, it is difficult to see how we can reverse the undesirable trend if we continue to do things the same old ways, some of which may not appeal to the present generation of people we wish to reach and evangelize. In truth, our approach to a number of things has not changed in many of our parishes and among our laity and lay organizations. More importantly, the sense of mission is still very poor. As John Maxwell remarks, "What you put in always impacts on what comes out."[73] If we are not putting in something new and effective, we are not likely to stem the present tide and our Church may not experience the exponential growth she is capable of if only we can reawaken our mission, consciousness, and zeal.

Living on Our Past Glory

Perhaps some people will be familiar with the statement, "The Catholic Church is second to none." This statement always draws loud cheering from Catholics and we should not be surprised at all. It is natural to praise one's own thing. But beyond that natural instinct in us to praise our own thing, there is something fundamentally true about the assertion. The Catholic Church is actually second to none if we consider her long history, her rich catechism, her rich art, her rich tradition, her population and a host of other things. Nonetheless, what those who hide under the achievements of the past must know is that the Church's greatness did not come easy.

Her rich history gives evidence to a strong conviction about Christ on the part of the Christians. The heroes and heroines of the past, who collaborated with the Holy Spirit to build the Church and make it great, laboured relentlessly and made huge sacrifices for the spread of the Gospel. Their only or primary concern was the proclamation of God's kingdom and the spread of the Church everywhere, rather than themselves or the material benefits that accrue from the Gospel. In fact, their lives were characterized by complete selflessness, strong zeal for mission, and faithfulness to Christ and the Church in the face of rejection, loss of relationships, persecution, suffering, and even martyrdom. If they had not been so selfless in their labour for Christ and the Church and had chosen to use the Church (their offices or positions or privileges) as stepping stones to the attainment of self-glory and fulfilment, the Church would never have developed to the point of being "second to none."

While some Church leaders tend to flatter themselves and tout their successes, the truth is that we are handing on to the next

[73] J. MAXWELL, *How Successful People Think* (New York: Center Street, 2009), p. XI.

generation a weak Church that is not too conscious of her identity and mission, a Church that is content with half-measures and a priesthood that is highly compromised. This is because the ideals have been so lowered and almost forgotten over time that most people now think that they are no longer possible. If the heroes of our faith made extreme sacrifices to make the Church great, then our responsibility is not just to maintain it, but to build upon their solid foundation and successes. Put differently, we have a duty to make it even greater in our own time so that we can pass on a healthier and stronger Church to the next generation of Catholics. Sadly, this has not been the case. That sense of selflessness and sacrifice seems to have vanished in many different ways as a significant number of our ordained ministers now "use" God and his Church for their own purpose, rather than allow God to use them for his own purpose or the salvific mission of the Church.

Our Biases and a Weak Explanation of a Serious Reality

Rather than study this phenomenon of Pentecostalism objectively to know why they are experiencing rapid growth and how we can stem the drift of our members, some Catholics prefer to hold on to their biases. On closer examination, some of these biases often arise from a lack of spiritual depth,[74] unfounded assumptions that have never been thoroughly investigated, and ignorance of the teachings of the Church, especially Vatican II.

Oftentimes, they cite the attractiveness of the "prosperity Gospel," craze for miracles, ignorance, music, and the longing for entertainment as the reasons for the drift to these Churches. Even though some of these reasons have their own merits, they are not the only ones. There are more serious reasons to explain this exodus from the Church. Even some of the reasons we often cite to explain "away" the drift of our members to these Churches, such as igno-

[74] There are many baptized and confirmed Catholics as well as ordained persons who are not spiritually conscious and tend to practice Christianity as a religion rather than as a faith, which involves an intimate personal relationship with God and a life lived in the power of the Holy Spirit. They see things solely from the human point of view.

rance of the Catholic faith, music, and the search for miracles and solutions to the problems of life, raise some important questions for us as a Church on mission. Why are most of our members ignorant in spite of our rich catechism and other spiritual resources at our disposal? Why do they need to go out in search of miracles and solutions to the problems of life? Do the Catholic clergy and lay people not have *charisms*—for example, even the power to heal and conduct minor exorcism? My investigation and interaction with some former Catholics, some returnees to the Catholic faith, and some Pentecostals who are coming into the Church because of marriage to a Catholic, have been quite revealing.

When one considers the above and the ease with which many of us carry on unconcerned, one is forced to ask if these realities do not reveal a total lack of mission enterprise and zeal on our part or even indifference to the temporal and spiritual needs of our members? The point is that if people are leaving us because of ignorance of the Catholic faith, is it not one of the primary duties of our pastors and their collaborators to teach them and make them understand? If they want music—not profane music, but a religious music that is worthy of the liturgy and capable of lifting up their minds to God to give him glory, music that inspires them to worship better and satisfy their authentic spiritual yearnings—then why can't we give that to them without tampering with the Mass or its structures or sacredness?

We cannot run away from the fact that there is a cultural dimension to evangelization and worship. As Pope John Paul II observes,

> …'[I]nculturation' may be a neologism, but it expresses very well one factor of the great mystery of the Incarnation. We can say of catechesis, as well as of evangelization in general, that it is called to bring the power of the Gospel into the very heart of culture and cultures. For this purpose, catechesis will seek to know these cultures and their essential components; it will learn their most significant expressions; it will respect their particular values and riches. In this manner it will be able to offer these cultures the knowledge of the hidden mystery and help them to bring forth from their own living tradition original expressions

> of Christian life, celebration and thought.... On the one hand the Gospel message cannot be purely and simply isolated from the culture in which it was first inserted (the biblical world or, more concretely, the cultural milieu in which Jesus of Nazareth lived), nor, without serious loss, from the cultures in which it has already been expressed down the centuries.[75]

A vital thing we must always remember is that God has also passed through the African culture in general and left his marks in it in different ways, even before the advent of the white missionaries. Hence, we must factor this into the way we worship while maintaining the appropriate decorum, profound reverence for the mysteries we celebrate at Mass and, of course, the structure of the Mass. For example, singing can be more lively and spirit-filled.[76] The fact that a significant number of Christians—both young and old—from the established Churches are attracted to Pentecostal churches by music has a great deal to tell us about the mentality and yearnings of our people if we are open enough to hear and courageous and humble enough to listen. Although a few of them tend to return to the Church after a period of time, an overwhelming majority of them do not.

---

[75] Cf. POPE JOHN PAUL II, *Catechesi Tradendae – On Catechesis in Our Time,* October 16, 1979, n. 53.

[76] In a particular parish in Lagos metropolis, I observed that some parishioners who travelled abroad for their vacation would often say that they missed Mass in the parish, especially "the second collection." On a closer investigation, it dawned on me that the manner of singing and dancing during this time appealed to them. Without advocating that "choruses" should take the place of our hymns, we need to study what inspires our people to pray and worship well and compose Scripture-based and theologically sound hymns with the kind of melody that will inspire them. A popular hymn titled "In Thanksgiving and Love" by Jude Nnam is a good example of such hymns. If we are to achieve the goals of evangelization in the light of Vatican II, we cannot completely impose the Western way of singing on our people who like to express themselves. There should be a healthy balance in this area.

A Positive Response to the Phenomenon of Pentecostalism

Our usual approach to the new phenomenon of Pentecostalism is "attack" or "harsh criticism." Oftentimes, we busy ourselves complaining and criticizing the new churches. We tend to focus only or mainly on their visible shortcomings but ignore their strength, which is the reason people are drifting to them. At other times, our bias makes us quick to condemn things we do not even understand ourselves just because they are foreign to our conditioning over time. Unfortunately, we are not the only ones because they too do the same thing to us in different ways.[77] What is certain is that this cannot be the best way to tackle the phenomenon of Pentecostalism in Nigeria.

Great people who search for truth tend to be more open-minded. If truth is our quest, then the correct approach should be objectivity. This requires us to carefully investigate what Pentecostalism is all about and acknowledge its positive contributions to the spread of God's kingdom and the life of the Church as a whole. The temptation to throw both the baby and the dirty water away is not in our best interest or that of the Christian mission as a whole. Even if we do, they will continue to thrive in spite of their shortcomings while we continue at the same slow pace due to the present lack of apostolic zeal among many of our pastors and lay people. The ineffectiveness of the Church, especially in the area of mission *ad gentes* and the new evangelization, is traceable to a number of reasons. These include lack of personal conversion,[78] ignorance of the Church's mission or indifference on the part of many of our pastors

---

[77] That they too behave in a similar way towards us and condemn some of our noble practices is no justification for doing the same. Truth should be our quest and should make us investigate things objectively. In particular, we need patience and the help of the Holy Spirit to investigate those things we may not understand or agree with because of our conditioning in order to avoid any hasty conclusion or generalization.

[78] According to Pope Paul VI, it is unthinkable that anyone who experiences a personal conversion will not go out to convert others. Thus, if a person is not interested in evangelizing others to convert them, then we can question his own conversion.

and lay people, lack of accountability in this vital area, spiritual blindness or backwardness and the unwillingness to change, arising from an unwillingness to make the necessary sacrifice and invest more time and energy in the mission of evangelization.

If truth must be said, it is not everything about Pentecostalism that is bad. Pentecostals have many positive things to bring on board[79] if only we pay more attention to what they are doing well rather than their lapses. Although we have the fullness of the truth about God and salvation in comparison to the other churches, the Church does not claim or teach that truth cannot be found at all outside the Catholic Church. The willingness to grow and excel will make any reasonable and astute evangelizer pay attention to the truth and the "riches" which others possess and adopt the "positive" elements to enhance what he already has. No right-thinking and progressive business man will ignore the reasons other businessmen around him are thriving, especially if he is losing his customers to them. Most likely, he will investigate to know the positive things they are doing and learn some new tricks or methods that he can apply to his business to achieve better results.

To think that Pentecostals have nothing to offer society and the Church as a whole is delusive. We should not forget that God did not create anyone without an intellect to reason or without one or more talents that are meant to help him develop himself. The Church herself teaches that fact. She teaches that at the time of baptism the Holy Spirit bestows one or more spiritual gifts (*charisms*) on every baptized person. Such gifts are meant to help him participate in the building up of the Church and in her mission, in addition to fulfilling his own purpose in life. Like every other human being created in the image and likeness of God, Pentecostals too have talents.[80] Many of them are educated and have

---

[79] For example, the Pentecostal churches have a way of getting people—I mean people who were passive in their former churches—to become more interested and active in the life of the church. The more popular ones are professional in their approach to so many things. They expose their members to the Bible and strive to lead them into a personal relationship with God. Nonetheless, this does not suggest they do not have their own shortcomings.

[80] Talents and *charisms* (spiritual gifts) are not the same. We shall shed

achieved success in their different fields of human endeavour, such as banking, legal practice, medicine, lecturing, business and so on.

It is not impossible that some Catholics will argue that since *charisms* are given at the time of baptism, then those Pentecostals whose baptism is not accepted by the Catholic Church cannot have *charisms*. As plausible as that may seem to our human logic, experience seems to suggest that they too can manifest both the spiritual gifts (*charisms*) and the fruits of the Holy Spirit.[81] Besides, many of them were former Catholics, Anglicans, Methodists, and Baptists[82] who were validly baptized and confirmed. Now, do such Christians lose their baptism and their spiritual gifts once they leave their churches to join the Pentecostals? It does not seem so. Hence, they take with them many positive elements and practices from their former churches, which continue to support their spiritual growth.[83]

As former insiders, many of the Pentecostals know the strengths and the weaknesses of their former churches. Armed with such knowledge, a good number of them have come to fashion programmes and new ways of doing things, which many Africans, especially the younger generation, find attractive and enriching. Even though the Church continues to teach that we have to revise our methods of evangelization in the light of the new realities in society, in practice we continue to place "methods" above the "mission" itself. This can be likened to making secondary things more important than the primary ones or paying more attention to one's body rather than one's soul. Jesus Christ who instituted the Eucharist did not say the first Mass in Latin, but today we say Mass in Latin and other local languages to make it more intelligible to the

---

more light on this point much later. Every human being has one or more talents by birth, but Christians come to possess the *charisms* following baptism.

[81] The Spirit blows as he wishes and sometimes it is difficult to understand his actions because of our own limitedness. Certainly, we need serious discernment in many areas of the Christian life.

[82] The Catholic Church accepts the baptism done in these churches.

[83] For example, I have met some former Catholics who continued to say the rosary and prayers to particular saints, even after moving to a Pentecostal church.

faithful and enable them to participate better. So, while the mission is always constant and the message is unchangeable, the manner of delivering the message or pursuing the mission can change when necessary to achieve greater success.

No one can claim there are no abuses or erroneous theology or wrong practices among the Pentecostal churches. Certainly, we cannot copy their shortcomings or excesses. But a more reasonable and progressive approach is to appraise their methods, practices, and strengths objectively and revise some of our own methods that may need change or revitalization, if we are to achieve greater success in our mission—whether primary or secondary. At least, this is consistent with the objectives of the new evangelization. Refusing to learn a few positive things from them simply because they are Pentecostals and we are the mother Church with a profound theology and a rich history is not to our own advantage, because they too have taken a lot from us and are still learning from us in many areas.

Even in concrete human life, parents and adults can learn a few things from children, just as a wise, humble, and open-minded teacher can also learn a few things from his own students who are inferior to him in knowledge. The point is that no matter how intelligent and experienced people are, nobody knows it all such that he cannot learn anything from others. In the same way, nobody is so completely empty that he has nothing at all to offer others. The lack of openness and the mutual suspicion, rivalry, and intense criticism we witness among the members of the different Christian denominations do not serve the overall interest of Christianity, especially in our own clime where the danger of Islamization is real. "Christian disunity" is not a blessing. On the contrary, it weakens the cooperation between churches and thus compromises the mission of the Church as a whole.

A Wake-up Call to the Catholic Church

Some people have repeatedly described the Catholic Church as a "sleeping giant." They can see the enormous resources at our disposal and the too many untapped potentials. But unfortunately, many of our pastors do not realize this. They bask in the euphoria of "success" and do not bother about the drift of Catholics to other churches because they are comfortable and our churches are still full on Sundays. This in itself is worrisome. To put it mildly, how can a shepherd lose some of his sheep and not worry or go after them? Can a businessman sleep comfortably when he is losing some of his customers? Can a parent be comfortable and do nothing when his household is being decimated? So, why are many of the pastors unperturbed? Can this be a sign that something fundamental is wrong with their understanding of their vocation and the mission of the Church? Is it a case of ignorance or lack of personal conviction about Christ, the faith, or the Church's mission?[84] Can it be the case of failure in the area of apostolic formation or have they lost faith in the Church? No matter how we choose to look at it, something serious is definitely wrong somewhere.

Now that the years of denial are over and reality stares us right in the face, we can no longer remain complacent or inactive. We need to think of a way out of this situation. The drifting Catholics are our members and our brethren. We have a responsibility to strive to keep and feed them in the Church and to go after them when they stray. Not to go after them gives the impression that we do not care about them. The task at stake is urgent and of utmost importance, and we need to approach it with a high sense of responsibility and commitment in order to prevent a worse situation in the near future. From the standpoint of demography, the drift of many young Catholics (youths and young adults) from the Church has far-reaching implications for us in the near future. If the trend is not reversed, in about ten to twenty years' time, the Pentecostals may clearly outnumber the Catholics in Nigeria and other places, if that has not happened already in some places.

At this juncture, it is vital to state that the primary source of concern here is not that the Pentecostal churches exist in the first place. No doubt, they have a right to exist according to our constitution. Besides, we should be complementing one another rather

[84] It is important to state that some of our ordained ministers do not believe in the Church's mission of evangelization, while others have various misconceptions about evangelization, which keep them in their comfort zones and cause them to rationalize their inaction in this area.

than competing with one another.[85] But the problem is that we are not evangelizing as we should, and they are taking our members away rather than converting non-Christians to the faith. To reverse this situation, we must begin by asking ourselves a very critical question: Why are people leaving us? Any attempt to rationalize things or cast aspersions on the Pentecostals will not be a good starting point. Again, rather than focus only on their shortcomings as some of us often do, we should pay greater attention to our own attitude to mission and their own areas of strength, which keep attracting people to them.

On a general note, the rapid spread of Pentecostalism, just as the persecution of the early Christians in Jerusalem, should be a wake-up call to us—that is, the Church and her leaders—to leave our comfort zones and pay greater attention to the mission we received from our Lord and Saviour. We cannot turn our backs on the Great Commission or continue to pay lip service and do little or nothing in practice and expect all to be well with the Church. We need to rethink mission at all levels of the Church's life and administration and give priority to things of primary concern instead of the secondary ones.

Put differently, both in theory and in practice, priority should be given to mission *ad gentes*, new evangelization, and proper spiritual and apostolic formation of our priests, seminarians, religious lay leaders and the entire laity, rather than to some less important aspects of our ministry, such as buildings.[86] Today, it is absolutely

[85] In fact, the primary focus of all the churches should be to bring Christ, especially to the non-Christians around.

[86] Today, there is a strong tendency in the Church to put the cart before the horse. Similarly, there is a serious loss of focus of our identity and mission. We tend to pay greater attention to secondary things, such as buildings. Even in our schools and other institutions, there is the temptation to focus primarily on academic success or profit, rather than the primary reasons for establishing those institutions, namely: mission and the salvation of souls. In the actual sense, proper and intensive evangelization is not going on in many of our institutions. Oftentimes, people are led to the Church and the sacraments without being led to Christ and conversion first. In view of this, we must not forget that the reason behind every move the Church makes or anything she does is "mission"—to win

clear that the present maintenance culture in the Church is hurting us badly and can no longer be sustained without further harm to our real mission. As Pope Francis states, we need to move away from sheer maintenance culture and return to the culture of mission that was clearly present in the Church in the past. Put in his exact words,

> In our day Jesus' command to "go and make disciples" echoes in the changing scenarios and ever new challenges to the Church's mission of evangelization, and all of us are called to take part in this new missionary "going forth." Each Christian and every community must discern the path that the Lord points out, but all of us are asked to obey his call to go forth from our own comfort zone in order to reach all the "peripheries" in need of the light of the Gospel.[87]

The Measure of Church Growth

In the early Church, population growth was from their intentional and intensive efforts to evangelize the Jewish people and other non-Christians. Our membership growth should not come mainly from new births among our members or from those who enter the Church through marriage to Catholics as is the case now. Instead, actual Church growth, measured by growth in membership and in the number of those who come to experience conversion and are willing to go on mission for Christ and his Church, cannot be left to chance. It should be the natural outcome of our intentional and intensive evangelizing activities within and outside the Church.

On this point, Warren maintains that Church growth is measured by both quality and quantity. God expects his Church to be both faithful and fruitful in the numerical sense. He desires the two (quality and quantity, or faithfulness and fruitfulness) and one

---

souls for Christ and bring them into his body, the Church, where their ongoing formation and discipleship continues.

[87] See POPE FRANCIS, *Evangelium Gaudium* (EG) – On the Joy of the Gospel, November 24, 2013, n. 20.

without the other is incomplete.[88] However, the numerical strength that can attest to the fact that a Church is growing is not to be measured by the number of births by members which swells the population of a Church, but the increase in the number of new converts among non-Christians that enter the Church. The latter is what shows that evangelization is actually taking place in a Church. As a matter of fact, the ultimate measure of the fruitfulness or success of a Church is how it is fulfilling the Great Commission of Jesus Christ.[89] As he rightly points out, "Any Church that is not obeying the Great Commission is failing its purpose no matter what else it does,"[90] and this cannot be called fruitfulness by any standard. Even where we are bringing in new people into the Church, our parishes should also be places where members are experiencing both initial and ongoing conversion on a regular and progressive basis.

To say the least, we need a dose of humility and objectivity to appraise the reasons some of our members are drifting. Another value that can guide us in this investigation is openness of mind in an effort to reach the truth, which alone can set a person free. Perhaps, a good starting point in this important exercise is to beam our searchlight first and foremost on our understanding of mission as a Church—both in the strict sense and the broad sense—and our commitment to every aspect of it. Once we understand our mission clearly and determine what we are either not doing well or are neglecting altogether, our next move will be to change our mental attitude and to strategize to enable us to come up with a mission and pastoral plan, which will help us realize our goals. As the Church teaches, we need to continually reappraise the signs of the times, renew ourselves, revise our methods, and rekindle our zeal for mission as a matter of urgency.

---

[88] Cf. R. WARREN, *The Purpose Driven Church* (Grand Rapids, Michigan: Zondervan, 1995), pp. 62-64.

[89] *Ibid.*, p. 64.

[90] *Ibid.*

Chapter Three

WHY ARE PEOPLE LEAVING US? THE ACCUSATION THAT CATHOLICS DO NOT READ THE BIBLE

In Chapter Two, we tried to establish that many of our members and those of the other traditional churches are drifting to Pentecostalism. As a people called to scrutinize the signs of the times on an ongoing basis and respond appropriately to new situations and challenges that arise, we need to be a listening Church. In other words, we need to interact with them to know why they are leaving. The danger of closing our minds or refusing to listen is that we will continue to lose some more. The main thrust of this book is to examine the reasons people are leaving us, with the hope of addressing their concerns and finding appropriate solutions. In this chapter, we shall focus on one of the major ones, which is the accusation against the Catholic Church that we do not read the Bible.

Certain Truths About the Bible

Before addressing this accusation, there are certain truths we must know about the Bible and its place in the life of the Christian. The Bible is the greatest book ever written and the first to appear in print.[91] It is also "the most printed and read book in history."[92] The Bible contains seventy-three books—forty-six Old Testament books and twenty-seven New Testament books.[93] The different books of the Bible, written by more than forty human authors over

---

[91] Cf. E. SRI, *The Bible Compass, A Catholic's Guide to Navigating the Scriptures* (West Chester, PA: Ascension Press, 2009), p. 7.

[92] H. ROSE, *How to Study the Bible: Bible Study Made Easy*, pamphlet (Torrance, California: Rose Publishing Inc., 2004), p. 5.

[93] The Protestants have 39 Old Testament books and 27 New Testament books.

a period of 1,600 years, were not written to be simply historical books or a piece of literature that merely tells us about events that took place in the past.[94] On the contrary, the Bible is a divinely inspired book, which has God as its author. To put it differently, the books of the Bible were inspired by the Holy Spirit. The Greek word *theópneustos,* which is translated as "inspiration" in English, literally means "God-breathed."[95] The idea is that God "breathed" his own divine word through the words of men.[96] What this means is that it was the Holy Spirit who influenced the human writers of the different books of the Bible to write what they wrote, thus making him the real author of the Bible.

This does not in any way imply that the Bible is a dictation from God to man, as if the human writers had no input in what they wrote. On the contrary, they contributed to the writing of the Bible. As Sri puts it, "they made full use of their own freedom, creativity and writing style to communicate their [God-given] message to their particular audiences."[97] In spite of this collaboration between God and the human writers in producing the Bible, the Church teaches that the books of the Bible are sacred because they were "written by the inspiration of the Holy Spirit" and thus "have God as their author."[98] In this sense, while the human writers who collaborated with God to produce the books can be called authors in some sense, God himself is the primary author of the books of the Bible. The Holy Spirit did not merely prevent the human writers from error, he positively influenced what they wrote, making him the real author, not an editor.

Unlike the deists who believe that God does not interact with creation, Christians believe that the Creator God is not only interested in the world, but he also actually interacts with us. The Bible

---

[94] Cf. H. ROSE, *How to Study the Bible,* pamphlet…, *op. cit.*

[95] 2 Tim 3:16. See *CCC* 105; Also cited in E. SRI, *The Bible Compass…, op. cit.,* p. 7.

[96] E. SRI, *The Bible Compass…, op. cit.,* p. 8.

[97] *Ibid.*

[98] VATICAN I, *Dei Filius* (DF) –Dogmatic Constitution on the Catholic Faith, Chapter 2 (*DS,* 1787); See E. SRI, *The Bible Compass…, op. cit.,* p. 8.

is one of the main ways he chooses to communicate himself to us and reveal his divine plan or purpose for us.[99] *The Penny Catechism* teaches that "God made us to know him, to love him, to serve him and to be happy with him in this world and in the next."[100] The Bible was written for this purpose. It is meant to help us discover God and his Christ and enter into an intimate loving relationship with the Godhead that will culminate in eternal life.

Additionally, the Bible is the Word of God and thus God's mind. It reveals God's thoughts, his expectations, and his will to us. It is equally the first prayer book of the Christian. Besides the Psalms, different parts of Scripture can be used for all forms of prayer—petition, meditation, and even spiritual warfare (cf. Eph 6:12-17). More importantly, the Bible, in its totality as the Word of God, is given to us as a guide (cf. Ps 119:105). It is God's blueprint for Christian life without prejudice to the Sacred Tradition and the Magisterium.

The whole point of emphasizing God's authority on the books of the Bible earlier is to emphasize the importance of the Bible itself. If God considered it so important to pass on his Word to men and women of every generation and positively influenced what the human authors wrote, it was because he wanted everybody to come to know him and his divine plan that he intended to communicate to us and thus be guided by his Word. Put differently, if we consider the Bible to be God's "love letter" to his beloved children; if the Bible is one of the main ways (and, the easiest to access) that God chose to communicate himself to us and draw a personal response from us, then it should be a must-read for all. A letter to an individual, and more so a loving letter from a loving Father to his children to reveal his mind, his will, and his plan for them and the whole of creation, ought to be read as a matter of necessity to know the heart of the Father and the Son whom he sent. Besides, how can we know God more fully and possibly respond to what he is communicating to us in Christ if we do not read his Word?

---

[99] *Ibid.*, p. 10.

[100] *The Penny Catechism* is a simple catechism book we use in the Catholic Church.

The central focus of the Bible is Jesus Christ, the fullest revelation of the Father. In one of his homilies, Pope Paul VI described Jesus Christ in the following terms: "the One who reveals the invisible God; the foundation of everything created; the teacher of mankind and its redeemer; the centre of history and of the world; the secret of history; the bridge between heaven and earth; the key to our destiny; and our happiness."[101] If Jesus is all of this and the whole Bible revolves around him as the centre and the ultimate communication from God, then ignorance of the Bible, as Saint Jerome maintains, is ignorance of Christ.[102] Bringing us in contact with the person, words and deeds of Jesus, the Bible allows us to know and meditate on God's character and his principles for living.[103] Similarly, if the Holy Spirit in his wisdom inspired men to write the Bible to reveal God to men and call them to faith in him, and then entrusted it to the Church, it is because he trusts that the Church will get it across to all men for their salvation.

This puts the Church under obligation to be at the forefront of getting all of mankind to read this most precious book containing the best love story ever told. This is in view of the fact that frequent study of the Bible and meditation on the Word of God has a great potential to transform lives and mold people more into the image of Jesus Christ, who is the ultimate communication from God.[104] But if we think that the frequent study of the Bible and meditation is not necessary, then one can safely conclude that to have a personal or family Bible is superfluous, just as buying a car one does not intend to use will not make sense.

Just like a beautiful car (though not comparable to the most beautiful car or any material thing), the role of the Bible is not to decorate a home or an office. Also, it is obviously not a *talisman* meant to protect people from nightmares. Rather, it is first and foremost God's Word to humanity that we are expected to read,

---

[101] POPE PAUL VI, "We preach Christ to the far ends of the world." Homily given in Manila on November 29, 1970. Cited in the Office of the Reading of Sunday Week 13 of the Year.

[102] SAINT JEROME, *Commentariorum in Isaiamlibri, Prol.:* PL 24, 17B.

[103] H. ROSE, *How to Study the Bible,* pamphlet…, *op. cit.,* p. 6.

[104] Cf. *Ibid.,* p. 8.

meditate on, act upon, and share with others. Here, however, it is crucial to state that it is not enough to read the Bible merely to know, to teach, and quote Scripture passages. What is critical is obedience, that is, to act on what the Word says and allowing it to transform the way we think, the way we speak, and the way we live (Cf. Mt 7:21-28; Jas 1:22-25.). The only reason we are not witnessing commensurate spiritual growth and moral transformation in society, in spite of the fact that the Word is preached everywhere and people read and quote the Bible always, is that most people do not obey the Word or act upon it. Nevertheless, the solution is never to stop reading altogether, but to train people to read, to meditate, and to act upon what the Word tells them.

Jesus himself affirms the need to know and live by the Word of God when he says: "Man does not live on bread alone, but on every word that proceeds from the mouth of God" (Mt 4:4). Just as we eat material food daily to nourish our bodies and safeguard our physical life and health, we also need to study and meditate on the Word of God daily as a spiritual food for our souls and a healthy Christian life.[105] Commenting on the importance of the Bible, Saint Ephraem asserts that "He [the Lord] has hidden many treasures in his word so that each of us is enriched as we meditate on it."[106] According to him, "the word of God is a tree of life that from all its parts offers you fruits that are blessed. It is like that rock opened in the desert that from all its parts gave forth a spiritual drink."[107]

The Accusation That the Catholic Church Does Not Read the Bible

The accusation that Catholics do not read the Bible is a major one. In my last book, *When Salt Loses Its Saltiness,* I talked about the need to make the Bible better known among Catholics. Here, I

---

[105] This is in addition to the Eucharist and other spiritual activities that nourish our spiritual life.

[106] SAINT EPHRAEM, "The Word of God is an inexhaustible fountain," commentary on the Diatessaron. See the Second Reading of the Office of the Reading, Week 6 of the Year: Sunday.

[107] *Ibid.*

wish to take up the theme again. But this time around it is to show how the culture of not reading the Bible as individual Catholics or as Catholic families has contributed to the drift of a significant number of our members to Pentecostal churches. But first, let us make an important distinction here. Who does not read the Bible—the Catholic Church or Catholics?

Does the Catholic Church Read the Bible?

Most of the Pentecostal churches constantly, but erroneously, accuse the Catholic Church of not being a Bible church. This is something that affects a good number of our young Catholics. While some are quick to defend the Church, others are swayed by the accusation and tend to drift away. Unfortunately, what reinforces that belief is that as soon as they join these other churches, they are led to read the Bible regularly in the church as well as individually and as a family. With this growing knowledge of the Word of God and growth in the spiritual life on this account, many tend to conclude that the Church had kept them in the dark for too long.

Now, if what is meant by the Catholic Church not being a Bible church is that the Bible is not all we do or the centre of our faith, then they are absolutely correct. First and foremost, the Word of God is indispensable to the Catholic faith. But in spite of the great importance we attach to it, we also have the sacraments, especially the Holy Eucharist which is the centre and summit of our faith. Besides, even though the Word of God occupies a place of pride in our life and liturgy, the Bible is not the only source of our Catholic faith. The Living Tradition of the Church and the Magisterium are also authentic sources of our faith. Perhaps, it is pertinent to recall here that at one time the books of the New Testament did not yet exist, the Christian faith was transmitted orally. The New Testament Bible itself came out of the Living Tradition of the Church. Before the first two books of the New Testament, 1 and 2 Thessalonians were written in AD 51 and 52, the Church was already in existence and so was Tradition.

Evidence from Scripture itself points to Tradition as an authentic source of the Christian faith. Besides the testimony of Saint John the Evangelist that many other things Christ said and did were not written down in the Gospel (Jn 21:25), we know that Saint Paul constantly made reference to Tradition in his writings. In 1 Corinthians 11 alone he made reference to Tradition twice. First, he says, "…and you keep to the tradition I handed over to you" (see 1 Cor 11:2). Then in verse 23, he writes, "This is the tradition of the Lord that I received and that in my turn I have handed on to you…." In 1 Corinthians 15:3-7, he says, "I have handed on to you as of first importance what I in turn had received…."[108] Still, in his second letter to the Thessalonians, he admonishes the people, saying, "…stand firm and hold on to the traditions that we taught you by word or by letter" (2 Thes 2:15).

Here, it is crystal clear that while "letter" refers to the written part of the Sacred Scriptures, "word" refers to Tradition. In addition to the written Word (Bible) and the unwritten Word (Tradition), the Magisterium exists as a source of our faith, for the Bishops, in union with the successor of Peter, are the correct interpreters of the Bible itself. So, the whole talk about *sola Scriptura* (belief in the Bible alone) as the source of the Christian faith is not only unbiblical in itself, but it is equally illogical, granted that the Bible came out of Tradition. Some Evangelicals and Pentecostals have also come to realize the limitation of *sola Scriptura*. Without denying the importance of the Bible, they tend to acknowledge extra-biblical truths, which are consistent with biblical principles even though they are not written in the Bible.

A second possibility is that what the Pentecostals mean by the Catholic Church not being a Bible church is that we (as a Church) do not accord the reading of the Bible the attention it deserves. Again, this is a gross misconception, which from the standpoint of history also reveals the ignorance of those who hold such a view. Here, it is crucial to find out how the canon of the Bible was established. Was this not determined by the Catholic hierarchy? In

---

[108] See THE HOLY BIBLE, *New Revised Standard Version–Catholic Edition* (NRSV-CE); The NRSV-CE is based on the New Revised Standard Version (NRSV), first published in 1989 by an ecumenical translation committee under the National Council of Churches in Christ U.S.A. Here Saint Paul is referring to the tradition which he received from those who were disciples before him.

reference to what took place in second century AD, Alan Schreck writes,

> The bishops also discussed what writings were to be considered as God's inspired word for the whole Church. Some people, such as Marcion, had rejected the inspiration of the Hebrew Scriptures (our Old Testament) and accepted a very limited selection of Christian writings. Other groups, like the Gnostics, wanted to consider some very unusual writings as inspired by God.... In response to this, the bishops began to develop official lists of inspired writings, called canons, which later resulted in a general agreement on what writings make up our Bible today. Even by the fourth century, however, the canon of the New Testament was not yet finalized....[109]

Similarly, at the time of his persecution of Christians (AD 303–313), the Roman emperor, Diocletian, decreed the destruction of their sacred books. The "bishops and priests were compelled to turn over the Bible and other sacred books" of the Christian to be burned.[110] Although some complied and others fled the persecution, there were those who refused to surrender the sacred books.[111] But, more importantly, it was the Cenobite monks who hand copied the books of the Bible to preserve them. Again, this goes a long way to show that the Church has always seen the Bible as a treasure to be preserved and actually did everything to preserve it.

It is a historical fact that the Word of God has always been given prominence in the Church's life and liturgy from the time of the Apostles until now. The Catholic Church has always read the Bible as a Church. Even though the Holy Eucharist is the most central celebration of Catholics, what most people, Catholics themselves and non-Catholics in particular, do not know is that the various aspects of the Holy Mass and the Catholic liturgy in general are grounded in both the Old and the New Testament Scriptures. For example, in his write up, Mark Hass records over 100 Scripture

---

[109] A. SCHRECK, *The Compact History of the Catholic Church, op. cit.*, p. 18.

[110] *Ibid.*, p. 21.

[111] *Ibid.*

references to the different things we do at Mass.[112] While some of the words at Mass are taken directly from Scripture, others are simply based on it.

The Mass itself gives enormous evidence to the great importance the Church attaches to Scripture in her liturgical celebrations and her entire life. At every Sunday Mass or a solemnity, we take three readings (one each from the Old Testament, the New Testament letters, and the Gospels) as well as a Responsorial Psalm and an acclamation verse directly from Scripture. It is the same with the weekday Masses, the only exception being that we take just one reading from either the Old Testament or the New Testament letters, including the Book of Revelation. Similarly, with the exception of the Sacrament of Reconciliation, the celebration of all the other sacraments requires the reading of a Scripture passage. This renders the claim that the Catholic Church is not a Bible church incorrect and grossly misleading. Perhaps, it will be correct to state that if the Catholic Church did not preserve the Bible she so much believes in against all odds, the Christian world would never have known the Bible in its complete form or be in possession of the New Testament writings.

Do Catholics Really Read the Bible?

Eliminating the first two possibilities and clearly establishing that the Catholic Church cherishes and reads the Bible leaves us with one last possibility as to what the accusation of our separated brethren is all about. The pertinent question to address here is, "Do Catholics Really Read the Bible?" When the Pentecostals in particular claim that the Catholic Church is not a Bible church, they may have two things in mind. The first is that we do not read directly from the Bible, but depend more on the lectionary or the parish bulletin in our liturgical celebrations. The other thing is that Catholics, as individuals, do not read the Bible. Perhaps, the Catholic Church does not insist that her members should bring their

[112] M. HAAS, "Who says Catholics don't hear the Bible at Mass?" See https://aleteia.org/2017/08/12/who-says-catholics-dont-hear-the-bible-at-mass/.

Bibles to Church or read it regularly at home as a family and/or as individuals.

This particular accusation merits our candid consideration. Experience actually shows that most Catholics do not seem to have the culture of daily or regular Bible study and reflection whether as individuals or as families. The 2010 Pew Forum Survey revealed that Catholics in the US scored lower than the Protestants (including Pentecostals), the Mormons, the Jews, the agnostics and even the atheists in religious knowledge of the Bible and Christianity.[113] The truth is that there is no strong emphasis on this in the Church by most of the pastors even though some continue to harp on it based on their personal conviction. From childhood to adulthood most Catholics are not specifically taught to read the Bible always or regularly as an integral aspect of their Christian growth. Until more recent times, there was no Bible study in most parishes. Even now, catechumens in many of our parishes are not consciously schooled on the importance of studying the Bible regularly, whereas Scripture is one of the main components in catechesis.

Although most Catholics have Bibles at home, they appear more to be for "decoration" or are used by some only or primarily as a *talisman* meant to protect them against evil. Sometimes we allow the missal and the bulletin to take the place of the Bible. The Catholic Church is one of the few churches where people (both the clergy and the laity) attend retreats, recollections, prayer meetings, and even Bible study (where it exists) without Bibles. The implication is that, for most Catholics, daily or regular study of the Bible is not cultural but rather a case of thinking outside the box. As a result, many are ignorant of the Word of God and tend to rely on the homilies at Mass. And since no one can give what he does not have, most Catholics cannot and do not transmit the practice of daily or regular study of the Bible and meditation to their children and others around them.

The white missionaries who brought the Catholic faith to us did so many good things, especially in the areas of the administration of the sacraments, education, healthcare and similar, and sure-

[113] M. HEALY, "Lectio: Evangelization and the Acts of the Apostles." An Augustine Institute DVD, New York: Ignatian Press, 2016.

ly deserve our commendation. Nevertheless, while praising them for their efforts and the huge sacrifices they made, we must equally admit that they did not hand on to us the culture of reading the Bible outside of the Church's liturgy. If we go back to history, we will discover that the Church did not really encourage individual Bible reading by its members at first. Although this may not appear to be the best decision when viewed from our own historical context or perspective today, we cannot but agree that the Church had some good reasons for maintaining such a position. It would be unfair and mischievous to think that she deliberately wanted to hide the Bible or the truths about the faith from the faithful. On the contrary, there were some challenges in this area which made it almost impossible for ordinary people to read the Bible, even though we cannot deny the distraction arising from institutionalization and worldly pursuits in later years as some of the underlying causes.

The work by some researchers can shed a great light on this subject. Going back to history, Art Sippo, Terry Donahue, Mark Bonocore, and Hugh attempt to establish whether or not the Catholic Church forbade the reading of the Bible by her members. Their finding, which I intend to expose here, is quite informative. They remind us that in the early centuries of Christianity, the Bible as we know it today (as a single collection of books) did not exist. Instead, it was on scrolls and parchments.[114] Up until the Middle Ages, printing was not invented and every single Bible was written by hand and thus rare. Naturally, this also made it very expensive, such that an average person could not own a Bible or even a Gospel.[115] Besides, at the time in question, "most people were, at best, functionally literate,"[116] meaning that they could barely read. But to connect the people to events and stories in the Bible and enable them to grasp the Bible story, images and scenes from the Bible were painted on Church walls and portrayed on stained glass

[114] A. SIPPO et al., *"Did the Catholic Church forbid Bible reading?"* See https://www.catholicbridge.com/catholic/did-the-catholic-church-forbid-bible-reading.php.

[115] See *Christian Community Bible* (CCB), p. 21.

[116] *Ibid.*

windows. According to the *Christian Community Bible* in its introduction,

> In 1460, Gutenberg's discoveries made the printing of books possible. Before that there were only expensive and rare books, written by hand. The average person could not have a Bible, or even a Gospel. The Bible was read in the Church and was a source of preaching. To make it more visible to the faithful, no Church was built without adorning it throughout with paintings, sculptures or stained-glass windows depicting Biblical scenes.[117]

In 1436, Johann Gutenberg invented the printing press, which was to change so many things as far as the printing of books was concerned. With this discovery, the Gutenberg Bible became the first book to appear in print in 1460 and "like every Bible before it, it contained the deuterocanonical books which the Protestants refer to as 'extra' books"[118] or *apocrypha*. From these historical facts, it is clear that before 1436, when the printing became possible, it was totally impossible for every Christian to own a Bible.

Following the invention of printing and the eventual printing of the Bible, which made it possible to own a personal Bible, Martin Luther interpreted the Bible into the local dialect and distributed it to the local people to encourage them to read. But then, it is crucial to note that even before Luther's translation and the publication in German, some Catholics already had over twenty versions of the whole Bible translated into the various German dialects (High and Low). It is equally true that there existed various versions of the Bible in other languages before and after the Reformation.[119] Although the Church condemned certain vernacular[120] translations, it was not to prevent people from reading the Bible, but because of what she considered bad translations and anti-Catholic.

Later, the Catholic Church had the Bible translated into Latin. This translation is called the Latin Vulgate. Although it was avail-

---

[117] *Ibid.*

[118] *Ibid.*

[119] *Ibid.*

[120] Vernacular refers to the native tongue of the people in a particular region or country.

able to those who wished to read it without restriction, there was a major challenge as Latin was still the language of the elite and those who were well educated. At that time, there were no public schools and the literacy level was still very low among ordinary peasants.[121] To make the Bible more readily available to a greater number of people, the Church came up with the Catholic *Douay-Rheims Version* of the whole Bible (Old and New Testaments) in English in 1610. This translation from the Latin Vulgate was actually completed a year before the popular *Authorized Version* or *King James Version* published in 1611.[122] Although the Old Testament version was completed in 1610, the New Testament version of the *Douay Bible* was completed as far back as 1582 and was actually one of the sources that the translators of the *King James Version* used in the translation.[123]

It is a known fact that the Bible is very technical and complex. As such, uninformed readers could end up in error, that is, with a wrong interpretation of biblical texts or even heresy that would be harmful to them and the Christian community. *Exegesis,* which is necessary to lead out the real meaning of a biblical passage or what is intended by the author, is a complex task. Proper interpretation should involve examining a given text or book in the context of the storyline of the entire Bible as well as the Living Tradition of the whole Church.[124] Precisely, according to Pope Benedict XVI, "The Scripture is to be proclaimed, heard, read, received, and experienced as the Word of God, in the stream of the apostolic Tradition from which it is inseparable."[125] Hence, it is important that the faithful be properly schooled and trained to approach the Bible in

---

[121] A. SIPPO et al., *"Did the Catholic Church forbid Bible reading…, op. cit.*

[122] *Ibid.*

[123] *Ibid.* Contrary to what most people think, it is important to note that the word "authorized" used of the *King James Version* or the *Authorized Version* of the Bible does not really refer to the fact that it is the authentic Bible. Rather, it was used by the printers to indicate their faithfulness to what they were authorized to publish.

[124] See *CCC* 112-114.

[125] POPE BENEDICT XVI, Post-Synodal Apostolic Exhortation, *Verbum Domini* (VD) – On the Word of the Lord, 7.

relation to the Church's Living Tradition.[126] In the early days of the printing of the Bible, the leaders of the Church entertained the fear that making it available for all to read would result in incorrect interpretations by many people. This concern was not out of place if we recall the division that occurred among the disciples of Luther following the interpretation of the Bible into local dialects.[127]

In spite of the whole effort to translate the Bible and make it more readily available to all, we need to also admit that the Church could possibly have done more to promote the culture of regular Bible study and meditation among the faithful. As it is often said, "Where there is a will, there is always a way." But unfortunately, that did not appear to be the case at that time in the history of the Church. As the introduction to the *Christian Community Bible* indicates, there seemed to have been a misplacement of priority by Church institutions, the clergy and the religious who gave more attention to worldly interests over the ministry of the Gospel and evangelical renewal. According to the writer,

> For centuries, Church institutions, clergy and religious upheld the culture and the unity of the Christian world; as a result of the social status, worldly interests tended to attract greater interest than did the ministry of the Gospel itself. But what was more grievous was that the institutional Church had become a very heavy religious system, often stifling intellectual research as well as evangelical renewal. Many outstanding religious and holy people protested and asked for reforms. But no reforms followed. With the printing of the Bible, many thought that the only way to reform the Church was to give the Sacred Book to everyone so that by reading it, people would appreciate the original message and correct the errors and evil customs which had become so entrenched.[128]

Continuing on the same note, it insists that, even though the Catholic Church eventually had a counter-reform following the Protestant Reformation, not much changed in the area of promot-

[126] *VD* 18.

[127] *CCB*, p. 21.

[128] *Ibid.*

ing individual reading and reflection on the Bible by the faithful. Again, this is well captured in this assertion below:

> Later, after the rift with the Protestants, the Catholic Church, impoverished on human riches reformed itself. Great things were achieved and saints with exceptional personalities abounded. Still the Catholic Church was unable to stress listening to the Word of God. On the contrary, it was more than ever under the control of ecclesiastical authority, restraining to a large degree the expansion of the role of the Christian laity. Preachers and missionaries did indeed preach the Gospel, but were more like knowledgeable experts than servants of the Word of God trying to discover, together with their sisters and brothers, its richness.[129]

This brief journey through history is meant to show the efforts of the Church to make the Bible (the Word of God) more visible to the faithful, the challenges she faced and her fears, and of course, the distractions which made it impossible to establish individual reading of the Bible by all the faithful as a practice in the Church. An important thing about history is that it offers us an opportunity to reflect and learn from the past in order to grow in the present and be better in the future. So, the pertinent question that arises here is, What have we learnt over the centuries with regard to promoting regular Bible reading and reflection as a culture among Catholics? What concrete steps are we taking in our dioceses and parishes to establish this culture among the faithful?

What the Church Says About Regular Study of the Bible

Although the Catholic Church sees the Eucharist as the "source and summit of the Christian life,"[130] she has "always venerated the divine Scriptures as she venerated the Body of the Lord."[131] In

---

[129] *CCB,* p. 21.

[130] *CCC* 1324.

[131] *CCC* 141; See also M. HAAS, "Who says Catholics don't hear the Bible at Mass…, *op. cit.*

different documents and writings of the popes, the Church continues to invite all her faithful to give the Word of God the crucial attention it deserves both in preaching at liturgical celebrations and in group or individual study of the Word. To establish a culture of regular study of the Word of God by Catholics, the pastors need to continually teach the faithful the importance of the Word of God for daily living and encourage them to read. One of the ways we build relationship with God is through his Word. The Bible connects us with God and the person of Jesus Christ and makes possible a deeper relationship with the Godhead.

As Pope Benedict asserts, the law of the Gospel sets us free from the law of sin and enables us, through grace, to share in the divine life and to overcome our selfishness.[132] He maintains that the Word of God is the foundation of all things. This is because many other things (money, possession, pleasure and power) in which we trust for building our lives are ephemeral and sooner or later proven incapable of fulfilling the deepest yearnings of the human heart.[133] Hence, "in building our lives, we need solid foundations which will endure when human certainties fail."[134] Seeing the Word of God as a solid foundation, he concludes by quoting the words of Scripture that "whoever builds on this word builds the house of his life on rock."[135]

In the prologue to the fourth Gospel, Saint John the Evangelist writes, "In the beginning was the Word. And the Word was with God and the Word was God" (Jn 1:1). The Fathers of the Church affirm that Christ himself "is present in his Word, since it is he who speaks when Scripture is read in the Church."[136] Pope Paul VI sees the study of Sacred Scripture as the soul of sacred theology.[137] Thus,

---

[132] *VD* 9.

[133] *VD* 10.

[134] *VD* 10.

[135] *VD* 10.

[136] SECOND VATICAN ECUMENICAL COUNCIL, Constitution on the Sacred Liturgy, *Sacrosanctum Concilium* (SC). Promulgated by Pope Paul VI on 4 December 1963, n. 24; Cf. *VD* 52.

[137] POPE PAUL VI, *Dei Verbum* (DV)–Dogmatic Constitution on Divine Revelation. Promulgated November 18, 1965, n. 24.

echoing the thoughts of the bishops at the Twelfth Ordinary General Assembly of the Synod of Bishops in the Vatican in 2008, Pope Benedict XVI sees "the rediscovery of God's Word in the life of the Church as a wellspring of constant renewal."[138] He sees the Church as "the home of the Word"[139] and recognizes the central place of the Word in the Sacred liturgy. On this, he maintains,

> Every liturgical action is by its very nature steeped in Sacred Scripture. In the words of the Constitution Sacrosanctum Concilium, "Sacred Scripture is of the greatest importance in the celebration of the liturgy. From it are taken the readings, which are explained in the homily and the psalms that are sung. From Scripture, the petitions, prayers and liturgical hymns receive their inspiration and substance. From Scripture the liturgical actions and signs draw their meaning."[140]

Additionally, the Liturgy of the Word is a decisive element in the celebration of each of the Church's sacraments.[141] Speaking specifically about the relation of the Word to the Eucharist, the Church maintains that the two are so deeply bound together that we cannot understand one without the other. In fact, she honours the Word of God with the same "reverence" as the Eucharistic mystery, although not with the same worship.[142] In view of all this, Pope Benedict XVI exhorts all the Church's pastors engaged in pastoral work to see that the faithful appreciate the profound meaning of the Word of God in the liturgy.[143] To further stress the importance the Church attaches to the Word of God, the Synod Fathers at the Twelfth Ordinary General Assembly of the Synod of Bishops went to the extent of proposing that a visible place of honour should be given to the Sacred Scriptures, even outside of liturgical

---

[138] *VD* 1.

[139] *VD* 52.

[140] *VD* 2, 52.

[141] PONTIFICAL BIBLICAL COMMISSION, The Interpretation of the Bible in the Church, IV, c, 1: ENCHIRIDION VATICANUM 13, n. 3123; also quoted in *VD* 53.

[142] ORDO LECTIONUM MISSAE, 10; see also *VD* 55.

[143] *VD* 52.

celebrations.[144] In agreement with this, Pope Benedict XVI writes, "It is good that the book which contains the word of God should enjoy a visible place of honour inside the Christian Temple, without prejudice to the central place proper to the tabernacle containing the Blessed Sacrament."[145]

Still, to encourage the enhancement of the Word of God in our liturgy, he maintains that songs which are of clear biblical inspiration and which take faith back to the Word of God in the Sacred Scriptures should be given preference.[146] As part of the effort to give the Word its proper place in the life of the Church, the pope encourages pastoral commitment that fosters the centrality of the Word of God. The Bible should inspire all pastoral work.[147] In this light, there should be an effort to look into the ordinary activities of the parishes, the small Christian communities, associations and movements in the Church to see if they are truly committed to promoting among their members a personal encounter with Jesus Christ through his Word in the Bible. According to him, "making the Bible the inspiration of every ordinary and extraordinary pastoral outreach will lead to a greater awareness of the person of Christ."[148] Seeing this critical emphasis on bringing the Bible to the fore in the Church's life as one way to deal with certain pastoral challenges, he writes:

> For this reason, I encourage pastors and the faithful to recognize the importance of this emphasis on the Bible. It will also be the best way to deal with certain pastoral problems which were discussed at the Synod and have to do, for example, with the proliferation of sects which spread a distorted and manipulative reading of Sacred Scripture. Where the faithful are not helped to know the Bible in ac-

---

[144] Cf. *VD* 68.

[145] POPE BENEDICT XVI, Post-Synodal Apostolic Exhortation, *Verbum Domini* (VD)–On the Word of God in the Life and the Mission of the Church, September 30, 2010, n. 68. Here, the pope cites POPE BENEDICT XVI, *Post-Synodal Apostolic Exhortation Sacramentum Caritatis* (SC)–On the Eucharist, 69: AAS99 (2007), 157.

[146] *VD* 70.

[147] VD 73; Cf. also DV 24.

[148] VD 73.

> cordance with the Church's faith and based on her living Tradition, this pastoral vacuum becomes fertile ground for realities like the sects to take root.[149]

Here, it is absolutely clear that the Church favours the culture of reading the Bible. In fact, she insists that pastoral activity should favour associations and movements in the Church that are committed to helping the Church foster formation, prayer, and knowledge of the Bible (in accordance with the Church's faith) among her faithful.[150] All the Christian faithful and in particular catechists who form others should be given suitable training in the knowledge of the Bible. For this purpose, "centres of formation should be established where laity and missionaries can be trained to understand, live and proclaim the word of God."[151] With particular reference to catechesis in the Church, Pope Benedict XVI maintains that catechesis, if it is used wisely, is a wonderful tool that can aid the Church in rediscovering the centrality of the Word. He sees the Emmaus encounter of the two disciples with Jesus in Luke 24:13-25 as a good example of a model of catechesis centered on "the explanation of Sacred Scriptures."[152] In fact, he calls for a biblically inspired catechesis which is something that is lacking in many of our parishes. On this, he asserts:

> I wish to first and foremost state that catechesis must be permeated by the mindset, the spirit and the outlook of the Bible and the Gospels through assiduous contact with the texts themselves; yet it also means remembering that catechesis will be all the richer and more effective for reading the texts with mind and the heart of the Church, and for drawing inspiration from the two millennia of the Church's reflection and life.[153]

[149] VD 73.

[150] *VD* 73.

[151] *VD* 75.

[152] *VD* 74.

[153] Cf. CONGREGATION FOR THE CLERGY, *General Catechetical Directory* (August 15, 1997), 94-96; *ENCHIRIDION VATICANUM*, 16, no. 935; POPE JOHN PAUL II, *Apostolic Exhortation, Catechesis Tradendae* (October 16, 1979), 27: AAS71 (1979), 1299; VD 74.

Continuing the important point he is making here, he states that:

> Knowledge of biblical personages, events, and well-known sayings should thus be encouraged; this can also be promoted by the judicious memorization of some passages which are particularly expressive of the Christian ministries. Catechetical work always entails approaching Scripture in faith and in the Church's Tradition….[154]

Stressing the relationship between Sacred Scripture and the *Catechism of the Catholic Church*, Pope Benedict XVI concludes that both of them in their different ways are meant to nourish catechesis in the Church today.[155] Thus, he encourages the study of the Bible in the Church by lay people and their pastors and insists that they "need to be trained to discern God's will through a familiarity of their legitimate pastors."[156] On the other hand, dioceses should make adequate provisions for the ongoing formation of lay persons entrusted with responsibilities in the Church.[157]

The reading of the Bible should not end in the parish church. The Christian family is a domestic church where the whole family needs to constantly gather around the Word of God. As part of her duties to promote the centrality of the Word of God among the entire faithful, the Church and her pastors should support and help families in embracing and fostering "family prayer, attentive hearing of the word of God and knowledge of the Bible."[158] In view of this, the Synod of Fathers recommend "that every Christian family or household should have a Bible, to be kept in a worthy place and used for reading and prayer."[159] Similarly, they encourage the establishment of small communities of families where people can be led to cultivate the habit of common prayer and of reading

---

[154] *VD* 74.

[155] *VD* 74; *GENERAL CATECHETICAL DIRECTORY,* 128; *Enchiridion Vaticanum* 16, n. 936; VD, 74.

[156] *VD* 74.

[157] POPE JOHN PAUL II, Post-Synodal Exhortation, *Familiaris Consortio* (November 22, 1981), 49: AAS 74 (1982), 140–141; Cf. VD 84.

[158] *VD* 85.

[159] *Ibid.*

and meditating on Scripture and striving to live it out.[160] Finally, Pope Benedict XVI encourages the use of *Lectio Divina* as a form of prayer that leads one to read and meditate on the Word of God. He encourages individuals, communities, and associations to say Marian prayers, especially the Holy Rosary, which leads us to reflect on the mysteries of the Lord Jesus in Sacred Scripture.

From all that we have said in this section, the position of the Church regarding the importance of the Bible and the centrality of the Word of God in the life of the Church, the parish community, small Christian communities, the associations in the Catholic Church, the family and in the life of every Christian is crystal clear. Hence, the universal Church invites all her pastors, catechists, and the faith leaders in the communities to make the Bible inspire their pastoral work and activities. She calls on all Christian families and the entire faithful to commit to prayer, knowledge of the Bible (that is, regular reading and meditation on the Word) and dedication to living it out as an integral part of their spiritual development. The teaching of the Church here can be summarized as: Read the Bible or study the Word of God regularly; meditate on it and live it out daily; share it with others and spread this culture among all the faithful.

This vision of the universal Church is certainly awesome and seeks to move us along the right direction as a Church and a people. Unfortunately, this beautiful teaching, like many others like it on different important subjects (such as evangelization and family) is yet to reach the vast majority of the Catholic faithful in our parishes. Most of the groups and associations in the Church and majority of the faithful do not even know about the existence of this rich document. Consequently, they are ignorant of this clarion call by Pope Benedict XVI and the Synod Fathers to promote the centrality of the Word of God and build a culture of daily or regular Bible study and meditation among the faithful.

One can reasonably presume that when bishops from all over the world gather with the pope to deliberate on certain issues in the Church and world, such issues must be critical. In other words, they have some serious implications for the faithful and the institutional

160 *VD* 85.

Church as a whole to merit such attention at the highest level of the Church. If that is true, then it is expected that dioceses should organize seminars around these teachings or seek other effective means to disseminate information to the people. This is necessary to keep the clergy, religious, and the laity in tune with what the Church is saying in order to shape their thinking and the direction of their pastoral work.

Similarly, one should expect the pastors to draw the attention of the lay leaders and the faithful to new teachings or documents from the pope or the Synod of Bishops that affect their lives and that of the Church. In fact, the response by dioceses and parishes in collaboration with institutions, movements, and associations in the Church should be to devise ways to incarnate or domesticate the rich teachings from the pope and the Synod Fathers once they are published. This requires them to promote discussion on the documents and find ways to implement the contents as they apply to their different situations, granted that circumstances may differ from continent to continent and from region to region.

Unfortunately, this is not the case with most dioceses. Most of these beautiful teachings often end up in the documents in which they were published. Worse still, many of the pastors themselves are either ignorant of the existence of the documents or are simply not familiar with their rich contents or are simply indifferent. This attitude is harmful to the Church and her development because the indifference or ignorance of the clergy in most cases often translates to ignorance on the part of their parishioners as far as these documents are concerned. For example, I asked a congregation in a city parish about the new evangelization which was launched by Pope John Paul II in his 1990 encyclical, *Redemptoris Missio*, but to my surprise, only a few (less than 5 percent) knew about it 27 years after its publication. It was not surprising then that they did not know what it is all about and did not give it the serious attention it deserves.

Perhaps, what is even more surprising is the fact that many priests do not have a clear understanding of the subject as they tend to confuse it with the whole of the Church's mission of evangelization. Thus, to bridge this wide gulf between the official teaching of the Church on topical issues, such as the need for regular Bible study and meditation by Catholics, there has to be a paradigm shift in our dioceses and parishes. That is to say, they must, as a matter of urgency, devise ways of getting the people to know and implement important teachings contained in Church documents.

The Response of Catholics to the Accusation That Catholics Do Not Read the Bible

An important feature of today's Christianity is the centrality of the Bible or the Word of God. Among most Christians in Nigeria and other places, the Bible has become a major determinant of true teaching and who teaches the truth or not. Going back to the accusation that Catholics do not read the Bible, what appears to be the common reaction by most Catholics is to quickly point out the number of Scripture readings during our Sunday and weekday Masses. There is no doubt that the Holy Mass and the celebration of the other sacraments of the Church involve an encounter with the Word of God. Nevertheless, if we are truly serious about evangelization and the growth of our people through an ongoing encounter with the Word, some critical questions to ask are, What percentage of those who attend our Sunday Masses really pay attention to the readings? How many of them are able to recall the readings after Mass or two days or a week after? How many of them strive to live or apply the readings to their daily lives? These questions are without prejudice to those Catholics who strive on all these grounds.

Following a careful investigation, my experience is that the majority of our faithful are not able to recall the readings one or two days after Mass and some immediately after Mass or even after the Gospel reading. In a particular parish, I interviewed seventeen people after Sunday Mass and my finding was an eye-opener. While one of them was able to recall all three readings at Mass, another could only remember the first reading. The remaining fifteen people could neither remember any of the books from which the readings were taken nor a simple sentence from any of them.[161] Another Sunday, I interviewed thirteen youths in the evening and

[161] The sad thing is that this has become the normal disposition of many Catholics to the Word of God.

none of them could recall a single sentence from any of the readings at Mass. In the same parish, I asked some of the key functionaries at Mass (the altar servers, the choristers, and welcoming ministers) the same question immediately after the Gospel reading and found that over 94 percent of them could not recall any line from the readings or their sources.

Again, at a programme with about 500 of our Catholic youths in attendance, I discovered that only about 12 of them (about 2.4 percent) read the Bible regularly. Besides, none of them could remember the readings of that Sunday or any sentence from any of them. Still, in another parish, only a few read the Bible regularly. Besides, most of them (about 96 percent of those present) could not remember anything from the readings or the books immediately after the Gospel reading. The question here is, "How can one strive to act on what he did not hear or cannot recollect in the course of the week?"

The point I am making here is that the "common defence" that we take three readings at Mass in response to the accusation that we do not read the Bible cannot be justified in many cases. The critical thing is whether the people are encountering God in the readings at Mass on an ongoing basis and in such a way that can lead to conversion, an ongoing transformation, and spiritual fruitfulness. Even if it were the case that everybody is able to recall the readings at Mass, the second question will be whether that should stop individuals from daily or regular reading of the Bible and meditation on the living Word of God. No doubt, most Catholics have Bibles at home. But then, is a Bible meant to decorate our shelves or to be used as a *talisman* to prevent bad dreams and repel the attack of enemies when we are asleep? Was it given to us for this purpose?

This practice of not reading and meditating on Scripture on a daily or regular basis is harmful to Catholics themselves and to the Church as a whole. It impoverishes many of the faithful and reduces their confidence before their Pentecostal counterparts who end up intimidating them with a few quotations from Scripture, which may or may not be misleading. This has led many Catholics to drift to other churches while others tend to doubt some Catholic teachings and practices, such as the intercession of the Virgin Mary and the saints, the use of incense in our liturgy, which Isaiah 1:13

calls an "abomination" unto the Lord, and the presence of statues and images in our churches when God commands us in Exodus 20:1-6 that we are not to make graven images for ourselves.[162] Such erroneous and misleading interpretation and application of the Scriptures are known to have created some doubts in the minds of some faithful who end up accusing the Church of idolatry and false worship. For example, there are some Catholics who drifted to the new churches because they cannot stand the presence of statues in our churches.[163]

As we know, a prayerful reading of Scriptures does not only bring one in contact with the living Word of God, but also with Christ himself. Every true encounter with Christ in his Word always has a positive impact on a soul. It exposes one to a heavenly perspective about life and things in general. Some years ago, I tried to convince a former Catholic to return to the Church, but her reply was quite emphatic: "I can't. They [the Pentecostal church] taught me to read the Bible." An elderly woman in a similar situation bluntly rejected the idea of returning to the Catholic Church. She attributed the growth she was experiencing in her spiritual life

[162] In all of these cases, many of our separated brethren tend to read these passages out of context and end up confusing a good number of our Catholics because of their lack of familiarity with Scripture.

[163] Sometime in 2003, I had an interesting encounter with a man who had been a Catholic for the entire 50 years of his life. Although he claimed to love the Church, he left for a Pentecostal church because he was misled into believing that Catholics worshipped idols. His confusion stemmed from the erroneous interpretation of Exodus 20:1-6 by some Pentecostals he encountered. Identifying the lack of familiarity with the Scriptures as his problem, I led him to read Exodus 25:17-22 and Numbers 21:4-9. Following little exegesis on the passages, he realized he was wrong and later returned to the Catholic Church. What was remarkable about the experience was his utter shock after reading Exodus 25 and Numbers 21. His expression was, "You mean this is in the Bible?" to which I responded, "Yes." This confusion, which many other Catholics have, stems from poor catechesis which excludes the Sacred Scriptures.

to daily study of the Bible, which she learnt in her new church. The truth is that there are so many like them out there who left the Church because of ignorance or lack of familiarity with the Bible. The question the Church and her pastors are called to answer is, "How long will this continue? How long will we continue to allow our members to drift away due to ignorance of the Bible?"

Many of our priests often look down on the Pentecostal pastors. Perhaps, to show that we are more knowledgeable and are better equipped for ministry, we often describe them as "people who went to a Bible college for three months." But in view of the concrete realities we face today, it becomes necessary to ask ourselves some questions. For instance, how long will the so-called pastors with "inferior knowledge" and "training" continue to take away our flock? How can this be justified in spite of nine years of seminary formation with degrees (and sometimes master's and doctorate degrees) in philosophy and theology? Does it not seem to us that something is seriously wrong somewhere? If the present situation of things is not enough of a "wake-up call" to have a rethink and do the needful to ground our lay faithful in the Sacred Scriptures and thus prevent them from straying, then will it be wrong for anyone to label us as mere hirelings instead of shepherds? Perhaps, we need to read what God says about the shepherds of Israel in chapter 34 of Ezekiel, and what Jesus says about shepherds and hirelings in John 10 and see how these statements apply to us.[164]

While we acknowledge the complacency of many of our priests in this area, we most equally admit that many of our lay faithful also have their fair share of the blame. This is because in parishes where the more concerned pastors labour to promote the Word and organize weekly Bible study, only a few people attend. The

[164] In Ezekiel 34, God accuses the shepherds of Israel (the rulers and their administrators) of not taking care of his flock while feeding fat themselves. Their lack of concern for the well-being of the flock caused some of them to be injured, some to be killed, and others to stray. In John 10, Jesus makes an important distinction between the true shepherd and a hireling who pretends to be a shepherd. While the former loves the sheep and is willing to defend them and even lay down his life for them, the latter is more concerned about himself or the benefits that accrue to him and is willing to sacrifice the sheep.

cheering news, however, is that some associations and movements in the Church, such as Catholic Biblical Instructors Union (CBIU) and the Catholic Charismatic Renewal Movement (CCRM) are doing a lot to expose their members to the culture of regular and prayerful study of the Bible in order to lead them into an encounter with Christ or a deeper communion with him in his Word.

Although this is commendable, they still need the close guidance of their trained pastors to avoid misinterpretations and error. Nevertheless, the task to enthrone the culture of daily or regular Bible study and meditation among Catholics and Catholic families is not for a few priests or interested individuals or associations in the Church, but for all. In fact, the family should be involved in creating this culture, and our catechism classes, small Christian communities, and the pulpit should be outlets for advancing this paradigm shift. To prepare themselves for this task, both catechists and parents should avail themselves of every opportunity to ground themselves in the Word of God through daily or regular prayerful reading of the Bible. As they encounter God intimately and derive enormous spiritual nourishment from this beautiful and rewarding practice, they, in turn, will recommend it to their catechumens and children.

Similarly, all major Church functionaries, such as the choristers, altar servers, lectors, and welcoming ministers should receive basic formation in Bible study and meditation as an essential part of their formation prior to and even after their official induction. This ongoing exposure to the Word of God will most certainly have a positive effect on their personal lives and their ministries in the Church. Moreover, it will better equip them to defend their faith more vigorously and to educate their non-Catholic counterparts who call their faith to question. In other words, this conscious effort to expose them to Scripture will contribute significantly to stemming the drift of Catholics to other churches as well as improve our worship experience within our parishes. The point is that, as the Word of God penetrates their hearts and transforms them from within, these liturgical ministers, especially the choir, are more likely to "operate" from a higher level of conviction, faith, and spirituality capable of adding huge spiritual value to our worship experience.

The universities and other higher institutions of learning are the main places we lose our young Catholics to the Pentecostals. As a part of the effort to stem this trend, we need to pay greater attention to the formation of our teenagers and youths, especially before they gain admission into these institutions. The purpose is to offer them basic formation in daily Bible study, meditation on the Word of God, and a solid formation in the *Catechism of the Catholic Church*. Similarly, it is absolutely necessary to expose them to the antics of the Pentecostals (and even the Muslims)[165] and teach them how to organize fellowships and prayers in the absence of a priest. As Pope Benedict XVI himself admits, young people represent the future of the Church and their pastors need to show adequate concern for them. According to him, "we need to help young people to gain confidence and familiarity with Sacred Scripture so it can become a compass pointing out the path to follow."[166] Even where others fail to measure to expectation, our institutions and formation houses, such as secondary schools and minor seminaries, will have no justifiable excuses whatsoever not to succeed in this area.

To concentrate on the Bible, which is the subject matter here, it is not debatable that the faithful can derive immense spiritual benefits from daily or regular contact with Christ in his Word. We equally cannot exclude the enormous spiritual and pastoral transformation that this can bring to our parishes, dioceses, and the universal Church as a whole. In particular, considering the immense benefits of familiarity with regular spiritual Bible study to stem the

[165] To draw them away from the Church, the Pentecostals often confuse many of them with all sorts of arguments that attack our Catholic doctrines and practices, based on their misinterpretation of Scripture. Today, the Muslims are seeking to convert Christians in general by attacking our core Christian beliefs, such as the doctrines of the Holy Trinity and the resurrection. We need to school our young people adequately in these areas and other areas of attack by the Pentecostals and the Muslims to prepare them to defend their faith convincingly and educate their counterparts.

[166] POPE BENEDICT XVI, "Message for the Twenty-First World Youth Day." February 22, 2006: AAS 98 (2006), 282-286; Quoted also in *VD* 104.

increasing drift of Catholics to other Churches, ecclesiastical authorities would need to establish a diocesan policy on regular Bible study for every parish to follow. This should be backed up with necessary structures rather than leave such decision to the wish of each pastor.

The diocesan policy should make Bible study compulsory in every parish as a matter of necessity. The decision to have or not to have Bible study in the parish should never be left to individual priests. This is because some may ignore it for various "unjustifiable" reasons, ranging from sheer laziness, complacency, inability to prioritize or even total lack of interest in this area. By making it a diocesan policy, the bishops themselves would be at the forefront of the "crusade" to change the present culture among Catholics and promote the centrality of the Word in their dioceses.

Anyone who has discovered the immense spiritual riches in the Word of God from regular study exhibits a particular attitude towards it. Quite naturally, he will cherish it deeply and see it as a compass that can give direction to his life and the lives of others in a world that is full of misleading ideologies and practices. Recognizing the value of a frequent, prayerful contact with the living Word of God to the deepening and flourishing of the spiritual life of every Christian, especially bishops and priests, Pope Benedict XVI challenges them to always put "in first place" frequent personal reading and meditation on the Word.[167] Addressing the entire clergy with regard to the nourishment of their spiritual life, he maintains:

> The Word of God is indispensable in forming the hearts of a good shepherd and minister of the word. Bishops, priests and deacons can hardly think that they are living out their vocation and mission apart from a decisive and renewed commitment to sanctification, one of whose pillars is contact with God's word.[168]

In fact, for Pope Benedict XVI, the Word of God is the "basis of all authentic Christian spirituality."[169] As such, bishops and

[167] *VD* 79.

[168] *VD* 78.

[169] *VD* 86.

priests should read and live it and form the faithful in the knowledge of the Bible. According to him, "Bishops and priests, in accordance with their specific mission, are the first to be called to live a life completely at the service of the Word and to form the faithful in the authentic knowledge of Scripture."[170]

He insists that the lay people ought to be trained to discern the will of God through familiarity with his Word, read and studied in the Church under the supervision of her legitimate pastors.[171] In view of that, the bishops as the chief promoters of the centrality of the Word of God should utilize every opportunity at diocesan events and gatherings to exhort the priests, religious, the leaders of the lay associations and movements, and the lay faithful as a whole on the need to change the present "undesirable culture" in favour of promoting the centrality of the Word of God and a Bible-inspired pastoral work in the Church. If Christ is at the centre of what the Church is and does (her mission) and we agree with Saint Jerome that "ignorance of Scripture is ignorance of Christ," then we must see and use Scripture as a basic tool to lead people to Christ and help them build intimacy with him.

However, to guide the faithful on how to study the Word of God meaningfully with their eyes on personal conversion, transformation, and spiritual fruitfulness, it will be extremely helpful to provide them a simple booklet with some necessary aids. In fact, to ensure that they do not fall into the error of fundamentalism or heresy, such aids should include the five keys for correct biblical interpretation articulated by the *Catechism of the Catholic Church*.

These are:

i. reading to discover the intention of the author,
ii. being attentive to the unity of Scripture rather than take each text out of context,
iii. reading the Scripture within the Living Tradition of the Church rather than making oneself the sole interpreter of Scripture,
iv. reading the Scripture within the symphony of God's Revelation,

[170] *VD* 94.

[171] *VD* 84.

v. paying attention to the four senses of Scripture—the literal, moral, allegorical, and anagogical senses.[172]

Actually, there are two senses of Scripture according to an ancient tradition: the literal sense and the spiritual sense. But then, the latter is subdivided into the moral, allegorical, and anagogical senses.[173]

Although we encourage everyone to read the Bible, the correct approach must be that of humility and prayer in recognition of the fact that we did not write it and can never be the final authority as far as the interpretation of a Scripture text or passage is concerned. In approaching Scripture, we need to search out information about the author, the circumstance in which he wrote, the literary style he employed, and the intended meaning or message he wished to communicate among other things. We need to see the whole Bible as God's Word and avoid the prevailing tendency among some Christians to quote particular Scripture texts out of context. It is crucial to note that the final interpretation of the Bible belongs to the Magisterium of the Church and, to help scholars in the task of Biblical interpretation, it has enumerated certain guiding principles to which all should pay attention.

No doubt, there are some Catholics who see the call to read and meditate on the Scriptures frequently as unnecessary. But the fact that the Church encourages us to do so highlights the importance she attaches to the Word and the great benefits inherent in the practice itself. If an individual, priest or lay person, is opposed to frequent Bible study and meditation, then we can only deduce that he either does not practice that himself, or he is yet to discover the treasures of the Bible or the immense benefits that derive from a personal reading and meditation on the Word. As we mentioned earlier, the truth is that those who have encountered God in his Word and have experienced the transforming power of the Word in their own lives will most certainly recommend the noble practice of daily or frequent reading of Scripture and meditation to others.

Still focusing on the urgent need to foster a new culture of daily Bible study and meditation, we cannot forget that the big picture

[172] See *CCC* 109-119.

[173] *CCC* 115.

of the Church's mission of evangelization involves the transformation of the secular order or the culture in society with the principles of the Gospel. Since no culture can be called Christian if it is not shaped by the Gospel of Christ, then we must understand that we cannot possibly fulfill the mission of the Church if the Word of God does not take root in people's hearts and convert and transform them from within into the image of Jesus Christ the Saviour.

Chapter Four

WHY ARE PEOPLE LEAVING US? THE ISSUE OF INSPIRING MUSIC AND A SPIRIT-FILLED WORSHIP

One of the characteristic features of the Christian Church is worship. Although God invites us to worship him and worship is for our own benefit and not his, Jesus makes it abundantly clear that it is not every form of worship that is acceptable to him (cf. Jn 4:23-24). God's interest is not primarily in the actual "worship experience," but in the worshippers themselves. The quality or acceptability of any worship is dependent on the life and heart of the worshippers themselves. In other words, there can be no true worship in the real sense without true worshippers who are obedient and dedicated to God and desire to worship him in spirit and truth (cf. Is 1:1-20; Jn 4:23).

Praise is a vital part of the Church's worship experience. Praise-singing from the heart is prayer. Psalm 22:3 says that the Lord dwells on the praises of his people and as we all know there is power in praise. An old adage which Saint Augustine cited says, "he who sings well [that is, from the heart and with faith] prays twice." Through praise-singing, King Jehoshaphat and the Israelites were able to rout their enemies according to the promise of the Lord (cf. 2 Chr 20:1-24). In view of the importance of praises in the life of a believer or a church, Hebrews 13:15 invites us to offer God a sacrifice of praise, while the Book of Revelation sums it up by telling us that the angels and saints worship God continuously night and day before his throne in heaven (Rv 7:15).

The Holy Mass is the highest act of adoration, praise, and worship in the Catholic Church and indeed the world. This is because it is both the re-enactment of the sacrifice of the Cross in an unbloody manner and the action of Christ. Good music and a spirit-filled singing[174] by the choir and the congregation are critical to worship and thus the Mass. They create a wonderful ambience for a profound worship experience and heighten the potential for a spiritual encounter with God, which can lead the faithful to personal conversion or an ongoing transformation.[175] Spirit-filled singing transforms the atmosphere, uplifts the soul, ushers people into the divine presence of God, and causes them to worship him from the depth of their beings. In addition, it has the ability to soften the heart and predispose the congregation to be more open and attentive to the living Word of God. These truths became clear to me over time from my personal experience at some Masses, our parish Life in the Spirit Seminar (LISS) and our annual "night of praise" in the parish tagged "Unusual Praise."

This whole issue of inspiring music and a spirit-filled and fulfilling worship is arguably one of the major reasons we are losing many of our members, young and old, to the Pentecostal churches. A significant number of them leave, not because of our theology or doctrines, but for lack of fulfillment in worship. Far from being peculiar to the Church in Nigeria, this is a universal phenomenon. For example, Sherry Weddell tells us that, "when asked why they chose to join a Protestant faith, the overwhelming majority [that is, of ex-Catholics in the United States] responded that they enjoyed their new faith's services and worship."[176] Some of us may be quick to judge them as ignorant and dismiss their point without proper reflection, but then Weddell has an important warning for us. She maintains that,

> As frustrating as it can be for Catholics to hear this, it is critical that we listen carefully when spiritual seekers give

---

[174] By Spirit-filled singing I mean a form of "ministration" or singing from the depth of one's heart which clearly has the pleasure of God or his glory as its primary goal. It is the form of singing that also aims at raising the souls of the faithful to God to get them to exalt him wholeheartedly and disposes them to open their hearts to him.

[175] As people are touched in their spirit as a result of a spirit-filled worship experience they tend to yield themselves to God, making conversion and/or an ongoing spiritual transformation possible.

[176] S. WEDELL, *Forming Intentional Disciples…, op. cit.,* p. 30.

> us their reasons for changing faiths. It is all too easy to project our own passionately held theological and ecclesial convictions upon people who are motivated by entirely different questions and concerns. I cannot tell you how many times I have heard intelligent Catholics casually dismiss evangelical worship as mere "entertainment" while showing no understanding of what motivated millions of their former Catholic brothers and sisters to embrace that form of worship in the first place.[177]

Judging from her own investigation in the US, she dismisses the "entertainment" thesis as weak. For her, it only reflects our Catholic insider judgment about what we presume must have motivated those who left the Catholic Church for evangelical communities. But none of us had ever heard a living former Catholic use that language.[178] On the contrary, what you hear from them is usually something like "I never met Jesus in a living way as a Catholic."[179]

Nevertheless, while I do not dismiss the issue of ignorance with regard to Catholics who leave the Church, my argument here is not whether or not they are right. Rather, my position is that we need to have a "listening ear" and then judge carefully on the basis of what we have heard. As a matter of fact, we need to look inward objectively and constructively critique what we are doing in most of our parishes, how we are going about them, and how spiritually impactful they are. The starting point of such an important and much needed reflection should be what we are doing in the area of worship, especially the Holy Mass, how well we are feeding or schooling our people in the Bible (the Word of God) and in our doctrines and practices, and the level of openness to the Holy Spirit among the faithful during worship.

In general, Africans like to sing and dance. Experience shows that people go to church for different reasons. Those who are seeking a spiritual encounter with God tend to have greater expectations during worship in comparison with those who merely go to church to fulfill an obligation or to "enjoy" the Holy Mass. Those

---

[177] *Ibid.*

[178] *Ibid.*, p. 31.

[179] *Ibid.*

who long for something more profound and inspiring are naturally attracted to the kind of music that can launch them into God's presence, or a worship experience that can facilitate a spiritual encounter with God.

Although the theology behind our traditional English hymns is profound, the melody or actual rendering of many of the hymns in some places may not appeal so much to a typical African. For instance, they can fall short of people's expectations from the standpoint of instrumental accompaniment. That aside, the mode and the quality of singing by the choir and the congregation, the lack of "spiritual power" (or faith) behind their singing, and the level of physical, mental, emotional and spiritual involvement and participation on their part can also affect the overall impact of the worship experience on the people.

Singing is a ministry in the Church. The choristers are supposed to be singing ministers who prompt and lead others to praise and worship God during Mass as a form of ministration to him. Here, it is important to note the distinction between "singing" and "ministration." The fundamental reason or driving force behind mere singing and conscious ministration through music is not exactly the same. In reality, while almost everybody sings at Mass, it is not everybody that truly ministers with their songs as far as a spirit-filled and inspiring worship that can give glory to God is concerned. While singing merely requires the ability and a desire to sing and the singer may not have a living relationship with God or actually achieve a spiritual connection with him, "ministering through music or singing" requires much more than that. Among other things, it requires a personal relationship with God, deep love for him, a strong faith in him and in his power, a burning desire to praise, adore, and glorify him, the ability to connect with him and maintain this spiritual connection during the singing-ministration, a genuine concern for the conversion and salvation of the worshipping faithful, and a strong desire to be used as a vessel to minister to them.

Sometime in 2014, I had the opportunity to attend a highly spirit-filled liturgical celebration at the National Shrine in Washington, D.C. The participants at the Mass were some trained liturgy ministers from different parts of the United States. The music was celestial, superb, and spirit-filled. The participants were visibly immersed—body, emotion, mind and soul—in worship and their countenance was like that of a people who were completely wrapped up with God in his glory. The worship experience as a whole was breath-taking, spirit-filled, inspiring, and overwhelmingly fulfilling. It brought about this strong feeling of heaven on earth. I felt God's presence in a very powerful and compelling way. I was drawn to renew my commitment to God, to offer myself to him in worship, and to remain there in his presence.

Although I lived in Italy for some years and have participated in Masses in some parts of Europe, North America, South Africa and West Africa, I tend to see that particular "celebration of the Holy Mass" as the celebration of the Holy Mass at its very best. It was my own "transfiguration experience" viewed from the perspective of the Apostles.[180] That day, I left the basilica deeply fulfilled and happy that I was there, even though it was by chance. In all, the point to note is that the worship experience was so awesome, deep, and spirit-filled that it made an encounter with God so easy. That spiritual encounter was so uplifting and impactful that I still share the experience with everyone who cares to listen to me today.

A serious point we should not lose sight of here is that the Mass in question was not a different type of Mass from what the Church specifies. It was completely faithful to the rubrics of the Mass stipulated by the Church. But the difference was in its packaging, that is, the quality of the "singing ministration" by the choir, the overall worship ambience it created, and the disposition, desire, commitment and the determination of the priests, choristers, and the congregation to worship God in a profound and acceptable way. Actually, the Church expects us (every worshipper) to "go forth" at the end of every Mass and announce the Good News and share

---

[180] During Jesus' transfiguration on Mount Tabor, the Apostles—Peter, James, and John—were completely overwhelmed, and Peter wanted them to remain there with Jesus (Cf. Mt 17:1-6). Although I had gone to the National Shrine for sightseeing and prayer that day, I was so glad that I witnessed that Mass. I too felt like Peter. As a matter of fact, I forgot all about myself and truly focused on God. That was how impactful the Mass was. The music and the whole worship experience facilitated the encounter.

our experience of God. But the truth is that people will do that naturally and with utmost zeal and joy if they have been seriously impacted during worship, and the quality of the singing-ministration by the choir has a great role here even though we all equally have our vital roles in the liturgy.

The natural but critical question that should arise from the foregoing is, "How can we make such spirit-filled singing and spiritually fulfilling worship the regular experience of Catholics at Sunday Mass rather than a rare or an exceptional one?" Even if we cannot replicate the exact quality of singing and the profound worship experience as the National Shrine in our parish liturgy, we can, at least, make it our goal and devote all our resources to achieving it. There is absolutely an urgent need to deal with the present undesirable situation in many of our parishes if we are to keep our people from drifting and if we hope to bring back those who have already drifted.[181] To take our choristers and congregation to a new height where the quest will be an inspiring and spiritually fulfilling worship that is pleasing to God, first, we need to identify the sources and the nature of our problems.

In reality, the problem is multifaceted. Ordinarily, it concerns both the priests and the choristers as the main "prompters" within the liturgy and the congregation as a whole. As we all know, the Holy Mass is the re-enactment of Christ's sacrifice on Calvary and it is rich in every sense. The fact that it is the greatest act of praise, worship, and prayer is not in doubt as no one can do it better than Jesus. In actuality, the real problem is not with the Mass or its structure or even many of our hymns, although we cannot discountenance the huge cultural difference between us and the whites (or the Europeans in particular) as far as music is concerned. On the contrary, the real problem is the way we approach the Mass, which is extremely important.

[181] This does not in any way suggest that music is the only reason people are drifting or that this is the only area we need to fix. Also, there may be people who actually go to some of these churches because they tend to relax some of the Christian teachings or because they focus on "prosperity Gospel." Nonetheless, we are interested in the more reasonable complaints that we need to look into as a Church.

It is a known fact that many of the priests, the choristers, and the people themselves do not prepare adequately for the Sunday liturgy and this naturally impacts the overall outcome of our worship experience. The deliberate decision to focus more on the choir here is because of their vital role in fostering an atmosphere for a spirit-filled worship. Given their vital role in the liturgy, they can either enhance or mar the liturgy by the quality of their singing.[182] While spirit-filled singing can uplift the congregation to worship God well, poor singing can distract people from true worship and cause enormous frustration, which is why some Catholics drift away in search of spiritual fulfillment during worship.[183]

From my interaction with different choirs and the faithful, it is obvious that the focus of an average chorister at Mass is to enjoy singing and entertain the congregation, while most people in the congregation simply want to "enjoy" the Mass. Here, the primary focus is still ourselves—primarily our pleasure, not God's pleasure or his glory even though this point is not applicable to all choristers.[184] On the contrary, the real goal of singing or ministration during worship is the glory of God and our sanctification. Worship is first and foremost about what we offer him. It is about rendering "service" to him to give him glory; to pour out our hearts to him in adoration, thanksgiving, and praise; and to offer ourselves to him as a living sacrifice, even though we also ask for the forgiveness of our sins and present our petitions to him. Singing is meant to unite the worshippers as one people—the people of God, and to usher

---

[182] Note that our focus here is on the packaging of the Mass because the Holy Mass, on its own, is deeply rich and is designed to foster a living encounter with God that can result in conversion, spiritual transformation, and fruitfulness.

[183] It should be noted that the longing for spiritual fulfillment during worship is not self-centred. Viewed in a positive sense, we mean the type of fulfillment that comes from an experience of connecting with God successfully to give him glory and offer him acceptable service. A spirit-filled worship atmosphere makes this experience possible.

[184] In actuality, some of the choristers have a relationship with God and try their best to sing for his glory. Nevertheless, the percentage of those in this category is low.

them into his divine presence and inspire them to minister to him and give him pleasure.

Spirit-filled singing inspires and uplifts the congregation. It facilitates encounter with God, makes it easier for the worshippers to offer themselves to him, to pray better and to experience greater spiritual fulfillment during worship. God is always at the centre of every true ministration or singing that merits to be called prayer. Since the goal is to enter into his presence and serve or minister to him, achieving a spiritual connection with him is of utmost importance. In fact, spirit-filled singing or ministration involves a union of hearts and persons—the union of the members of the worshipping community with God in a profound way.

Sadly, singing in many of our parishes does not measure up to what we can call a wholehearted ministration to God or describe as "spirit-filled and inspiring." Experience shows that most of us, including the choristers, often sing without first getting spiritually connected to God and without paying particular attention to what we are saying to him in our hymns or actually meaning it.[185] Strictly speaking, such mechanical singing from the head rather than the heart cannot be said to be prayer, understood as the raising up of our minds and hearts to God or communication with him. Now, if it is not prayer, then how can it be a ministration or service to God in the real sense?

God deserves our very best in worship. The quality of singing by the choir and the participation in singing by the congregation in some of our parishes is extremely poor and can appear "insulting" to God where it is nowhere near the best we can actually offer him. Sometimes, it is so poor and uninspiring that one can rightly conclude that most of the choristers themselves neither understand worship in general nor the real goal of music within the liturgy. To be candid, most of them love to sing and desire to serve the Church in this area and actually devote their time to this. But then, their poor understanding of worship or what it means to minister through singing is a major problem. As much as they love to

[185] For instance, it is easy to sing a hymn like "I Surrender all to Jesus" and enjoy ourselves without even thinking of what we are saying, not to mention having any real desire to surrender even 20 percent of our lives to him.

sing, many of them often do not have their eyes on wholehearted, God-centred, Spirit-filled and acceptable worship that can uplift the congregation spiritually and inspire them to worship God sincerely and enthusiastically. This is because a significant number of them do not invest adequately in their own spiritual lives and formation as well as in the acquisition of the practical skills that will enable them to function at their best. This greatly harms those faithful who go to Mass with a strong desire to encounter God and worship him in spirit and truth.

At other times, the mindset or disposition of the choir is that of "performance." Many of our choristers erroneously see their role as that of "performance" or "entertainment." Again, the primary focus here is not God or his glory. It is not primarily about offering an acceptable sacrifice to him or inspiring the congregation to worship him in spirit and truth. Rather, it is more about entertaining the people. This explains why they actually behave as "performers" who sing "for" the people rather than as "prompters" whose main role is to inspire and lead the congregation to sing and worship God wholeheartedly. Hence, some of them have a strong tendency to reduce the congregation to mere spectators and recipients of their action.

No doubt, we have many talented and committed singers in the choir in many parishes who can sing beautifully. But then, while having a good voice and singing beautifully may be good enough for professional singers or an opera, it is certainly not good enough for a singing minister and for worship. Ministration through singing requires something more. It requires a level of spiritual consciousness and relationship with God. Unfortunately, most of our choristers lack that strong consciousness of God's presence and can hardly connect with him and maintain that connection during singing.[186] Most times, they do not pay attention to the lyrics of the songs they sing and may even lack faith in what they say. This kind of mechanical and uninspiring singing or "so-called worship" often lacks "spiritual power" behind it and can be extremely frustrating

[186] However, this problem is not limited to the choir alone. Many of the priests and the members of the congregation are equally guilty. Just like the choristers, a significant number of them who actually sing often do so mechanically without "spiritual power" or faith behind their singing.

to those members of our congregation who long for a living encounter with God at Mass.

A significant number of former Catholics actually cited this lack of spiritual connectivity and fulfillment arising from poor and uninspiring singing as the primary reason they left the Church for the Pentecostal churches. Some Pentecostals who came into the Catholic Church through marriage consider singing and worship as a whole in many of our parishes too dull and uninspiring. Even some convinced Catholics who are desirous of a profound worship experience complain about this same feeling of frustration and lack of spiritual fulfillment during worship from time to time. Interestingly, some even confessed to attending Mass in their parishes on Sundays only to go to Pentecostal churches afterwards in search of inspiring music and spiritual encounter and fulfillment during worship.[187] Although they cherish their Catholic faith and wish to remain Catholic, their hearts are beating for more in the sense of an inspiring worship.[188]

To further buttress the point being made here, I have celebrated Masses in some urban parishes in Nigeria and abroad and my experience in some was that of a deep-seated frustration. Singing by the choir and the congregation was uninspiring and the overall participation of the people was extremely poor. In a particular city parish in Nigeria, some members of the congregation who could no longer bear the situation openly expressed their deep frustration during worship. But unfortunately, the choir resisted every effort to effect a positive change through proper training, hard work, and

[187] For example, the particular response a Catholic woman I confronted on this matter was simply: "Father I have not left the Catholic Church. I go to the Pentecostal church just because of music." Another active Catholic confessed that although she attended Mass every Sunday and said her rosary, she always went to one of the Pentecostal churches for soul-uplifting music that offers her a fulfillment in worship. There are many other Catholics like them. But the truth is that some of those who go to these churches every Sunday because of music or spirit-filled singing eventually remain there.

[188] Here, I am not justifying their decision to leave the Church. Instead, I am stating things as they are even though I believe that a better thing to do is to remain and work with others to find a solution to the problem.

growth in spiritual consciousness. They were simply oblivious of the harm they were causing the worshipping community in keeping them at that level of dissatisfaction and frustration during worship.

Certainly, this does not represent the situation in every parish. In some parishes, the choristers and their pastors who are conscious of the spiritual yearnings of their people strive to promote an inspiring music and a spirit-filled worship experience. Even though there is room for improvement in those places, my major concern here is that if we continue to expose our members to poor and uninspiring liturgy over time, it will get to a point where those who long for more may not be able to stomach it and will go elsewhere in search of spiritual fulfillment. Even those who choose to remain either continue in their frustration or are gradually conditioned to accept as normal the undesirable situation or the aberration to which they are exposed every week rather than aspire for the ideal, thinking that it is impossible to attain.

Again, my interactions with many choristers in different parishes reveal that the vast majority of them are not well-informed about their ministry, though it is due to no fault of theirs. About 90 percent or more have a poor understanding of worship in general and ministration in particular. They neither see themselves as ministers in the true sense of the word, nor comprehend their real role in worship. Worse still, most of them do not know the goal of music in the liturgy, especially the Mass.[189] This problem arises from inadequate or a total lack of intellectual, spiritual, and apostolic formation for the choir in the art of worship and ministration, a problem which affects the congregation as a whole. Most people

---

[189] The issue here is that if most of our choristers do not understand worship and what it means to "minister" through singing; if many of them are yet to experience an initial conversion and have no personal relationship with God; if they are not spiritually conscious or even conscious of the goal of music in the liturgy, then it will be wrong to expect that their singing will be spirit-filled. Almost all the choristers I have interviewed did not seem to understand the goal of singing or the concept of "ministration." Again, beyond technical preparation, the vast majority of them do not prepare well for Mass.

join the choir because they like to sing, whereas singing in the choir as a ministry demands much more than that.

Again, most of our choristers have a poor understanding of the Mass and some neither show adequate reverence for it nor participate fruitfully in it. Some of them are concerned only about singing as if it constitutes the whole of Mass. This is clear from consistent late-coming by some and the way some discuss, walk about, and distract during the Liturgy of the Word in particular. As a result of this poor understanding of the Mass and the seriousness of their role as singing ministers, their preparation for worship is often inadequate from the mental, emotional, and spiritual standpoints, even where the technical one is sound.

Most of our choristers do not have a living relationship with God. As we said earlier, they lack the necessary spiritual consciousness expected of singing ministers. In many of our parishes, there are a good number of choristers who are communicants but never receive Holy Communion for months, and yet continue to sing at Mass every week in that spiritual state. This should not be treated as a piece of unimportant information to be overlooked. On the contrary, it gives us an idea of what goes on inside. For example, it is clear evidence of a lack of spiritual preparedness for both the Mass and the ministry of singing at Mass. Besides, the fact that this goes on for months unattended, in spite of the availability of the Sacrament of Reconciliation in the parish, calls to question the spiritual state of such individuals, their relationship with God, their level of spiritual consciousness, personal understanding and conviction about the Mass and the ministry of singing among other things.

The crucial question is, "Can a person in that spiritual state or who is not in the state of grace effectively minister to God in an acceptable way and connect people to him when he himself is 'disconnected' from him?" "Can someone who is not concerned about his own spiritual well-being be truly concerned about evangelizing others through the ministry of singing?" Put differently, "Can he glorify God in that state and genuinely set his mind on the conversion, ongoing transformation, and salvation of the congregation?" Owing to this inadequate spiritual consciousness and clarity about the spiritual and evangelical dimensions of singing, most of our parish choirs tend to rely more on technical competence where that exists. Often, they fail to take into cognizance the power of the Holy Spirit and his irreplaceable role in making their singing fruitful in inspiring, converting, and transforming the congregation.

A close appraisal of the situation in question shows that the choristers themselves are not culpable to a large extent. The root of the problem we are facing in the area of inspiring music is that, although the choristers have been sacramentalized, most of them have never been properly evangelized, even though this observation is not limited to them or their ministry.[190] While many of them may have received technical training in music, the intellectual, spiritual, and apostolic formations they require to be effective in their ministry are often lacking. For instance, most choristers are not conscious of their identity in Christ and the power of praise or spirit-filled singing.

In almost all the parishes, there is no carefully structured programme for the proper evangelization of intending choristers prior to their induction. At best, many who indicate interest in the choir are merely tested in music and voice (that is, auditioned) and admitted if successful. In other words, beyond being communicants,[191] the issue of a living relationship with God often does not arise. Similarly, most choirs do not have any serious ongoing

[190] Pope Saint John Paul II made the observation that a good number of Catholics who have been sacramentalized have never been properly evangelized and converted. The same observation is applicable, not just to a significant number of the choristers, but also to those in the other ministries, such as the lectors, the welcoming ministers, and the altar servers. There is no programme for evangelization before admission and commissioning or a clear programme for ongoing discipleship within their specific ministries.

[191] Actually, most Catholics have a reductive understanding of the word "communicant" as merely one who receives Holy Communion. They do not understand that, beyond receiving Communion, he is actually one who communes with God, which in itself implies a living relationship with him. But then, it is also not the fault of the vast majority of the faithful, considering that they were really not led into such a relationship before they were given the sacraments of the Holy Eucharist, confirmation, holy matrimony, and sometimes the priesthood.

formation programme aimed at discipling their members, even though some may hold an occasional recollection or retreat in their parishes. We must never forget that the "real power" behind the kind of singing that can pierce and convert hearts and inspire people to worship wholeheartedly does not come from mere technical ability on the part of the choristers or from the songs themselves no matter how wonderful the melodies may be. Rather, it comes from faith—real faith in God, faith in his Word, and faith in the mysteries being celebrated—and their reliance on the power of the Holy Spirit. As such, a chorister, as a singing minister, should be a man or a woman of faith.

Correspondingly, the ability to sing and glorify God in an acceptable way comes from a deep love for him and intimacy with him. For a chorister to be authentic in what he sings and be very effective as a singing minister, he must be equally one who is truly passionate about God and about glorifying him and leading people to encounter him, to glorify him, and to yield their lives to him. As a great lover and friend of God, a chorister or singing minster must be sufficiently familiar with his Word and his promises. He should be one who strives to follow Jesus and obey him. Since worship is also a lifestyle and not just what happens in the Church, a singing minster must strive to make praise and worship a lifestyle. In other words, his life should be a form of praise to God and offer authentic witness to Christ. As Saint Augustine would say, he should be someone who does not merely sing to God with his lips, but more importantly with his life. Just as other ministers who wish to be effective in their different ministries, he should be one who has connection with the Holy Spirit, enjoys intimacy with him, and depends mainly on his power to minister.

One of the reasons our Pentecostal brethren are doing better in the area of music is that their choristers are better prepared both intellectually and spiritually for their role of ministration during worship. There is an effort to evangelize them and lead them to Christ or into a personal relationship with God before they can become singing ministers in the church. Additionally, they teach them what real worship entails, build up their confidence and faith in God, and properly school them on the importance of singing from the heart as a form of prayer. In the same vein, they build up their prayer life, expose them to Scripture, the power of praises, and teach them to depend on the assistance of the Holy Spirit in the course of exercising their ministry. Thus, their solid formation prepares them, not just to sing, but to worship God in a way that inspires others and moves them to worship him wholeheartedly.

If we are to lead our congregation at Mass in a spirit-filled worship that can satisfy their spiritual yearnings and bring them immense spiritual benefits, we need to invest heavily in music and in the spiritual formation of the choir as a group. The emergence of a Music Commission in some dioceses is a welcome idea and a step in the right direction. But if the focus of such a commission is merely or primarily technical formation and discipline, as opposed to spiritual and apostolic formation (that is, evangelization and discipleship), the result will be "good singing" with little spiritual impact on the congregation. In other words, most people will enjoy the Mass without necessarily feeling its "power" or reaching the real goal of worship, which is beyond personal enjoyment. Keeping in view this goal of worship—the glorification of God and the transformation and sanctification of his people to make them more spiritually mature and fruitful—is of critical importance. Until we are able to achieve this in our liturgy, we may not be able to keep a good number of our Catholics, especially the younger generation, in the Church.

In the past we have left too many important issues (including the quality of our Sunday liturgy) to chance. But to get better results there is an urgent need for a paradigm shift in the way we (the priests, the liturgy ministers, and the entire congregation) approach worship in general. Without mincing words, we need to approach worship as an extremely serious spiritual event that deserves our undivided attention. Put differently, we should plan, consciously prepare for and celebrate as a "new" and "living encounter" with God to glorify and please him and at the same time renew and empower the worshiping community spiritually. To realize this objective, the yardstick for choosing the leaders of the choir should go beyond mere technical knack.

The prevailing atmosphere within the choir should be that which favours an ongoing re-evangelization of members' conversion, transformation (discipleship), and spiritual fruitfulness. In addition to possessing the necessary music ability, choir leaders should be people who have been properly evangelized themselves and discipled. They should have received adequate formation in worship, knowledge of the Mass, and what it means to minister to God and his people through singing. The blind cannot lead the blind. The importance of having properly evangelized and discipled leaders at the helm of affairs is that they, in turn, will be in a position to guide, evangelize, and lead their members to a personal relationship with God and so better prepare them for the ministry of singing in the Church. To complement this initial formation, it is necessary to plan a quarterly recollection, ongoing seminars, workshops, and retreats for the choir both at the parish level and the diocesan level. This will most likely help to foster their continuous growth in spirituality and their specific ministry.

Naturally, people want to go where they can find happiness and fulfilment. The Mass is a banquet—a joyful celebration and we should add life and a spirit of joy to it and all our liturgical celebrations.[192] As much as possible, music or singing should be lively[193] and spiritually uplifting and so contribute to the joy of the occasion. The joy of being in the presence of the Lord should be visible and contagious, especially as this can be a source of evangelization to visitors. However, making the Mass joyful should not in any way tamper with the solemnity of the liturgy. Similarly, it does not imply turning the homily into a comedy or the liturgy into a "show" or misplaced emotional display just to thrill people and make them happy. Conversely, the liturgy is a serious spiritual event and the joy which is lasting is that which comes from a living encounter with a loving God who forgives our sins, nourishes us with his

---

[192] Cf. J. McKEEVER, "What Pastors Need to Know about Church Growth," September 27, 2016. https://www.crosswalk.com/blogs/joe-mckeever/what-pastors-need-to-know-about-church-growth.html.

[193] Lively music does not necessarily imply "noise." The emphasis should really be on spiritually uplifting music that inspires us to worship. That is to say, we are more interested in music that uplifts the soul and enables more and more people to connect intimately with God and offer him the best of themselves in worship. A worship atmosphere needs not be rowdy, but certainly spirit-filled. A healthy balance of emotions and spirituality is needed.

Word, hears our prayers, and gives us the food of Christ's Body and Blood to renew and strengthen us. External manifestation of joy or balanced emotions must be rooted in and should flow from that intimate encounter with God in the heart of the worshipper.

The choice of music as well as singing at Mass should take cognizance of the different moods for the different parts of Mass to ensure that the congregation is led into the appropriate mood and achieve the goal that is intended for each part. For example, while the *Kyrie* before the absolution can be more solemn as a cry to God for mercy and forgiveness, the singing of the *Gloria* and the four acclamations at Mass (the *Alleluia*, the *Sanctus*, the proclamation of the mystery of our faith, and the Great Amen) should reflect the joy of a true encounter with the God of the universe. We should always bear in mind that the Mass is a commemoration of a joyful event—the death and resurrection of Jesus Christ—and not a mourning event.

For most worshippers at our Sunday Masses, the level of connectivity throughout the entire liturgy measured in percentage is less than ten percent. This is because most people merely go through the motion and never get to enter into God's presence most of the time to minister to him. This is the definition of "mechanical worship," which is no worship in the real sense as it can neither give glory to God nor transform the "worshipper." One of our major goals at Mass is that the Mass should permeate all the worshippers and get them to encounter God in a new and living way throughout the entire celebration. Every true encounter with the Lord yields some spiritual fruits. Some examples in the Bible include the experiences of Mary (cf. Mt 26:6-13; Lk 7:36-50), Zacchaeus (cf. Lk 19:1-10), the Samaritan woman (cf. Jn 4:4-42) and the two disciples on their way to Emmaus (cf. Lk 24:13-35). The importance of such an encounter at Mass does not merely lie in the spiritual fulfillment that can result from it, but also in the fact that it can lead the faithful to a personal conversion, ongoing transformation, and fruitfulness in evangelization—both in the area of witnessing and in actual sharing of the Gospel or the experience of one's meeting with God in the liturgy.

At this juncture, it is pertinent to remind ourselves that, although we have focused on the choir all this time, inspiring singing during worship is the responsibility of all the worshippers, not just the choir or the pastor or the other liturgy ministers. The role of the choir is to prompt, inspire, and lead the congregation in singing, not to take over. The task to create a spirit-filled worship environment that can foster an encounter with God, as a collective responsibility, requires the conscious and active collaboration of the entire congregation.

In view of this, there should be a conscious effort on the part of the pastors and their pastoral councils to give proper formation to the faithful as a whole that would enable them to participate consciously, meditatively, actively, and fruitfully both in singing and the entire Mass. Within the context of a well-prepared liturgy, this collaboration between an inspiring choir and a spiritually conscious congregation is absolutely necessary. It will most certainly foster that spirit-filled worship environment that can make possible the spiritual fulfillment which many Catholics yearn for today.[194] Once this happens, people will not only look forward to Sunday worship, but also, we are more likely to attract newcomers to our churches.

The desire to get the best out of the faithful calls for a total re-orientation, especially in the area of worship as a lifestyle. If the overall goal is the glory of God and the sanctification and transformation of the people; if it is to achieve a true worship of God in spirit and truth that will equally benefit them, then our first major task will be to form the members of the choir and our entire congregation into true worshippers. Worship is not merely what we do in Church, but also the way we live our concrete daily life in the presence and righteousness of God. Jesus himself is absolutely clear about what God wants. According to him, he does not just want worship or an inspiring worship event, but true worshippers (cf. Jn 4:23-24). The reason is not far-fetched. Only true worshippers

[194] It is important to note that what is being advocated here is not sheer sensationalism during worship but rather the need to prepare the faithful to worship God with their whole mind and heart through ongoing intellectual and spiritual formation and also to actually create an enabling spiritual environment during Mass or our worship events that can truly foster a living encounter between the members of our congregations and God.

who know him, love him, and live in obedience to him can truly worship him in spirit and truth. This is a crucial aspect of worship that most people often ignore, preferring to focus more or solely on the worship event.

Considering that the approach of most of our members to Mass is mechanical, we need to do something concrete to ensure that they do not continue to flow with the motion, internalizing little or nothing and failing to yield themselves to God during worship. No doubt, the task to re-orientate them and move them away from the present "mechanical worship,"[195] to which most of them have been conditioned over time, and form them into true worshippers will certainly not be an easy one. Habits are not formed in a day and are quite difficult to break. Ordinarily, people need conscious and consistent practice to break out of them. Realizing that this mental and spiritual re-orientation is necessary to change the way most of our people understand and approach worship, we cannot run away from it, but must face it headlong.

Although every form of formation is necessary, the most critical one is the spiritual formation. As much as the intellectual formation of the faithful (in the form of catechesis) is absolutely necessary, the truth is that we will not go far without properly evangelizing them to open, not just their intellects, but also their hearts to God and yield their wills to him. It is unthinkable that anyone can worship God in spirit and truth or in an acceptable way without first yielding his will to him or desiring to live for him and serve him wholeheartedly. The truth is that even when a person possesses vast "intellectual" knowledge about God, the heart needs to be converted to him before he can live out what he knows. Consequently, the ongoing evangelization of our congregations to lead them to Christ as well as an ongoing discipleship to mature them into disciples and transform them into true worshippers are absolutely critical to

[195] By "mechanical worship" we are referring to a mechanical approach to worship whereby people say and do things mechanically without getting connected to God or reflecting deeply on what they do. The outcome is that what they say and do on a regular basis are not from the heart and do not affect their lives positively as they should.

the formation of a congregation capable of worshipping God in a spirit-filled way during Mass and as a lifestyle.[196]

The first responsibility this creates for the pastor and the leaders of the parish community is to devise ways of leading the people to encounter God experientially. This entails leading them into a deep intimate, loving, personal relationship with him.[197] Once they encounter God, fall in love with him, and yield themselves completely to him, worship becomes their loving response to the invitation of a loving Father. Put differently, true worship is something that flows naturally from an interior conversion and truelove for the One true God whom we have come to know personally and not something we do out of fear or a desire to fulfil an obligation (cf. Ex 20:8-11) or to quiet our consciences.

Worship is a serious affair and God has great expectations where it is concerned. He knows that getting it right in this area is for our own good, whereas failure to get it right has serious negative consequences for us and the overall well-being of the world.[198] Although it is not God who benefits from our worship, but ourselves, he still expects us to present ourselves to him as a living sacrifice without blemish or defect (cf. Nm 28:9-11, 26-28; 29:1-2). In other words, he does not just require worship, but acceptable worship. This is

---

[196] Although this spiritual formation is the main key to a spirit-filled worship, it does not in any way make the intellectual formation and re-orientation of the faithful unimportant. Still, they need to understand what true worship is and how God wishes to be worshipped.

[197] There are too many people who frequent our churches today and still do not understand this whole notion of experiential knowledge of God and an intimate personal relationship with him. Beyond words, many of them do not even understand his nature as a loving, merciful, good and kind God. In theory, they acknowledge these attributes, but in practice they cannot relate to them.

[198] To appreciate this assertion, we need to look beyond our regular worship events and see worship as a lifestyle. Besides, for the communal worship in the Church to be true and acceptable from the perspective of the individual worshipper, it must flow from a life lived in God and for the glory of his name. In this sense, it is impossible to live in a way that contradicts his ways and offer him authentic worship in the Church without repentance.

the kind of worship that meets his worth as Almighty God and that can gradually transform us to reflect his glory more and more. Leviticus 19:5 states this clearly when it says, "When you offer a sacrifice of peace offering to the Lord, you shall offer it so that you may be accepted." True worship aims at giving God glory and pleasure and should change us over time to be godly and become better vessels in his hands to change the world. To achieve true worship as a community, everybody should come to Mass fully prepared mentally and spiritually to offer him or herself to God as a living, holy, and acceptable sacrifice that is worthy of his majesty as God and thus pleasing to him (cf. Rom 12:1-2).

This takes us to the very core of what true worship entails. It is not just about our praise, material gifts, petitions, and similar, but first and foremost about the offering of our lives to God in obedience and total surrender to his will. Once we, by virtue of our lives, become an acceptable sacrifice to God, then our sacrifice will also be acceptable to him. Jesus Christ is the best worshipper ever known. His entire life was a life of obedience to the Father and total surrender to his will (cf. Mk 14:34-36; Jn 4:34). Each time the Father gazed upon him, he saw only one who was pleasing to him (cf. Mt 3:17; 17:5). His ministry was exercised in total faithfulness to him and his missionary action in the world. Finally, on the Cross of Calvary, Jesus offered himself sacrificially to him on our behalf as a lamb without spot or blemish. This is what true worship entails and it makes Jesus our model as far as worship in spirit and truth is concerned.

In living worship as a lifestyle, Jesus' life was completely focused on God, not on himself. Even on the Cross the glory of the Father was his ultimate goal without losing sight of man's salvation. What his life or continuous worship and his sacrificial death on the Cross teach us is that worship is primarily about God and his pleasure, not us. As such, the more relevant concerns of worshippers should be, "Did we offer him acceptable worship?" "Did he enjoy us or take pleasure in our worship event?" "Was he truly glorified by our so-called act of worship?" Both Cain and the Israelites took this for granted. No doubt, they saw the need for worship. But the problem was their failure to note that it is not just any sacrifice (in the name of worship) that pleases God. Hence, their offerings and worship were not accepted (cf. Gen 4:1-7; Is 1:1-20; 58). Any worship we offer God that does not require our obedience to his commandments, a form of sacrifice on our part, and total surrender to his will can neither please him nor measure up to true worship in spirit and truth. This is because worship, as a lifestyle, includes the way we live at home, the way we work, the way we relate with others, and the charitable things we do for the glory of God among other things.

One way to measure the quality and effectiveness of our worship or worship events is to see their ongoing impact on our lives. If our worship is not making us more and more Christlike in character, then we need to critically reexamine what we are doing. In fact, the main reason God invites us to worship him is because he wants us to become like what we worship over time.[199] His desire is to transform us gradually and conform us more and more to the likeness of his Son, Jesus Christ, so that we can mirror his divine life in society. This call to live the divine life is actually the second aspect of the salvation Christ won for us.[200]

Here, a crucial thing to which we all must pay attention is that any worship or devotion that is not fostering the ongoing conversion and spiritual growth of the individual to mature him as a Christian disciple over time cannot be a true worship or devotion. In other words, some of the clear indicators that we are worshipping God well include conversion, ongoing transformation, growing intimacy with God and spiritual fruitfulness that is visible in service, and unalloyed commitment to God's action and mission in the world. To focus on spiritual transformation in particular, what we are doing, that is, our ongoing worship, should gradually transform our mindset, our worldview, our character and our desires to be more Christlike. Over time we should begin to reflect those

---

[199] Cf. B. JOHNSON, "Hosting the Presence: Unveiling Heaven's Agenda," an 8-session Bible study course on 2 DVDs (Shippensburg, PA: Destiny Image Publishers Inc.), disc 1.

[200] The first aspect of the salvation Christ won for us by his death and resurrection is redemption from sin, and the second aspect is the invitation to live the divine life of God in imitation of his only begotten Son, Jesus Christ.

Christlike qualities, such as sincere love for God and neighbour, truth, justice, peace, selflessness, sacrifice and similar.

The mission of the Church and Christians in the world is to change the world and win it for Christ. Technically, we call this evangelization, and regular worship is one of the key ways that Christians are prepared for this important task. This then implies that if we (Christians) are not changing the world or the society in which we live in spite of our so-called robust weekly or daily "worship" of God, then we need to stop and reappraise what we are doing to see if it measures up to acceptable worship or worship in spirit and truth. The whole point is that, as individuals are transformed spiritually through worship and grow in the love of God and serve him with greater intensity, they should ordinarily become more fruitful and be better instruments in his hands to change the world in which they live.

Again, the crux of the mission that Christ entrusted to his Church is to make everyone his disciple. Every Christian worshipper shares in that mission. In fact, he is sent forth at the end of every Mass to take Christ to the world in order to change it and win it for God. But the bitter truth is that he cannot bear fruit in this area unless he has first encountered Christ personally and has been transformed by him and conformed to him in his mind and behaviour. To conclude everything we have said in this chapter, it is pertinent to note that once we succeed in building the members of our congregations into true worshippers who worship God in spirit and truth as a lifestyle, we—not God—will be the primary beneficiaries since our worship does not add anything to his inner greatness but transforms and positions us for greater favours in life and for eternal life as his external glory.

Chapter Five

WHY ARE PEOPLE LEAVING US? SOME ISSUES REVOLVING AROUND THE CLERGY

Lack of Personal Conviction and Commitment to Mission

The Fathers of the Second Vatican Council remind us that the priests of the New Testament act *in persona Christi.*[201] Commenting on how a priest can act *in persona Christi,* Pope John Paul II describes the priest as "a sacramental representation of Christ, Head and Shepherd."[202] The implication of this teaching, according to Thomas Lane, an Irish Theologian, is that "a man is ordained to be a face, a presence, a voice, in the name and with the authority of Jesus Christ who is the shepherd...the priest...the prophet."[203] To this, I wish to state that,

> If this is what a priest is called to be, then it can be said that, today, a significant number of us have lost focus of our priestly identity, integrity and mission. This poses a fundamental problem. It poses a serious challenge to the effectiveness of our ministry and continues to harm the Church in a significant way. No doubt, we are producing more and more priests and some have wrongly interpreted that as "vocation boom." But a careful appraisal of the

---

[201] See VATICAN II, Decree on the Ministry and Life of Priests *Presbyterorum Ordinis,* 7 December 1965, n. 2.

[202] POPE JOHN PAUL II, Post-Synodal Apostolic Exhortation *Pastores Dabo Vobis* (PDV), 25 March 1992, n. 1.

[203] T. LANE, *A Priesthood in Tune: Theological Reflections on Ministry* (Dublin: The Columba Press, 1993), p. 100.

> reality on ground reveals that the way many of them conceive the priesthood is a far cry from what the Church teaches. Their notion of the priesthood is "upside down" which is why some behave as if the priesthood were a private thing and that everyone should be allowed to live it the way he wants.[204]

This wrong notion of the priesthood is changing its face in practice. More than ever, our life is characterized by growing shallowness or poverty of the mind, individualism, self-centredness, worldliness, corruption, tribalism, inordinate ambition for money, position and power, sexual laxity, and disordered priorities among other things. Given the above, it will not be too surprising, as funny as it may sound, to state that the clergy is another reason for the drift of some Catholics to the new generation churches. It does not seem many of our priests are getting it right as far as their vocation and the mission of the Church are concerned. Without sounding pessimistic, the more visible signs suggest that things are getting worse by the day and we are not doing enough to reverse the situation.

Catholic priests contribute directly or indirectly to the drift of some Catholics to the Pentecostal churches in different ways. If we are serious about finding a solution to this problem and if "mission" and not "maintenance" is our primary goal, then the clergy as a whole need a dose of humility to admit that most of us are underperforming or have lost focus of our vocation and mission altogether.

Just as any proud Catholic we are quick to remind others that the Catholic Church is the real Church founded by Christ and that all others were established by human beings. No doubt, we are saying the obvious and need not apologize for that. In the same vein, many are quick to scorn and dismiss the Pentecostal pastors as self-appointed ministers who became pastors "overnight" or after three or six months training at a Bible college, which again may be true of most pastors. At other times, we are quick to remind our

---

[204] P. NWAEZEAPU, "A Year of Faith and the Priestly Ministry: Challenges and Prospects." A paper presented at the Seminary of Saint Peter and Saint Paul, Bodija, Ibadan, on Wednesday, 26 June 2013, pp. 4-5.

audience that most of the Pentecostal pastors, if not all, established churches for business and, perhaps, fame. In truth, we are not totally wrong even though this may not be applicable to every one of them, granted that some may have done so primarily to propagate the kingdom of God.

Compared to the Pentecostal pastors, the Catholic clergy receive training in philosophy and theology for about nine years. Ordinarily, this should give them an edge over their Pentecostal counterparts. But, in practice, whether or not this is the case is a different thing altogether. In some cases, people wonder if many of our priests are justifying the efforts committed to their long training and the huge investment the Church makes in this area. Given some undesirable situations or excesses we witness on a regular basis, especially in more recent times, most people will agree that all is not well. But then, what is the source of this problem?

Although some lay people and even priests will be hasty in putting the whole blame on the priests, I think that the issue needs proper investigation considering the important role of priests as drivers of the Church's mission. A reasonable question we need to ask in this area is, "Does the problem arise from the quality of the formation in our seminaries and dioceses, or the mental and spiritual environments in these places, or the personal disposition of the individuals who are being formed, or a combination of many things?"

Catholic priests are trained in philosophy and theology and, after the initial seminary formation, some go on to acquire expertise in these disciplines. Ordinarily, philosophy as a discipline trains us to ask the most fundamental questions, which can help us appraise the signs of the times critically, investigate present challenges, and proffer reasonable solutions. This ancient discipline should make us ask pertinent questions regarding our identity and vocation as priests as well as the identity, vocation, and the mission of the Church we serve. Some of the questions that our philosophical studies should help us confront on a constant basis include: Who is a Catholic priest? What is his vocation about? What is the mission of the Catholic Church and the Catholic priest? Are we really fulfilling that mission? If not, why are we not fulfilling it? Why are a good number of our people leaving us? What can be done? These are only some of the questions we need to ask to regain our focus and be authentic in living our vocation and more effective in pursuing the mission of Christ for his Church.

Sadly, in spite of our degrees, it does not seem that, in practice, our training in this discipline is aiding us well. The point is, how can married people who were probably trained for three or six months turn out to be more industrious and effective than priests in propagating the Gospel to the extent of attracting our members? Where is our philosophy? Where is our theology? Where is our nine years of studies and formation within the seminary walls and beyond? Is all this a sheer waste of time and resources? Even if the seminary formation has not been perfect, should not our philosophical studies lead us to rethink things and come up with workable solutions?

Some of us are quick to point out that the Pentecostal pastors are aggressive in propagating the faith because of money. That is to say, they are doing business with church. As I pointed out in "The Model of the Astute Businessman," regarding models of evangelization in my book, *When Salt Loses Its Saltiness*, most people will agree that this is the case with most of them. But then, it can also be argued that if money is what drives most of them (either primarily or even entirely) to propagate the Gospel zealously, and we consider the love of God and the salvation of souls to be more important than money, then should not our commitment to evangelization be even greater? Is money or fame a greater force or motivation than Jesus Christ? Is it possible to be Jesus-driven in this matter? Is money more important than souls? Did Saint Paul not embark on extensive missionary journeys and work even when money was not the consideration? How about the Apostles and many of the saints and martyrs—Saint Francis Xavier, Saint Dominic, Saint Francis of Assisi, Saint Anthony of Padua, Saint Thomas More and a host of others—were they driven by money and fame or the love of God and the salvation of souls?

To be honest with ourselves, the presence and activities of the Pentecostals have exposed some of our shortcomings. The lame excuse that their pastors are driven by the love of money is not convincing enough. In fact, it cannot hide the present uninspiring attitude of many priests to pastoral work, the spiritual growth of their people and mission, which are some of the reasons for the continued drift of some Catholics to Pentecostal churches.

In some parishes, this poor attitude to pastoral work and the spiritual growth of our lay people has become a source of frustration and discouragement to many of them. In fact, some of them are of the opinion that a good number of their priests are not spiritual. They think that, besides celebrating the sacraments, they are more interested in money-generating activities, physical projects and social events than in pastoral and spiritual programmes that can impact positively on the spiritual and moral life of the faithful and the parish as a whole.

Although the sacraments are the primary responsibility of priests, the pastoral life of the parish cannot be reduced to the celebration of the sacraments alone. Spiritual programmes that can advance the proper evangelization and discipling of the faithful to ripen their faith and better equip them for their specific mission in the world are also necessary in the parish.[205] The complaint by some of our lay people in this area is very important, especially if we consider that ignorance of the faith and lack of spirituality are some of the major reasons why some leave the Church.

If we are serious about stemming the drift of Catholics to other churches, then this situation cannot be allowed to continue. The authorities in the universal Church were not foolish in choosing philosophy and theology as the key fields of study that future priests must undertake before ordination. As trained philosophers and theologians, we must be constantly appraising the pastoral situation before us and the challenges they present, ask the necessary questions, and chart a way forward rather than concentrate all our energy in criticizing our Pentecostal counterparts while some more lay people continue to leave us.

---

[205] Even at the time of writing, many parishes do not hold weekly Bible study or "know your faith" or proper evangelization and discipleship programmes aimed at conversion and the maturing of the faith of parishioners. Many Catholics and lay associations are still ignorant of the real mission of the Church in the world and their own specific roles in that mission due to lack of information and training by their pastors.

Lack of a Personal Conviction about Christ and the Church

If the early Church was extremely successful in her mission, one of the major reasons was because she had a clear focus on mission. But then, this strong focus on mission came from something else—the personal conviction of the disciples about Christ, his message, his mission and heaven. The lack of commitment to mission that we talked about earlier, which can be said to be one of the greatest problems militating against the success of the Church today, arises from other fundamental problems. These include the lack of personal conviction about Christ, the personal spirituality of the clergy, and lack of commitment to the Church.

When compared to the reality today, the level of conviction of the early Christians about Christ, their total commitment to their vocation, the Church and the Great Commission, and their sense of sacrifice cannot cease to amaze us. Saint Paul in particular was so strong in his conviction that he declared, "Life for me is Christ" (Phil 1:21). For him, spreading the Good News was a duty. He saw his mission as proclaiming Christ and his Gospel everywhere and was prepared to give up everything, including his life, just to have Christ and spread his Gospel (cf. Rom 1:14-15; 1 Cor 1:17-18, 9:16).

Similarly, we can learn a great deal from the life of Saint Ignatius of Antioch. Although he lived at a time when martyrdom flourished in Christendom, his conviction about Christ was remarkable while his commitment was total. He was ready to give his life for Christ. In his Letter to the Romans, he declares, "The chains are schooling me to have done with earthly desires." Then he adds:

> This is the first stage of my discipleship and no power, visible or invisible, must grudge me my coming to Jesus Christ. Fire, cross, beast-fighting, hacking and quartering, splintering of bone and mangling of limb, even the pulverizing of my entire body–let every horrid and diabolical torment come upon me, provided only that I can win my own way to Jesus Christ.[206]

[206] IGNATIUS OF ANTIOCH, Letter to the Romans, 3:1-5; See the Office of the Reading in the Breviary, vol. 3.

Such conviction about Christ and total commitment to his Church and the Great Commission are rare today among the shepherds (pastors) even though they are not completely lacking. Self-love, inordinate ambition, self-advancement and self-glorification have replaced selflessness, self-sacrifice and abandonment in the priesthood.

Jesus rejected the kingdom that the devil offered him during his temptation (Lk 4:5-6), but sadly, a significant number of the shepherds are trying to take it back. The pathetic thing is that the Church and the priesthood are sometimes used as the means to achieve and sustain such vain pursuits. This explains why the much expected commitment to pastoral work, evangelization, discipleship, spirituality, and Christian witness is weak or non-existent among a significant number of the clergy. It is also the underlying factor why many clerics and religious venture into activities that are not consistent with their chosen vocations.

The Claim That Catholic Priests Do Not Preach Well

There is power in the Word of God, whether written or spoken. In our discussion on Scripture, we saw clearly the importance of the written Word of God to authentic growth in the Christian life. Similarly, when the same word is proclaimed in its richness with conviction, it has the power to convict, convert, liberate, encourage, transform, and foster authentic spiritual growth in the hearer and the Christian community as a whole. This clearly underlines the important place of preaching within the liturgy with particular attention on the Holy Mass. Bearing that in mind, the Church makes the homily a compulsory component of the liturgy on Sundays and solemnities and encourages a brief homily during the weekday Masses.

In her long history, she has been blessed with great teachers and preachers, such as Saint Anthony of Padua, Saint John Chrysostom, and a host of others. In recent times, we can talk about great ministers like Archbishop Fulton Sheen, and others. Here in Nigeria, there are many great preachers who have not only contributed immensely to the spiritual growth of the faithful through deeply inspiring homilies, but have actually been instrumental to the conversion of some non-Catholics to the faith. But on the other side of the spectrum, there are also many ordained ministers who constantly bore their congregations with dry and uninspiring homilies. It is on this basis that some Catholics claim that the Pentecostal pastors are better preachers than many of our priests and tend to follow their televangelism or go to their churches after Mass on Sundays to listen to their preaching. There are also those who think that the more popular ones possess better communication and organizational skills and pray better than our priests. From such comments, it is easy to see some sort of dissatisfaction among some Catholics and a growing admiration for some of these pastors. Besides, some Catholics who hold these views are vexed by the fact and tend to show signs of disappointment in many of their priests.

As we attempt to investigate why some Catholics are drifting away from the Church, it is pertinent to examine this concern carefully rather than simply dismiss it and remain complacent. The accusation is serious and the different reactions of some lay faithful to it are worth investigating. Some of the very conservative or "die-hard" Catholics who see nothing good in other denominations, especially the Pentecostal churches, are quick to dismiss the claim as untrue. There are others who admit that, on the average, the Pentecostal pastors preach better than most Catholic priests, but are not swayed by that fact to go to their churches for any reason. Still some who cherish their Catholic faith and do not wish to leave the Church, have devised ways to deal with the problem of poor preaching by their priests. While some of them simply attend Mass on Sunday and go back home to listen to the preaching by Pentecostal televangelists, others actually sneak to their churches just to listen to the Word of God. But then, experience shows that some Catholics who go to these churches for so-called "inspiring preaching" with no intention of becoming their members actually end up joining them, just as there are some who leave to join particular Pentecostal churches because of the preaching skills of their pastors.[207]

[207] Without contesting the fact that some Catholic priests do not preach well, it is equally necessary to state that nowadays some people are merely

At this juncture, it is extremely important to state that preaching the Word of God is one of the most essential duties of a priest. The Holy Mass, which is the center of our faith as Catholics, is divided into two main parts: the Liturgy of the Word and the Liturgy of the Eucharist. Although the Gospel Reading is the high point of the Liturgy of the Word in Catholic teaching, most Catholics tend to focus more on the homily as the real high point of that part of the Mass. Here, it is vital to note that, beyond going to Church on Sunday to fulfill their obligation, most Catholics go to Mass for two main things: to listen to the homily and to receive Holy Communion. To further show the great importance Catholics and, perhaps, people in general attach to the homily, some clearly stated during investigation that the quality of the homily influences what they give as offering during Mass even though that should not be the case. During a Bible study class in an urban parish in Lagos, a particular lady put it thus, "I decide what I will give as my offering at home. But if the homily is good [that is, inspiring], I give more." The simple point we are trying to establish here is that most people listen to homilies even though they do so for different reasons, which also explain why some get transformed over time and others do not. Whatever is the case, the truth is that those who listen to homilies to receive encouragement or to apply the Word of God to life circumstances or to grow in their spiritual life are most likely to be unfulfilled with anything that is uninspiring.

Considering the importance of preaching to the spiritual growth of the faithful and families, that is, its potential to shape their thinking and behaviour, to deepen their commitment to the mission of the Church and thus foster the pastoral life of a parish, an important question arises. If it is true that many of our priests do not preach well, then who is to blame and what can be done to correct this?

Here, we can think of some answers. Using Nigeria as a case study, our experience is that most priests who work in busy parishes in the cities are often overburdened or overwhelmed by the

---

looking for homilies that psyche them up or motivate them, but not the ones that challenge them to repent and live authentic Christian lives. While a homily should encourage the people, it should also call them to conversion among other things.

challenge of parish administration and pastoral work. For example, it is a common thing to find just two or three priests in a parish with over 2,500 parishioners. The fact that things are not well-structured in Nigeria as a whole as in the Western world only adds to the burden of administration as "everybody" wishes to see the priest for even problems that some lay people are better suited to handle. As a result, many priests become so immersed in daily administration and pastoral work in the parish that they end up burning themselves out and not having adequate time to prepare their homilies well. While it is good to commend the profound commitment of these priests to pastoral work and parish administration, it is also necessary to remind ourselves that this is not a justifiable excuse as far as preaching is concerned. Preaching should have preference in the order of priority because it is one of the primary duties of the priest. For whatever reason, it should never be relegated to the list of secondary things. Rather than sacrifice the quality of their homilies, priests should learn to prioritize and give the much needed attention to things that are more crucial.

Poor and uninspiring homilies can also arise from the natural inability of the preacher himself. But again, this cannot be an excuse for boring the faithful with dry and uninspiring homilies that do not help them to grow in their relationship with God. Although people are not equally endowed, a more positive and acceptable approach will be to study harder than others and spend more quality time in silence before God as a prelude to preparing their homilies. Besides, recognition of their personal limitation and the importance of preaching an inspiring homily should lead them to seek the help of their more gifted colleagues in preparing. Another possibility is to identify some gifted lay people and constitute them into a study group with whom they can meet on a weekly basis for a prayerful study and reflection on the readings of Sunday with an intention to draw useful spiritual insights that can be applied to the homily at Sunday Mass.

Consistently poor and uninspiring homilies can also be the fruit of inadequate preparation by the priest. In this case, they do not result from lack of capacity or too much work, but for other reasons, such as sheer laziness, complacency, or lack of interest, self-imposed distraction, irresponsibility or even pride, which causes a priest to underrate his congregation. Today, a good number of our pastors are too distracted. Rather than spend more quality time on preparing their homilies, many devote excessive time and energy to some harmful activities as well as some "harmless" ones of less consequences. Some spend the greater part of their time watching European football, tennis (Grand Slams), and films. These, in themselves, are not bad, since as the saying goes, "All work and no play makes Jack a dull boy." No doubt, priests also need to recreate in order to be healthy, but then, there has to be a proper or healthy balance between his important pastoral duties, socializing, and recreation. Where priority is given to the latter ahead of a more important duty like preaching, then we can only speak of a sheer loss of focus and discipline. To prepare to preach to their Sunday congregation or on television, most pastors often spend over ten hours researching the theme of their message and reflecting on the Word of God. Similarly, if our priests wish to preach well, they too must do likewise.

The issue of poor and uninspiring homilies can equally arise from inadequate formation in the art of preaching and communication skills during seminary training and afterwards. Even though preaching is a crucial aspect of the priestly ministry, sometimes the candidates for the priesthood are not properly trained and equipped for preaching. While some of those saddled with the responsibility of training students in this area may not be well-grounded in it themselves, at other times, the problem is that of inadequate practical formation in preaching as a result of the busy schedules operated in most seminaries. Proper training in the basics of preaching and communications and, more so, formation in prayerful study of the Word of God and meditation are critical to preaching. Formation in this area should be not merely theoretical and should not be limited to one or two semesters in the course of seminary training. Considering the importance of preaching, it should at least span through the whole period of theological studies even though we recognize that paying attention to good preachers is as well formative.

If we want our priests and future priests to be great preachers of the Word of God, then our investment in this area should be ongoing and should know no bounds. Experts in preaching techniques and communication techniques should be brought in to assist the formators in training the students, who should also be exposed to constant practice to sharpen their communication and preaching abilities. Since preaching is critical to parish life and what the priest does on a daily basis, then to help seminarians to internalize the seriousness involved, the formation team can go the extra mile of making practical preaching a compulsory course, which every student must take and excel in at least a semester of each of the last four years of formation in the seminary. Introducing this practice will enable the formation team itself to determine the ability of each student and to decide early on what more needs to be done to assist those who do not measure up to the expected standard. Given the enormity of the programmes in the seminaries, the different dioceses should show specific interest and collaborate with the seminary formation team to provide such trainings for their seminarians in their respective dioceses or provinces. We need to apply practical wisdom to the resolution of teething problems in the Church.

No doubt, intellectual formation is needed, but we need to get our priorities right. If we give adequate attention to certain philosophy and theology courses and secular discipline because that is necessary for university certification, why can we not give more time to practical formation in preaching, which is what the priest does in the parish every day and that with which the people appraise the quality of his formation most of the time. The truth is that the faithful expect first and foremost a preacher who can nourish their spiritual lives daily than a scholar who has nothing much to offer them in this area.[208]

Recognizing the harm that priests do to both the lay faithful and the Church as a result of poor and uninspiring homilies, Pope Benedict XVI reminds bishops, priests, and deacons who exercise this ministry of preaching in the Church of the need to improve the quality of their homilies. His words are crystal clear in the statement below:

[208] Scholarship is good, but a priest should be first and foremost a preacher before a scholar.

> In the Apostolic Exhortation *Sacramentum Caritatis*, I pointed out that "given the importance of the word of God, the quality of homilies needs to be improved. The homily 'is part of the liturgical action' and is meant to foster a deeper understanding of the word of God, so that it can bear fruit in the lives of the faithful."[209]

Continuing his exhortation on this salient issue, he asserts that a homily should be Christocentric and goes on to list some other things a good homily should focus on. According to him,

> The homily is a means of bringing the scriptural message to life in a way that helps the faithful to realize that God is present and at work in their everyday lives. It should lead to an understanding of the mysteries being celebrated, serve as a summons to mission, and prepare the assembly for the profession of faith, the universal prayer and the Eucharist liturgy. Consequently, those who have been charged with preaching by virtue of a specific ministry ought to take this task to heart... The faithful should be able to perceive clearly that the preacher has a compelling desire to present Christ, who must stand at the centre of every homily.[210]

The emphasis on making Christ the centre of our homilies is very critical. Oftentimes, we hear homilies that are "generic and abstract." Homilies should focus people on Christ, but tragically, at other times, useless digressions which do not serve the real goal of a homily enter the preaching of some priests. Worse still, there are others who seem to shift the primary attention of their homily from Christ to themselves or attempt to turn the homily into a "comedy" with their primary focus on making people to "laugh" and "enjoy" themselves. While studying in Rome, I encountered a priest who was feeling excited and proud of himself because some lay people who met him somewhere (after he left their parish) had told him how much they missed him because of his jokes during

---

[209] POPE BENEDICT XVI, *VD* 59, citing Apostolic Exhortation *Sacramentum Caritatis,* n. 46: AAS 99 (2007), 141.

[210] *VD* 59; Cf. *DV* 25.

his homilies rather than the spiritual content of his homilies. Similarly, at a particular priestly ordination anniversary Mass I witnessed some years back, the homily was about 80 to 85 percent "comedy" or "jokes." The content was not primarily focused on Christ or his Word, but on entertaining the people to a feast of jokes that made them laugh hysterically. Clearly, this was a case of playing to the gallery. On closer examination and reflection, it only reveals the absence of an encounter with God in his Word; that is, a lack of a prayerful reflection on the readings of that Mass or the mystery of the priesthood on the part of the preacher prior to mounting the ambo to preach. Homily is not centred on exalting self or pleasing others, but on proclaiming Christ and leading the faithful to encounter him in his Word in a way that is personal and transforming.

To forestall such abuses, Pope Benedict exhorts preachers to prepare their homilies carefully by close and constant contact with the text and by meditation and prayer, so as to preach with conviction and passion.[211] In preparing for the homily, the preacher must first encounter the Word of God as it applies to his own concrete life and then move from that to what God wishes to communicate to that particular community in the light of its concrete life experience and challenges.[212] We get to know God's thought and feel his pulse by being with him. There is great value in silence in his presence and in a prayerful contact with his Word in the Bible. When we speak from the standpoint of a prayerful study of the word and meditation, our words carry greater spiritual "power" to change and transform hearts, because in the real sense, they are not our own words, but God's Word placed on our lips. Thus, careful study and prayerful meditation on the Word of God in addition to some communication skills are necessary to improve our homilies.

There is a huge difference between preaching from the head and preaching from the heart or from a personal conviction. In fact, some people can actually make the difference between the two when they listen to homilies. What is really needed is preaching from the heart or from a position of conviction, passion, and moral

[211] *VD* 59; See *DV* 25.

[212] Cf. *VD* 59.

authority flowing from a life of virtue, witness, and constant striving for holiness which is clear to the people. This aspect of conviction and personal witness is crucial because one serious thing that can weaken even a carefully prepared homily in the long run and distract the faithful from the message itself is a life of anti-witness on the part of the preacher. In conclusion, it must be clear to all that, although the preacher himself is human and capable of making mistakes like other men and women, he is personally convinced of what he preaches and strives sincerely to live it out with the help of the Holy Spirit.

Anti-Witness Behaviour of Some Priests

The first stage in the Church's mission of evangelization is Christian witness. This happens when Christians in a place live in a constructive way that is different from what one finds in society. They share life and destiny with other people and show solidarity with the efforts of all for whatever is noble and good. At the same time, they radiate faith in values that go beyond current values or the disvalues they find in society in a way that reflects their hope in something beyond the present life, that is, heaven.[213]

As Pope Paul VI asserts, through their wordless witness to the life of Christ, Christians in general can stir some questions in people who wish to know why they are different and what inspires them. "Such a witness is already a silent proclamation of the Good News and a very powerful and effective one. Here we have an initial act of evangelization."[214] As the pope maintains, such an act of witness can offer these Christians an opportunity to proclaim Christ to those who see how they live. This is because, "Modern man listens more willingly to witnesses than to teachers, and if he does listen to teachers, it is because they are witnesses."[215]

[213] See POPE PAUL VI, Apostolic Exhortation *Evangelii Nuntiandi* (EN) – On Evangelization in the Modern World (Nairobi, Kenya: St. Paul Publications Africa, December 8, 1975), n. 21.

[214] *EN* 21.

[215] *Ibid.* 41; See also POPE PAUL VI, *Address to the Members of the Consilium de Laicis* (2 October 1974): *AAS 66* (1974), p. 568.

These statements stress the importance of Christian witness and its role in the propagation of the Gospel of Christ. While there are some lay faithful whose faith can be described as strong, there are others whose faith is very fragile. As the leaders of the Christian communities, the ordained ministers cannot easily hide from the people. While their faith and exemplary Christian life (i.e., witness of life) can have a positive impact on the faith of the people and their spiritual growth, so too, serious forms of anti-witness can pose some obstacles to their growth or scandalize them altogether.

Today, there are many good priests in the Church who are sincerely pursuing perfection and who are dedicated to their pastoral duties. Even if they are not perfect yet, their commitment to the priestly life and ministry is not in question. This category of priests makes huge sacrifices for the Church and the people on a daily basis and can be said to be witnesses even to a large extent. Also, there are some who are struggling, but are not consciously striving for perfection. Yet, we cannot also deny that a good number of priests appear to consistently live lives that are clearly opposed to the faith and their priestly calling. This anti-witness or unchristian behavior on their part is a serious source of concern to many of the people of God. In our time, this anti-Christian witness manifests itself in different ways and in different places. Here, we shall briefly focus on some of them to see the role they have played in the past and continue to play in leading Catholics away from the Church or to complete loss of faith.

In the Western world as a whole, the anti-witness of some of the ordained ministers is known to have led many people either away from the Church or to total loss of faith in God and the Church. In America and other parts of the West, the scandals arising from the sexual abuse of children by Catholic priests and high-ranking prelates have caused many to stumble and abandon the Church or the Christian faith altogether. In reality, such scandals are not restricted to the Catholic priests, but extend to the ministers of the other churches and the lay people themselves. Nevertheless, it seems that the Catholic Church has faced the greatest attack in this area probably because of her high moral teaching, which some find too strict and conservative and also because of the efforts of some of her opponents to destroy her.[216]

Although the scandals are not solely responsible for the crisis of faith in the West or the closing or merging of Catholic parishes due to the dwindling of church members, we cannot deny the fact that they have contributed immensely to the present undesirable situation in the Church.[217]

It will be presumptuous to think that the Church in Africa and Nigeria in particular are free. The crisis within the priesthood is growing and is becoming more and more visible by the day. As the saying goes, a stitch in time saves nine. The Church must be wise and nip the crisis breeding in the priesthood in the bud, noting that prevention is better and less expensive than a cure. As I mentioned in my previous book, *When Salt Loses Its Saltiness,* it is positive, prudent and courageous actions, not lamentation or procrastination that can change things and prevent the doomsday. If we do not honestly look inward and do the needful as a matter of urgency, the same situation in the West may befall the Church in Nigeria faster than we think. Objectively, while there are many good things happening in the Church, we cannot allow them to blind us to the "time bombs" waiting to explode and cause serious damage if they are not proactively and wisely detonated early enough by the Church hierarchy.

From experience, it is clear that, in spite of a sincere effort to be good Christians or priests, all men sometimes do wrong or fall into error or make mistakes in different ways. But then, persistence in wrongdoings and glorying in them can be serious pointers to a complete loss of identity of who the priest is called to be. In my previous book, *When Salt Loses Its Saltiness*, I took time to describe some of the anomalies that plague our ordained ministers in Nigeria

---

216 Also, we cannot rule out the fact that some criticisms against the Catholic Church in this area are launched by some Catholics who wish to see the Church they love purified and renewed.

217 Many of the big churches in Europe are empty and more and more churches in America are being sold while some parishes are being merged. Thus, while the Evangelical churches are growing in number, the population of former Catholics is growing significantly, meaning that the Catholic Church is losing some of her members.

and distract them from total commitment to their vocation and priestly duties, such as vanity, materialism, lack of a sound prayer life, and similar. Without repeating them all over, it may be useful to mention a few more which require serious and urgent attention to avoid a forced "fire brigade" approach to some deep-seated problems that may arise in the future if nothing is done now.

There is always wisdom in projecting and being proactive. Egypt survived a severe famine of seven years because Pharaoh heeded the wise counsel of Joseph and adopted a proactive measure (cf. Gen 41-45). Even in our time God, through the Holy Spirit, continues to raise people with prophetic insight to guide and warn us. He continues to send spiritual waves to his people to show us what is wrong and the right direction to follow. But unfortunately, most leaders are too busy with the administrative demands of their office and physical projects. Oftentimes, we allow the noise from within and without to completely blind us to what the Spirit is saying to the Church of our time and place (cf. Rev 2:29). Having said that, let us consider some serious issues in the priesthood that impact negatively on the faithful and cause some of them to drift or give up going to church altogether. These need to be dealt with from the standpoint of a thorough investigation with our eyes on potential solutions that will be enduring.

The Pursuit of Materialism and Vanity

Charisms, including that of healing, are good and desirable in the Church. Jesus himself who is our teacher and model was involved in the ministry of healing and exercised other *charisms*. When he sent out his twelve disciples on mission, he commanded them to proclaim the Gospel and gave them power and authority over demons and to heal the sick (cf. Lk 9:1-6). Again, when he sent out the seventy disciples, he empowered them and commanded them to cure the sick and cast out demons (cf. Lk 10:17-20). In what seems to be Mark's version of the Great Commission, some of the signs that believers in Christ will manifest include the *charisms* of healing and speaking in tongues (cf. Mk 16:15-18). An important thing we need to emphasize here is that the giving of the *charism* of healing and deliverance reveals the loving heart of the Saviour who is not merely interested in the spiritual well-being of his children, but also their physical and mental well-being and freedom from the forces of evil. Hence, this ministry should be accorded the importance it deserves in the life of the Church.

In today's Nigeria, there are many sick and spiritually oppressed people in need of physical, psychological, and spiritual healing and deliverance from the forces of evil. Unfortunately, some priests pay little or no attention to the sufferings of some of the faithful in the area of healing and deliverance. Many of them live in denial in this area. Rather than refer such cases to other priests who are in a position to assist the victims, they simply dismiss them as having psychological problems, thereby evading their duties. Certainly, this attitude is wrong. Instead, proper discernment on a case-by-case basis is required in this area to know the real sources of people's problems to determine the ones that need spiritual healing or deliverance and the ones that require the attention of a medical doctor or a psychologist or even a psychiatrist. Besides, rather than send people away out of ignorance or sheer inability to deal with such cases, a priest can easily refer the complainant to another priest who is gifted in that area.

Another challenge is that most dioceses in Nigeria do not have a concrete ministry of healing and deliverance to deal with cases of spiritual affliction, oppression, and possession affecting their people, which is a grave omission. The bitter truth is that some Catholics who are in need of spiritual help in this area often do not receive it from many of their priests. When they can no longer bear it, some go to other churches in search of solutions to their problems and may end up remaining there. In the absence of such an important provision in most dioceses, the efforts of some priests who are genuinely exercising the ministry of healing and deliverance in the Church to alleviate the sufferings of the people and who use it to lead the faithful to a practical faith in God and a deeper relationship with him is highly commendable.

Nevertheless, the sad thing we witness today in the exercise of this ministry and sometimes the *charism* of teaching and preaching is the abuse of spiritual gifts for personal enrichment rather than for selfless service to the people of God or the building up of the Church. The level of greed and impunity in this area is growing by the day. While some so-called "preachers" charge or negotiate exorbitant fees to preach retreats or help parishes raise money, some "healers" are building business empires. Nowadays, it seems that more and more priests and even lay people are venturing into this important ministry in the Church with uncommon speed for money and fame. In some places, there have been cases of abuses, playing to the gallery to impress people, and shady practices that seem strange to the Catholic faith. In fact, the activities of some so-called healers and preachers are worrisome and raise serious doubts as to their maturity and the real motives behind their ministries—that is, the glory of God and the temporal and spiritual good of his people, or self-enrichment, fame, and vainglory on the part of those who are involved in these ministries.[218] In the Book of Kings, the prophet Elijah prayed thus in the presence of the prophets of Baal and the people of Israel:

> O Lord, God of Abraham, Isaac and Israel, let it be known this day that you are God in Israel, that I am your servant, and that I have done all these things at your bidding [command]. Answer me, O Lord, answer me, so that this people may know that you, O Lord, are God, and that you have turned their hearts back [to you].[219]

The vital point to note here is the noble motive of Elijah in praying for a miracle. Clearly, it was not for his exaltation or profit or vainglory, but the glory of God and the conversion of his people. In general, *charisms* are given to individual Christians for service—for the good of others and the upbuilding of the Church. Among the *charisms* that are known, the more extraordinary ones include prophecy, healing, and speaking in tongues.[220] In general, *charisms* are free gifts that ought to be dispensed freely. Thus, any form of commercialization for personal gain amounts to a wrong use of a spiritual gift. Although this may not be one of the main reasons people leave the Church, it does not remove the fact that it

---

[218] This observation does not in any way suggest that we do not have very disciplined priests and even lay people in the ministry who are motivated by the love of God and neighbour and a desire to serve the Church with their gifts.

[219] 1 Kings 18:36-37 in NRSV.

[220] *CCC* 799-800.

is an anti-witness behaviour that can discourage some of the faithful.

So, the points we are emphasizing in this section is that while the non-provision of the service of healing and deliverance can force some Catholics to drift to other churches, abuses in the exercise of the same ministry or anti-witness in this area can equally discourage a few and make them give up their faith. In the absence of the office of an official diocesan exorcist in the meantime, what is needed are checks and balances by the ecclesiastical authorities to ensure that while the services are available to those who need them, abuses that can weaken or destroy the faith of the people are avoided or dealt with decisively when they arise.

Goodbye, Good Men: Activities of the Enemy Within

Every human being is created in the image and likeness of God and has an inherent dignity. In virtue of this, no one can deny that every man or woman has the personality of a child of God. In the area of sexual morality, the Church teaches that marriage is a union between a man and a woman and that the sexual act is reserved for married couples. Every unmarried person is called to chastity and that makes the sexual relationship or act between unmarried persons wrong irrespective of their sexual orientation—heterosexual, homosexual or bisexual.[221]

Although the Church considers the homosexual orientation objectively and intrinsically disordered, my argument here is on the difference between "bad" and "evil" or between "being bad" and "being evil." In this context, being bad implies consistently engaging in a morally bad act without intentionally promoting it or influencing others to embrace it. On the other hand, being evil

---

[221] This does not, however, put the sexual relationship or act between unmarried heterosexual persons and two single homosexual persons or couples at the same level. As the Church teaches (and I totally agree), although homosexual persons have dignity and should be respected, the homosexual orientation itself is objectively and intrinsically disordered, meaning that all homosexual acts are morally wrong irrespective of who is involved.

implies consistently indulging in a morally bad act and deliberately promoting it or influencing others to embrace it.

On the basis of the Church's moral teaching and with specific reference to this distinction between "being bad" and "being evil," an individual (regardless of his sexual orientation) can be said to be living a morally "bad life" if he consistently engages in sexual relationships or acts, while he will be living an "evil life" if he consistently engages in any of this and deliberately promotes it among others. It is in this context I wish to approach the issue of gay lobby in the Church as a serious evil that needs to be tackled.[222]

Now, the title, *Goodbye, Good Men*, used in this section is from a book by an American author, Michael Rose. There is a popular saying that those who do not learn from history live to repeat the same mistakes. The wisdom in this is that we should be careful and learn from the experiences of others. As the American writer, Og Mandino, maintains, there are three types of people in relation to history. The first consists of those who learn from the mistakes of others and these are the wise ones. The second group comprises those who learn from their own mistakes and they are the happy ones. The last group comprises those who neither learn from the mistakes of others nor their own and they are the foolish ones.

The book, *Goodbye, Good Men*, by Michael Rose, gives a clear insight into what went wrong in the Church in America, which is largely responsible for the present crisis in the priesthood and the Church there. The widespread sex abuse scandals, which are causing many Catholics to abandon their faith or leave the Church can be traced back to two main reasons. The first is a well-orchestrated agenda by some enemies of the Church to infiltrate the priesthood and destroy the Church from within. And the second is carelessness or lack of vigilance on the part of the authorities and sometimes compromise by some of them as unfortunate as that may sound. Speaking about the existence of homolobby within the Church, Dariusz Oko writes,

[222] My view here is also applicable to any other type of evil lobby or practice, even if it is heterosexual in nature.

> I began my work as a struggle against a deadly, external threat to Christianity, but then gradually discovered that the division is not that simple. The enemy is not only outside the Church, but within it as well, sometimes perfectly camouflaged, like the Trojan Horse. We are dealing not only with the problem of a homoideology and a homolobby outside the Church, but with an analogous problem within it as well, where homoideology takes the form of a homoheresy.[223]

In a paper I delivered to some bishops, priests, and seminarians in Ibadan some years back, I had made a similar observation that the homolobby within the priesthood is here with us in the Church in Nigeria even though it may not be at this same scale we witness it in the Church in America. In that paper, I stated categorically that,

> Today, the global secular culture has become entrenched in many places and the Church is not an exception. This is a real problem. Some priests have acquired a secular or an extremely liberal mindset that does not conform to the teaching of the Catholic Church, while some others are guilty of syncretism. Still, there are a few who exhibit traits of subtle atheism to put it mildly. The bottom line is that a significant number of the clergy (in spite of having been ordained), are not yet converted and need to be properly evangelized and led to conversion and intimate friendship with Christ. The Republic of Benin saga where some bishops and priests were implicated in shady practices is a clear example of what I am saying. But it will be foolish to think that that is Republic of Benin and not Nigeria because the same reality is here with us as well as

[223] D. OKO, "With the Pope Against the Homoheresy," posted by New Catholic, 2/16/2013, p. 2. See also https://www.lifesitenews.com/news/with-the-pope-against-homoheresy/.

the issue of "gay-lobby," which Michael Rose pointed out in his book, *Goodbye, Good Men,* is here with us.[224]

Apparently in reference to the strong homolobby within the priesthood, Pope Benedict XVI states that "the greatest persecution of the Church comes not from her enemies without, but arises from sin within the Church."[225] He acknowledges that it is a great crisis which seems to present the whole priesthood as a place of shame because every priest is looked upon with suspicion as being one of them.[226] Speaking on what the homolobby has caused the Church, Oko maintains:

> .... it is therefore important to note that scandals involving sexual abuse which have shaken the global Church were mostly the work of homosexual clergymen. The Church has paid a very painful price for the tremendous offences which have been exposed, losing much of its credibility. This has caused dramatic difficulties both in spiritual and material terms in many dioceses, monasteries and seminaries, with churches becoming empty in entire provinces of the Church. It is estimated that the Church in the U.S.A. has had to pay more than one and a half billion dollars in damages so far.[227]

Still on the negative impact of homolobby within the Church, Oko asserts, "The more organized the offenders are successful in protecting their own interests, the more successful they are in bringing harm to others and in destroying the credibility of the Church. This way, a powerful impulse towards de-Christianization comes forward from within the Church itself."[228]

---

[224] P. NWAEZEAPU, "A Year of Faith and the Priestly Ministry..., *op. cit.*

[225] POPE BENEDICT XVI, *Light of the World: The Pope, the Church and the Signs of the Times, A Conversation with Peter Seewald,* transl. by Michael J. Miller and Adrian J. Walker (San Francisco, CA: Ignatius Press, 2010), p. 27.

[226] *Ibid.,* p. 23; Also cited by D. OKO, "With the Pope Against the Homoheresy..., *op. cit.,* pp. 11-12.

[227] *Ibid.,* p. 3; Cf. D. MICHALSKI, "The Price of Priestly Pederasty," Crisis Magazine, October 2001, pp. 15-19.

[228] *Ibid.,* p. 6.

In truth, every monster or evil always has a small beginning and then begins to grow if it is not checked or destroyed immediately or at its early stages. Going by the information offered by Rose, the Church in America neither paid attention to the emergence of homolobby in their seminaries nor to its gradual but steady growth in planting their agenda. The consequences have been devastating for the Church and the Catholic priesthood, leaving both with seriously battered images, which undermine the mission of the Church and her witness to truth, justice, and holiness. While we cannot undo the wrong of the past, we can at least manage and reduce the negative effects and be more proactive in preventing new problems. True love for the Church and zeal for her mission should compel us to protect her now from the attacks of the enemies from within and without. The same love for the Church should make us consider how best we can pass on a healthy and flourishing Church and priesthood to generations after us by building on right foundations and rebuilding foundations that have been compromised or destroyed.

Conspiracy of silence or inaction in matters of grave consequences for the priesthood and the Church and her future cannot be a mark of love and commitment to her or to her founder or her mission. Speaking on the silence of many priests and the fear to speak out against the evil of homolobby in the Church, Oko observes,

> This can also be seen in the fear and confusion of the clergy, particularly in certain dioceses and congregations, when faced with that topic–they escape into silence, unable to articulate even elementary statements on the teaching of the Church on the subject. What are they afraid of? Where does that fear in entire groups of mature, adult men come from? And where do the neuroses, heart diseases and other complaints come from in priests who nevertheless try to oppose such phenomena, especially to protect children and youth? They must be afraid of some influential lobby which wields its power and which they may fall into disfavour with.[229]

---

[229] D. OKO, "With the Pope Against the Homoheresy…, *op. cit.,* p. 5.

The most annoying and frustrating aspect, which can cause neurosis for any right-thinking person or lead to disillusionment is that, in practice, we are not doing enough in the dioceses (or in some cases anything concrete) to arrest this shameful situation. We talk and lament, but without any "serious" action. Instead, some choose to pamper or cover up "evil" and continue to erode confidence in the priesthood among the laity.[230] No doubt, while all of us are sinners, not all are evil or, better still, glorify and entrench evil as a way of life. Insisting that denial of the existence of homolobby within the priesthood will harm us more, Augustyn maintains that "If we make an *a priori* assumption that no lobby of homosexual priests has ever existed, exists now or will exist in the future, we actually support the phenomenon. The homosexual lobby of the clergy gets off scot-free and becomes a serious threat."[231]

One of the clear evidences life offers us is that it is easier to destroy than to build or rebuild. We see that in the experience of the Church in America. In spite of all the efforts that some of the dioceses and Church institutions are making to bounce back and rebuild the battered image of the Church and the priesthood, the wrongs, bad choices, and negligence of the past continue to haunt them in the present. Again, this suggests that prevention is better and more economical that the cure.

The experience of the Church in the Republic of Benin is another interesting saga. The scandal that rocked the Church and the faithful was the disheartening discovery a few years back that some of the ordained ministers were into syncretism and the occult. In the confused minds of these ministers, Jesus Christ (the Light of

---

[230] Cf. P. NWAEZEAPU, "A Year of Faith and the Priestly Ministry…, *op. cit.,* p. 6. At other times, we trade blames and are never proactive in finding practical solutions, which makes one question the essence of the four years we spend studying philosophy as a discipline. Concrete reforms are needed rather than a cosmetic approach to very serious matters that can destroy the image of the Church and continue to erode confidence in the priesthood.

[231] Cf. J. AUGUSTYN, *Bez oskarżeńiuogólnień* [*Without Charges and Generalizations*], an interview by T. Królak about homosexuality among priests for the Catholic News Agency, March 23, 2012, http://ekai.pl. See also D. OKO, "With the Pope…, *op. cit.,* p. 7.

the world) and the devil (the prince of darkness) seemed to "coexist without any tension"[232] even though Jesus' statement makes it clear "that no man can serve two masters" (See Mt 6:24). Deep down in their minds, there was really no difference between the "altar of God" and the "altar of Satan." Their inordinate lust for wealth, power, and pleasure distorted their reasoning and deadened their consciences. The negative impact of that scandal on the lay faithful was huge. Here, we can cite cases of weakened faith and complete loss of faith in the Church and the priesthood. Some of the faithful drifted to other churches and the whole episode left the Church grossly weakened with her image seriously battered.

The Church in Benin cannot undo the wrong or change this sad story, which is now a dark part of her history. At best, she can only strive to rebuild by painfully struggling over time to re-present to the people of God and their nation the true image of Christ's Church characterized by a sincere adherence to the Gospel and to holiness of life. Even though this will take some time to achieve given the suspicion and dissension in the air, the truth is that it is achievable provided the Church there can learn from this ugly experience and renew herself from within. This renewal should be visible in sincere conversion, atonement, and striving for holiness of life by all, especially the priests and the religious.

More importantly, other churches spread all over the world and Africa, and the churches in Nigeria in particular, have a great deal to learn from the experiences of the churches in North America and the Republic of Benin. If these evils can happen in these places, then they can equally happen elsewhere. This is why we need to be cautious and highly proactive in our study and appraisal of what happened in these places to unravel why and how they occurred as well as how they grew and became so entrenched, undetected, or unchallenged. It is equally important to reappraise the damages or the undesirable situations in the different dioceses where these evils occurred, keeping in mind that it is easier and better to build

[232] The truth is that Jesus and the devil cannot coexist the same way light and darkness cannot coexist. It is not possible to give one's allegiance to God and the devil at the same time. In the case of these priests, the truth was that they were simply using the Church and the priestly ministry as a cover-up.

properly from the beginning than to attempt to rebuild a collapsed structure. That is to say, it is better to check and prevent the "undesirable" now than to invest time, money, and energy in the future to try and manage or correct the damage that could have been prevented in the first place with due diligence and courage.

This infiltration of the occult into the Church is not a new phenomenon. On the contrary, it was a carefully hatched plan by the members of secret cults in the 18th and 19th centuries. Speaking of their plan to infiltrate and destroy the Church from within, Pope Leo XIII writes,

> The race of man, after its miserable fall from God, the Creator and the Giver of heavenly gifts, "through the envy of the devil," separated into two diverse and opposite parts, of which the one steadfastly contends for truth and virtue, the other of those things which are contrary to virtue and to truth. The one is the kingdom of God on earth, namely, the true Church of Jesus Christ; and those who desire from their heart to be united with it, so as to gain salvation, must of necessity serve God and His only-begotten Son with their whole mind and with an entire will. The other is the kingdom of Satan, in whose possession and control are all whosoever follow the fatal example of their leader and of our first parents, those who refuse to obey the divine and eternal law, and who have many aims of their own in contempt of God, and many aims also against God.[233]

He identifies the Freemasons as the main force behind the plan to destroy the Church from within and possibly despoil the nations of the earth of Christendom in order to enthrone the kingdom of Satan. Drawing insight from the writing of Saint Augustine in *The City of God* about the "two loves," he contends that the motivation behind the evil plan of the secret societies is inordinate self-love. In their case, this self-love has reached a level of contempt for the Creator himself that they plot to overthrow his kingdom on earth

---

[233] POPE LEO XIII, *Humanum Genus* (HG) – Encyclical on Freemasonry, April 20, 1884 (Tan Books & Publishers Inc., United States, 1992), n. 2.

and build a world without any reference to God. These points are absolutely clear in the statement,

> This twofold kingdom St. Augustine keenly discerned and described after the manner of two cities, contrary in their laws because striving for contrary objects; and with a subtle brevity he expressed the efficient cause of each in these words: "Two loves formed two cities: the love of self, reaching even to contempt of God, an earthly city; and the love of God, reaching to contempt of self, a heavenly one." (1) At every period of time each has been in conflict with the other, with a variety and multiplicity of weapons and of warfare, although not always with equal ardour and assault. At this period, however, the partisans of evil seem to be combining together, and to be struggling with united vehemence, led on or assisted by that strongly organized and widespread association called the Freemasons. No longer making any secret of their purposes, they are now boldly rising up against God Himself. They are planning the destruction of holy Church publicly and openly, and this with the set purpose of utterly despoiling the nations of Christendom, if it were possible, of the blessings obtained for us through Jesus Christ our Saviour.[234]

In actual fact, the Freemasons planned to achieve their evil plan by targeting seminarians, young priests, nuns, monasteries, and young people in schools. Their strategy was to corrupt the doctrines, morals, and the theology of the Church, among other things, by exposing their targets to modernist and secular humanist ideals that attempted to do away with everything supernatural in the Christian faith.[235] As a true shepherd of God's people, Pope Leo XIII considered it to be his duty to point out the danger, to

---

[234] *Ibid.,* n. 2; See also *De civ. Dei*, 14, 28 (PL 41, 436). Cited by the pope.

[235] T. MARSHALL, "Truth About Infiltration of Catholic Church," interview with Taylor Marshall on his new book, *Infiltration: The Plot to Destroy the Church from Within.* https://taylormarshall.com/2019/06/257-truth-infiltration-catholic-church-faith-goldy-interviews-dr-taylor-marshall-podcast.html.

expose the adversaries, and to resist their plans and devices in order to protect the faith and the salvation of God's people and foster his kingdom entrusted to his charge all over the world.[236] Thus, to resist their evil incursion and activities, the pope mounted a strong opposition to the plan. His resistance was twofold. This involved acting or "doing something concrete" and praying as well. First, he counseled all to expose them, that is, to "tear away the mask from Freemasonry, and to let it be seen as it really is."[237] This is to be achieved through preaching, publication, the promotion and sustenance of virtuous organizations such as religious guilds for workmen[238] and the Third Order lay associations (of Saint Francis),[239] and by devoting special care to the instruction of the young people in our schools who are the hope of human society.[240] Acknowledging that our united human efforts will not be sufficient to defeat the Freemasons and their evil plot to overthrow the Church and impose a new state of things (that is, a new world order) founded on mere naturalism or secular humanist ideals.[241] In his exact words, the pope maintains,

> We well know, however, that our united labors will by no means suffice to pluck up these pernicious seeds from the Lord's field, unless the Heavenly Master of the vineyard shall mercifully help us in our endeavours. We must, therefore, with great and anxious care, implore of Him the help which the greatness of the danger and of the need requires. The sect of the Freemasons shows itself insolent and proud of its success, and seems as if it would put no bounds to its pertinacity. Its followers, joined together

---

[236] *HG* 3.

[237] *HG* 31.

[238] *HG* 35.

[239] *HG* 34.

[240] *HG* 36.

[241] *HG* 10. See also B. MILES, "Revolution in Tiara and Cope: A History of Church Infiltration – Part II," in https://musingsofanoldcurmudgeon.blogspot.com/2020/03/revolution-in-tiara-and-cope-history-of_17.html. Posted Tuesday, 17 March, 2020. Originally published on April 20, 2015.

> by a wicked compact and by secret counsels, give help one to another, and excite one another to an audacity for evil things. So vehement an attack demands an equal defence–namely, that all good men should form the widest possible association of action and of prayer. We beseech them, therefore, with united hearts, to stand together and unmoved against the advancing force of the sects; and in mourning and supplication to stretch out their hands to God...[242]

The Lack of Will to Tackle Evil Within the Church and Priesthood

In one of his writings, Saint Boniface pointed out that "the Church is like a great ship sailing the sea of the world and tossed by the waves of temptation in this life."[243] In our time, the challenge that the Church faces has taken a new dimension. The attack is not just from the world, but also from within. It is as if the enemy has finally infiltrated and planted his army within, to carry on the crusade to destroy the Church, the priesthood, and the religious life from within. Although the plot may not have started in recent times, the facts on the ground indicate that some people who are firmly entrenched in the Church are pursuing an agenda that is opposed to her mission in the world.

The Pope Emeritus, Benedict XVI, did not mince words when he wrote that the Church is under attack from within, meaning that some people within the ranks of the clergy are involved. As a cardinal, he recognized as far back as 2004 that there is so much filth, so much pride and self-complacency in the Church "even among those who, in the priesthood, ought to belong entirely to Christ."[244] More recently in Fatima, he sternly warned us that, "the

---

[242] *HG* 37.

[243] SAINT BONIFACE, Letter 78; See the Second Reading of the Office of the Reading on June 5.

[244] JOSEPH CARDINAL RATZINGER, A reflection on the Ninth Station during "The Way of the Cross" at the Colosseum, Rome, Good Friday 2005.

greatest persecution of the Church does not come from outside enemies, but arises from sin in the Church.... And that the Church therefore has a profound need to re-learn penance, accept purification, learn forgiveness but also the necessity of justice."[245]

The crisis in the Church and the priesthood in particular is increasingly becoming visible to some of the lay people themselves. In actual fact, some of them are worried about the well-being and future of the Church and are asking questions. But in the face of all this, there seems to be a strange and uncomfortable silence among many of the clergy, especially those who wield some power to address the situation and change things. This has given rise to some probing questions among some priests, religious, and lay people themselves, even though many of them make their remarks mainly in private, perhaps, out of fear of victimization or persecution, or to protect their positions or ambitions.

Now, a question we cannot avoid is, "Are not those clergymen who are in a position to change things aware of the crisis and the serious negative consequences for the Church and her mission both at present and in the future?" Most people believe that this is very unlikely. But then, if they are aware, why are they silent? Why are they doing little or nothing to safeguard the best interest of the Church they claim to love dearly and serve? Could it be fear? But fear over what? Is it about safeguarding their positions or rising further in the hierarchy of the Church? Is it about losing popularity and favour? Is it about persecution? What is the silence all about when evil continues to thrive? Are we not supposed to be shepherds instead of hirelings who do not really care about Christ—the Chief Shepherd, the Church and our flock? Is there something (maybe a hidden agenda) that some of us do not know? These are the questions being asked by a significant number of priests who are disillusioned over what seems like a "conspiracy of silence" in the face of evil.

---

[245] POPE BENEDICT XVI, "3rd secret of Fatima: A persecution will come from 'inside the Church.' Pope Benedict XVI Warns." A comment on the Third Secret of Fatima while on a visit to Fatima. See https://mysticpost.com/3rd-secret-of-fatima-a-persecution-will-come-from-inside-the-church/.

Although the crisis in the Church and priesthood is yet to explode in Nigeria as we have it in the West, especially in the United States, the truth is that it is brewing and will eventually explode if we are not proactive enough to do penance, to purify the system now, and re-establish virtue in the priesthood. In the US, the crisis is affecting the population of Catholics. For example, the number of those who claim that they have no religion has risen to 23.1%; Catholics are 23%; the Evangelicals are 22.5%; mainland Protestants are 10.8%; while other religions together make up the remaining 20.6%.[246] The important thing to consider here is that, from being a fast growing denomination in the US in 1957, today we are declining and becoming less relevant to the people, especially because of the sex abuse scandals mainly orchestrated by the homosexual network and the failure of many of the priests to satisfy the spiritual yearning of the faithful.

Back home, even though it is true that we do not have a full-blown crisis yet, we cannot ignore the warning signs, which are there for those who have eyes. Moreover, the world is now a global village and some Catholics, especially the informed young adults who are aware of the ugly situation abroad and the manner in which it is being handled, are becoming disillusioned about it all. In fact, some are no longer too excited about the Church while others tend to stay away on this ground. Even though these are clearly in the minority, we should be worried. It should compel the more to ask how long this "conspiracy of silence" or inaction in the face of a serious crisis will last. How long will it take for the crisis to explode here as in the United States? Really, do we need to wait until that happens, bearing in mind the grave consequences for the faith?

Regarding this lack of will to tackle some of the evils plaguing the Church and the priesthood, one can easily identify a number of reasons. The different factors that are responsible for this may include fear of victimization or persecution, fear of blackmail, lack of courage, lack of moral authority, compromise, lust for financial gains, careerism, and utter selfishness.[247] Nevertheless, while these

---

[246] What we need to understand here is that, while the Evangelicals are growing in population, the Catholic Church is declining.

[247] The sad reality is that money and the inordinate ambition to rise in the

may be the immediate reasons for our inaction or the failure to take a decisive stand against evil, the root cause is the loss of supernatural faith or lack of spirituality among most of the clergy and religious. Put another way, the lack of a personal conviction about Christ, the Church, and her mission is a major problem.

It is a well-known fact supported by experience that evil spreads and takes root where there is no concerted effort to stop it. According to a British statesman, Edmund Burke (1729-1797), all that is necessary for the forces of evil to prevail in the world is for enough good men to do nothing. Also, the words of Pope Saint Gregory the Great are very apt here. According to him, "A religious leader [I mean the entire clergy] should be careful in deciding when to remain silent and be sure to say something useful when deciding to speak….ill-advised silence can leave people in their error, when they could have been shown where they were wrong."[248] Furthermore, he states that when we hide behind the wall of silence in the face of a serious crisis that can adversely affect the faith or the physical and spiritual well-being of the flock or the Church, then we can be described as taking flight at the approach of the wolf, which makes us hirelings rather than shepherds, and dumb dogs that cannot bark.[249]

Saint Boniface's position is clearly in agreement with this. Writing to his fellow shepherds, he insists that we must stand firm in battle, which includes that from within. In his letter, he states, "Living under pagan emperors, they [the Fathers of the past] steered the

---

ecclesiastical ladder are contributing seriously to the silence people often maintain in the face of certain evils that are devastating the Church. The "godfathers" have so much money to share among their loyalists, and in some cases they have the connections to push them up the ladder. Nevertheless, what I consider to be the greatest problem is that many of the ordained ministers aren't properly evangelized and converted. Hence, their level of commitment to the Church and her mission is weak just as their level of openness to martyrdom for the cause of Christ and the Church.

[248] POPE SAINT GREGORY THE GREAT, A reading from *The Book of Pastoral Rule* of Pope St. Gregory the Great, Bk 24. See the second reading of the office of the Reading, week 27 of the year: Sunday.

[249] *Ibid.*

sheep of Christ, that is, the Church, his beloved spouse. And they did this by teaching, defending, working and suffering even to the shedding of their blood."[250] On this ground, he concludes, "Let us not be dumb watch-dogs or silent spectators: let us not be hirelings that flee at the approach of the wolf. Let us be watchful shepherds guarding the flock of Christ…."[251]

The key words here are, "With the shedding of their blood." Certainly, these Church Fathers did that because they were personally convinced about Christ, his Church, and the mission of the Church, and placed the interest of the Church above self or any narrow or misguided interest or ambition. Today, where is the same conviction and commitment to Christ and his cause among the clergy, especially those who have some influence in the Church? Where is the zeal to maintain sanity and preserve the right values among the clergy and in the Church as a whole? The truth is that until our ordained ministers and leaders die to self and make Christ and the mission of the Church their first, if not their only priority, not much will change.

Talking about confronting evil, we can learn from the resistance of Pope Leo XIII and more so of Pope Pius X who actually did a lot to deal with the challenge posed by the secret societies, that is, the bold obstinacy of Freemasonry in their times. These leaders did not keep quiet or look the other way, or maintain a conspiracy of silence, or refuse to act decisively in the face of a serious crisis or a threat aimed at weakening and destroying the Church. On the contrary, they faced the battle headlong.

If Christians and the clergy in particular are unwilling to do similar battle to save the Church and the priesthood from gradual or total collapse, it may be because they have never allowed themselves to be transformed by Christ's power into fervent disciples who are totally committed to his Church and her mission in the world. Ardent followers of Christ who prioritize their relationship with him above all other relationships and interests are not likely to sit back and watch or do nothing. Instead, they are more likely

---

[250] SAINT BONIFACE, "Letter (78)." See http://totus2us.org/vocation/saints/st-boniface/.

[251] *Ibid.*

to sacrifice everything to defend the priesthood and the Church from any serious attack which tends to undermine her integrity and mission.

Jesus' demand is that his followers should die to self and carry their cross and follow him (cf. Lk 14:25-27). But it seems that the commitment of most ordained ministers is to self. In practice, the "self" seems to come before Jesus Christ and his mission. This is why many no longer frown at wrongdoings, and there seems to be no desire to practice what is preached or to enforce discipline or seek renewal. Also, it explains why some remain unperturbed or silent while evil continues to ravage the Church and the priesthood almost unchallenged. Even if we claim that we do not know the extent of the crisis on the ground, then the fact that we can no longer smell or detect the presence of evil and deal with it speaks volumes. It shows the level of spiritual consciousness and decay in the system even though the Church is a universal sacrament of salvation.

On the contrary, it is easy to see where there is a resolute will to confront evil in a place. Clear and unmistakable signals—both in words and actions—by those in authority make it abundantly clear what is allowed and what is prohibited. This is what is needed to tackle the issues of homolobby, occultism, and other evils in the Church and priesthood, which continue to batter the image of the Church and undermine her mission. The body language should be clear to all. For example, in making important appointments in the diocese or a congregation with regard to the office of the director of vocations, vicar general, chancellor, deans, consultors, and pastors of the more financially buoyant parishes, caution should be exercised to ensure that they are not members of any group which promotes an ungodly agenda or individuals who are indifferent or sympathetic to such agendas.

Besides safeguarding the dioceses and religious congregations from evil intrusions, appointments must make it crystal clear that every form of ungodly association is prohibited without necessarily discriminating against anyone on the basis of his orientation.[252] A

[252] We should note that an inclination or even a somewhat permanent proclivity towards a homosexual or bisexual orientation is not a sin in itself. However, to engage in illicit sexual practice is sinful, while con-

valuable contribution to this discussion is that made by F. Professor Józef Augustyn, cited by Oko. According to him,

> The problem, in my opinion, is not "in them" but in our reaction "to them." How do we, ordinary priests and superiors, react to their behaviour? Do we yield to fear, step back, call for silence, pretend the problem does not exist? Or do we face the problem, are explicit about it, take away their influential positions, remove them from their offices? They should not work in seminaries or hold any important positions. If the homosexual lobby exists and has anything to say in the structures of the Church, it is because we give in, withdraw, pretend, and so on....[253]

The truth is that we can find solutions to many human problems where there is a will to do so. God has not only blessed us with intelligence, but Christ also assured his Church of divine assistance. In the case of the homolobby within the priesthood, one of such attempts to proffer a solution was by Pope Benedict XVI. According to him,

> Homosexuality is incompatible with the priestly vocation. Otherwise, celibacy itself would lose its meaning as a renunciation. It would be extremely dangerous if celibacy became a sort of pretext for bringing people into priesthood who don't want to get married anyway. For, in the end, their attitude toward man and woman is somehow distorted, often centred, and, in any case, is not within the direction of creation of which we have spoken.... The Congregation for Education issued a decision a few years ago to the effect that homosexual candidates cannot become priests because their sexual orientation estranges them from the proper sense of paternity, from the intrinsic nature of priestly being. The selection of candidates to the priesthood must therefore be very careful. The greatest attention is needed here in order to prevent the intrusion

---

sciously promoting it as an agenda is evil. The observation here is applicable to both heterosexual and homosexual activities and every other evil agenda.

[253] *Ibid.*, pp. 6-7.

> of this kind of ambiguity and to head off a situation where the celibacy of priests would practically end up being identified with the tendency to homosexuality."[254]

Given the above, it is definitely not out of place to state that, at the point of entry or admission, candidates should be made to run certain psychological tests to further discover themselves and receive proper help where necessary. In the same vein, we should ensure seminarians on pastoral work are not posted to priests who are likely to influence them negatively or expose them into ungodly agenda or associations. The authorities should offer seminarians a form of protection and encourage them to promptly report any attempt to abuse or lure them into an evil network or clique. To send a clear message to all the serious wrongdoing in these areas and other areas will no longer be condoned, the authorities must exhibit uncommon courage in sending those who have been carefully identified to be promoting such evil agendas for psychological therapy, retreat, and other effective spiritual programmes.

The focus of such therapies or spiritual exercises should be their healing, conversion, and reformation rather than ignore and leave them to destroy themselves and others or to inflict serious injuries on the Church, the priesthood, the religious life, and the faith of individuals. In all of this, we should always look out for the best interest of the Church and the potential victims of the perpetrators' activities. But, of course, we must consider the good of the perpetrators of the evil agendas themselves who, though are in bondage and in dire need of liberation and conversion, may not realize it or have become powerless over time to free or help themselves due to the formation of deep-seated bad habits from long practice.

In general, the most important response of the Church to grave issues undermining her image and mission today is a well-thought-out, well-rounded and solid formation of future priests and ongoing formation of priests. These should include ongoing seminars, workshops and similar around the identity, vocation, and spirituality of a priest in a way that is compelling. Such exercises should squarely address grey areas that are already known, and identify

[254] POPE BENEDICT XVI, *Light of the World…, op. cit.,* pp. 152ff; Also cited by D. OKO, "With the Pope…, *op. cit.,* p. 14.

concrete measures to deal with them, and at the same time make use of proactive measures to prevent or greatly minimize their future occurrence.

One of the best proactive measures we can take is to invest heavily in discerning the quality of vocations we have at the different levels of formation—at the point of entry or prior to admission; at the end of the spiritual year programme before the candidate proceeds to the major seminary; in the course of seminary training and pastoral work; during pastoral year; and before diaconate ordination in particular. This is very crucial because a significant number of people enter the priesthood with wrong motives. This fact should not be ignored because the motive behind the choice of a vocation will likely shape or influence the goal the individual will have in mind unless he encounters God personally at some point during his formation and experiences conversion, a change of mindset, a change in his priorities, and a change in his motivation. For this to happen often, the authorities must prioritize formation with particular focus on the spiritual dimension.

Priests are not angels, but mortal human beings. They are taken from the society and are exposed to both the positive and the negative influences in society. In spite of the sincerity of many of them in responding to God's invitation to serve as priests in the Church, we should never forget that they too remain human beings who are plagued by the same weaknesses affecting all other humans. Contrary to the superhuman labels we often place on them, they can be vulnerable. The point is that many of our ordained ministers, though not perfect, have the right motive for choosing the priesthood. However, this does not remove the fact that also, over the years, many people have found their way into the seminary with some sinister or wrong motives or a very wrong perception of the priestly vocation, life, and ministry.

In more recent times, many come in with self-centred motives, such as economic or material security and careerism, while some use the priesthood as a cover or see it as a place to hide from the prying eyes of society and practice their sinister activities. The sad thing is that most of those who harbour such hidden agendas often succeed in making it to the priesthood without these motives being detected and challenged in a decisive way to convert and purify them. This fact rubbishes the whole idea of vocation boom if we are to measure real boom, not in terms of number, but by the availability and commitment of priests who, though weak, have pure motives and actually strive to live an authentic priestly life and are willing to give their lives unreservedly to the service of God and the Church. Thus, to achieve a self-rediscovery, the reordering of priorities, purification of motives, and commitment to our mission among the entire clergy, we need to remind ourselves that a Catholic priest is "not a social worker with a religious tag; instead, he is a servant-leader of the community, whose members he teaches, guides, administers the Sacraments to, and reaches out to bring healing and unity where there is despair and division. He does this through the proclamation of the Word, public worship and close-relatedness with the people in service, witness and God-centredness."[255]

There is another dimension to the problem. In spite of the many good priests we find around, we must be honest to admit that the practical environment within the priesthood itself characterized by materialism, vanity, unhealthy rivalry, social climbing, and lack of Christian witness among others tend to promote a false notion of the Catholic priesthood and may likely attract the wrong vocations.[256] Ordinarily, most people find it easier to copy bad examples than good ones. This is because bad examples often do not require a serious effort or self-discipline or sacrifice as opposed to good ones, which require strict discipline and sacrifice. Besides, the case of mental poverty, vacuum of sense, and spiritual blindness witnessed more among the younger generation of priests has reached a point where virtue or the insistence on what is right is not celebrated, while certain wrongdoings or aberrations are accepted or ignored for different reasons. In some cases, the level of degeneration is alarming and, sometimes, it is not clear if priests still share the same Christian beliefs or if some actually believe in

[255] Cf. MANNATH, J., "Who Is a Priest?" Contemporary Religious Update–II, *The New Leader*, November 1-15, 1995, pp. 13-15.

[256] We should note that there are a good number of priests who are truly making an effort to be true witnesses to the Gospel. Sadly, when people focus on the wrongdoings of priests, they often do not remember these others and their huge sacrifices for the faith and the people of God.

some of the truths we profess, teach, and celebrate, or share the same lofty goals of the priesthood as they relate to disciple, pastoral work, and the overall mission of the Church. This new or emerging situation can make relationship and communication among some priests extremely difficult. As such, some are forced to abandon fraternal correction and discipline in order to maintain peace.

It is a well-known fact that the environment in a place (that is, the physical, mental, moral and spiritual environments) can shape the minds or worldviews of those who live there. If the Church must be proactive in raising good priests, our seminaries, parishes, and dioceses ought to provide the necessary healthy environment (from a practical standpoint) so that future priests can be influenced positively and purify their own negative mindset and wrong motives, in order to embrace a healthy notion of the priestly life and ministry.

The tendency to expect a bumper harvest of good fruits, that is, holy and efficient priests, without first focusing on or assuring the potential goodness of the seeds, the richness or fertility of the soil, and the necessary conditions for growth and fruitfulness of harvest is surely misguided and will always end in futility. As a matter of fact, if we do nothing to reengineer the environments (especially the moral, spiritual, and apostolic environments) within the priesthood and our seminaries as a whole, it is not only that nothing positive will result, but we shall end up harming the priesthood and the Church and her mission further.

Again, as part of the proactive measures to restore the glory of the priesthood and further the mission of the Church, we must seek to create a new formation programme that can upset the present mindset and psychology of seminarians. Such a programme should make intimacy with God, sainthood, and an unusual commitment to mission the primary goals to be aspired for during seminary formation, and the actual exercise of the priestly ministry after ordination. Sometime in 2017, I attended a month programme organized by the Fellowship of Catholic University Students (FOCUS) in Florida, United States. One of the inspiring things that struck me deeply was that the call to personal holiness and commitment to mission were given critical emphasis. The participants were made to see sainthood, not as an option or as something for a chosen few, but as a goal for everyone. In a similar way, everyone was made to see mission as a personal vocation to which one must offer his personal best with a huge sense of sacrifice.

At the practical level, the whole intellectual, moral, and spiritual environment or atmosphere was designed to move all the participants towards these goals of sainthood and mission. Having imbibed that, everyone encouraged everyone else to grow towards holiness of life and to go on mission for Christ. If success is possible with FOCUS, a lay missionary organization with a higher population of followers, then it is possible in our seminaries. But then, that is if all hands are on deck to collaborate closely with some carefully chosen, intellectually and mentally sound and spiritually conscious and mature formators who understand disciple-making and see sainthood and mission as projects in their own lives, which ought to be communicated to others as well. Without doubt, their positive influence on those being formed will be unquantifiable in the long run.

On Tribalism in the Church and the Priesthood

In his book, *The City of God,* Saint Augustine speaks about two cities and two loves whose ways and goals are opposed to one another. The first is the city of God and the other is the city of man. According to him, there are two loves by which things are accomplished in these cities. The "love of God, reaching to contempt of self," is the principle of the city of God or the heavenly city, while [inordinate] self-love, "reaching even contempt for God," is that of the city of man.[257] Ordinarily, the city of God and the city of man can coexist in the same country or city or town or village or an institution, yet their ways and standards of operation are never the same. While one seeks the glory of God, the other seeks the exaltation of self, that is, self-glory. The love of God will imply the love of his creation of which man, irrespective of his race or tribe or language or culture or social status, is the crown. But the love of self focuses on "self" understood as an individual himself or "self" as "my family" or "self" as my "particular race, tribe, or group." This

[257] SAINT AUGUSTINE, *De civ. Dei*, 14, 28 (PL 41, 436). Cited also in *HG* 2.

takes us to the issue of tribalism in the Church in Nigeria. From my personal experience, I know how deadly tribalism can be. It is like a dangerous virus and can destroy the victim emotionally, socially, and even health-wise, depending on the level of exposure, the duration of the exposure, and the mental-spiritual coping mechanism of the victim. If it is as harmful as we have stated, then we need to make a judgment here: Does tribalism belong to the city of God governed by the Gospel principles or the city of man? Are those who promote it, either publicly or secretly by words or actions or even silence (omission or inaction), promoting the city of God or the city of man, considering that the two ways are opposed?

Let us begin with the ways or standard of the city of God by delving into Scripture itself. A major truth that emerges from the genealogy of Jesus Christ in Matthew 1:1-17 is that with the coming of Jesus into the world, discrimination on the basis of race or tribe is knocked down. This fact is clear in the inclusion of two women, Rahab and Ruth, who were non-Israelites, in the genealogy of Christ. Similarly, the biblical event of the Epiphany or the visit of the Wise Men from the East (cf. Mt 2:1-11) is another pointer to the same truth, namely that Christ will be the unifying factor among those who accept his light.

The sociopolitical environment in Nigeria is deeply tainted with tribalism. Sadly, at the national level there has been no serious effort by the political leaders to address it decisively and seek out ways to unite the people of the different tribes, ethnicities, and religions into a nation or one united people. Instead, most politicians use it as a basis for manipulating the populace to achieve their own selfish political and economic ambitions. The reason why this reference to the sociopolitical environment in Nigeria is crucial is that Christians, and more so priests and religious, do not fall from heaven. They are born in society, reared in society, and largely become products of their social conditioning within society. The difference is that rearing with family can contradict or affirm the conditioning in the larger society and shape the mindset and character of each individual child. The unfortunate reality is that most Nigerian families have been overcome by the evil of tribalism. Consciously and unconsciously it has come to define most Nigerians, their worldview, and how they approach national issues. Every tribe is suspicious of the others. Oftentimes, they appraise most national issues as to how they affect their tribes rather than from the position of objectivity, truth, and justice. Today, we have many tribe-based sociocultural groups in Nigeria. There is Afenifere in the West, Arewa in the North, and Ohaneze Ndigbo in the East. Similarly, we have different tribal militia groups whose main agenda is tribe-based. From all this, it is easy to see that, in practice, the sociopolitical environment in Nigeria tilts more to the city of man. But considering that although Christians are in the world but not of the world (cf. Jn 15:18-21), the big question that arises is, "What is the situation in the Church of Christ which ordinarily should belong to the city of God and with a clear mission to change the world?"

As we know, the Church is made up of the same human beings who live in the larger society. Yet, there is a huge difference. Although Christians are in the world, they are not supposed to be of the world (cf. Jn 15:18-21). Their mindset, values, and mode of operation cannot be the same as those of the world because they have been called out of the world and sent to be salt to the earth and light to the world (cf. Mt 5:13-16). The Church is supposed to be a people set apart to proclaim God and promote the principles of his kingdom everywhere (cf. 1 Pt 2:9). What this means is that, even where Christians live in an evil and corrupt society, they are meant to redeem it by their lives and Christian witness and not to be overcome and guided by the same worldly principles that society promotes. The Scriptures are very clear in this matter in stating, "Do not be conformed to this world, but be transformed by the renewing of your minds, so that you may discern what is the will of God—what is good and acceptable and perfect" (Rom 12:2).

Unfortunately, experience shows that there is little or no difference between those in the Church and their counterparts in the world as far as the issue of tribalism is concerned. What this simply suggests is that conversion is yet to take root in the hearts and lives of many Christians, including the clergy and the religious. A very good example that bolsters this point was the big scandal witnessed in Rwanda. In the face of the tribal war in the country, some bishops, priests, religious, and lay Christians from one side of the divide are known to have participated actively in handing over their fellow Christians and Catholics, including priests and lay people from the other tribes, to the enemy soldiers to kill.

No matter what they preached about the waters of baptism and the redemptive blood of Jesus Christ on the Cross, it would seem that, in practice, the "tribal blood" which runs in them proved to be "thicker" than the blood of Jesus which redeemed the whole of mankind. Although Christ calls his followers to prioritize their relationships and put him first (cf. Lk 14:25-27), their real loyalty was to their tribes, not Christ. Their weekly profession of faith in God or their so-called loyalty to Christ in baptism, confirmation, holy orders, holy matrimony, and in religious profession was superficial and a great lie.

In spite of the apologies they rendered after the war and the forgiveness that was offered and received, their action remains a huge scandal, and so it is with all acts of racism, tribalism, and ethnicity among God's people in the Church everywhere. To put it in another way, if Christian disunity is a scandal, then the disunity among people of the same denomination arising from tribalism or ethnicity can be said to be an even greater scandal.

Regrettably, the situation in the Church in Nigeria is not different. The tribal agenda looms large in the hearts of many of the ordained ministers, the religious and lay people. Conditioned by society and failing to convert and become Christians at heart, many of them are blinded and plagued by the deadly virus of tribalism. In practice, they seem to consider the tribal agenda to be higher than the Christ agenda, even though we continue to pay lip service to our unity or oneness as a Church. In practice, the tribal battle is fiercer when it concerns appointments into ecclesiastical offices or other "important" appointments in the Church. We can cite the cases of Oyo, Benin-City, and especially Ahiara, which have brought so much negative attention both at home and abroad to the Catholic Church in Nigeria.[258]

---

[258] Even in Ijebu-Ode there were serious grumblings based on ethnic considerations, following the appointment of a new bishop from a different ethnic group and province, in spite of his proven ability as an administrator. Such a negative attitude is common in almost all the different parts of Nigeria. It should be noted that I am not a judge here as to who is right or wrong in any of the cases that I mentioned. My intention is simply to

Some individuals who are interested in particular offices in the local Church or at the provincial or national level sometimes play the tribal or ethnic card to manipulate their equally immature, narrow-minded and unconverted brethren, for their own selfish individual or group advantage. Just as the emphasis on tribe or region has mortgaged the development of the Nigerian State, the sad thing in the case of the Church is that there is no guarantee that the "son of the soil" will do the job well or do it better. Moreover, this narrow-mindedness, self-love, lack of conversion and commitment to the Church and her mission has not only created disunity, mutual suspicion, and lack of proper cooperation among the presbyterate in some dioceses, but it is actually driving the Church along the path of self-destruction.[259]

These strong tribal sentiments and the secret activities of some priests and religious motivated by tribe testify to the fact that the tribal mindset many people carry into our seminaries and formation houses from their families and our corrupt society is often not challenged intellectually and spiritually and consciously evangelized in the course of their seminary training. Just as most average Christians in Nigeria, many of the ordained ministers still define themselves first and foremost by their tribes or ethnic groups than by their Christian identity, which is extremely sad in view of their privileged position as the spiritual leaders and guides of God's people. Here, we have a great deal to learn from the experience of a

---

state that tribalism and ethnicity exist in our Church in Nigeria and that it is unchristian.

[259] If we are not careful, we may begin to witness the emergence of "religious" *Afenifere*, "religious" *Arewa,* and "religious" *Ohaneze Ndigbo* within the priesthood in our metropolitan archdioceses if it is not happening already. Already in some dioceses, there exist some lay associations with deep tribal orientation and agenda. These associations are not open to people of other tribes whether or not they are baptized and confirmed. Sometimes, only carefully chosen individuals from the same town are admitted, which signals that some of these associations are into something sinister. Nonetheless, one thing that is absolutely clear in all of this is that such cases of tribalism and ethnicity often arise from improper human formation, deep-seated ignorance about Christianity, lack of conversion, and inordinate ambition for power among others.

Belgian Moslem who was interviewed on Cable News Network (CNN) sometime in 2017 over his support for radical Islam.

Given the radical views he expressed, the interviewer was quick to remind him that he was a Belgian whose allegiance should be first to the State. But, to the surprise of the interviewer, he too was quick to declare that he was first and foremost a Moslem. In other words, he meant to say, I may be a Belgian by birth, but my "Muslimness" is my primary or only identity, and it comes before race or nationality. How many Christians or priests and religious in Nigeria can unequivocally state that their Christianity comes before their tribe or ethnicity?[260] Without supporting any form of radicalization in religion, one cannot fail to see the fact that, following his conversion to Islam, he now sees his "Muslimness" as what defines his identity, at least primarily. The contrary is the case with many of our ordained ministers, religious, and lay Catholics and Christians in Nigeria. For the vast majority, their *afenifereness* or *arewaness* or *ohanezeness* often comes before our Christian identity and Catholicism. Some mentally and spiritually liberated and converted lay people find tribalism or ethnicity in the Church and priesthood absolutely scandalous. In some cases, it is known to have caused some of them to abandon their Catholic faith or to simply withdraw from being active in the Church.[261]

Against this backdrop, we need to remind ourselves that through baptism we are initiated into the life of Christ. Priests everywhere are ordained for Christ and his Church, not for the people of a particular tribe or race, even though they exercise their ministry in dioceses located in particular regions in a given country. A particular case that has rocked the Church in recent times is

---

[260] The point is not that such convinced Catholics or priests and religious do not exist in Nigeria but rather that the percentage will be low.

[261] I have encountered some Catholics who stopped going to church because of this, and many more whose level of commitment has dropped drastically in their parishes. These often complain that, while their money, services, and sacrifices are needed, they themselves do not seem to count once it comes to being assigned particular positions in the Church. Their worth seems to be tied to what they can give. In other words, tribalism only affects them, but not their money or services. Here, we should note that this negative attitude also exists in other Christian churches.

the "stalemate" arising from the appointment of a bishop for the Diocese of Ahiara. The appointment met with prolonged protests and the total rejection of the bishop that was appointed by the vast majority of the indigenous priests, religious, and the people of Ahiara.[262] The sad reality about the way we approach issues sometimes is that once a diocesan bishop is successfully installed for the diocese, we may consider the problem solved. The tendency may be to declare a "Sabbath" and go to rest until another serious case arises in another part of Nigeria.

The Church always instructs her children to carefully study the signs of the times and interpret them in the light of the Gospel. It is not certain that we have done that with the Ahiara saga in order to unravel the real causes and devise proactive measures to prevent such embarrassing and anti-witness occurrences in the future. It seems more that most people have chosen to dwell on the surface of things, focusing more on whether the ecclesial authorities or the priests of Ahiara diocese are to blame for the problem rather than look at the big picture and see the whole episode as a clarion call from God to reform the formation of our future priests and rethink tribalism, ethnicity, godfather-ism, and nepotism in the Church.[263] As bad as the case may be, it offers us ample opportunity to review all the different cases we have had and proffer a more enduring solution that can serve the best interest of the Church. That is to

[262] Again, my interest here is to state what happened, but not the underlying currents which I do not know with certainty. Nevertheless, the issue of ethnicity played out in the whole saga no matter the angle from which we wish to look at it.

[263] I was alarmed at a given place when an elderly priest defined the Church in his diocese in terms of tribe. According to him, their Church is Tribe-A Church, rather than the Church of Christ located within the region of Tribe-A. In truth, is there really an Hausa Church or Igbo Church or Yoruba Church? Is not the correct thing the Church in Hausaland or Igboland or Yorubaland? Is it baptism or tribe that makes one a member of the Church? If the Church and her priests, religious, and lay people think in such a narrow way, how then can she permeate society with the spirit of the Gospel? If the civil society or world must listen to the Church, then the leaders (the clergy) need to strive to practice what they preach.

say, we must aim at solutions that can protect her image and that of the priesthood, safeguard her moral authority to speak to society, and to save the innocent people of God from unnecessary scandal and embarrassment that can impact negatively on their faith or weaken their interest and commitment to the Church.[264]

Ordinarily, a tribe is a blessing in itself and there is nothing wrong with working for the progress of one's tribe. Nonetheless, whether we wish to admit it or not, tribalism and ethnicity as practiced in Nigeria and in the Church today are deep reflections of a lack of personal conversion and Christian maturity among the clergy, religious, and the laity. The Christian standard is love—love of God and neighbor (cf. Mk 12:28-31; Jn 13:34-35; 15:12-15). Love should be the primary motive of what the Church does and what drives us as Christians. But this is not the case with the promoters of tribalism. Instead, they are driven by fear, arrogance, self-love, and Charles Darwin's law of the survival of the fittest, which itself arises from an erroneous worldview that life is a product of chance and has no definite purpose or goal. Tribalism or ethnicity is equally a reflection of mental and moral immaturity. This is the case when a Christian or an ordained minister or leader allows a tribal agenda to override his personal convictions as a Christian and his judgment about what is right or wrong.[265]

As against the disunity fostered by tribalism and ethnicity, the Bible which is Christ's rule of life for his people as well as the sacraments speak of the oneness of believers as something to be safeguarded. Many Biblical passages speak to this point. In his Letter

---

[264] Even after a bishop is eventually installed in dioceses that have experienced such a crisis, the divisions that arose during those times of strife never completely go away. Respect for priests is eroded in the hearts of some lay people who were involved in the unhealthy struggle. Besides, it is not everyone who got scandalized by the negative actions of their religious leaders that recovers from the whole saga. So, in the end, the Church in the place and sometimes beyond is significantly harmed, especially in places where the media got involved.

[265] There are some priests and lay people who accept membership of tribal groups to avoid being labeled traitors. Sociologists often describe such as others-directed. They have no mind of their own or lack the courage to take a stand on issues based on their personal convictions.

to the Ephesians, Saint Paul instructs the Christian community thus:

> "... make every effort to maintain the unity of the Spirit in the bond of peace. There is one body and one Spirit, just as you were called to the one hope that belongs to your call, one Lord, one faith, one baptism, one God and Father of us all, who is above all and through all and in all.[266]

Again, in the same Letter to the Ephesians he continues:

> For he [Jesus Christ] is our peace, who has made us both one, and has broken down the dividing wall of hostility, by abolishing in his flesh the law with its commandments and ordinances, that he might create in himself one new humanity in place of the two, so making peace, and might reconcile us both to God in one body through the cross, thereby bringing the hostility to an end. And he came and preached peace to you who were far off and peace to those who were near; for through him we both have access in one Spirit to the Father. So then you are no longer strangers and sojourners, but you are fellow citizens with the saints and members of the household of God, built upon the foundation of the apostles and prophets, Christ Jesus himself being the cornerstone, in whom the whole structure is joined together and grows into a holy temple in the Lord; in whom you also are built into it for a dwelling place of God in the Spirit.[267]

Furthermore, in 1 Corinthians 10:16-17, he asks: "The cup of blessing which we bless, is it not a participation in the blood of Christ? The bread which we break, is it not a participation in the body of Christ? Because there is one bread we who are many, are one body for we all partake of the one bread."

Finally, he maintains:

> For just as the body is one and has many members, and all the members of the body, though many, are one body,

[266] Eph 4:3-6.

[267] Eph 2:14-22.

> so it is with Christ. For in the one Spirit we were all baptized into one body—Jews or Greeks, slaves or free—and we were all made to drink of one Spirit. Indeed, the body does not consist of one member but of many. If the foot would say, "Because I am not a hand, I do not belong to the body," that would not make it any less a part of the body. And if the ear would say, "Because I am not an eye, I do not belong to the body," that would not make it any less a part of the body. If the whole body were an eye, where would the hearing be? If the whole body were hearing, where would the sense of smell be?[268]

From these passages, it is clear that tribalism and ethnicity are unchristian. Turning to the sacraments of the Church with particular reference to baptism and the Holy Eucharist, it is easy to see the critical emphasis that the Church places on the unity of believers founded on Christ rather than tribe or ethnic considerations.

One of the four most powerful symbols inside the Church is the baptismal font, and it is carefully displayed in a visible spot in the Church to remind us, among other things, of our spiritual rebirth and our membership of his spiritual family (the Church) irrespective of tribe or race or any other worldly consideration. Ideally, there should be only one chalice and one ciborium on the altar during Mass from which everyone receives the Body and the Blood of Christ, as a sign of our oneness or unity founded on Christ. This makes any form of ungodly unity based on racism or tribalism or ethnicity or any form of party-sprit in the Church, especially among the ordained ministers, a scandal and a huge mockery of what we celebrate and receive on the Altar of God. As Saint Ignatius of Antioch writes to the Magnesians, we too must see that there is a "godly unity" among us and a spirit that is above all divisions.[269]

The leaders of the Church must exhibit great courage in confronting this issue rather than considering it an impossible task, which it is not. This calls for serious and ongoing discussions within the Church and among the clergy. Besides, the matter itself

---

[268] 1 Cor 12:12-17.

[269] SAINT IGNATIUS OF ANITIOCH, "Letter to the Magnesians," n. 10, 1-15.

should receive the critical attention it demands in our seminaries and houses of formation by way of organizing seminars around it. The goal is to challenge the mindsets of seminarians and conscientize them with regard to the evil of tribalism and ethnicity as practiced in Nigeria and the reality of our identity as Christians and a new spiritual family of Christ. If the ordained ministers and the religious men and women who have been exposed to a level of formation cannot rise above tribe and ethnicity, then what right or moral authority would they have to recommend it to ordinary Nigerians?

The Shepherds and Inadequate Spiritual Awareness

Right from the early Church until now, the Church has enjoyed the services of many true guides as pastors. In different dioceses all over the world, there are many priests who can be described as real pastors and guides to the flock of Christ. Although these may have their own imperfections, they are real guides to their people. They want to see the growth in their faith and spirituality and actually invest time, energy, and resources into making this happen.

At the other end of the spectrum, the Church in our time is suffering from the absence of many pastors who are real spiritual guides to the flock of God in their charge. Some of these shepherds themselves do not understand the difference between religiosity and spirituality, or the difference between mechanical "worship" and real worship in spirit and truth. As such, they tend to keep their people at the level of religiosity and mechanical "worship." People are led to the sacraments, but not to an intimate personal relationship with Christ. Others are led to work "for" Christ without being taught to walk with Christ. Those yearning for more do not often get it.

In other words, these shepherds keep their congregations at the level of mechanical Christianity. Most of them are not properly evangelized and cannot speak of any real "spiritual turning point" in their lives whereby they give their concrete "Yes" to God. Many remain at a level whereby they may be religious and active in the Church, but have no intimacy with God. They do not understand Christianity as primarily a relationship, but rather as a mechanical observance of certain religious practices and duties. In this way, the ignorance and spiritual blindness of the shepherds or pastors pose serious threats to the spiritual growth and apostolic empowerment of the faithful in their parishes. They keep the people in ignorance just as the case of the Jews under the spiritual leadership of the chief priests and Pharisees who were so blind and closed to the Spirit of God that they kept them in a state of mental and spiritual blindness or sheer religiosity that did not transform their lives and make them godly. Often, this failure to recognize, nourish, and satisfy the spiritual yearnings of the faithful and thus empower them to be vessels that God could use to propagate his kingdom is known to have contributed immensely to the drift of some Catholics to Pentecostal churches.

Chapter Six

WHY ARE THEY LEAVING US? IMPROPER FORMATION AND EMPOWERMENT OF THE LAITY

Ignorance of the Bible and the Faith by Many Catholics

Knowledge is wealth, and ignorance is a disease, for most people. In Hosea 4:6, God says through his prophet that his people perish for lack of knowledge. This statement is applicable to many Catholics who drift to the Pentecostal churches. As we saw in Chapter Two, even though it was the Catholic Church that approved the list of the books in the Bible, most Catholics are ignorant of the Bible because they do not study it regularly as the Pentecostals do.[270] When people accuse us of holding certain beliefs that are not explicit in the Bible, our main defence is that our faith is not based on the Bible alone, but also on Tradition and the Magisterium. While this is true, the fact is that the vast majority of the Catholic faithful are even more ignorant of these other two sources of our faith. The natural outcome is that most of them are unable to defend some of our Catholic beliefs and practices when confronted by our Pentecostal brethren.

Focusing on Nigeria in particular, the major attacks are launched from the standpoint of Scripture by those who erroneously think that anything about the Christian faith that is not explicitly stated in the Bible is unacceptable. They fail to understand that what we

[270] Most Catholics are not familiar with the contents of the Bible when compared with the Pentecostals. This is due to a total lack of emphasis on this in the Church in spite of the call by the universal Church to make regular Bible study a culture within families and in our individual lives as Christians.

know of Jesus Christ in the Gospels are merely sketches of his life rather than his biography.[271] From experience, some of the main areas of attack by the Pentecostals include the use of images or statues in the Church, which they see as idolatry in reference to Exodus 20:1-6 that prohibits the making of idols. Also, some of them condemn the use of incense at Mass because in Isaiah 1:13, God says "incense is an abomination to me."[272] In these instances, they often take Bible passages out of context and twist them to suit their positions and end up swaying some of our Catholics to join them. The other accusations include the following: that Catholics are not born again Christians; they are not Bible Christians; they worship the Blessed Virgin Mary; they pray to Mary and the saints; they call Mary a virgin when in fact she had other children who were mentioned in the Bible (cf. Mt 13:55-56; Mk 6:3). In all, the Pentecostals attack certain Catholic beliefs erroneously and confuse many unsuspecting Catholics.

On close examination, the major reason they often succeed is that most Catholics are ignorant of the faith of the Church. The level of ignorance varies from persons to persons and from groups to groups. Although this can be blamed on individual Catholics who do not take it upon themselves to understand their faith, a greater part of the blame goes to the local churches and their pastors who are not investing adequately in the proper evangelization, formation, and empowerment of the lay faithful as their close and indispensable collaborators in the work of evangelization.

Rethinking the practice of Catholicism, I have come to identify the lack of proper evangelization and formation of our people to equip them for the Christian life and their crucial role in the mission of the Church as a major reason many of them are drifting to Pentecostal churches. In this chapter, we shall examine the problem under two headings: improper evangelization of Catholics prior to sacramentalization, and the inadequate formation and empowerment of the laity for mission by way of catechesis or discipleship.

---

[271] Cf. W. BARCLAY, *The Daily Bible Study – The Gospel of Luke..., op. cit.,* see commentary on Luke 10:13, p. 134.

[272] NRSV, see Isaiah 1:13.

Improper Evangelization of Catholics Prior to Sacramentalization

The mission of the Church is evangelization, and the goal is interior conversion. We can speak of conversion from two angles. There is the initial conversion, which arises from the kerygmatic proclamation, and then an ongoing conversion (or a deepening of the conversion experience), which occurs during catechesis or the discipleship phase of evangelization. In general, conversion involves a change of heart—a change in one's mindset, worldview, interests, priorities, and activities. As Pope Paul VI asserts, the purpose of evangelization is to convert the mindset and conscience of an individual or the collective consciences of a people, as well as the way they live their lives and the activities in which they engage.[273] The full process of evangelization is supposed to lead a person or a people to imbibe a Christian culture or outlook to life and then to embark on the mission of evangelizing others.

Our common experience as Catholics is that the vast majority of us were baptized as infants on the basis of the faith of our parents and godparents whose duty it is (as it is that of the Christian community) to nurture and help us come to a profound understanding of the faith. As a minimum requirement, an initial conversion is expected to have taken place in individuals who present for First Holy Communion and Confirmation, and more so the priesthood and the married life, prior to sacramentalization. But the sad reality is that this is not often the case as the vast majority of sacramentalized Catholics were never properly evangelized and have never had an initial conversion.

The fact that some of our Catholics are drifting to the Pentecostal churches is a clear sign that they are not properly evangelized and discipled. But then, this does not merely apply to those who are leaving but also to the vast majority of those who are still in the Church. In fact, studies done in North America and Canada reveal that only about ten percent (10%) of Catholics who attend church on Sundays are properly evangelized.[274] The implication is

[273] *EN* 18.

[274] Cf. M. DOPP, "Relit–The Heart of Evangelization..., *op. cit.*

that even less than 10% of this number can be said to have been discipled or are spiritually mature Christians who can feed others.

The root cause is that a vast majority of Catholics were baptized as infants and have never heard the kerygma proclaimed intentionally to them in their adult lives to consciously elicit a response—that is, that of belief in Christ and at least an initial conversion that launches them into an intimate relationship with him. Although most people continue to attend church and receive the sacraments, some come to discover at some point that something is missing in their Christian life. For example, most of them cannot really point to a time in their lives when they consciously and personally gave their life to Christ, or a time they can refer to as their spiritual turning point in life, to use the words of Weddell.

This point was absolutely clear to me in the Life in the Spirit Seminars we ran in parishes. The testimony of many adult Catholics was that they experienced their real, spiritual turning point in life during the seminar. This was not strange to me because of the high kerygmatic components in the proclamation or Messages during this seminar. But then, what percentage of Catholics has undergone this life-changing seminar or similar seminars or programmes with strong kerygmatic components?[275]

During the Life in the Spirit Seminar, I equally became aware that most Catholics do not understand meditation. Although they go to Mass on Sunday, recite the rosary and other prayers, many are not familiar with meditation or what some call "quiet time with the Lord." Similarly, although Catholics believe in the Trinity and confess the Holy Spirit to be God, most of them still see him as an impersonal force rather than a person with whom they can have a personal relationship. In practice, a majority of them do not understand the role of the Holy Spirit in their lives and the spiritual gifts he bestowed on them during their baptism and confirmation. Also, many Catholics do not know that they can hear God, because

[275] Here, we should note that I am not claiming that the Life in the Spirit Seminar is the only spiritual programme through which one can encounter Christ personally and experience an initial conversion. Certainly, there are other programmes, such as the kerygma course, the Alpha Course, and so on.

they were never taught how to hear him in prayer and other ways, as well as how to do a proper discernment.

What this means is that the prayer life of most Catholics is a monologue rather than a dialogue with God. For example, in a congregation, I found out that most people have been receiving Holy Communion between five and fifty years and yet over ninety-five percent (95%) claimed that they never heard Jesus say anything to them all this time. To revisit what we said in Chapter Three, Catholics in general are not schooled in the practice of a regular study of the Bible in order to derive from it something concrete, which they can store in their spiritual bloodstream through meditation and practice daily in order to grow in the spiritual life.[276] Even though the practice of *lectio divina* has a long history in the Church, most Catholics are neither familiar with it nor are trained to practice it.

As a Catholic, I was in this situation for a long time and now know the huge difference between sheer religiosity and the spiritual life. An experience of the latter at even the most basic level makes you feel you have been wasting your time all the time, and this is why the phrase "I have seen the light" is common among Catholics who probably encountered Jesus outside the Church. The sad thing here is that the Catholic Church sees Christianity as something more than a religion. Precisely, she sees it as an "event" or a "faith" whereby God draws us into a living relationship with him through Christ in the Holy Spirit.

The first component of catechesis as the Church teaches is "prayer and the spiritual/sacramental life." Prayer is communication with God; it is a relationship with him. Growth in the spiritual and sacramental life implies growth in this relationship with him. Essentially, the spiritual life entails three main things—avoiding evil or detachment from sin (purification), acquiring virtue or attachment to doing God's will (illumination), and an entering into communion or union with God.[277] From this fact alone, it is clear that the Church sees the Christian life first and foremost as a life

[276] See L. EIMS, *The Lost Art of Disciple Making* (Grand Rapids, Michigan: Zondervan, 1978), p. 21.

[277] Cf. DIOCESE OF METUCHEN–OFFICE OF EVANGELIZATION, "Fire Upon the Earth," Parish Evangelization Team Manual, 2014-2015; See Session on Discipleship, p. 3.

of relationship or communion or fellowship with God. Unfortunately, most Catholics, due to improper evangelization and poor formation, do not understand or speak this beautiful language of an intimate relationship or communion with God and tend to reduce everything to sheer religiosity which favours the mechanical approach many of us bring to the practice of our faith.

In practice, the emphasis in most of our churches is not on personal conversion, relationship, the quality of the faith, disciple-making, and mission. The maintenance culture in our parishes leads us in the direction of sheer sacramentalization, mere numerical growth and financial strength. These become the main criteria we use to measure our growth as a Church or parish. Hence, once our churches have huge populations and more and more people come to the sacraments and we have enough funds to embark on physical projects, we feel satisfaction and a deep sense of success.

At other times, some of us strive to get the non-sacramentarians in our parishes to receive the necessary sacraments and try to reach some inactive parishioners to get them more involved in parish life[278] and to render service. As good as this may be, it is not enough because our mission as a Church definitely goes far beyond that. True or proper evangelization must begin with an interior conversion in response to the Gospel message that is proclaimed, and it should culminate in discipleship and mission, which are two essential things we often overlook in most of our parishes.[279]

Baptism signifies repentance.[280] The reason for undergoing baptism is conversion and the willingness to follow Christ and live his life. A major problem we witness in most parishes is that intentional kerygmatic proclamation to lead people to conversion and faith in Christ is almost non-existent either before or during the period of catechism. The result is that a majority of catechumens who pass through our catechism classes are never challenged to consciously respond to the kerygma and have never given their personal "Yes"

[278] Cf. M. SWEENEY and S. WEDDELL, *The Parish: Mission or Maintenance?* (Colorado Springs, CO: The Catherine of Siena Institute, 2002), p. 5.

[279] Cf. *Ibid.*

[280] Cf. *AG* 6.

to Christ beyond the "Yes" of their parents and godparents at the time of their baptism as infants. Reflecting on the present situation in the Church, Dimitri Sala rightly observes,

> In the early Church, the preaching of this Message [the kerygma] was clear and people knew the terms of it. That's why it stirred up so much trouble and people were even killed for it. But now we have settled for a practice of baptism in which people are welcomed to the sacraments externally without necessarily having heard a clear proclamation of the Gospel. And so many are baptized without making the baptismal choice of conversion.[281]

Hence, most catechumens attend catechism class more for the purpose of receiving specific sacraments than to discover Jesus Christ in a personal way and learn more about his life with an intention to become more like him in character, service, and mission. In other words, the transformation of life or the maturing of the faith, which ought to be the goal of catechesis, is sacrificed for sheer sacramentalization due to improper evangelization and conversion on the part of the candidates.

Inadequate Formation and Empowerment of Catholics for Mission

In addition to the absence of an ongoing and intentional kerygmatic proclamation in our parishes, another problematic area worthy of note is the inadequate formation and empowerment of the laity for personal Christian maturity and for mission. This problem is the outcome of our failure in the area of intentional disciple-making in the Church, especially during catechesis. In fact, if the vast majority of our sacramentalized lay faithful were never properly evangelized, then it follows automatically that they could not have been discipled either, since the latter presupposes the former.

Although we stated earlier in this work that no other church can boast of a richer catechism than that of the Catholic Church,

---

[281] D. SALA, *The Truth About Evangelization* (Liguori MO: Liguori Publications, 1997), p. 18.

we must note that it is one thing to have a rich catechism and another thing altogether to communicate it well. This is where we need to make an important distinction between the catechism of the Church and catechesis. The two are not exactly the same. The catechism is the rich deposit of our Catholic faith, a summary of the principles or the fundamental truths of our Christian faith formulated by the Church. On the other hand, catechesis is education in the faith. More specifically, as Pope John Paul II maintains, "it is an *education in the faith* of children, young people and adults which includes especially the teaching of Christian doctrine imparted, generally speaking, in an organic and systematic way, with a view to initiating the hearers into the fullness of Christian life."[282] Similarly, the *General Directory for Catechesis* sees catechesis as "nothing other than the process of transmitting the Gospel, as the Christian community has received it, understands it, celebrates it, lives it and communicates it in many ways."[283]

In *Catechesi Tradendae*, Pope John Paul II states that, "accordingly, the definitive aim of catechesis is to put people not only in touch but in communion, in intimacy with Jesus Christ who alone can lead us to the love of the Father in the Spirit and make us share in the love of the Holy Trinity."[284] Poor catechesis can undermine a rich catechism. More than ever, we need a solid catechesis to lead our numerous catechumens and the faithful in general into the riches of our faith in a way that will bring about a personal conviction about Christ and the truths of the faith and challenge Catholics to live out the faith.

The stage of catechesis is the third stage of the Church's mission of evangelization. In practice, this is the stage of discipleship, and it has as its goal the transformation of the candidates for the sacraments to make them more like Christ in character and to be totally committed to his saving mission. Our common experience in the Church in Nigeria and in many other places is that the quality of

---

[282] POPE JOHN PAUL, Post-Synodal Apostolic Exhortation *Catechesi Tradendae (CT)*– On Catechesis in Our Time, October 16, 1979, n. 18.

[283] CONGREGATION FOR THE CLERGY, *General Directory for Catechesis* (GDC), promulgated in 1997 by the Congregation for the Clergy updates the General Catechetical Directory published in 1971, n. 105.

[284] *CT* 5.

catechesis that is offered in our catechism classes in most parishes often does not achieve this vital goal of catechesis. Even though most Catholics continue to attend Mass every Sunday and some are active in their parishes, it does not necessarily imply that all are converted and have been discipled. To be candid, most of them are yet to attain Christian maturity due to a lack of discipleship. Although many of them actively *work for God,* they do not *walk with him* or enjoy intimacy with him. This lack of proper conversion and discipleship is largely responsible for the lukewarm or nonchalant attitude of most Catholics to the mission of evangelization.[285] Narrating her own experience with regard to the Church in the West, Sherry Weddell writes:

> The answers we received – from hundreds of ordinary Catholics and parish leaders all over the world – were consistently revealing and astounding. And we have learned a great deal more by listening to over 1,600 diocesan and parish leaders from 60 dioceses who have attended our evangelization seminar, Making Disciples, over the past eight years .... We have learned that there is a chasm, the size of the Grand Canyon, between the Church's sophisticated theology of the lay apostolate and the lived spiritual experience of the majority of our people. And this chasm has a name: discipleship. We learned that majority of even "active" American Catholics are still at an early, essentially passive stage of spiritual development. We learned that our first need at the parish level isn't catechetical. Rather, our fundamental problem is that most of our people are not yet disciples. They will never be apostles until they have begun to follow Jesus Christ in the midst of his Church.[286]

[285] Converted and discipled people always do mission because they have been taught to *walk* with Jesus and *work* with him through the process of discipleship.

[286] S. WEDDEL, *Forming Intentional Disciples* (Huntington, Indiana: Our Sunday Visitor, Inc., 2012), p. 11.

Poor Catechesis: Lack of Disciple-Making

Intentional disciple-making is critical to the making of apostles or missionaries. As a matter of fact, the stage of catechesis should be the real stage of making disciples in the Church. Yet, this is not what actually takes place in most of our catechism classes. The vast majority of our catechists do not disciple their catechumens or help them achieve an appreciable level of spiritual transformation required of a true disciple of Jesus Christ. The major reason is that most of them neither understand the concept of discipleship nor realize that catechesis is the stage of conscious and intentional disciple-making in the process of evangelization. The emphasis is often more on intellectual formation and some lessons on morals.

At the expiration of the stipulated period for catechism, the candidates that the vast majority of the catechists often present for the reception of the sacraments are mostly those who merely memorized some Church doctrines or teachings about Christ, but who may never have had a personal encounter with God or experienced an interior conversion or enjoy intimacy with him. As Pope John Paul II states, it is "Only in deep communion with him [Jesus Christ] will catechists find light and strength for an authentic, desirable renewal of catechesis."[287] But then, in most cases, the fault is not really that of the catechists because they cannot give what they do not have.

Further, from the intellectual point of view, the catechists in many of our parishes are either not too educated or are not well-grounded in the teachings of the Church and the spirit that underpins them. What this implies is that most of them are not even adequately equipped to teach catechism from the intellectual standpoint. Even in places where we have educated catechists, many of them may still be at the level of sheer religiosity and may not have attained Christian maturity themselves. Thus, what takes place in their classes is the passing on of religious information about God and the transmission of doctrines that many of the young ones cannot sufficiently grasp as opposed to a discipleship-oriented catechesis geared towards practical spiritual life or personal spiritual transformation and mission.

---

[287] *CT* 1, 9.

The major fruit of a successful catechesis is the spiritual transformation that occurs in the life of an individual. This is visible in personal holiness, authentic witness of life, and strong commitment to the mission of Christ and his Church. But in practice, it seems we are more interested in actual sacramentalization or in the number of people who receive the sacraments than in the spiritual transformation of the individuals or their fidelity to the actual Christian life and mission associated with each sacrament. As a result, most people emerge from our catechetical formation in the parish without clear evidence of a real transformation in their worldview, priorities, character, and choices.

Similarly, according to the 1977 *General Directory for Catechesis,* this "formation for the apostolate and for mission is one of the tasks of catechesis."[288] But sadly, in spite of two or more years of catechesis in the parish, most confirmed Catholics often lack the much-expected mission consciousness and zeal that a mature or discipled Christian should exhibit as a lifestyle. This is because they are often not taught that the Church has a mission and then discipled to prepare them for an active role in that mission. On this note, Sherry Weddel maintains that, "If formation for mission is essential to true catechesis, then the overwhelming majority of lay Christians are not being truly catechized."[289]

The truth is that she is absolutely right. Even the lay associations in the Church are not doing a good job in this area as most of them neither know the mission of the Church nor have a mission mindset. Sometime in 2018, I asked the archdiocesan officers of a major lay organisation in the Church in a particular archdiocese in Nigeria what the mission of the Church is, but to my utter surprise they did not know it. The story is the same with almost all the lay associations we have in the Church and the fact that the parishes themselves are no better goes a long way to show the clear loss of focus on mission in the Church and thus the failure of our catechesis to produce mature Christians (that is, disciples) who are committed to intentional sharing of the Gospel or mission.

---

[288] *GDC,* no. 30.

[289] M. SWEENEY and S. WEDDELL, *The Parish: Mission or Maintenance..., op. cit.,* p. 15.

This, in itself, is overwhelming evidence that the goal of Christian growth and spiritual transformation is not being achieved in our catechesis. In fact, this evidence is overwhelming for those who understand what catechesis or the discipleship phase is all about.

Again, most of our catechists in Nigeria do not seem to know that catechesis has two dimensions which are education and the maturing of the faith. They focus a great deal on what the Church believes, but tend to pay little or no attention to the formation and maturing of catechumens in the spiritual life that is critical to the actual practice of the faith. Similarly, many of them do not seem to know that catechesis has four main components, namely: prayer and spiritual life, Scripture, doctrine, and the moral life. As the Office of Evangelization in the Diocese of Metuchen puts it,

> The third stage in the Process of Evangelization is known as the Discipleship Stage [or catechesis] because the individual is now a learner or student of the Master.... The fire of faith that was ignited or fanned back into flame in the soul will need a lot care and attention to keep it burning bright and long. It must be systematically fed and stoked with Christ-centred teaching and mentoring in several areas, namely: 1. Prayer and the sacramental life; 2. Sacred scripture; 3. Doctrine; 4. Communal life/stewardship and 5. Service/mission. Only as one grows in these areas will one be transformed into the bonfire of God's love that he is intended to be.[290]

But due to ignorance in this area and the fact that they are not adequately equipped for their task, most of them invest their energy in some aspects of the catechetical formation while neglecting the others. Quite often they focus on doctrines and to some extent on morality and ignore formation in the Sacred Scriptures, prayer, and the spiritual life from the standpoint of a relationship, communal life/stewardship, and mission. The consequence is that those who emerge from our catechism classes are not very familiar with Scripture because they were never exposed to regular Scripture reading and meditation or mission during catechism. Also, beyond

---

[290] DIOCESE OF METUCHEN – OFFICE OF EVANGELIZATION, "Fire Upon the Earth..., *op. cit.*, p. 1.

the regimented prayers in our prayer books, most of them lack the confidence to lead spontaneous prayers, especially in public. This is because most catechists do not take practical steps to train their catechumens in this area.

This situation has a lot to reveal about the state of the spiritual life of many of the catechists themselves and parents too who certainly have a large chunk of the blame for failing in their role as the first evangelizers and teachers of their children in the faith. The point is that if many of our catechists and parents see Christianity more from the standpoint of religiosity or faithfulness to religious practices instead of an intimate loving relationship with God, which manifests itself in authentic Christian living and spiritual fruitfulness, then we cannot expect a miracle from them.

Actually, in most cases, the fault is not really that of the catechists because they are not adequately equipped for their ministry. Ordinarily, one may argue that this is where the priests should come in to redirect things. But in spite of being the chief catechists of their parishes, most of the pastors too are neither personally involved in the teaching of catechism nor pay enough attention to what goes on in the classes or to the retraining of their catechists to enlighten them and make them more effective in their work.

On the other hand, it is also true that some of the priests themselves are either plagued by the same ignorance as the catechists, as far as the goal of catechesis is concerned, or have insufficient interest in catechesis and mission. It is not only that they do not intentionally invest in disciple-making in their parishes, but they equally do not promote mission among their members and the lay associations in their parishes. In reality, disciple-making and apostleship are not household terms in our parishes and formation houses and this problem is not limited to Nigeria. The story is the same everywhere. For example, speaking of her experience in the United States, Sherry Weddell maintains that whenever she used the term "disciple," Catholics sometimes told her that she was betraying her Protestant roots because (they erroneously believe) that the word "disciple" is a Protestant term, not a Catholic one.[291]

[291] *Ibid.*, p. 6.

Furthermore, as a result of poor catechesis and formation, most Catholics do not understand the concept of true worship in general. As critical as the Mass is to our life as Catholics, catechumens are often not led to a deep intellectual and spiritual understanding of the Mass or trained to approach it with a lively faith and from the standpoint of a loving relationship with God that should result in personal spiritual transformation and spiritual fruitfulness. As such, most people neither come to offer themselves completely as a living offering to God nor do they come with expectations to encounter him personally and be transformed on an ongoing basis. The truth is that a mechanical attendance at Mass cannot build up anyone spiritually or result in that interior transformation that can lead to an authentic practice of the faith as a lifestyle and spiritual fruitfulness.

The harms that poor catechesis has caused the Church and her members are enormous and cannot be easily quantified. Most Catholics who emerge from such catechism classes do not develop an authentic spiritual life or a sound prayer life as most of them do not understand the language of a personal relationship or intimacy with God. Many of them have a shallow understanding of Christianity as a faith and the role of the Holy Spirit as far as the Christian life and mission are concerned. Many do not have the culture of regular Bible study and meditation as we saw in an earlier chapter. They seem so content with a form of "mechanical Christianity" characterized by keeping obligations and fulfilling certain rituals from the standpoint of obligation rather than a Christianity marked by a deep loving intimacy with God and where prayer, worship, and service to him flow from the place of love and intimacy with him.

Today, people connect more with teachings which come from practical experience than with those arising from what we read in books or heard from others. A common thing among most of our catechists is that they merely teach the doctrines of the Church but do not take time to see if the catechumens in their care are evangelized or not and then make an effort to evangelize them where necessary to lead them to that initial conversion before catechizing them. In the same vein, they do not often share with their students the story or experience of their personal encounter with Jesus

Christ as the reason for their own conversion and continued belief in him. Why this happens is that many of them may not have a personal conversion story or may not have experienced what can be called a "spiritual turning point in life."[292]

According to Pope John Paul II, proclamation (and even the catechetical formation of catechumens) should not be "a matter of merely passing on a doctrine but rather a personal and profound meeting with the Saviour."[293] So, catechesis, as an essential stage in the Church's mission of evangelization and a stage which also aims at preparing catechumens for their evangelizing mission, should involve a personal testimony of the catechist's walk with Jesus. In other words, it involves communicating our own experience of the doctrine of the Good News of Jesus Christ as our personal Saviour and Lord. In actual fact, the type of catechesis needed in the present time is evangelical catechesis, which incorporates evangelization into catechetical formation to achieve the overall goal leading the catechumens to the fullness of the Christian faith both in word and in practice.

As a matter of fact, every catechist who wishes to be effective should be able to tell his or her catechumens the reason for their own conversion, continued belief in Jesus Christ and his Church, and why they live the way they do, which is different from the currents of the secular world. If we consider that what is more important to catechesis is getting people to "know God" rather than to "know about God," and to lead people to a personal transformation and spiritual fruitfulness in the areas of authentic Christian witness and intentional mission, then one cannot but liken what takes place in our catechism classes most times to the case of the blind or partially blind leading the blind or a so-called guide who does not have clarity about the destination leading others.

---

[292] The phrase "spiritual turning point" was used by Sherry Weddell to indicate a conversion experience.

[293] POPE JOHN PAUL II, Message for World Mission Sunday, 2001.

The Important Connection Between Catechesis and Evangelization

Catechesis is the third of the four stages in the Church's mission of evangelization, while kerygma or the initial proclamation of the Gospel is the second. Although evangelization flows through all four stages, the real stage committed to actual proclamation or evangelization is the second stage which has as its goal the initial conversion of hearts to Jesus Christ. A major challenge we face in the area of catechesis is that most priests and catechists fail to see the important connection between evangelization, or more precisely, kerygma, and catechesis. Although the two are not exactly the same, they are interconnected.

Speaking on this, Pope John Paul II makes it abundantly clear that, although catechesis and evangelization (that is, kerygma) are not exactly the same, they are interconnected and should always go hand in hand. As a matter of fact, catechesis cannot succeed without prior or ongoing evangelization. Evangelization involves the proclamation of the Good News of salvation in Jesus Christ with an aim to convert the hearer, while catechesis involves a systematic and integral formation with its goal as the complete transformation of life. The latter involves sound spiritual, intellectual, moral and scriptural formation, and communal teaching and mentoring.[294]

Still on the difference between the kerygma (the initial proclamation) and catechesis, the observation of Marybeth Bonacci who was a director of evangelization and catechesis in a large parish in Denver, United States, is quite instructive.

> Until recently, I was the director of evangelization and catechesis at a large parish here in Denver. And in that time, it became clear to me that (1) there is a significant difference in meaning between those two terms and that (2) most parishes don't fully understand that difference, and that hurts our ability to reach the people in the pews.... To put it simply, "evangelization" is the process of introducing someone to Jesus Christ. It is about sharing his

---

[294] *CT* 25.

> Good News with them, and inspiring them to make the radical decision to follow him.[295]

Continuing, she maintains that,

> It [evangelization] is the fundamental turning of the heart toward God, the reorientation of one's entire life to live not primarily for self, but for him. Evangelization is the "why." Why do I renounce this world for the next? Why do I follow Christ? "Catechesis," which happens after evangelization, is the nuts and bolts of instruction – the "how." It is where we learn in a systematic way what we need to do in order to follow Christ, how to live as a Christian, how to grow in faith and love and grace.[296]

From the above, it is easy to see that the success of this second stage is critical to the success of catechesis or discipleship, which is the third stage. Where personal spiritual transformation of the individuals and not sheer sacramentalization is the real goal, then those who present for catechesis should be people who have been evangelized and have experienced an initial conversion. They should be individuals who are now open and ready and are deliberately seeking the maturing of their own Christian life through intentional disciple-making that will culminate in personal transformation and mission.

Strictly speaking, catechesis is the period we deepen the conversion experience that began at the second stage. By implication where an initial conversion has not taken place prior to catechesis, it will be almost impossible to achieve this goal of transformation unless a form of evangelization first takes place during the catechism class. What this means is that candidates who have never had an initial conversion are not really ready for catechesis because we cannot possibly deepen the conversion experience if it was non-existent in the first place.

Oftentimes, many of the catechumens who present for catechism in our parishes have never been properly evangelized and

---

[295] M. BONACCI, "Evangelization before catechesis" in *The Arlington Catholic Herald* of 9/12/12. See https://www.catholicherald.com/article/columns/mary-beth-bonacci/evangelization-before-catechesis/.

[296] *Ibid.*

have not had an initial conversion. Most of them tend to approach catechesis from the standpoint of a church requirement to be satisfied, with their eyes set almost completely on the actual reception of the sacrament. In other words, they hardly spare any thought for the maturing of their Christian life or faith and the mission that is tied to the specific sacrament, especially the Sacrament of Confirmation.

This has been the pattern for a long time, but the truth we need to stress here is that we cannot effectively catechize the unevangelized or the unconverted who have not made a personal decision to follow Jesus more closely. In other words, investing so much energy on catechesis (stage 3) without paying attention to the proper evangelization of the candidates (stage 2) is a bad strategy. In fact, some trained catechists in North America came to this conclusion from their personal experiences on the job. Many of these have been calling for the reintroduction of kerygma prior to catechesis. For example, the statement by Marybeth Bonacci offers a clear diagnosis of the problems in this area. Based on the distinction she made earlier between evangelization and catechesis, she asserts:

> Catechesis, then, presupposes evangelization. It would make no sense to teach people how to live a certain way if they don't understand why they would want to live that way. It would be like giving someone a road map to a place they have no interest in going. They'd have no use for the map. They'd be more likely to use it to line the bird cage than they would be to actually follow it.[297]

Going further, she states,

> And here is where I see the disconnect in most parishes. Most Churches operate on a presupposition. They assume that their congregations consist of the "faithful" – people who have been evangelized, who have made the decision to follow Jesus Christ, who desire to become "new creations" in him. They are gathered together to pray, to worship and to learn how to deepen that relationship. The Church's catechesis exists to help those people, who have already

[297] *Ibid.*

> made the decision to follow Christ, to follow him more closely. Only, in many cases, that presupposition is wrong. It may have been true, in previous generations, that a majority of the people in the pews on Sunday mornings were fully evangelized, committed Christians who had given their lives to following Jesus Christ. That may still be the case in some evangelical congregations. But it is not the situation in the average Catholic parish here at the dawn of the 21st century.[298]

Still, on the need to seek to evangelize people before catechizing them, she maintains:

> I believe that there are a lot of people in those pews who have never been evangelized. They're probably sincere people, for the most part. They're there. They want to be "good." They want to meet nice people, maybe please the grandparents, maybe fulfill some kind of obligation. But they don't get it. They don't understand the power of Christ to transform their lives. They don't see the need for the radical, life-altering transformation that he offers. It's no wonder our catechesis doesn't seem to be getting us too far. We're offering them a road map to a place they have no interest in going. And hence, the primary need in the average Catholic Church is not for catechesis. It's for evangelization.[299]

The whole point in this area is that, in spite of the difference between them, neither catechesis nor evangelization (Gospel kerygma) is supposed to stand on its own. Just as catechesis needs evangelization to thrive, so does evangelization need catechesis in order to deepen what was begun at the initial proclamation or the Gospel kerygma. We can infer this from the statement by Pope John Paul II to stress the importance of catechesis in the formation in the Christian life. According to him,

> Thus through catechesis the Gospel kerygma (the initial ardent proclamation by which a person is one day

---

[298] *Ibid.*

[299] *Ibid.*

> overwhelmed and brought to the decision to entrust himself to Jesus Christ by faith) is gradually deepened, developed in its implicit consequences, explained in language that includes an appeal to reason, and channelled towards Christian practice in the Church and the world. All this is no less evangelical than the kerygma, in spite of what is said by certain people who consider that catechesis necessarily rationalizes, dries up and eventually kills all that is living, spontaneous and vibrant in the kerygma. The truths studied in catechesis are the same truths that touched the person's heart when he heard them for the first time. Far from blunting or exhausting them, the fact of knowing them better should make them even more challenging and decisive for one's life.[300]

Inadequate Preparation of Catechumens for the Sacraments

Besides the problem of catechizing the unevangelized, it does not seem that most of us—catechists, priests, and in fact dioceses and parishes—accord the sacraments, especially confirmation, the level of seriousness and attention they deserve both in our thoughts and in the actual preparation of catechumens. Commenting on the quality of preparation for the sacraments, as Pope John Paul II maintains,

> [There should be] a thorough preparation for this sacrament [that is, Confirmation] which will allow those who receive it to renew their baptismal promises with full awareness of the gifts they are receiving and the obligation they are assuming. Without a long and serious preparation, they run the risk of reducing the sacrament to a mere formality or external ritual, or even losing sight of the essential aspect by insisting exclusively on the normal commitment involved.[301]

[300] *CT* 25.

[301] POPE JOHN PAUL II, "General Audience of January 4, 1994."

Again, as one commentator rightly observes, the development of doctrinal knowledge by catechumens during the period of catechesis should equally coincide with a development of faith.[302] It should not only manifest in the knowledge of truth but also in love for Christ, communion with him, and service. The proper communication of doctrine should stir up in the recipients "an allegiance to Christ in the intellect and in the heart and enlarges the Christian community."[303]

Examining the attitude of Catholics to the sacraments in general, it appears that the mindsets of many of us have been secularized. In practice, this is why we tend to focus more on the actual sacramentalization of catechumens without paying adequate attention to their living out the fruits of the sacraments and the mission or apostolate attached to them. Some attitudes that we exhibit consciously or unconsciously actually lead to such a conclusion. Some examples will suffice here.

It is a known fact that some parents try to influence the priest or catechists to admit their children to First Holy Communion or Confirmation even when they have not been adequately catechized and prepared for the sacraments. The attitude of some parents in this regard and the fact that some priests and catechists actually yield to such requests in order to foster friendship or for some other unjustifiable reasons reveal our secularized mindset as far as the sacraments are concerned. We see the same attitude is the case of a priest who asked his parishioners who were not yet confirmed to put down their names for confirmation less than a month to the ceremony without adequate preparation just to impress the bishop who was visiting his parish with a long list of names and thus show that he is efficient.

Confirmation is the sacrament that is meant to create soldiers for Christ and his Church on earth. Viewed from the standpoint of the old Roman Empire, one can easily identify three main functions of soldiers or an army. These include: quelling an internal insurrection, defending the State or Empire against foreign aggression,

---

[302] See S. CYRENO, https://www.slideshare.net/SimonCyreno/pope-john-paul-ii-catechesis, August 21, 2011.

[303] M. BONACCI, "Evangelization before Catechesis"..., *op. cit.*

and conquering new territories for the emperor and the Empire for both physical expansion and the extension of the culture and influence of the Roman Empire. This makes soldiers extremely important to the State, especially if we consider that the security of a State is also critical to economic growth and the overall well-being of its people.

As soldiers of Christ in the Church, confirmed Catholics are expected to fulfill all the roles of a soldier mentioned earlier. They are supposed to defend the faith and the teachings of the Church against heresies, misinterpretation, and all forms of attack against her. Beyond that, they have also an expansionist role—that is, mission. This involves reaching and winning the world for Christ by conquering new territories for him through the witness of their own lives and the explicit proclamation of the Gospel to lead people to him and his Church. This mission also includes fostering the Gospel values everywhere, planting new churches and working to Christianize the culture in society among other things.

Concerning the above, the formation of Christian soldiers or confirmed Catholics cannot be merely an academic or intellectual exercise or minor thing that can be left to those who do not understand what is at stake. Ordinarily, policemen or immigration officials or even soldiers who have never worked outside an office do not train soldiers for battle. Only experienced soldiers who have fought battles can do that effectively. But unfortunately, this often happens in the case of preparing the candidates for confirmation. In most cases, the catechists themselves do not have an experiential knowledge of Christ and a living relationship with him.

Furthermore, the test to determine who or not will receive the sacrament is a test of the candidate's intellectual capacity rather than his Christian maturity also. What this means is that any intelligent person can pass it and receive the sacrament whether or not transformation has occurred in his life or he is convinced of the doctrines that are transmitted. On the other hand, there are cases involving others who have a strong conviction about Christ and the doctrines and have a personal faith but lack the intellectual capacity to memorize doctrines. These may likely not pass the test and receive the sacraments. The outcome is that intellectually gifted individuals who lack conviction and Christian maturity will receive the sacrament quite alright, but are not likely to bear the necessary spiritual fruits or be involved in mission as confirmed Catholics unless they come to have a personal encounter with God at some point in their lives.

In some cases, many of the children who present for the Sacrament of Confirmation in particular are too young and actually come out of obedience to their parents. In many cases, most of these parents themselves are equally ignorant of the demands of their Christian vocation and the specific apostolate that is tied to the sacrament and as such cannot help their wards come to terms with the same realities. The result is that most people pass through our catechism classes but end up not being transformed in character and empowered for mission. They end up not being changed to reflect the life of Christ in their own lives.

Again, we all are aware of the key areas of attack on Catholicism by our Pentecostal brethren and the areas of attack or objection to the Christian faith by the Muslims and the atheists. In spite of that, there is no concerted effort by many catechists and priests to address those issues extensively from the standpoints of Scripture, Tradition, Magisterial teachings, and simple logic in order to better equip the candidates for confirmation or Catholics in general to be able to defend their faith when it is called into question or to educate their ignorant inquisitors. Due to ignorance, on their part, especially in the area of Scripture, some Catholics often get blown off by the Pentecostals and begin to question some of our beliefs and practices.

In more recent times, the Moslems are converting Christians, including Catholics, to Islam while the atheists and secular humanists are causing some to doubt the existence of God altogether by exposing them to harmful teachings. But the point to note here is that some Catholics give up their Catholic faith or Christianity or belief in God as a whole due to a lack of a personal conviction about Christ and proper grounding in the Catholic faith and practices during the period of catechism, even though catechesis is ongoing and should extend beyond the reception of the Sacrament of Confirmation.

In general, to use secular terms, the whole process of catechesis leading to confirmation can be likened to setting out to create combatant soldiers (a fierce army that is supposed to conquer territories) only to end up creating *boy scouts and girl guilds* clothed in *military uniform* and then calling them soldiers.[304] This is why the Church of Christ on earth which ought to be Church militant in name and in practice is now *Church militant* in name, whereas in practice it is almost turning into *Church passive*. Thus, a beautiful process—catechesis—that is meant to produce committed disciples or *militant* soldiers for Christ ends up making immature and passive Christians.

This passivity is very clear in the inability of most confirmed Catholics to share the faith. Consequently, a highly-gifted Church entrusted with a serious mission of winning the whole world to Christ is not only unable to defend her territory (that is, keep her members) but is actually losing significant territories to the modernists or secular humanists, the Pentecostals, and even the Moslems, whether the focus is on the Catholic Church in Nigeria or Ghana or Brazil or the Western world as a whole.

Inadequate Formation of the Candidates for Marriage

Marriage is both a sacrament and a serious institution in society. It is marriage that gives rise to family. Considering that family is the basic cell or nucleus of society where values are built and the foundation of society is established, we cannot but accord marriage from which it arises the critical attention it deserves. It is even more so if we remember that the family is a domestic church and the first centre of evangelization where children come to know and love God through the word and example of their parents.[305]

---

[304] Boy scouts and girl guilds clothed in military uniform cannot be said to be military men and women and cannot do the work of the military the same way that Coca-Cola when poured into a bottle of cough syrup can neither be said to be a cough syrup nor do the actual work of a cough syrup.

[305] Cf. POPE JOHN PAUL II, Apostolic Exhortation *Familiaris Consortio*–On the Role of the Christian Family in the Modern World, promulgated November 22, 1981, nos. 21, 59-60; PONTIFICAL COUNCIL FOR JUSTICE AND PEACE, *Compendium of the Social Doctrine of the*

The natural conclusion from this is that preparation for Christian marriage should be robust in terms of its contents and the level of seriousness with which it is pursued by the Church, the marriage counsellors, and the candidates for marriage themselves.

Sadly, this is not often the case, especially from the spiritual standpoint. Again as Sala observes, our present experience with the Sacrament of Marriage in the Church is not different from our experience of admitting to baptism people who are yet to make a sincere and practical baptismal choice of conversion. As he maintains, the Sacrament of Marriage like any other sacrament is not magic, and without a personal acceptance of the reality that it is supposed to celebrate, it has minimal effect in the couples' lives.[306]

Today, the reality in many places is that many of those who marry in the Church are not well-prepared for the sacrament as a vocation and for the apostolate which arises from it. Although they are mature from the standpoint of biology, most are not spiritually mature and ready for a vocation as serious as Christian marriage with many implications for children, the family, the Church and her mission, and the overall stability and well-being of society as a whole. Again, this problem boils down to the quality of catechesis in our parishes and our homes and the actual practice of the faith within the family and the Christian community.

My experiment with the marriage preparatory class in my parish reveals that most of the young people who present for marriage are not properly evangelized and do not have a personal or a living relationship with God, even though most of them are confirmed. A majority of them do not have a sound prayer life or the culture of regular Bible study, meditation, and mission, among other things. They are weak in the knowledge of Catholic doctrines and can hardly recall most of the things they learnt during their catechism days. Although most continue to attend Mass on Sundays, they neither understand the Holy Mass nor are they active in the Church. The summary of all we are saying here is that they are not properly evangelized and discipled, meaning that they are not yet

Catholic Church (Vatican: The Pontifical Council for Justice and Peace, 2004), Chapter V, paragraph III, nos. 238-240.

[306] D. SALA, *The Truth About Evangelization…*, *op. cit.,* p. 18.

mature Christians who can truly raise their own children to Christian maturity over time.

This situation has several implications which contribute to the drift of Catholics to the Pentecostal churches. If a majority of those who present for marriage are Christians or confirmed Catholics only in name (by virtue of their baptism or confirmation), but not in their mindset and deeds, then it will be extremely difficult for them to live out the marriage vocation fruitfully and to build a family that will be a truly domestic church.

The formation of children involves both teaching and example (that is, the witness) on the part of parents. Although most parents continue to take their children to church on Sunday and to catechism class, if they are not properly evangelized and discipled themselves, then they cannot adequately transmit the faith to their children or provide them with a strong Catholic Christian upbringing that will enable them live the faith, defend it when challenged, and at the same time engage in intentional mission. As a natural consequence, many of these children who grow up without a solid Christian and Catholic foundation tend to become easy prey to those who call their faith into question.[307]

Inadequate Preparation of Godparents for Their Role

In more recent times, we have witnessed the watering down of some important practices in the Church meant to nurture and protect the faith of Catholics. One of such is the issue of godparents for those presenting for baptism, especially infants. Ordinarily, we baptize infants and children on the basis of the faith of their parents and godparents as well as their firm commitment to take responsibility for their Christian upbringing. By word and example they have a duty to raise these children to understand and practice the faith as handed on by the Church.[308] The godparents in par-

---

[307] On this basis, the most important thing we need to do for a good number of those who present for marriage in our parishes is evangelization to help them become converted Christians in name, in mindset, and in deed.

[308] In the course of the celebration of the Sacrament of Baptism, ques-

ticular have the role of mentorship in the Christian life. Although this is still a requirement for the sacrament today, in many cases some people take up the role for some social reasons or to satisfy a Church requirement and fulfil all righteousness rather than for the noble purpose of mentorship intended by the Church.

Sometimes, parents pick total strangers or close family members or friends who do not have interest in the work involved or people who are not in a position to help their children on their Christian journey because they themselves are not properly evangelized and are not striving to live the Christian life. The author himself was once in this situation. As a young man, he stood as a godfather for a number of children without a clear understanding of the important role or duties of a godparent. Sadly, his work, like that of many other ignorant or minimal godparents, began and ended immediately after the baptism.

What makes this even more serious is that some of the parents of such children are not in a position to raise them with strong Christian convictions because they too are not properly evangelized or are nominal Christians who are in need of serious spiritual mentoring themselves. In fact, when exposed to Pentecostalism and other anti-Catholic teachings, some of these parents are the ones who often drag their children to the Pentecostal churches.

Inadequate Preparation of Catechumens for Mission During Catechism

Another area of major concern is that people emerge from our catechism classes without knowing the mission of the Church. Indeed, most Catholics are not adequately schooled on the mission of the Church and carefully prepared for their specific role in it. Even many priests display a great deal of ignorance in this area. Sadly, some actually claim that they are not interested in evangelization, which is a major disaster, considering that this was the primary reason they were ordained priests.

---

tions are put to the parents and godparents of the children to be baptized and they freely undertake the responsibility to bring them up in the practice of the Christian faith as handed on by the Catholic Church.

Similarly, the vast majority of the Catholic lay faithful do not even know that the Church has a clear mission, while others believe that the mission of evangelization is the exclusive duty of the ordained ministers and the religious and so do not get personally involved in sharing the Gospel. Even the lay associations in the Church are not doing a good job in this area. For example, sometime in 2018, I asked the archdiocesan officers of a "prominent" lay organisation in the Church the mission of the Church. To my utter surprise they did not know the answer. The story is the same with almost all the other lay associations in the Church, and it partly explains the clear loss of focus on mission in the Church today.

However we wish to look at it, this problem is the outcome of poor catechesis. During catechism class, there is little or no emphasis on mission. Although catechesis should culminate in mission, catechumens are neither exposed to practical evangelization nor taught the methods of evangelization. Besides, most of those who graduate from our catechism classes are not familiar with the books of the Bible. Some search for some New Testament books in the Old Testament, while many others depend on the index to find the books. What this lack of familiarity with Scripture means is that they were never trained to study the Bible regularly. Perhaps, this is because the teachers themselves do not know the importance of the regular study of the Word of God and meditation to the formation of a Christian. Stressing the importance of Scripture in catechesis, Pope John Paul II asserts,

> To speak of Tradition and Scripture as the source of catechesis is to draw attention to the fact that catechesis must be impregnated and penetrated by the thought, the spirit and the outlook of the Bible and the Gospels through assiduous contact with the texts themselves; but it is also a reminder that catechesis will be all the richer and more effective for the reading of the texts with the intelligence and the heart of the Church and drawing inspiration from the 2,000 years of the Church's reflection and life.[309]

[309] *Cf.* 27.

If truth be said, one of the main reasons things have remained the way they are for a long time is that we are not mission and goal oriented in our approach to the teaching of catechism. Perhaps in practice, we have moved the goal of catechesis set by the Church from being "complete transformation of the individual" to sheer sacramentalization. Another serious reason for our underperformance is a lack of spiritual accountability in the areas of mission and catechesis in our parishes. We do not hold ourselves accountable before God and the Church with regard to the quality of formation we offer our catechumens, provided we are presenting enough people for the sacraments.

Additionally, we do not do proper appraisal of what we are doing based on verifiable indices to see if we are getting the required result of making real disciples and spiritual soldiers for Christ with a passion to win souls and conquer new territories for him through intentional missionary endeavours. This absence of a feedback system or a critical appraisal or accountability is not to our own advantage as a Church. So, to redeem this situation, there is a need to review our goal and our strategy, and re-orientate Catholics towards what ought to be. For this to be effective, there is need to hold our bishops, priests, catechists and lay leaders accountable in the areas of evangelization and catechesis to ensure that no one leaves his work undone.

The Gap Between Theology on Lay Apostolate and Practice

The vast majority of the lay people in Nigeria, including the active ones, are not familiar with the Magisterial teachings of the Church. In reality, there is a wide gap or total disconnect between the rich theology of the Church, concerning the apostolate of lay people in the Church and world, and actual practice. What makes the situation even more pathetic is that most of the clergy and the leaders in the Church seem to have accepted this disconnect. On the one hand, most of our lay faithful are ignorant of the teachings of the Church in this area and cannot practice what they do not know. On the other hand, some of the priests do not seem to know any better while many others are hesitant when it comes to educating and empowering the laity for their proper apostolate and role in the Church.

In practice, most of our pastors are neither intentionally discipling the lay faithful to empower them for their apostolate nor are we intentionally sending them on mission. They do not emphasize disciple-making as a necessity because they do not fully comprehend it and its importance to the success of our mission as a Church. Commenting on this, Sherry Weddell expresses her shock in discovering that "many pastoral leaders [in the Church] do not even possess a conceptual category for discipleship," meaning that "the Church's teaching on social justice and evangelization will remain beautiful ideas that are, practically speaking, dead letters for the vast majority of Catholics."[310] Certainly, this is not good for a Church with a serious mission to reach and win the world for Christ. If the leaders do not understand discipleship as a strategy and do not adequately empower the laity, then they will not only render them impotent as far as their mission or apostolate is concerned, but also, this will make them vulnerable to the evangelical activities of the Pentecostals and others.

In view of all we said about the inadequate formation and empowerment of Catholics, the Church needs to invest more in the area of catechesis. Since evangelization is critical to the success of catechesis, such an investment must include a plan to properly evangelize and convert the candidates either before or during the normal catechism and the RCIA/OCIA programme. It is vital that modern day catechists receive adequate training in evangelization to enable them to evangelize their candidates prior to catechesis proper.

Furthermore, these catechists themselves should be spiritually mature Christians who have been discipled. Experience clearly shows that they are likely to be more effective in their ministry if they themselves have been properly evangelized, converted and discipled, and are walking in intimacy with God. Conversely, if they are merely communicators of the Church's doctrines who have no personal encounter with God or intimacy with him arising from

[310] S. WEDDELL, *Making Intentional Disciples..., op. cit.*, p. 11.

a personal conversion and discipleship, then they cannot be very effective in their ministry.

The challenge this poses to the Church and her pastors is the need to re-evangelize, disciple, and retrain the trainers, that is, the catechists themselves or get them to work hand in hand with some trained evangelizers during the period of catechism or the RCIA/OCIA progamme in our parishes. No doubt, some catechists will not be open to this while others who prefer the status quo, which does not challenge them to grow, may resist it. Nevertheless, in such a case, a pastor who is mission and goal oriented must insist that only properly evangelized and discipled catechists should teach catechism in his parish. An important point that arises here as we think of a lasting solution to the challenge of improper formation and empowerment of the laity is the need to re-establish a culture of evangelization and disciple-making in the Church. We shall take this up in chapters nine and ten.

Chapter Seven

WHY ARE PEOPLE LEAVING US? OTHER REASONS

Man is a social being and thrives better in an atmosphere where he enjoys a healthy interaction with others. In life, first impressions, as they say, matter a lot. When you walk into a church on Sunday, whether as a regular parishioner or as a visitor, you want to feel welcomed. Usually, most people want recognition and tend to go where they feel wanted. One of the accusations levelled against the Catholic Church by some of our former members and even some Catholics is that many of our parishes are not welcoming or friendly enough, especially if we compare them to some of the new generation churches. In truth, the general attitude of most Catholics in this area is not praiseworthy. Sometimes, visitors and newcomers can walk in and out of our churches on Sundays for weeks unnoticed.

Church Wardens and the Issue of a Welcoming Environment

The first people you encounter in our parishes are the security men and the church wardens, or welcoming ministers or the ministers of hospitality. More importantly, the latter are the first church officials that parishioners, visitors, and newcomers encounter when they come to Mass on Sundays. In most cases, these officials are not intentionally trained to be welcoming in their approach and dealings with people who come to our churches. Although we have some excellent church wardens who understand their job, the simple truth is that most church wardens, who are supposed to be the official welcoming ministers at our liturgical celebrations, operate more as many of the unprofessional traffic wardens on Nigerian roads that are unfriendly and sometimes aggressive and abusive. As a matter of fact, such attitudes make people, especially visitors and newcomers, feel unwelcome to our churches. They can keep them away altogether or make it difficult for some of them to integrate themselves easily into the parish where they choose to remain.

The ministry of church wardens or welcoming ministers or ministers of hospitality in the parish is a very important one, which should never be left to all-comers as is the case in many places. Their role includes welcoming people warmly to church and making them comfortable as much as possible to enable them to participate fruitfully at liturgical celebrations. Additionally, they maintain order in the church during such celebrations and assist the minister and people in different ways as the situation dictates. In general, their work is oriented towards maintaining an enabling atmosphere for worship as well as safeguarding the well-being of the members of the congregation before, during, and after the liturgical celebration, with their eyes ultimately on the salvation of their souls. In view of this, they should ensure that everything is ready before Mass or the actual liturgical celebration to greatly minimize distractions during the celebration.

Strictly, their work is more spiritually inclined than technical, even though we cannot ignore the technical dimension of it. Equally, their work has a serious evangelical dimension, which we often ignore. Their privileged position and special role at the Holy Mass enables them to identify regular late-comers, those who distract or do not participate well at the Holy Mass, non-communicants, those who do not receive Holy Communion regularly, and those parishioners who always leave the church before the end of Mass. Surely, this category of people need further evangelization. It is an important aspect of the work of the welcoming ministers to identify and befriend them and try to evangelize them in a manner that depicts genuine interest and love for them. Also, it is their role to identify newcomers or first time visitors and warmly welcome them and help integrate them into the life and activities of the parish. They should assist in registering them in the parish and ensure that they visit them or call them on the phone when a real visit is not possible before the following Sunday. If they are unable to handle the evangelical aspect effectively themselves, they can collaborate with a team of known evangelizers in the parish or the Parish Evangelization Committee where such exists.

In view of the vital role they fulfil in our liturgy, a great deal is expected of the welcoming ministers, not only from the standpoint of their performance, but also from that of the human qualities they possess. Given the nature of their ministry, they should exhibit a strong sense of humility, discipline, calmness, punctuality, sacrifice and patience, since some members of the congregation will always be difficult to manage. It is advisable that they are in the church at least an hour or thirty minutes before Mass or any liturgical event to ensure that everything is properly arranged and to organize themselves properly and assign roles to one another rather than do that during Mass and cause distraction to the worshippers.

Prior to the arrival of the congregation, some welcoming ministers should be at strategic locations near the church entrances to warmly welcome parishioners and visitors with smiles, greetings, and kind words that will make them feel valued and welcomed. Similarly, this should be repeated at the end of Mass. Although the large crowds that throng our churches in Nigeria in contrast to Europe and America may pose a challenge of its own in this area, they should still endeavour to reach as many people as possible.

As some parishes are already doing, there should be a time after the post-communion prayer when the presiding priest himself or the person who handles the announcements recognizes and welcomes the newcomers or visitors to the parish.[311] As our parishes become more welcoming and warm, we will not only attract people to our churches, but also, we will end up fostering a family spirit among parishioners capable of raising the percentage of engaged parishioners who serve the parish with their time, talents, and gifts.

In spite of their crucial role in our liturgical celebrations, we do not accord the welcoming ministers the attention they deserve. Just as in the case of the choir, we tend to admit every individual who shows interest in the ministry without paying adequate attention to their natural abilities and spiritual gifting. This explains why most of them do not possess the necessary qualities required for their ministry. Additionally, when they recruit new members, these

---

[311] Our churches should not be places people can walk in and out unnoticed. The security situation in Nigeria makes it even more compelling to engage visitors to our parishes.

are not sufficiently trained and prepared (technically, emotionally, and spiritually) for their ministry. In most cases, their leaders offer them some advice and give them directives that will help them settle into the job. But the basic understanding most of them have of their work is that of a function rather than a ministry. Even some view their role more from the standpoint of "power and prestige" instead of a service to God and his people, and sometimes this affects their treatment of the very people they are called to serve.

Today, if we are to raise a body of highly effective welcoming ministers in the church, formation is of utmost importance. Formation is of different dimensions—technical, emotional, and spiritual. But as important as the technical dimension of their training may be, the most critical things they require are spiritual formation and training in human relation skills that can endear them to parishioners. The ultimate goal to which our life on earth is ordered is eternal life with God,[312] and conversion is critical to it. Thus, from the spiritual standpoint, welcoming ministers need to be properly evangelized and discipled and led to view their work as a ministry. In addition to this, they should be trained in the technical and relational aspects of their ministry prior to their official induction. Their discipleship training should make them see themselves as servants and missionaries sent to witness to Jesus before the congregation and to serve his people in humility. As a matter of fact, it should equip them to evangelize in the course of discharging their duties with their smiles, politeness, patience, kind words, and their overall behaviour.

God has given the faithful all the charisms they require for service in the Church. Unfortunately, in recruiting welcoming ministers we do not often watch out for the important charisms needed for the exercise of this ministry, such as hospitality, service, and administration. The natural outcome is that we have too many people in the wrong roles and this greatly affects their efficiency. Hence, a training or formation that can be considered adequate for the welcoming ministers should be such that will help discern their

[312] Our purpose on earth is to glorify God and this is expected to culminate in eternal life with him in heaven where we glorify him forever.

natural talents and their spiritual gifts (or charisms) and call them out for a fruitful service among the people of God.

In general, the formation of welcoming ministers, just as that of other ministers in the Church, should also be Scripture-based. More specifically, we should carefully expose them to the teachings of the Holy Bible on the love of neighbor, service, and hospitality.[313] This is to ensure that their approach to service or their ministry is Scripture or God-driven. Some of the useful passages related to their ministry, which should be studied in-depth with them, include Luke 10 (the story of the good Samaritan); Mark 12:30-31, John 13:34-35, and 15:12-15 (on the commandment on love of neighbours); Leviticus 19:9-18, 33-37 (on the care of the poor, the newcomers and the foreigners) and so on. Besides, every ministry is a type of service to God in his Church. As such, they should be formed to love God wholeheartedly and above all to see their work as a service to him that deserves their greatest devotion and commitment.

Since the exercise of their ministry takes place primarily within Mass, they should have a profound understanding of the Mass and worship in general. Their deep love for the Mass and reverential attitude to it at all times should be visible and contagious. Their personal conviction, faith, and devotion in this area will be a form of witness and provide a good example for the congregation to emulate. In virtue of the nature of their ministry, they should exhibit a strong sense of discipline and always avoid becoming a source of distraction to the congregation through unnecessary movements and discussion with one another during Mass.

Moreover, they should be men and women of faith who approach their duties from the standpoint of prayer. Deep faith in God and prayer will enable them to bring God into what they do and constantly remind them both of their need for him and their dependence on him if they are to be fruitful in their ministry. At the same time, these will reduce the danger of becoming self-referential or overdependent on self, as well as the tendency to go through their work as another routine or something mechanical. Besides,

[313] Cf. J. McKEEVER, "What Pastors Need to Know about Church Growth…, *op. cit.*

prayerfulness aided by charity will lead to a situation whereby they make it a point of duty to pray for the congregation they serve and their respective needs.

The Issue of an Unwelcoming Congregation

The priests and the congregation can also contribute to an unwelcoming environment in our churches. At times, a good number of us could be unfriendly or hostile. In the more financially strong parishes, we sometimes get complaints about some parishioners who find it difficult to extend the sign of Christ's peace to others during the Holy Mass. In some cases, it is not impossible to find among some members of our parishes cliques based on tribe or social class or on some other unjustifiable grounds. Some find this extremely irritating and prefer to stay away altogether rather than get involved in the life of the parish.

These discriminatory attitudes in themselves show that some of us are yet to grasp our identity as Christians and thus as one family of God. All these things put together can create an ambience that is not very welcoming. Hence, there is a serious need to continue to emphasize the fact of our oneness as the spiritual family of Christ to our congregations in strong and appealing terms on a continuous basis. This is necessary to break down all discriminatory tendencies among the people and forge unity and friendship among them.

In addition, many of our parishes in the cities are too busy. Due to the large population and the number of Masses celebrated in some of them every Sunday, people are expected or even encouraged to leave the church immediately after Mass to make room for those coming for the next Mass. This practice does not foster adequate interaction among the faithful. It makes it a lot more difficult for most parishioners to get to know each other and develop cordial relationships that can help build an engaged family church.

Another strong accusation some people level against our parishes is that a parishioner can be away from church for weeks as a result of sickness or something else without anybody being aware or trying to find out why.[314] Although this is true and largely in-

[314] They are not completely right here because this is why we have associations and prayer groups in the Church.

excusable, the fact is that the same priest does not always celebrate the same Mass every Sunday. Similarly, some parishioners do not attend the same Mass every Sunday, while others who attend particular Masses on Sunday do not always maintain the same seat or position. All this makes it absolutely difficult for the priests and the parishioners to keep track of everyone on Sunday.

In spite of these excuses, we cannot run away from the fact that most Catholics, at least in Nigeria, are weak in the area of looking out for each other. The challenge this brings to the fore is the absence of "communities" in some of our parishes, and some ways to deal with it include the establishment of Small Christian Communities in every parish and getting parishioners to join an association or group in the parish.

Ordinarily, these associations are supposed to look out for their members and bring to the central administration led by the priest whatever they consider necessary. But then, our lived experience at least in Lagos is that most Catholics neither identify with the parish societies, nor the Small Christian Communities, nor attend parish programmes outside the Sunday Mass. What this means is that the problem will remain for a long time unless people go beyond being a Sunday only type of Christian.

The Church is the House of God and should be open to all-comers who are seeking him. Nonetheless, we need to reject certain erroneous notions of "openness" or "inclusiveness" that some people have. If openness to all-comers or inclusiveness means admitting both saints and sinners who are searching for God for the salvation of their souls, then that is praiseworthy. But if by inclusiveness we mean the extreme position of allowing people to bring into the Church ideologies and practices from the prevailing secular culture that are in conflict with the Gospel values or could be misleading to the younger generation, then we must reject it.

Openness or inclusiveness should not be synonymous with "just anything" or the lowering of standards or acceptable practices just to win more parishioners or keep those who are already with us. The ways of the kingdom of God are different from the ways of the kingdom of the world. Since the Church represents the kingdom of God on earth and possesses the truth, it should dictate the pace and show the way to the secular world, not vice versa.

Nevertheless, there are some positive things that the Church of our time can do to deal with this challenge of an unwelcoming environment in our parishes. We need to do some sort of rebranding to make our parishes more welcoming and attractive to people, especially visitors and newcomers. Whatever we are doing in this regard should extend to those who work in every department of the church. The parish office workers, the security committee (where it exists), the security men, and all other church functionaries should be trained to be kind and friendly in their dealings with parishioners and visitors to the parish. The church should be a place where people look forward to going to, not just because it is the House of God, but also because of the friendship they enjoy there.

Location of our Parishes, and Financial and Security Implications

In siting a business, one of the factors we consider in economics is the nearness of the business to the market. In relation to the Church, this particular point may come as a surprise. Although most convinced Catholics brave every condition to locate the nearest Catholic Church to them, this does not happen in every case. Some nominal Catholics as well as some poor families in remote areas or even in some parts of the city are known to change their denomination or give up going to church altogether because of the distance of the church to their homes.

Even though the lack of a personal conviction about the Catholic faith is the real problem here, the truth remains that the issue of distance and the financial implication for the family as regards transportation can be a major source of temptation to some people. In the course of our field evangelization outside the parish, this was cited as a factor by some former Catholics who started attending the other churches nearest to them or stayed away from church.

A potential solution to this problem is to work towards locating more parishes or outstations closer to the people as much as we can and go the extra mile to establish Small Christian Communities in areas where we do not yet have a church and ensure that they are functional.[315] Their presence will make it easier to identify

[315] Although I mentioned earlier that most Catholics are yet to embrace

such families and respond to their specific challenges and needs as much as possible.

Besides the category of people who move to other churches in the absence of a Catholic Church in their neighbourhood, distance can equally pose a problem in other ways. For those who live far from the church, the traffic jams in our cities and security challenges can affect their active participation in the life of the parish during the weekdays.[316] For these reasons, many parishioners stay away from programmes, such as Bible study, know your faith, retreats, social activities, and similar church activities, which offer them countless opportunities to grow in their faith and build friendship with other parishioners.

Even though this does not directly encourage the drift of Catholics to other churches, the point is that anything that keeps them away from proper formation and ongoing socialization within the community can indirectly expose them to that danger considering the factors we discussed earlier in this chapter and the previous chapters. However, bringing the church nearer to the people can help overcome these challenges to a large extent.

Here, it is pertinent to state that Church growth in the real sense does not merely involve gaining new members or converts, but also keeping—not losing—the ones we already have, and working hard to keep all of them spiritually healthy[317] by converting and making them evangelical in the mindset. The emphasis on all here is not by chance. In fact, to keep Catholics from drifting to other churches, our ministry must be all-embracing. That is to say, we need to reach and engage every category of person in the Church—children, teenagers, youth, adults, the elderly and even the physically challenged persons, such as the blind and the deaf.

---

the idea of Small Christian Communities, we should continue to work towards making it a reality, especially in areas where there are no churches or outstations.

[316] Due to distance, the stress of traffic after a long day's work, and fear for security, most people tend to stay away from church activities during the week, which usually take place sometime between seven and nine o'clock in the evening.

[317] Cf. R. WARREN, *The Purpose Driven Church..., op. cit.,* pp. 17, 32, and 64.

This is because everybody needs Christ and God desires the salvation of all (cf. 1 Tim 2:4). In all, to achieve Church growth so conceived will require us to transform our parishes and the different ministries, societies, and organizations in our parishes into places for promoting initial and ongoing conversion and the raising of mature Christian disciples who imitate Christ and invest heavily on mission as a matter of intentionality and total commitment to him.

The Issue of the Holy Spirit, Charisms, and Prayer

Another reason some Catholics drift to the Pentecostal churches is the issue of the Holy Spirit, the charisms, and prayer. These individuals argue that the Catholic Church is not Spirit-filled and lively. In their opinion, we are dull and boring, and too ritualistic, rigid, and mechanical in our approach to singing, prayer, and worship in general. Worship is also a celebration and should be a joyful experience, but oftentimes we give the impression of a people who are mourning.

In addition, they claim that (in practice) we neither emphasize the role of the Holy Spirit in the life of the Christian and the Church nor the charismatic gifts he bestows. Put differently, they feel that we do not allow the Holy Spirit free reign or enough room to operate or manifest himself in our lives and corporate worship. Although every baptized person in the Church has received one or more gifts from the Holy Spirit for service and the development of the Church, we do not encourage their exercise by all.

Besides, in the Catholic Church, lay people are not sufficiently helped to discover their gifts or equipped to exercise them. Many of them do not know their specific mission due to a lack of exposure. Almost everything is concentrated in the hands of the priests when, in fact, some of them may not be gifted in certain ministries or be sufficiently interested in the spiritual growth of parishioners and the overall growth of the Church. In fact, some of these former Catholics are quick to cite cases where some priests ended up running down their parishes rather than fostering the growth of the people.

Still, some Catholics and former Catholics are of the strong opinion that most of us do not know how to pray. No doubt, the Catholic Church has a rich tradition of prayer. Here, we can talk of the *lectio divina*, contemplative prayer and similar. Nevertheless, they claim that most Catholics are taught to merely recite prayers from books. Most of us cannot pray spontaneously and lack the basic confidence to lead public prayers outside the rosary and other known prayers we say in church. Although some of the points raised in this chapter could be true to some extent, I will not dwell extensively on the issue of the Holy Spirit, the charisms, and prayer here. I intend to address them later. But what is worthy of note is that these issues are contributing to the drift of some Catholics to the Pentecostal churches.

Chapter Eight

PROPER FORMATION OF FUTURE PRIESTS

In the previous chapters, the major focus has been to expose the reasons that underpin the continuous drift of many Catholics to the Pentecostal churches. In this chapter and other chapters that will follow, I intend to make suggestions as to what we can do to reposition the Church. This would not just be to keep her faithful from leaving the Church, but to keep Christ's faithful healthy and to better empower the priests and the lay people to fulfil their specific missions in the Church and world. The first of such recommendations is on the proper formation of future priests in our seminaries and dioceses.

The Importance of the Priest in the Catholic Church

Archbishop Charles Chaput describes the Church as a community rooted both in God's Word and in the Sacrament.[318] The Catholic priest occupies a very important place in the life of this community. According to the Fathers of the Second Vatican Council, a priest acts in *persona Christi capitis,* that is, in the place of Christ, the Head—in his three-fold role as sanctifier (priest), teacher (prophet), and shepherd (king).[319]

---

[318] C. CHAPUT, "As Christ Loved the Church: A Pastoral Letter to the People of God in Northern Colorado on Forming Tomorrow's Priests," September 8, 1999; n. 5.

[319] VATICAN COUNCIL II, *Presbyterorum Ordinis* (PO) – Decree on the Ministry and Life of Priests, promulgated by Pope Paul VI on 7 December 1965, n. 2; Also cited by C. CHAPUT, "As Christ Loved the Church..., *op. cit.,* n. 9.

The Sacrament of Holy Orders, just as marriage, is a sacrament that calls for commitment of service to others. According to the *Catechism of the Catholic Church*, "Two other sacraments, Holy Orders and Matrimony, are directed towards the salvation of others; if they contribute as well to personal salvation, it is through service to others that they do so. They confer a particular mission in the Church and serve to build up the People of God."[320] In view of his calling as a shepherd of the flock of Christ, his duty is to feed and lead them to Christ. He is a minister and servant of God. As a matter of fact, his work is to serve God, his Church, and his people with his life. To emphasize the importance of the priest in the Church, Archbishop Chaput asserts that, "no matter how many other things bear good fruit for the Gospel in our day, there is no ongoing presence of Jesus Christ in the world without the Church; there is no Church without the Eucharist; and there is no Eucharist without the priest."[321]

By virtue of his ordination and celibacy, he is married to the Church, the bride of Christ. In view of this marriage, "his vocation is not merely to do things in and for the Church, but to be a lover of the Church who is expected to love her as Christ loves her and gave his life for her."[322] The language is always that of sacrifice, following in the footsteps of Christ himself. This sacrificial love for Christ and the Church is the compelling reason for the celibacy of the priesthood.[323] His love, commitment, and fidelity to the Church of Christ should be exemplary and thus be a visible sign to those in the married state of the love, commitment, and fidelity they owe one another. As Archbishop Chaput puts it, through the priest's love for the Church to which he is married through celibacy, "he becomes a sign to those in the married state of the radical love God asks of them. It is in recognition of his vocation as a husband to the believing community he serves that we traditionally call priests 'father.'"[324]

---

320 *CCC* 1534.

321 C. CHAPUT, "As Christ Loved the Church…, *op. cit.,* n. 10.

322 *Ibid.,* n. 9.

323 *Ibid.,* n. 10.

324 *Ibid.*

Prayer and the Spiritual Life of a Priest

The priestly ministry requires a great sacrifice, holiness of life, and total commitment to the demands of his vocation on the part of the priest. Hence, the spirituality and the prayer life of priests are critical, not only to their personal spiritual advancement and their ministry in the Church, but also to the spiritual development of the people of God. In other words, if an essential aspect of his ministry is to lead people to God and to intimacy with him, then he also should enjoy intimacy with him.

According to one of the great eastern fathers, Gregory Nazianzus, "we must [first] become light to illuminate. Draw close to God to bring him close to others, be sanctified to sanctify…."[325] As Archbishop Chaput maintains, a priest "cannot be just a man who prays; he must be a man of prayer, a man transformed by constant prayer."[326] According to him, and rightly so too, "Without [an intimate relationship with God and] a deep familiarity with the 'plan of mystery' revealed in Christ (cf. Eph 3:9), a priest cannot disclose that mystery to others."[327]

In his writing, Pope Benedict XV alludes to the same point, citing the words of Saint Bernard to fellow preachers that, "if you are wise, be a reservoir, not a conduit, be full yourself of what you preach and do not think it enough to pour it out to others."[328] Addressing to the people of his time words that are equally applicable to us today, Saint Bernard maintains, "Today we have in the Church a profusion of conduits, but how few are the reservoirs."[329] Every priest is called to be a reservoir because he is connected to the source—God—through prayer and communicates, not his own

---

[325] See *Ibid.,* n. 11.

[326] See *Ibid.,* n. 22.

[327] *Ibid.*

[328] See POPE BENEDICT XV, Encyclical Letter *Humani Generis Redemtionem* (HGR) – On Preaching the Word of God, June 15, 1917, n. 19. Here, the pope cites Saint Bernard in *Cant. Serm.* 18; See also J. TREMBLAY, "The Papal Letter of 1917," in Catholic News Agency, February 8, 2013, https://www.catholicnewsagency.com/column/52456/the-papal-letter-of-1917.

[329] *Ibid.*

words, but the words that are made available to him in prayer by God.

Thus, this intimacy with God is critical to the priestly ministry. Strictly, it is through prayer that a priest or any other Christian for that matter maintains communion with him. Prayer equips and transforms the individual. In fact, the fruits of the spirituality and the prayer life of a priest are seen in ongoing transformation and personal holiness. The root of almost all the challenges priests face in the ministry is the lack of a spiritual life characterized by a sound life of prayer.[330] Commenting on the abrupt surge of secularism in the world in a letter to her nephew, Father Valinho, Sister Lucia (one of the seers of Fatima) wrote, "....the principal error is that they [Catholics] have abandoned prayer. The principal cause of evil in the world and the falling away of so many consecrated souls is the lack of union with God in prayer."[331]

Although some priests work in busy parishes and are often overburdened with both administrative and pastoral duties, prayer and spirituality cannot be relegated to the list of secondary things because this often comes with grave consequences for the individual and the ministry. On this, Archbishop Chaput maintains that, "Our modern schedules can make time for prayer a scarcity—but a priest must schedule God first and other duties second. Without the first, he won't have much to offer those who follow."[332]

In a similar way, Sister Lucy counsels those in spiritual authority to keep close to God. And to stress the importance of prayer in the life of the clergy and Catholics in general, she says, "Let time be lacking for everything else, but never for prayer."[333] To that effect, a priest's spirituality and prayer life should be rooted in a number of things. These include a prayerful celebration of the Holy Mass, daily Eucharistic adoration, daily prayerful study of the Word of God and meditation, regular recourse to the Sacrament of Reconciliation, commitment to the divine office, prayerful recitation of

---

[330] The stark reality is that while some strive after the spiritual life and invest in a sound prayer life, others do not pay attention to them.

[331] See J. TREMBLAY, "The Papal Letter of 1917..., *op. cit.*

[332] C. CHAPUT, "As Christ Loved the Church..., *op. cit.*, n. 23.

[333] Cf. *Ibid.*

the rosary and similar. These are necessary tools and conditions for any meaningful advancement in the spiritual life.[334]

The *Catechism of the Catholic Church* teaches that the Sacrament of Ordination is "directed towards the salvation of others."[335] The priest is a fisher of men who fishes, not for himself, but for Christ and his Church. As Archbishop Chaput insists, for the Church to succeed in her mission, she needs well-formed priests. Since their ministry is directed to others, a good and well-formed priest is one who, in addition to being a holy man and a man of prayer and faith whose personal life radiates the life of Christ, is not ruled by self-love or self-preservation, but places greater premium on the love of God and the Church and is eager to serve God's people selflessly.[336] Having said that, the question that arises is, "How do we produce such priests?" This leads us to the issue of the proper formation of future priests even though we equally recognize the need for the ongoing formation of those who are already ordained.

The Goal of Seminary Formation and the Situation in the Priesthood

According to the *Ratio Fundamentalis Institutionis Sacerdotalis* by the Congregation for the Clergy, the goal of seminary formation is discipleship—to form missionary disciples for Jesus Christ.[337] Simply put, a disciple is one who strives to replicate the lifestyle of Jesus and is totally committed to his mission, that is, the mission of winning new converts and making them into disciples who also make other disciples. The seminary training takes place for about eight to nine years and during this time the candidates are exposed to philosophical and theological studies and other aspects of formation. The whole training is meant to transform the candidates into spiritually mature men who think and act like Christ and are

---

[334] See C. CHAPUT, "As Christ Loved the Church..., *op. cit.,* n. 21; See *CCC* 1566.

[335] *CCC* 1534.

[336] See C. CHAPUT, "As Christ Loved the Church..., *op. cit.*

[337] CONGREGATION FOR THE CLERGY, *The Gift of the Priestly Vocation – Ratio Fundamentalis Institutionis Sacerdotalis*, Libreria Editrice-Vaticana, 2016, (Printed by Belt Konsult Limited, Nigeria), p. 14.

committed to his mission. As we begin to look for ways to stem the drift of many of our faithful from the Church, it is absolutely important to see if we are achieving this goal. To be more specific, are we really raising missionary disciples who are configured to the celibate Christ?

Sadly, it is not easy to answer this question in the affirmative. Today, we witness so much self-centredness, materialism, consumerism, careerism, tribalism, politicking, the loss of focus and other anti-witness behavior among the clergy, and some no longer have hunger for Jesus and his mission. The priesthood appears to be in a deep crisis, which some attentive priests and lay people tend to describe as a "time bomb" waiting to explode.

More so, in recent times, priests have come under intense criticism for their anti-Christian witness and complacency in the area of mission among other things. While many are quick to criticize them, a careful investigation shows that most of them may actually be victims of their formation whether they realize it or not. The truth is that their formation of many years has not adequately prepared them spiritually and pastorally for their ministry and the concrete situations and challenges they face in the course of discharging their duties after ordination.

In actual fact, the mindset of some priests at the time of ordination is what we can call the "I have arrived mentality," which is opposed to the "mission mindset" whereby the individual views his priestly ordination as the beginning of the real mission for which he has been prepared over the years. Naturally, the thinking of a person who has arrived at his destination and that of a man who is about to begin a serious journey are never the same. While the former can easily think of rest or sleep or even enjoyment, the latter is more likely to be awake and focused on the journey and what it will take to make it to his destination. "I have arrived mentality" focuses primarily on the benefits of the priesthood than on the ministry itself. A good example of such a mindset was clearly exhibited by a young priest whose advice to seminarians during his visit to his alma mater was that they should do everything possible to be ordained because there is money and so much enjoyment in the priesthood.

This mindset which a good number of our priests exhibit at the time of ordination (whether it is subtle or more pronounced) signals the failure of formation. This failure may arise from the seminary or the diocese or the student himself or others who were involved in formation or all these factors put together. Whatever the source may be, what is abundantly clear is that it has a direct negative implication for the ministry of the priest and thus the drift of Catholics to other churches. The point is that where many priests are more interested in worldly pursuits than in pastoral work and the spiritual formation of the faithful, some people may likely become disillusioned over time and leave.

In every sense, this situation is worrisome. If the present formation of our future priests is not transforming them to be more Christlike; if it is not empowering them to increasingly love God and neighbour and be totally committed to the soul-winning mission of the Church, then we need to reappraise the whole exercise. Also, if our seminaries are producing "faithless" men who are no different from or are sometimes worse than those who have never been exposed to seminary formation, then we should be asking ourselves some serious questions about the quality of the formation in our seminaries and dioceses. Besides, we need to examine the overall culture in these places, otherwise we will continue to ordain and inject into the priesthood men who are not adequately prepared and ready for the priestly ministry.

Is there a Way out of the Problem?

If one considers the enormity of the challenges we are discussing here, one may ask if there is a way out. Is there something the ecclesial authorities, the seminary formation team, the directors of vocations and the rest of us can do? The tendency to live in denial or complain endlessly and pass the buck will not get us anywhere. Likewise, the tendency to think that there is no way out will amount to pessimism and a hasty generalization. Without any iota of doubt, we can do a lot to salvage the situation to a large extent if not completely. This requires intentionality, strong will and prayer on the part of the formators, but more particularly the ecclesial authorities.

Man is a rational being and, by employing this God-given power, he has been able to gain mastery over many things that seemed impossible in the distant past. We can talk about enormous progress in the areas of the physical and biological sciences, medicine, and technology. We can equally point to the huge successes recorded in the areas of psychology, sociology, and other disciplines. What this goes on to tell us is that the "rational power" that man possesses cannot be underestimated in spite of his natural limitations.

More importantly, our Church is God's Church, not man's, and we do not have to depend only on limited human reason and abilities. Jesus Christ our Head did not leave the Church and her mission completely in the hands of limited mortal men. Rather, he promised to remain with her through the Holy Spirit (cf. Mt 28:20). Since he to whom nothing is impossible is always with her, there will always be a way out of every difficult situation (cf. Lk 1:37; Is 43:18-19). So, we need to prayerfully reflect and come up with potential solutions that can take us out of the present situation and step out boldly and invest time, resources, and energy in them.

Perhaps, to accomplish more in the formation of future priests in our seminaries and dioceses, we need to look beyond ourselves and our time and think of the big picture and the future. We need to reason more, listen more, ask more questions, discern more, pray more, be more proactive in our approach, and act more decisively in dealing with issues even where they require some tough and painful measures. There is a clear need for intentionality and total dedication in this area if we are to succeed. But in all of this, we must seek the counsel of God and listen to the Holy Spirit. We cannot expect to roll out saints if we are not consciously investing in the making of saints, or roll out missionary disciples if we are not investing conscientiously in making disciples. With this in mind, let us see some of the areas where we can do something meaningful.

Re-evangelization of New Intakes Prior to Seminary Formation

One of the greatest problems I see in the area of achieving discipleship during the usual seminary training is the level of evangelization of the new seminary intakes. Are they men of faith? Have they experienced at least an initial conversion? Are they open and ready for formation? The Church's requirement is that those to be admitted to the seminary should be "men of faith." In practice, this is watered down to mean individuals who are confirmed or are active in their parishes or are products of a minor seminary. But, in the real sense, it refers to people who have been properly evangelized and converted and have a living faith and a relationship with God. Although conversion is ongoing until death, it is expected that such individuals should have experienced an initial conversion and are willing to be discipled.[338]

Most of our dioceses are culpable in this matter. They often admit and send candidates (including minor seminarians) who are not properly evangelized and converted and open to formation, which greatly compounds the difficult task of the seminary formation team. It is absolutely important to note that it is a big mistake to carry on with seminary formation aimed at discipleship without first dealing with the issue of improper evangelization and conversion among the candidates. In that case, the work of formation will be extremely difficult and sometimes futile because no one can disciple a person who is not evangelized and open to discipleship. As the saying goes, you can lead the horse to the river, but you cannot force it to drink water. In the case of seminarians, the fact that they keep all the seminary rules does not necessarily imply that all of them are open to formation. The fact is that many do so in order to survive and be ordained.

Without denying the fact that human beings are born with particular personality traits, we cannot overlook the enormous impact of socialization within the family, school, and the larger society, that is, its power to shape and condition people. The world is now a global village thanks to technology. The effects of the secular culture spreading out of the Western world on people are enormous. Those who are pursuing the secular agenda are using social media, entertainment, art, education, and similar as strong tools to exert enormous negative and anti-Christian influence on young people

[338] Ordinarily, the preparations for the sacraments up until confirmation ought to have dealt with this issue of discipleship to a large extent, but unfortunately, it is not so in practice.

in particular. At an alarming rate, the world is moving from God and godliness towards secularism. Some of the negative trends that characterize our world are the craze for robust freedom without a corresponding responsibility, individualism, selfishness, greed, and sexual liberation among others. The negative impact of this state of affairs on young people all over the world is clear. Reflecting on the situation of young people today, Pope John Paul II, writes,

> The many contradictions and potentialities marking our societies and cultures – as well as ecclesial communities – are perceived, lived and experienced by young people with a particular intensity and have immediate and very acute repercussions on their personal growth.... The lure of the so-called "consumer society" is so strong among young people that they become totally dominated and imprisoned by an individualistic, materialistic and hedonistic interpretation of human existence. Material "well-being," which is so intensely sought after, becomes the one ideal to be striven for in life, a well-being which is to be attained in any way and at any price. There is a refusal of anything that speaks of sacrifice and a rejection of any effort to look for and to practice spiritual and religious values. The all-determining "concern" for having supplants the primacy of being, and consequently personal and interpersonal values are interpreted and lived not according to the logic of giving and generosity but according to the logic of selfish possession and the exploitation of others.... of these tendencies.[339]

This truth also captures the situation in Nigeria in a way. Over the years we have experienced a gross erosion of our values. In addition to the things listed above, our society now thrives on lies, self-centredness, tribalism, greed for money and power, high scale corruption, fetish practices and the sort. This has a serious implication for the formation of future priests. People are largely products of their environment, by which I mean, not just the physical, but

[339] JOHN PAUL II, Post-Synodal Apostolic Exhortation *Pastores Dabo Vobis* (PDV) – On the Formation of Priests in the Circumstances of the Present Day, March 15, 1992, n. 8.

also the mental, moral, and spiritual environments in which we live and operate.

It is a fact that we all get conditioned within society. Those we admit into our seminaries do not fall from the sky or a different world. They are not exempt from the anomalies or the intellectual, social, and moral contaminations we witness either in the family or our immediate society and the world around us. The sad reality is that many of those who have been exposed to and so negatively conditioned by these corrupting influences will end up carrying them to the seminary. So, what do we do?

First and foremost, we should admit only students with the right intentions who are open and have the potential to excel, and recruit the best hands for their formation. Bearing in mind that, if seminary formation does not succeed in penetrating them to lead them out of their negative conditioning within the family and society and re-evangelizing them (that is, their mindset, their way of thinking, their desires, their priorities, their points of interests and their activities), then the outcome will be comparable to that of an old wine poured into a new wineskin. That is to say, we shall be producing largely unconverted priests with a worldly or even a pagan mindset that is a reflection of the larger society.

Although the human character or behaviour is formed early in life and most of those who come to our seminaries come with their own baggage, re-formation is possible no matter how difficult it may be. The fact that we are aware that most of them are largely exposed to the negative conditioning with the family, the corrupt society, and the secular world means that we are forearmed. Such knowledge should partly shape our approach to formation. To ignore this reality is suicidal.

In view of this, it is expected that the first stage of formation should be to engage the new intakes conscientiously in order to identify any unchristian mindset, worldviews, and conditioning they are bringing with them from these places. Following this, formators should spend quality time to address all the issues they identify squarely and educate and re-evangelize them.[340] The aim

[340] Formators should confront the different issues from both the intellectual and the spiritual standpoints to help students see the flaws in them

should be to convert them and thus prepare them for the real formation aimed at transforming them into missionary disciples who are Christlike in their character and intention about mission. The process will involve re-teaching them to think as Christ and training their wills to act accordingly.

If society or peer groups can shape and corrupt people in certain ways in spite of their good upbringing, then our seminaries should be capable of reforming people in spite of their previous negative conditioning. On the other hand, if we subscribe to the view that people cannot change once they are formed, then the whole point of preaching the Gospel is defeated. Fortunately, experience shows that people do change when exposed to spiritual truths, or new situations and ways or new associations, or when challenged intellectually and made to see the big picture or to see things from a different perspective. This does not suggest that everyone will change once they are exposed to new realities or the best environment. Our human experience does not justify this either, because the disposition or openness of each person and his willingness to strive for change also count.

But the point is that formators need to critically address with superior arguments certain prejudices or negative conditionings that students bring, and carefully expose them to the truth and the right values. Once they succeed in this area, and support their teaching with the authentic witness of their own lives, many of their students will be led to conversion and transformation even where they themselves are not perfect.

Investing in Proper Disciple-Making

One of the solutions some formation teams have come up with to tackle the challenge of formation is "auto-formation." It means that an individual should also play a major role in his own formation with major input and proper supervision from the seminary formation team. Indubitably, every individual has a serious role to

---

and their negative consequences for them, their future ministry, and the society. The goal is to get them to reject their negative conditionings based on their personal conviction arising from this new understanding of issues.

play in his own formation. In principle, the idea of auto-formation seems wonderful, especially as we are dealing with adults.

In general, formation should be seriously guided at all times. But more importantly in our present circumstance, it should be handled by capable and spiritually aware individuals who genuinely love Christ and his Church passionately, and clearly understand discipleship and mission both conceptually and practically. In practice, disciple-making requires a close relationship with the disciple-maker and the modeling of what discipleship entails by him. An individual who does not understand discipleship conceptually and practically cannot disciple others.

Formation will make greater sense where an individual has attained a considerable level of maturity and focus and is interested in his own development and willing to take responsibility for it. As experience shows, most students in our seminaries do not often exhibit that level of understanding and responsibility that favours their own wholistic formation. Is not that why many of them are experts and masters in the art of manipulation, that is, invest more time and energy in mastering and applying Robert Greene's 48 Laws of Power than studying the Sacred Scriptures?

To be honest, within the present seminary environment, even auto-formation, as good as it is and no matter how heavily guided, may still not be adequate to achieve discipleship in practice. Something more is urgently required if we wish to achieve that goal. A step in the right direction may be to seek out priests who understand disciple-making and mission and place students in their care for mentorship. Another step may be to create diocesan schools or centres for discipleship and make it compulsory for those seeking admission into our seminaries (especially the minor seminaries) to pass through them for about six months or a year prior to being admitted. Similarly, provision should be made for them to go back to these centres for ongoing discipleship training throughout the period of their seminary formation. Dioceses should complement the efforts of the seminaries rather than leave everything to them.

Need for a Proper Understanding of Discipleship

Oftentimes, the formation team is not to blame for the failure in formation. If truth must be said, most of them are never adequately prepared for this all-important task beyond acquiring academic degrees. Although discipleship is the goal of seminary formation,[341] a close interaction with some former and present formators sometimes reveals that they do not have a clear understanding of what discipleship entails conceptually and in practice. In other words, we use a beautiful concept we do not understand, which is extremely problematic in itself because a person cannot possibly lead others beyond what he knows or, worse still, to what he does not know.

My personal interaction with some senior seminarians and young priests is quite revealing. Most of them do not understand the notion of discipleship as well as the idea of charisms and their specific mission within the priesthood and the general mission of the Church. Often, they appear confused and lost when questions regarding discipleship, *charisms*, and similar are put to them, which are clear signs of inadequate formation. To put it mildly, it is not out of place to expect them to be familiar with these terms from their spiritual-year days or in their first few years in the major seminary or even before they are admitted into the seminary.

The fact that the vast majority of seminarians are not conscious that they are being discipled in the course of their seminary formation is a major problem. This is because true disciple-making involves intentionality, trust, and cooperation between the disciple-maker and the disciple, and the goal is clear to both parties—in this case, the formator and the formandi.[342] When we begin to do the needful and consciously invest in the spiritual and apostolic formation of those who show interest in the priesthood, we will discover that it is possible to evangelize and disciple them before they are admitted into the spiritual year programme.

---

[341] CONGREGATION FOR THE CLERGY, *The Gift of the Priestly Vocation…*, *op. cit.*, p. 14.

[342] The one who is discipling clearly understands that he is discipling the other, while the person being discipled understands that he is being discipled and freely submits himself to the exercise.

Evangelizing the Environment in our Seminaries and the Priesthood

The overall intellectual, moral, and spiritual environments or culture[343] in a place can shape the worldview and character of those who live there. The seminary training takes place for about eight to nine years within the environments of the seminary and our parishes[344] and this makes them critical to formation. Naturally, an evangelized environment with a Christianized culture will contribute to the evangelization and discipling of the students.

The fact that some priests and seminarians have, at one time or the other, confessed that their faith in God was stronger prior to going to the seminary than while in the seminary or even in the priesthood should be a matter of grave concern to all. It is something worth investigating because it is a clear indication that something serious and undesirable may be going on in our seminaries. Could it be that the manner of teaching philosophy or theology in our seminaries does not foster faith as a whole? Could it be that those who teach these disciplines are not properly evangelized and discipled themselves and as such do not have a personal conviction about the Christian faith or a living relationship with God? Could there be some forms of anti-witness among the formators themselves and within the priestly circles in the different dioceses that affect the faith of seminarians?

To produce holy and dedicated priests who will be missionary disciples, the environment and culture in our seminaries and the priesthood as a whole must be consciously evangelized. Sadly, in many cases, it is difficult to see the fruits of the theological studies and formation in many priests in the areas of practical faith, spiritual life, prayer, fear of God, love of God and neighbour, selflessness, dedication to service, sacrifice, deep concern for lost souls, and a serious commitment to the Church and her mission.

---

[343] Culture here is understood as the way of life within a given society, and in this case, our seminaries.

[344] During their training, seminarians spend as much as about ten months of the year in the seminary and the parish. Even when they are on holidays, most of them report at their parishes regularly.

On the contrary, what we see is so much self-centredness and a clear loss of focus among them. In reality, it appears that many of them are more concerned about material comfort, position, power, pleasure, politicking and the sort. While we acknowledge and celebrate the heroic example and sacrifice of many good priests who are selfless and dedicated to their ministry, we must state unequivocally that the serious anti-witness of the clergy in these areas, which is too evident today, is harmful to the Church and her mission and the spiritual growth of the people of God.

More specifically, an anti-witness environment in the priesthood and the seminary in particular constitutes a major obstacle to the formation of missionary disciples. It is not only that it can scandalize and destroy the faith of many good seminarians, but it can equally cause some of them to be less enthusiastic about the Church, to become worldly in their mindset, priorities, and pursuits or even cause some of them to stumble and drift away.[345] No matter how we choose to look at it, it does not always favour actual disciple-making because discipleship involves modeling the life of Christ.

No doubt, we all know that formators are also human beings with limitations and can make mistakes.[346] But then, they must never allow their lifestyle to become a form of anti-witness to the students they are meant to disciple because actions speak louder than words and people are influenced more by what they see than what they hear. So, they too must back up whatever they teach the seminarians with practical example or witness of their own lives. Their students must always see them to be striving to live out all

[345] No doubt, many of our priests are trying in spite of the different signs of imperfection we see. Besides, we must admit that even most of those who are lagging behind are not as worldly and materialistic as their counterparts in most of the Pentecostal churches. Nevertheless, it should not be an excuse or a justification for being worldly and materialistic because Jesus Christ, and not these others who are getting it wrong, should be our model.

[346] We should note here that there is a major difference between "falling into sin" as a result of human weakness and actually "living in sin." The latter implies an acceptance of sin.

they are teaching them.[347] Anything less than that will be counter-productive as far as formation is concerned.

As I have consistently maintained, to a very large extent, man is a product of his environment. If we can evangelize the environment in our seminaries, houses of formation, and clergy houses by creating an intellectual, moral, and spiritual culture in these places which favours a positive change in attitude, interests, priorities, and commitment to mission, then this, in turn, can help evangelize those who pass through them. The challenge that this poses to the Church is that we must strive to turn our seminaries and formation houses into real centres for conversion and authentic transformation. If we want results, then it cannot and should never be business as usual.

Lack of Openness on the Part of Seminarians

In farming, it is not only the quality of the seed that matters, but also that of the soil. Planting good seeds in poor soil is not likely to result in a rich harvest just as planting a bad seed in good soil. This was clearly illustrated by Jesus in the Parable of the Sower (cf. Mt 13:1-23). Although the seeds of the sower fell on four different soils, only the ones that fell on a good soil produced their fruits by a hundredfold, sixtyfold, or thirtyfold. Formation is not a one-way thing. Its success does not depend on the formators alone, but also on those undergoing formation. It is the fruit of a healthy cooperation between them.

Even though the formation of future priests in our seminaries and dioceses is inadequate, no one can honestly say that nothing is happening altogether. While we look forward to something better, we should not discard what we have now. Seminarians need to be interested in their own formation and open to receive what is positive in what they are being offered at present. A major thing

[347] Our seminaries and formation houses should be evangelizing and discipling environments both from the standpoints of teaching and practical witness. If they teach them that the right thing is to fly airplanes and avoid driving Caterpillars, then they should constantly see them fly airplanes and striving hard to avoid driving Caterpillars.

that reveals the deep-seated crisis in formation is the sharp contrast between what students are exposed to during their eight or nine years in the seminary and the way many of them live as priests afterwards. This ranges from their dress code to their prayer life, punctuality, modesty and similar.

In the seminary, the students are trained to dress up properly and to be punctual at prayer, Mass, lectures, and other events. They are taught to live as a community—at least, to pray together, eat together, and do a few other things in common. Also, they are exposed to the daily reading of the divine office, meditation, Eucharistic adoration, and the rosary for nine years. The whole essence is to ensure that they develop themselves in the spiritual life and acquire certain virtues or good habits that will help them function effectively as priests.

Regrettably, many seminarians do not often internalize this training and tend to abandon it or some aspects of it after ordination. Two things may be responsible for this. The first is that the formators may not have schooled them properly on the value of the different elements of their formation to enable them to reach a personal conviction about them. As such, many go through them as essential requirements for ordination rather than something to be internalized and lived even after leaving the seminary. The second reason is that many of the seminarians were never properly evangelized and converted prior to being exposed to seminary formation and, therefore, were not really open to formation.

In fact, as we know from experience, many of them pretend and merely go through the formation in order to survive and be ordained priests. It is only after their ordination that they begin to show their true colour. It is as if the priestly ordination frees them from what they consider to be some sort of "burdens" or a "bondage" to which they have been subjected all the while in the course of their formation. Thus, following their "liberation" at ordination, some tend to devote greater attention to things that do not foster their own spiritual growth and development. Many formators have expressed their frustration about this situation and, to defend themselves, some claim that they do not really "know" most of the students. In fact, someone claimed that they do not really know over seventy-five percent (75%) of them. This in itself is a major problem because it means they keep proposing for ordination people they do not really know and can hardly vouch for. This is not surprising because they are dealing with a crowd, whereas proper disciple-making involves a close (one-on-one) relationship that makes it possible for the discipler to discover his student.

This reality should necessarily force the ecclesial authorities, the seminary formation team, and all those who are involved in the formation of seminarians to review what we are doing at present to see what will serve our interest the most. The owners of a company that was set up to produce shoes of great quality should be overtly worried if they are producing only a few good ones in spite of their investment. As a matter of urgency, they will be interested in unraveling what the problems are and deal decisively with them to save their name, their business, and to maximize profit. As we mentioned earlier, priests play a critical role in the Church and if the healthy survival of the Church and the realization of her mission are important to us, then we all can learn from such astute business owners.

It is so easy and convenient to explain things away and absolve ourselves of any blame. Too often we hear comments such as, "We have done our own bit," or "It is the fault of the individuals who failed to internalize the formation they were offered." But then, we should not forget that the negative consequences of their future choices and actions will affect all of us, the Church and the priesthood. At other times, formators complain that some of the seminarians themselves were already formed in certain negative ways before they were sent to them, or may have bad "mentors" whom they imitate, or "godfathers" in or outside their dioceses that control and influence them negatively.

In all honesty, we cannot deny or ignore such complaints. On the contrary, we sympathize with those saddled with the burden of formation in our seminaries. But, no matter the excuses we come up with, what is paramount is that the situation is bad for the Church and the priesthood and needs to be addressed decisively. The question remains: Is there something more that they can do? Is there something more the diocesan authorities, the directors of vocations, and the rest of us can do?

Avoiding Certain Presumptions in Formation

Presumption can be a big problem in formation. In view of the present challenges we face in this area today, the seminary formation personnel should take nothing for granted. A more realistic and proactive approach is to believe that everyone who is admitted into the seminary may have been exposed to the corrupting influences in society and needs some help to overcome it. The only exception should be where a student clearly proves otherwise.

Similarly, we need to avoid presumption as much as possible as this may prove costly. Formators should never presume that students understand the need and the usefulness of the different aspects of formation for their lives and future ministry by merely exposing them to certain practices or activities. On the contrary, they should back up everything with a thorough explanation to lead out the sense behind each practice. The real target of formation is transformation (into missionary disciples) and it is necessary to help them reach a personal conviction about what they are taught and the practices to which they are exposed if they are to remain faithful to them after ordination.

Knowing the sense behind things will make many of them better appreciate the specific formation in question. The problem with this suggestion is that we may seem to be treating adults more like children. But then, this can be excused if it will help achieve the noble objective of formation rather than continue exactly what we are doing now and face the serious negative consequences, which may be even more devastating in the near future.[348] As a matter of fact, a disciple is supposed to be childlike in his attitude to learning. Even Jesus took his time to explain things to his disciples. They were like children and that made learning easier (cf. Mt 11:25).

Today, psychologists have come to a conclusion that the age of maturity is moving up and we should not shy away from an approach (even if imperfect) that has a potential to solve or significantly reduce the problems we are facing today. If we have adopted a particular approach for long and the result has not been satis-

---

[348] This is not a suggestion that the end justifies the means. In this case, there is nothing morally wrong with the means being proposed here to reach a good end.

factory, perhaps it is time to try a different approach, especially as experience shows that a good number of priests still have a wrong notion of Christianity and a flawed understanding of the identity and ministry of a priest even many years after their ordination.

We know that some students are admitted into seminary without an initial conversion and sometimes graduate worse than they were at the beginning.[349] Some go in as simple people with open minds and come out as politicians, schemers, social climbers, and experts in manipulation. While we cannot lay the whole blame at the doorsteps of our seminaries, we cannot absolve them of blame either. The seminary should be the place for challenging and breaking down worldly and unchristian mindsets and purifying all the negative conditionings and corrupt influences from social media and within family and society. If we are really serious about forming missionary disciples, then the seminary should be a place for transforming lives and planting a new vision about life—the Christian vision of life and ministry—in the minds and hearts of future priests.

The main challenge this places on formators is that they themselves must first be converted Christians, witnesses, and missionary disciples who can model these new ideals they are trying to inculcate in their students, if they are to succeed in the task of evangelizing and discipling the vast majority of them. The simple truth is that only a person who is already a disciple can disciple another. We must never forget that even though teaching is important, training is the key element in discipleship. Besides, disciple-making does not merely consist in beautiful words and lectures, but it involves an imitation of the personal lifestyle and example of the "master" by his apprentice.

Absence of Some Essential Conditions for Disciple-Making

It is easy to see that the present setting in our seminaries is not favourable to the making of Christian disciples, if we lack a conceptual and a practical understanding of discipleship. This is

---

[349] Some lose the sense of the fear of God and begin to rationalize and justify some wrongdoings.

because some of the important conditions necessary for success are clearly absent. Intentional disciple-making is a serious business and it involves time and sacrifice. Proper discipleship training can only take place where both the discipler and the one to be discipled sincerely want it and are willing to invest time, energy, and resources into the process. It is a mutual and reciprocal commitment where two hearts meet in their conviction to freely seek discipleship and to freely give it. The willingness of the individual to be discipled is manifested in a number of ways. These include the presentation of himself to another in trust for discipleship, his complete openness to formation, and a conscious effort to grow in the experiential knowledge and love of Jesus Christ with an overall goal to be transformed to be more like him in character.

Disciple-making requires a close relationship of openness, trust, and friendship between the disciple and the one who is discipling, and the goal is always transformation. Obedience to rules and the formation offered by the seminary should arise from a personal conviction based on a personal desire to be transformed into a missionary disciple who is like Christ in character.

But for most seminarians, as a deacon from one of the seminaries in Nigeria observed, everything is about survival. They keep the rules for fear of being expelled or because they want to be ordained at all cost. In other words, their goal is not personal transformation and this often leads to pretence and lack of growth. This happens because a close rapport of openness and trust does not exist between many of them and the seminary formators. This problem can arise from the students or the formators or both. But what is clear is that a relationship based on rules and regulations, suspicion, mistrust, and fear can never produce missionary disciples.[350]

---

[350] This observation does not suggest that our seminaries are mechanical, inefficient systems. Certainly, they are not. While there are important issues we need to deal with, the truth remains that the different seminaries have also produced efficient and admirable priests. While it is true that many of the formators need to offer more to the students, it is equally true that seminarians themselves should at least try to interiorize what they are offered and thus take personal responsibility for their own formation.

Again, if disciple-making involves a close relationship of trust and guidance on a regular basis, it is unthinkable that it can effectively happen in our seminaries with the current ratio of students to a formator, which is outrageous. Even if these priests were the best formators around, it would still be an impossible task to expect about thirteen men to disciple over four hundred seminarians.[351] The point is that you cannot disciple a crowd. Even Jesus Christ did not attempt that—he closely discipled twelve men for about three years.[352] Thus, to expect such a magic to happen can only mean that we do not understand what discipleship entails in practice.

The Four Areas of Seminary Formation of Future Priests

The new developments in the priesthood arising from the improper formation of future priests require us to revisit the components of seminary formation. In *Pastores Dabo Vobis*, Pope John Paul II lists four main components to which those involved with the seminary formation need to pay scrupulous attention. These are human formation, intellectual formation, spiritual formation, and pastoral formation.[353]

Human Formation: Human formation is the basis or foundation of all priestly formation. In this area, formators are expected to educate the candidates for the priesthood by word and their personal witness to "love the truth, to be loyal, to respect every person, to have a sense of justice, to be true to their word, to be genuinely compassionate, to be men of integrity and, especially, to

[351] At present we have about thirteen formators in one of our major seminaries in the western part of Nigeria. The number of resident students is over four hundred, while the students who come for lectures from their different communities are over two hundred.

[352] Even though the Bible tells us about seventy or seventy-two other disciples who were sent out on mission, our concern here are the twelve disciples (or apostles) he took to himself and invested heavily in their formation and preparation for a world mission. These were the real ones that lived with him and were with him up to the Last Supper.

[353] *PDV* 43-59.

be balanced in judgment and behaviour."[354] This is in addition to developing affective maturity which presupposes an awareness that love has a central role in human life and is prudent.[355]

Intellectual Formation: Seminary training should expose future priests to vigorous intellectual formation. This is necessary to enable them to cope with many of the faithful and others in society who have received enormous formation in the sciences and other disciplines or have been exposed to the different fields of human endeavour. To be an effective evangelizer in today's world that is increasingly growing cold towards God, the priests should be adequately equipped to engage these men and women in meaningful conversation that can open up an avenue for evangelization or the deepening of their faith as the case may be.

Spiritual Formation: Christianity is about intimate relationship with the Godhead. With regard to spiritual formation, the formation team is expected to lead the seminarians to an experiential knowledge of God. Put differently, they should lead them to a personal experience of Christ, to a personal conversion, to intimacy with God, and to a spiritual transformation. According to the Second Vatican Council's decree, *Optatam Totius,* which Pope John Paul II quotes, the spiritual formation of future priests should be conducted in such a way that they are formed "to live in intimate and unceasing union with God the Father through his Son Jesus Christ, in the Holy Spirit."[356]

Future priests are supposed to take on the likeness of Christ the priest through sacred ordination. Thus, in the course of their training, they should be led to form a habit of drawing close to him as a friend in both prayer and every aspect or detail of their lives.[357] To advance his spiritual life, a future priest should over time develop intimacy with Christ in the Eucharist and in the Word and draw daily strength from the reception of the Eucharist and his study and

---

[354] *PDV* 43.

[355] *PDV* 44.

[356] *PDV* 45, Quoting SECOND VATICAN COUNCIL, *Optatam Totius* (OT) – The Decree on Priestly Training, October 28, 1965, n. 8; See also CHARLES CHAPUT, "As Christ Loved the Church…, *op. cit.,* n. 19.

[357] *PDV* 45.

meditation on the Sacred Scriptures without discounting the importance of regular recourse to the Sacrament of Reconciliation[358] and other prayers in the Church, such as the prayerful recitation of the rosary. Holiness is important to the life and ministry of a priest, and his formation should lead to this. Stressing the importance of holiness in the life of priests and the need for formation to be directed consciously towards the acquisition of virtues, Pope Leo XIII asserts,

> Holiness of life, without which knowledge puffs up and does not edify, consists not only in good and honorable habits, but also in that group of sacerdotal virtues which makes good priests exemplars of Jesus Christ, the eternal High Priest. For this purpose there are sacred seminaries.... Choose teachers and spiritual directors for these institutions thoughtfully. They should be men of sound doctrine and good morals, men to whom you can confidently entrust a matter of such great importance. Choose rectors and spiritual guides who are outstanding in prudence, counsel, and experience. The common life and discipline should be so arranged by your authority that not only will the students never offend against piety, but that there will be an abundance of all aids which nourish piety. The students should thus be encouraged to make daily progress in acquiring the sacerdotal virtues. Your industrious and diligent labors in the education of priests will bear much desirable fruit, making your episcopal office easier to administer and producing a richer profit for all.[359]

Pastoral Formation: Today, some priests claim that they are not interested in evangelization. Others erroneously see it as one of the things the Church does, and tend to relegate it to the list of secondary things. This is sad considering that evangelization is the mission of the Church and mission is the reason she exists. This reality is a clear sign of an improper pastoral formation in our

---

[358] *PDV* 45; Cf. CHARLES CHAPUT, "As Christ Loved the Church..., *op. cit.*, n. 21.

[359] POPE LEO XIII, *Quod Multum* (QM) – Encyclical on the Liberty of the Church, August 22, 1886, n. 10.

seminaries and dioceses. As a matter of importance and necessity, seminary formation should pay serious attention to the pastoral formation of future priests. Basically, this should cover every aspect of the Church's mission of evangelization—mission *ad gentes*, new evangelization and pastoral care.

The Sacrament of Ordination is directed towards others. The priest is not a man for himself but a man for God and others. Hence, the formation of future priests in its different aspects must have a fundamentally pastoral character. It should lead future priests to this realization and prepare them to image Jesus Christ the Good Shepherd and to have pastoral charity that will enable them to give more and more of themselves in service of the Church and the people of God.[360] If the mission of the Church is to make disciples for Jesus Christ everywhere and to foster pastoral activity among those who have been baptized, then formation in the seminary should lead them to form a pastoral spirit and zeal that will also manifest itself both in their pastoral care for the faithful and in widespread missionary activities.

This emphasis on mission beyond the four walls of the parish is extremely important, considering that most of our parishes do not engage in mission *ad gentes*. In all, it is crucial that seminary training is directed towards the formation of shepherds who have a genuine concern for souls. According to Pope John Paul II, "The object of the whole training of future priests should be "to make them shepherds of souls after the example of our Lord Jesus Christ, teacher, priest, and shepherd."[361] Hence, Archbishop Chaput concludes that, "it is not enough that one [the priest] be emotionally, spiritually and intellectually mature. [Rather], all these attributes have to be placed at the service of others in the priesthood."[362]

---

[360] *PDV* 57; See C. CHAPUT, "As Christ Loved the Church..., *op. cit.,* n. 31.

[361] *PDV* 57, Quoting *PO* 4; Also cited by C. CHAPUT, "As Christ Loved the Church..., *op. cit.,* n. 31.

[362] *Ibid.*

Disproportionate Emphasis on Intellectual Formation of Priests

As uncomfortable as this may make us, an honest appraisal of our present seminary formation and the state of the priesthood today will make it abundantly clear to any discerning person that we are not achieving the desired goals of formation. Lives are hardly being transformed in our seminaries and most seminarians do not emerge from them as missionary disciples. In fact, it is more likely that things will get worse unless we rethink what we are doing now and become more goal oriented in our approach.[363]

To form priests who are configured to Christ and totally committed to his mission, seminary formation in the four areas we have seen should be rock solid. Regrettably, it is not often so. On the contrary, our seminaries focus principally on intellectual formation. That is to say, they do not often give the human, spiritual, and pastoral formation sufficient attention, even though it is not entirely their fault.[364] A more reasonable thing to do should be to give all the four areas the critical attention they merit but with greater emphasis on the spiritual and the pastoral aspects of formation.[365]

---

[363] If we continue to expose seminarians to the same level of formation which yielded only little fruit in the past when the level of sanity and morality in society was higher, then we will be deceiving ourselves to expect that things will change for the better now that our value system has collapsed and the exposure of young people to secular ideas is worse.

[364] Definitely, some of the seminary formators are competent and well-equipped for their work, but the authorities need to see to the re-orientation of formation in general in our seminaries. In addition, the dioceses need to collaborate more closely with the seminary formation teams in terms of vision and goals and how these are to be accomplished.

[365] Here, my emphasis is on actual practice and not merely the usual verbal emphasis on the importance of the spiritual life. Students need more concrete formation in prayer and the spiritual life. A person who does not know God experientially or enjoy intimacy with him can hardly lead anybody to him. Most likely, he will discuss him from what he "knows about him" as opposed to what he "knows of him" from a place of intimacy with him. The point is that intellectual knowledge of God is not the same as an experiential knowledge of him, which is more important to the spiritual life.

Although the intellectual formation is absolutely necessary, it cannot be said to be the only or the most important aspect of formation, especially in Nigeria or Africa where rationalism and the level of exposure to the secular culture is far less.[366] In his encyclical, *Quod Multum– On the Liberty of the Church,* Pope Leo XIII admonishes the bishops of Hungary to pay serious attention to the formation of priests because "the reputation of the Church and the eternal salvation of her people depend on priests."[367] Laying a critical emphasis on the holiness in the formation of a priest, he states that, "in the education of clerics, two elements are absolutely necessary: learning for the development of the mind and virtue for the perfection of the spirit."[368]

> If the education of all youth in general contributes a great deal to the true welfare of the state, this is much more true of the education of those aiming at ordination. To this matter you must give special attention; it should occupy the greater portion of your vigils and labors, since the youths destined for orders are the hope and, as it were, the incomplete form of future priests. You surely know how much the reputation of the Church and the eternal salvation of her people depend on priests. – In the education of clerics, two elements are absolutely necessary: learning for the development of the mind and virtue for the perfection of the spirit....[369]

Considering the over-exaggerated or disproportionate emphasis on intellectual formation, it is imperative to remind us that the fact that a person is an intellectual giant or a doctorate degree holder in philosophy and theology does not necessarily mean he will make a good and efficient pastor, as experience has shown. If truth be told, being an intellectual giant without Christ as in the case of

---

[366] Besides, the philosophical studies in the seminary relate more to the reality in the Western world than the practical realties people face in Nigeria and Africa as a whole.

[367] *QM* 10.

[368] *Ibid.*

[369] *Ibid.*

a priest who is not properly evangelized and converted (that is, a "pagan" at heart) can significantly harm the Church and the people of God. This is because, lacking intimacy with God and pastoral zeal, he may not show adequate interest in the spiritual growth of the faithful and the Church's mission of evangelization. Many examples abound in this area.

Additionally, experience shows that some not-too-educated lay people, especially in the Catholic Charismatic Renewal (CCR), the Catholic Biblical Instructors' Union (CBIU), and similar societies are known to be more spiritually aware and upright, more interested in mission, better equipped, and more effective in actual evangelization than many of the ordained ministers themselves. In practice, many of them can boast of an experiential (not intellectual) knowledge of God, a personal relationship with him through Jesus Christ in the Holy Spirit, and actually exude greater faith in him.

Some bishops, priests, and seminarians themselves constantly complain that the seminary formation of our future priests is inadequate, especially from the spiritual and practical standpoints. If we are serious about going forward, we must display an uncanny courage and critically look into this complaint and rethink what we are doing.[370] The fact that we are raising many intellectually sound priests who are seriously lacking in the other areas is undesirable. It is a case of a misplaced priority, which contributes gravely to our inability to achieve proper discipleship in the cause of seminary formation. Similarly, it is responsible for many of the challenges we face in the priesthood today and our backwardness in the areas of mission *ad gentes* and the new evangelization.

No doubt, some may disagree with a number of the views expressed here for different reasons. But my reaction is simple. If indeed we are achieving the goal of seminary formation and are truly making missionary disciples, then where are they? Why are most

---

[370] At present, the investment of time and energy in the other aspects of seminary formation (human, spiritual, and pastoral) is inadequate, especially from the practical standpoint even though the dioceses have a large share of the blame. Some of them are not doing enough in this area and tend to leave almost everything to the seminaries.

people (including the bishops and the seminary formators themselves) complaining about the quality of priests we are raising and different challenges in the priesthood bordering on lack of conversion and holiness of life? Why are we not as effective as we should be in fulfilling the mission of the Church? Why is disciple-making not being replicated in our parishes, considering that disciples naturally tend to repeat the process all over to make new disciples who can reach the world for Christ? Why are a significant number of our members drifting away instead? Why is it extremely difficult for the dioceses to find a priest to fill the role of official diocesan exorcist in spite of the huge number of priests around?

Perhaps we need to understand discipleship first—at the conceptual and the practical levels—and then orientate formation within the seminaries and the dioceses towards it instead of playing with concepts. In point of fact, if we are serious about raising a new generation of priests who will be missionary disciples, the Church has to take some concrete steps towards this direction that will necessarily affect what we do in the following areas: the entry point, that is, the point of admitting candidates for the seminary in the dioceses, the spiritual year formation, the major seminaries, the appointment of diocesan directors of vocations, and the choice of the members of the seminary formation team.

The same should be applicable to the minor seminaries from where we select a significant number of those we admit into our major seminaries. This point is clear in the writing of Pope Leo XIII. He advocates for thoughtfulness in choosing teachers and spiritual directors who are sound in doctrine and strong in good morals, and rectors and spiritual guides who are outstanding in prudence, counsel, and experience.[371]

In all, there should be a proper revisioning of the mindset of the key players in formation in the seminary and the dioceses to ensure that they have a common vision and goal and also for better collaboration among them. In addition to other considerations, an intense appreciation of the challenges the Church faces today, a profound understanding of the goal of formation at both the con-

371 *QM* 10.

ceptual and the practical levels, clarity of purpose, and love for God and the Church on their part are absolutely essential.

Also, the option for dioceses to have their own houses of formation outside the seminary may be seriously considered because this is more favourable to disciple-making from the standpoints of number, close interaction, training, and supervision. Moreover, proper and ongoing formation of the directors of vocations, spiritual directors, and the seminary formators themselves, especially in virtue and holiness, in the art of disciple-making, discernment, and mission will be valuable to our overall goal of raising true shepherds who are missionary disciples. In all of this, the authorities should make it a priority to create an enabling environment for those involved in the formation of future priests to do their work. Above all, there should be a way of holding everybody accountable to ensure that each plays his role.

Specific Formation in the Area of Sexuality

These times are certainly not the best for the Catholic Church worldwide. The clergy sex scandals that are rocking the Church in the West have been a source of crisis and loss of faith for many devoted Catholics. Although emerging evidences in the cases involving minors clearly indicate that it is a "homosexual problem,"[372] we cannot overlook the heterosexual priests altogether. All agree that a sexual relationship between an adult and a minor is always a crime. But the usual defence some priests often put up in the case of two consenting adults is that they too, like other human beings, are capable of making mistakes.

Although this is true, a more reasonable thing is not to make excuses for obvious wrongdoings, but to repent and readjust their ways. Their wrongdoings in this area have seriously wounded some members of the Church, especially the weak. It has endangered their faith and salvation, disfigured the image of the Church, and impacted negatively on her mission, even though some of them

[372] Statistics from the United States of America put the figure of cases involving homosexual priests at 81%, while in some parts of Eastern Europe the figure could be higher.

may also have acted in ignorance[373] at the time. As a starting point, priests should express their profound sorrow and repentance and call out to all who have been hurt or unjustly affected by their actions, saying *mea culpa, mea culpa, mea maxima culpa*. Every priest needs to ask for forgiveness for his own failings and/or those of his colleagues who faltered.[374]

Without a doubt, a sincere plea for forgiveness cannot undo past wrongdoings and the negative consequences arising from them. But then, it can at least lead to the healing of emotions among the victims and those affected by their actions and minimize the hurt. Nevertheless, for the Church, this confession and appeal for forgiveness is not enough. Not even the zero-tolerance policy that most dioceses all over the whole are adopting is enough. While this can save the face of the Church in some way, promote justice in favour of victims by ensuring that a person convicted of such offences suffers the consequence of his actions, the truth remains that this can never undo the act itself.

Honestly, if we critically appraise the situation or the overall picture, this certainly cannot be the best that the Church can do. The point is that even where the erring priest is severely punished and, perhaps, suffers public disgrace on account of his offence, this still does not remove the severe damage to the present and future psychological, emotional, and spiritual well-being of the victim. Equally, it does not remove the damage done to the image of the Church as an institution, considering that the news of such offences often weakens the faith of many people—Catholics and non-Catholics alike.

[373] The ignorance in question is spiritual in nature. It is such that arises from spiritual blindness as a result of an improper spiritual formation. Many priests often do no experience real conversion and/or attain an acceptable level of spiritual consciousness and moral maturity prior to ordination due to the inadequate formation they have received in these areas. In actual sense, some of them can become victims of their own "spiritual blindness" and weakness.

[374] It should be noted that not all priests are guilty, whether we are talking about sexual crimes involving minors or sexual sins involving consenting adults. Nevertheless, they can reach out to the victims and the faithful as a mark of charity and solidarity towards them.

Moreover, while the public disgrace and punishment meted out to the perpetrator himself can be justified, the ensuing situation can have an adverse negative implication for his spiritual well-being and salvation if it is not carefully managed. Thus, in addition to all that we have noted so far, even though the zero-tolerance policy in itself is highly commendable and should be encouraged, it does not remove the potential damage to the image and integrity of the priesthood, making it inadequate when it stands alone as a solution.

Philosophy is a discipline that asks all the right questions in pursuit of truth. Our rigorous philosophical studies in the seminary, and perhaps afterwards for some priests, was meant to equip us to think critically and appraise issues objectively and wholistically in order to reach meaningful solutions to life problems. The whole effort cannot be in vain. Today, in view of this situation that confronts us as a Church, the real question we should be asking is, "What more can the Church really do in this area?" Rather than being too quick to choose the easy way out and avoid the financial consequences of the clergy sex abuse, the Church can invest more in a potential solution that can eliminate or drastically reduce, not only the cases of sexual abuse of minors, but also their sexual sins with adults. The focus here is on what will promote a sincere adherence to the vows of celibacy and chastity among the clergy, considering that "prevention is better than cure."

The Church in Nigeria and all over the world must adopt a more proactive policy or measure in this matter. Based on a careful reflection, I think that what will qualify as a proactive and responsible measure that can help prevent or at least reduce to the barest minimum cases of sex abuse and sexual sins and their present and future damages to all the parties involved (the victim, the Church, the priesthood, and even the erring priest) will be to go back to the goals of seminary formation of future priests proposed by Pope John Paul II in *Pastores Dabo Vobis.*

An important truth which most people often ignore in the case of sexual sins involving adults is that some of the erring priests themselves are "victims" of the inadequate formation they received in the seminary and their dioceses and the prevailing environment within the priesthood itself.[375] In actual fact, so much is expected of them by all, and rightly so too, but yet they were not adequately equipped to handle their sexuality and some other challenges they face in the ministry. Hence, it is absolutely necessary to review the current approach to the formation of seminarians from a more practical and proactive standpoint. The authorities, the seminary formators, and other collaborators need to come up with something more comprehensive and practical (arising from a thorough research) that can address some specific nerve-racking issues in the priesthood, such as interior conversion, the use of sexuality, sound prayer life, priestly holiness and similar. This should be used in the formation of future priests in the seminaries and the dioceses and the ongoing formation of priests.

To be forewarned is to be forearmed. Since many priests seem to have issues in the area of sexuality, the Church needs to pay greater attention to this specific area in the formation of future priests and the ongoing formation of priests. Both vigilance and proper discernment are seriously required in the course of formation. More specifically, to prepare future priests to cope well in the area of human sexuality, those who have the responsibility to form them in the seminary and the dioceses should carefully and thoroughly expose them to such teachings as "the theology of the body" in ways that will be impactful. Rather than making it one of those classroom courses that most students go through to pass exams, they should organize serious seminars and workshops with focus on practical ways to handle human sexuality and sexual temptations. Also, these seminars and workshop (which experts in the subject should handle) should clearly emphasize the immediate and future practical consequences of compromising oneself in this area.

[375] This is not to take away personal responsibility on the part of the individual. But the point is that proper and in-depth human and spiritual formation can greatly reduce the issues we face in this area. When an individual experiences interior conversion and is led to intimacy with God, he is not likely to indulge in sin—including sexual sins. Although the cases involving minors can be traced to some deep-seated psychological problems, the fact also remains that proper human and spiritual formation will equally be helpful here. Nevertheless, it is advisable to expose students to different psychological tests before ordination to ascertain that they are all right.

Additionally, prior to admitting people to the seminary and in the course of their formation, it is pertinent to subject the candidates to a psychological test in the area of sexuality and to proper discernment by those entrusted with their formation both in the seminaries and the dioceses. This is necessary to discover those who might have deep-seated psychological problems in this area that can predispose them to aberrant and/or illicit sexual behaviours in the future. As a matter of fact, ongoing psychological testing and spiritual counselling should also be available to those who are already in the ministry on a regular basis in full recognition that the loneliness, frustrations, and serious exposure to temptations that often come with the ministry can overwhelm some priests.

But ultimately everybody will agree that indulging consistently in aberrant sexual sins and illicit sexual relationships is a clear reflection of the unhealthy state of the spiritual life of a person and more so a priest. Thus, to deal with the issues in this area (except in the case of a psychological problem), the most important thing is spirituality. In other words, we need to focus on fixing the spiritual life of priests by investing heavily in their proper evangelization and conversion and in their moral, spiritual, and pastoral formation more than anything else.

To that effect, ongoing *kerygmatic* retreats and seminars targeted at the conversion of future priests as well as practical discipling to lead them to Christian maturity, intimacy with God, and a lifelong commitment to Christ and the mission of Church are critical to our success. The truth is that a converted and discipled minister who is trained to pursue virtue and sainthood as a way of life will not only see certain sexual behaviours as deplorable, but also, he is most likely not to indulge in them and other grave sins as a way of life.

Forming Priests to Overcome Self—the Idol of "Self"

A priest is a fisher of men as distinct from a fisherman. A fisherman's interest in the fish is not in the best interest of the fish. He is not interested in the well-being or survival of the fish. The fish is only a means to his own survival and comfort. He catches it in order to kill and eat it or to sell it for monetary gains. On the other hand, a real fisher of men is motivated by three main things, namely: the love of God who wants all men to be saved (cf. Jn 3:16; 1 Tim 2:4); the love of the Church in whose name he fishes; and the love of the fish (neighbour) in need of salvation. He does not seek the fish—that is, men—for himself or his own selfish purpose, but to lead them to Christ.

So, while it is the fisherman who benefits primarily from his own fishing activity, the kingdom of God, the Church, and the individual who is saved are the primary beneficiaries from the activity of the fisher of men even though in evangelizing or fishing for Christ, he too shares in the reward of eternal life. Some distinctive qualities of a priest that arise from this are the love of God, love of the Church, love of souls and, of course, selflessness and sacrifice. The opposite of this outward-looking love mentioned here is self-love—inordinate self-love—which in itself is a serious form of idol worship.

In the past, people actually worshipped idols as gods. Those idols had shrines where people offered sacrifices and invoked them. With the advent of Christianity and some major religions, most people all over the world discarded their idols to worship God. Nevertheless, in our time most people—Christians and non-Christians alike—are immersed in idol worship in its more dangerous form. This idol which commands great attention among the people of every race, tribe, and language and religion is "self" or inordinate self-love. This idol—self—is so powerful that it controls the choices and decisions of most people on a daily basis. Whereas most believers can ignore God in their choices and actions, yet they find it extremely difficult to ignore this idol called self.

The influence of "self-love" on most human beings is so strong that it can be argued that it is the main reason many people worship God or the devil. In reality, it is doubtful if any right-thinking person can enter the service of the devil for his own sake. What we know from experience is that people worship the devil or join secret cults for love of self, that is, in search of money or power or a solution or other comfort for "self."

On the other hand, even though a good number of people have grown spiritually to the point of seeking God primarily for his own sake, the vast majority of believers, including many Christians, tend to seek him primarily for their self-interest—security, providence, deliverance from evil, eternal life, and other favours. This explains why the "material-prosperity Gospel" is more attractive to most people than the "kingdom-prosperity Gospel." This problem is not limited to our generation. On the contrary, it is a trait of our *fallenness* that man is selfish. Even Jesus Christ reminded the crowd looking for him that they were actually not looking for him but for what he could offer them—bread (cf. Jn 6:27). In other words, they were looking for him primarily for "self."

Nevertheless, what is more important to us here is that self-love or inordinate self-love is always opposed to Christ's Gospel. The "self" can be a monster where it has not been tamed. It tends to rear its ugly head everywhere and to seek the lion's share if not everything for itself. In a certain sense, "self" is the greatest obstacle to the worship of God and godliness. It is too greedy, domineering, and can use the worst means at times to achieve its purpose. The devil himself knows the power of "self" and actually employs it as a tool to tempt and destroy men. For example, Adam and Eve disobeyed God and listened to the snake in the garden because they sought "divinization" for self (cf. Gen 3:1-6); King Saul tried to kill the innocent David to protect his self-interest (cf. Sam 19:1:24 ff.); David had Uriah killed to cover up his sin (2 Sam 11 ff.); and Peter denied Jesus thrice to save his own life (Lk 22:54-62).

From all of this, it is clear that the greatest problem of humanity is the inordinate self-love. Jesus Christ who is the greatest teacher of all times knew the power of "self." He clearly understood that self-love will always be a major obstacle to godliness and true discipleship. Hence, in spelling out the cost of discipleship, he stressed that no man can be his disciple without denying the "self." According to him, "Whoever comes to me and does not hate father and mother, wife and children, brothers and sisters, yes, and even life itself, cannot be my disciple. Whoever does not carry the cross and follow me cannot be my disciple" (Lk 14:26-27). And to stress the importance of dying to self or subduing this powerful idol called "self-love," Jesus laid down his own life for the salvation of mankind. Speaking of modern paganism, Pope Benedict XVI identifies the source as "love of self." According to him,

> Do we nevertheless get the impression sometimes that by some law of nature paganism again and again wins back to some extent areas that were cleared and cultivated by Christianity? In keeping with man's fallen [selfish] nature, paganism breaks through in him again and again: this is an experience that runs through all the centuries. The truth of original sin is confirmed. Again and again man falls behind the faith and wants to be just himself again; he becomes a heathen in the most profound sense of the word. As Saint Augustine said: world history is a battle of two forms of love. Love of self to the point of destroying the world. And love of others – to the point of renouncing oneself. This battle, which could always be seen, is in progress now, too.[376]

Here, it is easy to see the danger that lies in inordinate love of self as opposed to the self-renunciation which Jesus proposes to his followers. Self-love has a way of blinding us. It narrows our whole mind and our worldview to the extent that we can no longer see the big picture. In this state of mental or spiritual blindness all we can see or think of is "self"—the power that "self" can wield, the width of the region that "self" controls, the number of persons that "self" controls and so on. Everything revolves around self or primarily around self-glory. God, the Church and her mission, and people are always secondary and sometimes only a means to the selfish end of the individual. As a result of this inordinate and blind worship of self, many good decisions that should be taken in the best interest of the faith—the Church and her mission of evangelization—are either not taken at all to protect self-interest or inordinate ambition or other vain pursuits or are taken at the convenience of "self," that is, only after the individual must have been fully satisfied.

One of the characteristics of self is that it likes to cling, not just to what is its own, but even to what is not its own or that which is merely entrusted to it. This self-seeking idol called "self" often longs to be worshipped and tends to love and listen to only those

---

[376] POPE BENEDICT XVI, *Light of the World: The Pope, the Church and the Signs of The Times* (San Francisco, CA: Ignatius Press, 2010), p. 59.

who massage its ego. It loves to remain in the dark because truth is light. Sadly, under the rule or dominion of self, we cannot understand that Christ and his Church and her salvific mission are bigger than any one of us. As a result of self-love, the presbyterate in many dioceses have been set on fire with hate and warfare arising from tribal or ethnic considerations, unhealthy power tussles and division, with serious negative implications for the priesthood and the mission of the Church.

Still, owing to this same problem and the attendant narrow-mindedness, Church growth and expansion in many parishes and at different times have been jeopardized or completely sacrificed by many of the clergy. The tendency is always to think that creating a new parish from "my" parish will lead to losing "my" territory, "my" people and part of "my" power and influence. This blindness from self-love makes it difficult to let go. It makes it almost impossible for the individual to see how his selfless move—letting go of a part of his territory—can ease administration, reduce unnecessary stress, and foster the mission of the Church and thus the spread of God's kingdom.

This same self-love is what makes it difficult for many priests to step out of their comfort zones and carry out evangelization and a fruitful pastoral work. In this case, Bible study, doctrinal class, involvement in catechesis, and other faith formation programmes that can deepen the faith of the people, foster their spiritual growth, and make them more spiritually fruitful are viewed as burdens and sacrificed on the altar of laziness and complacency. Meanwhile, many of the so-called "overnight" pastors who probably had only six months of training at a Bible college invest time and energy in all this to develop their members spiritually. This love of self and its attendant consequences are some of the major reasons we are losing people to other churches. The truth is that many people are searching for God and spiritual fulfillment and if their priests are not making the sacrifice to meet these expectations or satisfy their longing, some go elsewhere.

A way to challenge this nonchalant and lazy attitude of a good number of our priests is to seek to disciple them to imitate Jesus Christ who renounced himself and worldly glories to be the Saviour of mankind that the Father wanted him to be (cf. Mt 4:8-11;

Lk 4:5-8; Phil 2:6-11). A serious training revolving around self-renunciation should be an integral part of the ongoing formation of our priests and future priests. In practice, this same self-renunciation should be obvious at every level of the Church, especially among the leaders themselves because priests and the people learn more from what they see.

Nevertheless, priests are also human beings and the Church hierarchy should make every effort to secure their welfare, especially when they are retired or can no longer function effectively for any reason. This is absolutely necessary to ensure that it does not become a source of distraction and temptation to many of them. By and large, a serious battle that must be fought and won in the Church at all levels of the priesthood is not that against the evil spirits, but that of mastering the self or overcoming self-love. If this monster is not prevailed against, the mission of the Church will continue to suffer and some Catholics will continue to drift away, whereas on the other hand, dying to self will free the clergy from self-absorption and make them focus more on the glory of God and the mission of the Church.

The Need for a Thorough Self-Examination

Reflecting on the state of formation of future priests in our seminaries and dioceses, it is easy to see a lot of flaws in different areas, which ultimately affect the quality of priests we are raising. If truth be told, all of us without exception are contributing to the bad situation. In fact, there are so many questions we should be asking and many issues we need to address if we expect things to change for the better. I will raise some of them here.

As important as mission is, what is the level of emphasis given to it in the course of seminary training? How many seminars and workshops do we organize around discipleship and practical evangelization (especially mission *ad gentes*) for our future priests in the seminary and dioceses? Is this not why many of our priests, parishes, and the pious associations in most parishes are not evangelical in the approach? How many seminars or workshops do we organize around leadership, human sexuality, and other important subjects for seminarians?

We cannot expect to have excellent priests if we are not doing all that is expected of us to form such priests. In actual fact, how are seminary formators and the diocesan directors of vocations selected? Do some of them have a proper understanding of their work, the seriousness of formation, and the negative consequences of negligence on their part? Do some of them really have what it takes to properly guide and mentor the seminarians in their care? Are they trained in the work of formation and spiritual discernment? What level of attention do we devote to the proper discernment of the human, spiritual, and the pastoral development of seminarians prior to ordination? How many of the priests who host seminarians on pastoral work are in a position to help them grow in the spiritual life and in pastoral charity and zeal and thus complement the efforts of the seminary formators and the directors of vocations? Do many of these priests really have what it takes to help them? Do some not corrupt them with their anti-Christian witness? How sincere and objective are priests in writing the reports of seminarians on pastoral work? Do some not simply write good reports to avoid criticism and trouble, even when they are convinced that particular seminarians have serious issues? What measures does the Church have in place to hold people accountable when things go wrong in the area of formation?

These are only some of the questions that arise here even though there could be more. But it is important to note that the proper formation of our future priests has a direct implication for the spiritual well-being of the faithful and the success of our mission as a Church. To a great extent, our collective failure in the area of formation contributes to the inadequacies and crisis we witness in the Church and the priesthood today. It is a case of reaping what we are sowing and the truth is that nothing will change until all of us without exception begin to hold ourselves accountable to God and to the Church for our individual or collective negligence—omission or commission—in this area. Rather than leave a lot of things unattended or to chance and complain and trade blames when issues arise, we must give the formation of future priests our best attention. This is one area we cannot afford to toil with because of the grave consequences for the Church and all of us.

Regular self-examination is good for every individual who has his eyes on self-improvement and development. It exposes one's areas of strengths and weaknesses, and positions one to deal with those weaknesses that can slow down his development and progress. Those in the business world constantly hold business retreats to reappraise their progress, challenges, new opportunities, and strategies with a bid to making even greater progress. The art of objective self-examination or appraisal on the part of an individual or group, or more so an institution like the Church which is called to be light to the world and a beacon of hope in society, is not a sign of weakness, but a necessity from which we cannot run away.

In his time when Pope Benedict XV observed that the world was increasingly growing cold towards God, he willingly embarked on a serious soul-searching exercise on behalf of the universal Church rather than look outward.[377] He found the answer in the priesthood and, more precisely, in the poor and ineffective proclamation of the Word of God by priests. Addressing the problem in his 1917 encyclical, *On Preaching the Word*, he emphasized the need for diligence on the part of bishops in selecting, not only learned men, but holy men for the priesthood.[378] Here, he was simply recalling the position of the Lateran Council centuries before that, "If it should ever be impossible to maintain the present number [of priests], it is better to have good priests than a multitude of bad ones."[379]

To stress the seriousness of this matter, the pope maintains that, "If an unworthy priest leads souls astray through error or scandal, then the bishop who ordained him would share in his sins." Consequently, he stresses that, "If anyone [a bishop, or if you like, a rector or formation personnel or director of vocations or any priest to whom a seminarian is entrusted] acts carelessly and negligently in this duty, he clearly offends in a grievous matter, and on him will fall the responsibility of the errors which the untrained preacher

---

[377] See J. TREMBLEY, "The Papal Letter of 1917…, *op. cit.,* p. 1.

[378] *HGR* 7-8; Also quoted in J. TREMBLAY, "The Papal Letter of 1971…, *op. cit.,* p. 1.

[379] LATERAN COUNCIL, Quoted by Tremblay. See *Ibid.* Here, Tremblay cites the Lateran Council.

may spread or of the scandal and the bad example which the unworthy one may give."[380]

In view of this, he recommends that the bishops must act if any priest abuses his office, insisting that for the good of souls, false compassion for the erring or unworthy priest has to be set aside. Any priest found to use his office for his own glory or wanting in virtue or learning should be debarred.[381] For him, the three-fold criteria that we should use to choose worthy men for the priesthood are as follows: First, the individual should be holy—a man of virtue "who always fully conformed himself to God's will" and his glory above his own profit. Secondly, he should possess the spirit of sacrifice and service like Christ and the Apostles and should not avoid "labour or trouble of any kind" or immoderately desire the comforts of life or seek his own ease instead of the good of souls. Like Christ and the Apostles, he must possess the spirit of sacrifice. And lastly, such a candidate should not be merely someone who prays, but rather "a man of prayer" who enjoys intimate communion with God.[382]

Learning from Business Owners

We can learn a great deal from the proprietors of the major football clubs across Europe, such as FC Barcelona, Real Madrid, Juventus, Manchester United, Bayern Munich and others who have their eyes on results or major trophies. These do not sit back and do very little and expect a miracle to happen. On the contrary, they intentionally invest in the process that will lead to the realization of their dreams and mission. As part of their long-term plan for success, they invest in football academies that will help discover and develop talented young players for future exploits in their main teams.

To achieve their goal of winning trophies, they buy players with huge potentials and employ the services of some of the best coaches in the world and take time to school them on the vision,

---

[380] *HGR* 7; Also cited in J. TREMBLAY, "The Papal Letter of 1971…, *op. cit.,* p. 1.

[381] See *Ibid.,* p. 2.

[382] See *Ibid.*

mission, and the philosophy of their teams. To motivate them to give their best, they provide good training facilities, pay them mouth-watering remunerations, and give them their best attention and cooperation. At all times, their desire is to keep improving, to keep winning, to keep making more profit, and to expanding their influence.

Having done their part in creating the enabling conditions for success, they set targets for the coaches and players and monitor their progress to ensure that they are effective. In particular, they hold the coaches accountable and fire them when they underperform. The reason they do all this is to succeed—to secure their investments and accomplish their overall objectives. In other words, they strategize and keep investing time, energy, and resources to ensure success. For the club, administration is a serious business and they never take their eyes off their mission. In fact, they are goal oriented, committed, and totally focused on success.

Now, they do all this even though what is at stake—money, fame, earthly laurels—are nothing compared to what is at stake in the mission of the Church concerning the eternal salvation of souls and the proper formation of future priests who will drive this all-important mission. The Church in Nigeria has a lot to learn from them. We too need to be mission conscious and goal oriented in our approach to the formation of future priests if we want to succeed in our overall mission.

To a large extent, the success of the Church's mission depends on the spiritual and pastoral health of our parishes, which is a reflection of that of the faithful. In turn, the spiritual health and pastoral effectiveness of our parishes depends to a large extent on the spiritual health of the priests who run them and their total commitment to pastoral work in pursuit of the mission of the Church. Finally, the level of commitment and effectiveness of the priests will depend chiefly on the quality of the human, intellectual, spiritual, and pastoral formation they received in the seminary and in their dioceses in the course of their training. This explains why the authorities should endeavour to invest heavily in the seminaries and the directorates of vocations and create the right conditions for success in the formation of future priests.

Chapter Nine

RE-ESTABLISHING THE CULTURE OF EVANGELIZATION IN THE CHURCH

Today, Catholicism is dying in Europe, while Islam appears to be growing in some parts of the continent. In fact, recent studies cite Islam as the fastest growing religion in the world with an indication that it may become the world's largest religion by 2050, if the current trend continues.[383] Similarly, the vocation to the priesthood is decreasing in Europe and North America. Just recently, in his book, *Who Will Break Bread for Us?*, Irish priest Father Hoban states that in twenty years' time Ireland will not have priests anymore.[384]

This decline of Christianity in the West did not begin today. As far back as 1917, Pope Benedict XV had observed that the world was growing cold to Christ. What is even more fearful is that the modernists or secular humanists who wish to do away with God and build a new Tower of Babel (cf. Gen 11) have practically infiltrated the seven models of culture and now influence how most people think and act.

Sadly, this secular culture is gradually rearing its ugly head in the Church herself. Moreover, the Muslims in Nigeria are now converting some Christians, including Catholics. Their incursion

---

[383] See T. JOHNSON and B. GRIM, *The World's Religions in Figures: An Introduction to International Religious Demography* (Hoboken, NJ: Wiley-Blackwell, 2013), p. 10. Archived from the original (PDF) on 27 September 2013. The forecast for 2050 by Pew Research Center indicates that the Muslim population will experience a higher growth rate than the Christian population primarily because of the young age and high fertility rate of Muslims.

[384] See B. HOBAN, @IrishCentral on Twitter, published Tuesday, June 11, 2013. Fr. Brendan Hoban claims disaster is facing the Catholic Church in Ireland.

into the eastern part of the country, which is a stronghold of Catholicism in Nigeria, is a new reality that is extremely worrisome. Even more worrisome is the fact that they are gradually and strategically trying to Islamize Nigeria under our watch. For instance, at the time of writing, Christianity is not mentioned in the Nigerian constitution, although Islam, *sharia,* and similar are mentioned several times in spite of Nigeria being a secular State.

Some questions arise on the basis of these new realities. How did we get here? Why is the Church shrinking in the West? To be more specific, Why is the Catholic Church in Nigeria (and perhaps in many other parts of the world) losing some of her members? Why are there still so many non-Christians (Muslims and traditional worshippers) in many of our communities? Does the Church still have a mission? Why are many of our parishes and our pious associations and organizations not committed to evangelization?

The answer to all these questions is simple. To put it mildly, this is bound to happen when a Church with a mission loses focus of her mission or relegates it to the background or simply makes it one of the things she does. Again, this loss of members and territories is bound to happen where the clergy and lay faithful themselves are not trained to be evangelical or missionary in their mindset or approach to the practice of their faith. Where there is a shift of emphasis from the supernatural to the natural, or the Church is more interested in worldly affairs than in the salvation of souls and the growth of the kingdom of God, the kingdom of the world gains the upper hand.

Acknowledging the Problem and Tackling It

In my last book, *When Salt Loses Its Saltiness,* I was extremely clear that there is need for urgent reforms in the formation of future priests in our seminaries as well as an ongoing spiritual and apostolic formation of priests in particular. Nearly a decade after, it is clear that the situation is even worse and critical to the extent that some priests and lay people themselves are afraid of a potential crisis that will befall the Church if nothing meaningful is done as a matter of urgency.

Not knowing that there is a problem when one actually exists is a big problem in itself. Knowing that there is a problem and convincing oneself that there is none or that it is not one's problem (when actually it is) amounts to deceit. Still, knowing that there is a problem and not responding to it accordingly or leaving it for others to deal with in the future is a clear flight from responsibility, which is always morally culpable. When we talk about effecting positive change in the life of a society or an institution, an awareness of the problem is never enough. Awareness that there is a problem has never been known to resolve a problem the same way that incessant complaints and trading of blames are not known to resolve issues. No doubt, knowledge of the existence of a problem is good and vital, but ultimately, it is meant to lead to a solution or a search for one.

Thus, as we reflect on why a good number of our faithful have drifted from the Church, our solution should focus on how to stem this negative trend in three ways: how to prevent others from leaving, how to attract and bring back those who have left, and how to win those who have never been a part of us and convert the non-Christians. In clear language, the point is, "How do we bring about change and recover the years eaten by locusts?"

Two major potential solutions readily come to mind here. These also have the potential to stem the drift of Catholics to the Pentecostal churches. At the same time they can confront the present challenges posed by the spread of the secular culture and Islam. These solutions are as follows: the re-establishment of the culture of evangelization and the rediscovery of disciple-making as a culture in the Church among the clergy and the entire laity. In this chapter, I shall focus on the first.

Rediscovering the Culture of Evangelization in the Church

The general situation in the world points to the fact that there is an urgent need for full-scale evangelization in the Church or what George Weigel calls evangelical Catholicism.[385] The Church needs to rediscover herself and her essence and embrace her vocation as a missionary enterprise.

---

[385] See G. WEIGEL, *Evangelical Catholicism: Deep Reform in the 21st-Century Church* (New York: Basic Books, 2013), p. 3.

Beginning with the Second Vatican Council, the Fathers of the Church, the popes, and many Catholic theologians and writers have been stressing the need for the Church to rediscover herself and her essence and embrace her vocation as a missionary enterprise.

As a document of the Second Vatican Council, *Ad Gentes* states, "the pilgrim Church is missionary by her very nature."[386] In line with this, Stephen Bevans and Jeffrey Gros maintain that the Church's mission, in both its general sense and its specific sense, is not merely among the many assignments she has to carry out. Rather, "it is what makes the Church the Church, such that the Church will cease to exist if mission ceased to exist."[387]

Similarly, Weigel puts it thus: "[The Church] doesn't just have a mission, as if 'mission' was one of a dozen things the Church does. The Church is a mission. At the center of that mission is the proclamation of the Gospel and the offer of friendship with Jesus Christ. Everyone and everything in the Church must be measured by mission-effectiveness."[388] For the new evangelization to succeed there must be "a robust, unapologetic proclamation of the Gospel," as that is the only thing that can meet the challenge of today's *Christophobic* public culture that increasingly regards biblical morality as irrational bigotry.[389]

The Sad Reality: An Overview of the Problem

By virtue of our baptism, every Christian is called to participate in the life and mission of the Church to evangelize. This was the practice among the first Christians and the Christians in the early eras. But unlike in the distant past, the sad reality today is that

---

[386] *AG* 2.

[387] See S. BEVAN and J. GROS, in "Evangelisation," ed. S. KAROTEMPREL, *Following Christ in Mission: A Foundational Course in Missiology* (Kenya: Paulines Publication Africa, 1995), p. 32.

[388] G. WEIGEL, "Catholics Need a Pope for the 'New Evangelization.'" The next pontiff must nurture Catholicism where it is growing and revive it where it is not. An article by Weigel, published on February 13, 2013, p. 1.

[389] *Ibid.*

mission or the sharing of the Gospel is no longer a culture in the Church. The vast majority of lay people do not know that they are called to evangelize. They were never raised to see evangelization as a culture and are actually ignorant of their role in it.

Even many of those who have been exposed to this truth often shy away from sharing the Gospel while some seem to believe that donating money in the Church frees them from the duty to share the Gospel and witness to Christ. But this only creates a gap in God's plan for evangelization and slows down the process of reaching and winning the world for Christ. In fact, as one commentator puts it, "a dollar does not remove your duty to God; an excuse does not override your responsibility to God; nor does old age cancel out a calling bestowed upon a human by God."[390] Posing an important question every Catholic should ponder carefully, he writes:

> Where will the missionaries of today come from if no one "through faith" stands upon the Word of God to follow God as those listed in Hebrews chapter eleven? If you go away, how shall they hear? If you fail, who will tell the story? If you compromise, how can they see Christ in you? If you return home because of doubt and fear, who will fill your shoes? Will you also go away?[391]

Today, in the churches, there are many people, the clergy and lay people alike, who do not believe in the Church's mission of evangelization.[392] They are open to every benefit or service the Church can offer them, but show little or no interest in evangelization within or outside their parishes and are not willing to make any meaningful sacrifice to promote it. Skinner captures the situation very well when he says,

> There are always multitudes waiting in line for free handouts but when the words "work" and "sacrifice" are mentioned, they fall on deaf ears. Many so-called Christians

[390] J. SKINNER, *Miracles & Missions Digest,* April/May 2009, vol. 53, no. 3, p. 3.

[391] *Ibid.,* p. 2.

[392] In fact, some priests are known to state that they do not believe in evangelization, which is extremely scandalous granted that it is the very reason for which they were ordained.

> are blind to needs of lost worlds; although sinners live next door and surround them at the work place. Even in their places of worship, while singing and praising their Savior, they are ignorant of the world's need for missionaries.[393]

This is also true of the Catholic priests from the standpoint of mission *ad gentes*. Most of them are content with pastoral care. They neither engage in mission beyond their parishes nor labour to prepare the lay faithful as missionaries to be sent to the unevangelized at the marketplace. What makes the situation even more critical for the Church on mission is that the success of her evangelizing mission lies at the marketplace. To put it differently, our success does not lie in the four walls of our churches, but in the world or more precisely in taking control of the seven models of culture or influence in society.

The Church is the place for transforming those who are already inside into holy men and women and missionary disciples, and then equipping them as an army for Christ to be sent into the field of the world to make converts and bring others to him. Now, if the success of our evangelizing mission is at the marketplace and nobody is reaching these places for Christ, then certain conclusions are inevitable. First is that we need to review what we are doing because we cannot be said to be as effective as we should be. In other words, if our parishes are not centres for training and sending out intentional missionaries into the world where they are planted, we cannot make real progress as far as mission is concerned.

God wants the salvation of all men and women (cf. 1 Tim 2:4), but lack of commitment to evangelization on our part makes it difficult to lead more and more people to Christ and the salvation he offers. Again, this point is clear in Skinner's comment on the story of the woman caught in the act of adultery in John 8:1-11. According to him,

> There is a wonderful transformation that can take place not only in the outright sinner but also in the religious hypocrite when they come face to face with Jesus Christ. Not only did this woman go away from his presence changed but her accusers also left shamed. No man can

---

[393] J. SKINNER, *Miracles & Missions Digest…*, *op. cit.*, p. 3.

> do what Jesus Christ can do for a soul! But without man's missionary efforts, most may never find this transforming Saviour. The men that brought her to Jesus felt conviction of heart also and had the opportunity to be changed and to go and sin no more as did the woman they threw at Jesus' feet.[394]

During World War II, millions of Americans (one-third of the able-bodied American men) enlisted in the army to fight against Adolf Hitler and his army. Although they knew that there were dangers ahead and were aware that some of them may die in the course of the war, yet the aversion they had for the "evil" that Hitler represented in the minds of many was strong enough to make them volunteer to make a huge sacrifice to enlist in the army and fight it. They were ready to make sacrifices and die for their convictions.

Now, what is at stake in the Church's mission of evangelization is a much more serious battle. It is a battle for the souls of men with a far-reaching eternal consequence—eternal life or eternal damnation (cf. Mk 16:15-18; Jn 3:16-18). As a duty, all the baptized are called to enlist in the army of Christ and join the battle to save souls and win the world for Christ through Christian witness and the intentional sharing of the Gospel as a lifestyle or culture. No member of the Church is exempt from this task of evangelization. Thus, to run away from it under any pretext (except in the case of inculpable ignorance or serious mental disability) can only be a reflection of a deep-seated selfishness or perhaps lack of an interior conversion. If sending his Son, Jesus Christ, to save mankind is a mark of the Father's love for mankind, then the refusal to collaborate with him to save our fellow brothers and sisters through evangelization will amount to lack of love for the lost as well as lack of love for God and Christ.

The truth is that God does not want us to go to heaven alone; he wants us to bring his other children with us. So, lack of interest in mission is a case of disobedience and insensitivity to his will and his plan for the world. Granted the present situation and the fact

[394] *Ibid.*, p. 4.

that the Church exists for mission, a major question we must ask ourselves as a matter of necessity is, How can we re-establish the culture of mission or evangelization in the Church? Perhaps a good way to begin is to go back to our roots and the reason for which the Church was established in the first place.

The Great Commission of Jesus Christ

Although God's missionary activity in the world began long before the New Testament era of which the Blessed Trinity is the foundation, the Church's mission results directly from the Great Commission of Jesus Christ in Matthew 28:19-20. In fact, any serious talk about the mission of the Church must necessarily go back to the Great Commission. To emphasize the importance of this commission, all four Gospels and the Acts of the Apostles capture it in different ways (cf. Mk 16:15-18; Lk 24:44-49, Jn 20:21-23; Acts 1:8). These passages make it abundantly clear that the Church is a sent Church. She is sent to the world, that is, to go or carry a specific message to the world to win it for Christ and not to wait for the world to come to her.

The call of Peter and the Apostles and the Church of every age, which includes all the baptized—the clergy and the laity—is to be fishers of men. To some extent the work is similar to that of a fisherman even though the fisherman's interest is different.[395] The fishes are in the sea and the fisherman does not wait at home for them to come to him. Rather, he goes to the sea to look for them and catch them. Similarly, the people we need to seek out, convert, and bring into the Church are mainly in the world even though we recognize that many of those in the Church are also in need of conversion. But even while we continue to work on the re-evangelization of those in the Church, we need to step out of the comfort zone of our parishes in search of those in the world. The tendency to engage in pastoral care among those already in the fold and waiting for those outside to come to us arises from a clear misconception of our mission and role. In the early days of Christianity, the

[395] While the fishers of men (missionaries) are interested in Christ and the salvation of the men they need to reach with the Gospel, the fisherman is more interested in his own good rather than that of the fish.

Church was outward-looking. Every Christian was involved in the spreading of the Good News as a culture or lifestyle in spite of the work within to disciple or to make disciples of those already inside.

Revisiting our Mission of Evangelization

As we saw in Chapter One, the soul-winning mission of the Church is called evangelization. The word evangelization comes from the Greek *euangelion* which means good news. Some also trace the root to the Latin *evangelium* which also means good news. The Latin *evangelizare* means "to spread or preach the Gospel." Originally, the word was used by the Romans to refer to the gift that was given to the one who brought good news. Later the Church adopted the term and used it to denote the good news itself. However, it was not used to denote good news in general, but specific good news.[396] Specifically, evangelization is the proclamation of the Good News of salvation in Christ in order to convert an individual or a group of individuals to Jesus Christ.

The Two Senses of Evangelization: The Strict Sense and the Big Picture

We can speak of the Church's mission of evangelization at two different levels or in two different senses. The first is the strict sense of the term and the second is the broad sense or what some refer to as the big picture of evangelization. In the strict sense, evangelization means the proclamation of the Good News to a person or a group of individuals to convert them to Christ. This involves proclaiming the kerygma to them with a purpose to lead them to faith in him as Lord and Saviour and invite them into a relationship with him. This was exactly what Peter did on the day of Pentecost (see Acts 2). It is not the same as catechizing people. The latter actually should come after the initial conversion has taken place (in response to the kerygma) in order to deepen the faith of the new converts and make them more like Christ in character.

But viewed in its broad sense or the big picture, evangelization focuses on something more. It goes beyond proclaiming the

---

[396] M. HEALY, "Lectio: Evangelization and Acts of the Apostles ..., *op. cit.*

kerygma for the purpose of converting some individuals. Instead, the target is to convert and transform a people's culture—their way of thinking, their way of living and the activities in which they engage with the Spirit of Christ and his Gospel. It involves incarnating the Gospel in the culture and Christianizing society as a whole. According to Mary Healy, it refers to "the Church's whole mission to bring Christ into the world." As such, it covers such areas as "the kerygma, catechesis, the sacraments, ongoing faith formation, pastoral care, even transformation of communities, institutions, the culture and society as a whole."[397]

The Two Ways to Approach Evangelization

There are two ways to approach evangelization. The first involves the proclamation of the kerygma to an individual or a group of individuals in a way that evokes a personal response to Christ and his Gospel Message. The second is to evangelize the environment (intellectual, social, moral and spiritual environments) within an institution or a society by infusing it with the values and principles of the Gospel of our Lord Jesus Christ. The whole point behind this strategy is that the "evangelized environment" then shapes the thinking and behaviour of those who live in it.[398] Nevertheless, it is important to state that these two approaches are not mutually exclusive where the circumstance permits.

To achieve the big picture or the broad sense of evangelization, we need to pay strict attention to the models of culture in society, which influence the thought-patterns and behaviours of the people. These include the Church or religion, family, education, government, media, art, and business and finance.[399] Some other authors add sports and entertainment. These seven models of culture determine the type of influence to which a people living in a given society are exposed and equally shape their minds, choices,

---

[397] M. HEALY, "Lectio: Evangelization and Acts of the Apostles..., *op. cit.*

[398] L. WALLNAU, "Take All 7," The Lance Learning Group. A set of 4 CDs on the Seven Mountains. See CD 1; See also www.lancelearning.com.

[399] *Ibid.*

and activities. These areas in question can be said to be the marketplace where the success of our mission lies.

Until we are able to permeate them and influence what goes on in each of them with the Spirit of Jesus Christ and the values of the Gospel, it will be impossible for the Church to win society for Christ and fulfill her mission.[400] On the contrary, if the identified areas of culture are not evangelized, then evangelizers will end up producing Christians who live a life of double standards. In other words, they are "godly" within the environment of the Church, but worldly outside in order to survive or find acceptance. The truth is that if this continues over time the conscience is gradually weakened such that what is abnormal may become normal to them.

Getting Catholics to Embrace the Call of the Popes for Evangelization

Following the Second Vatican Council, all the popes (with the exception of Pope John Paul I whose pontificate was short) have been calling for evangelization in the world. They all see it as a necessity today, which the Church and all the members should embark upon as a matter of urgency. One of the ways we can stem the present drift of Catholics to other churches and properly evangelize the lay faithful and prepare them for their own evangelizing mission is by exposing them to the writings of the popes in this area and getting them to embrace their call for massive evangelization

[400] People are influenced by their environment, viewed, not only from the physical point of view, but also the intellectual, moral, and spiritual standpoints. Since the environment itself is shaped by the culture in a place, it makes the evangelization and Christianization of culture (a people's way of life) a real target for the Church on mission. It is crucial that the Gospel engages culture and transforms it in order to influence a people's mode of thinking, their criteria for judgment, the choices they make and the activities in which they engage in the society. Infusing culture with the principles of the Gospel will make it serve the purpose of the kingdom of God. But for that to happen, the Gospel must first penetrate and Christianize the seven models of culture in society and influence what goes on in each of them.

(mission *ad gentes*, pastoral care, and new evangelization) in the world. Here we shall attempt to summarize the positions of the different popes on the subject matter, beginning with Pope Paul VI.

Pope Paul VI's Call for a Worldwide Evangelization

Pope Paul VI (1897–1978) was pope from 1963 to 1978. His pontificate was at a time of significant change in the Church following the Second Vatican Council. He was a missionary pope and the first to embark on apostolic visits to other continents outside Europe. On December 8, 1975, he published his famous apostolic exhortation, *Evangeli Nuntiandi*–On Evangelization in the Modern World.

Noting the profound changes in the modern world and different situations of de-Christianization in his day, such as increase in unbelief, atheistic humanism, secularism and similar, he called for evangelization in the world. In his writings, he insists that in order to reach those who are distant from the faith, the Church "must constantly seek the proper means and language for presenting, or representing, to them God's revelation and faith in Jesus Christ."[401]

The salient point from this landmark document is that mission (evangelization) is the identity and vocation of the Church. In his exact words, "Evangelizing is in fact the grace and vocation proper to the Church, her deepest identity. She exists in order to evangelize, that is to say, in order to preach and teach, to be the channel of the gift of grace, to reconcile sinners with God, and to perpetuate Christ's sacrifice in the Mass, which is the memorial of His death and glorious resurrection."[402] The Church's mission is Christocentric. The proclamation of the kingdom of God and salvation for all people through Jesus Christ is at its very foundation and form the essential aspect of evangelization. The foundation and centre of evangelization is, "a clear proclamation that, in Jesus Christ, the Son of God made man, who died and rose from the dead, salvation is offered to all men, as a gift of God's grace and mercy."[403]

---

[401] *EN* 56.

[402] *EN* 14.

[403] *EN* 27.

He emphasizes the importance of personal witness, that is, an exemplary Christian life as a very powerful tool in evangelization. For him, "to evangelize is first of all to bear witness."[404] Besides, he insists that "Modern man listens more willingly to witnesses than to teachers, and if he does listen to teachers, it is because they are witnesses."[405] Nevertheless, he states clearly that a clear, explicit, and unequivocal proclamation of the Good News is absolutely necessary, for without it there can be no real evangelization.[406]

Furthermore, he identifies total interior renewal which the Gospel calls metanoia, that is, radical conversion—the profound change of mind and heart—as the goal of evangelization[407] and sees the work of evangelization itself as the responsibility of all Christians and not just the ordained ministers.[408] Every baptized person is called to share the Good News. In actual fact, getting involved in the evangelizing mission of Christ and his Church is one of the ways we demonstrate our own conversion. According to the pope, "here lies the test of truth, the touchstone of evangelization: it is unthinkable that a person should accept the Word and give himself to the kingdom without becoming a person who bears witness to it and proclaims it in his turn."[409]

In particular, the Holy Father stresses the important role of lay people in the Church's evangelizing activity. Since they are the ones who live and work in the secular world, he challenges them to exercise special forms of missionary activities there, which should cover the fields of politics, culture, economics, the sciences and the arts, the media and so on. Their vocation is to infuse these areas with the Spirit of Christ and his Gospel. Further, he stresses the need to prepare good instructors in the faith and catechetical instruction, that is, to raise effective faith-soldiers and communicators such as catechists, parents, and teachers. Again, he insists that we must

---

[404] *EN* 26.

[405] *EN* 41; Cites POPE PAUL VI, *Address to the Members of the Consilium de Laicis* (2 October 1974): AAS 66 (1974), p. 568.

[406] *EN* 21-22.

[407] *EN* 10.

[408] Cf. *EN* 21.

[409] *EN* 24.

employ the mass media or means of social communication to proclaim the kerygma, catechesis, or the further deepening of faith.[410] In other words, we must use every reasonable method available to propagate the evangelizing mission of the Church.

Finally, he makes an interesting and quite instructive statement, which is that "evangelization will never be possible without the action of the Holy Spirit,"[411] the same Spirit that descended on Jesus at his baptism. As he admits, "The Holy Spirit places on his lips [i.e., the lips of the evangelizer] the words which he could not find by himself, and at the same time the Holy Spirit predisposes the soul of the hearer to be open and receptive to the Good News and to the kingdom being proclaimed."[412] The indisputable conclusion to which this leads then is that for the evangelizing activities of the Church or individual Christians or groups to be effective and fruitful we need the guidance and help of the Holy Spirit.

Pope John Paul II's Call for a New Evangelization

The pontificate of Pope Saint John Paul II (1920–2005) was from 1978 to 2005. Interestingly, he said a lot about evangelization. His most notable contribution to the subject was his December 7, 1990, publication of the encyclical letter, *Redemptoris Missio*–On the Mission of the Redeemer. Here, he emphasizes the necessity and urgency of evangelization as the mission of the Church and stresses that it occurs most effectively when the Church engages the culture of those she evangelizes. We shall pay greater attention to his teaching.

The pope's timely encyclical, *Redemptoris Missio,* was a clear attempt to wake the Church up from her deep slumber and "redirect and refocus her priority for the third millennium."[413] According to

[410] *EN* 45.

[411] *EN* 75.

[412] *EN* 75.

[413] See D. NODAR, *Characteristics of the New Evangelization,* Second Edition (Baltimore, MD: Christ Life, 2013), p. 5. In this discussion on the New Evangelization, I also found the article by Dave Nodar, "What Are Characteristics of the New Evangelization?" quite helpful. See http://www.focusonline.org/images/content/pagebuilder/the_call/8_30/Dave%20Nodar%20article.pdf.

the pope, "…the moment has come to commit all of the Church's energies to a new evangelization and to the mission *ad gentes*. No believer in Christ, no institution of the Church can avoid this supreme duty to proclaim Christ to all peoples."[414]

Dave Nodar considers this call to direct the whole of the Church's energies to evangelization as a radical change in emphasis. His reason is that the vast majority of Catholics (clergy, religious, and lay people alike) are not inclined to evangelization as we have pointed out earlier.[415] In fact, most people tend to think that the term evangelization itself is protestant, considering the belief by Catholics and non-Catholics that the Catholic Church is primarily liturgical, pastoral, and hierarchical.[416] So, the pope's call embodies an urgent need for a paradigm shift in our thinking and focus. As a matter of necessity, he is challenging us to refocus our priorities by creating a new culture of evangelization in the Church that also challenges us to look within and convert our fellow Catholics rather than concentrating all our efforts on foreign lands.

New evangelization does not imply a new content for evangelization or a new message or a new Gospel. It is still the same Gospel of Christ and the same message of salvation that was preached over 2000 years ago. By introducing the new evangelization, Pope John Paul II simply expanded the original scope of the Church's mission. Prior to this time, evangelization used to be divided into two parts, namely: mission *ad gentes* and the pastoral care within the Church. But by new evangelization, he introduces an intermediate way between the two ways of understanding the mission of evangelization.

Put differently, with the introduction of the new evangelization, the pope identifies three situations in evangelization to which the Church must pay attention today.[417] The first situation that the

[414] *RM* 3.

[415] D. NODAR, "What Are Characteristics of the New Evangelization…, *op. cit.*, p. 1.

[416] D. NODAR, *Characteristics of the New Evangelization…, op. cit.*, pp. 5-7.

[417] *RM* 33.

Church's missionary activity addresses is mission *ad gentes.* This involves the missionary activity of the Church (particularly, the proclamation of the Good News of Jesus Christ) to people and groups and in social-cultural contexts where Christ and his Gospel are not known or in areas where the Church is yet to take root or the Christian communities lack sufficient maturity to incarnate the faith.[418] The aim is to convert the people and establish the Church there or Christian communities with adequate and solid ecclesial structures.

The second situation, which is pastoral care applies to Churches or Christian communities with adequate and solid ecclesial structures. In such communities, people are fervent in the faith and strive to live the Christian life. Also, they witness to the Gospel in their environs and have a sense of commitment to the collective mission of the Church.[419] The purpose of this second situation is to attend to the pastoral needs of the people and deepen their living experience of God and the faith.

The third but intermediate situation introduced by Pope John Paul II is new evangelization. This focuses particularly on "countries with ancient Christian roots, and occasionally in the younger Churches as well, where entire groups of the baptized have lost a living sense of the faith, or even no longer consider themselves members of the Church, and live a life far removed from Christ and his Gospel."[420] The aim of the Church's missionary activity here is to re-evangelize such de-Christianized peoples or countries and lead them to conversion and a living relationship with God.

With this shift in emphasis, the mission of evangelization will not only focus on Christians taking the Gospel to non-Christian territories or non-Christians to convert them or just pastoral activity among already sacramentalized Catholics to deepen their faith. Rather, it will also be about the re-evangelization of the baptized and sacramentalized Catholics in the established churches and original Christian territories. As Pope John Paul states in *Novo Millennio Inuente*, "Even in [these] countries evangelized many cen-

[418] *RM* 33.

[419] *Ibid.*

[420] *Ibid.*

turies ago, the reality of a 'Christian Society' which, amid all of the frailties which have always marked human life, measured itself explicitly on Gospel values, is now gone."[421]

Alluding to this same situation which necessitates the new evangelization, Marybeth Bonacci states, "Our mission fields [that is, the mission fields of the countries in the West] are no longer in far-off lands. They are right here, in our own cities, amongst the people who gather with us for Mass on Sunday mornings. Those are the people we need to introduce, or reintroduce, to the truth about salvation in Jesus Christ."[422] So, the new evangelization is actually directed to sacramentalized Christians. As Michael Klopp puts it, the term focuses on the baptized and can be explained in five words—the re-evangelization of the baptized.[423]

So, the call for a new evangelization reminds us that many of our baptized and confirmed brethren including those who attend Mass every Sunday may not have been properly evangelized and converted. Although they are Christians in name and they know about God, they neither know him experientially nor have a living relationship with him. If that is the case, they, in turn, cannot evangelize others to lead them to Christ, a fact that slows down the success of the Church's mission. The wisdom here is that if this category of people are properly evangelized and converted to Christ, then we will not only have succeeded in increasing the number of the converted and saved, but also we would have succeeded in increasing the number of the soldiers of Christ who can embark on the evangelization of non-Christians or mission *ad gentes.*

Speaking about the new evangelization, the pope also states that "evangelization can be new in its ardor, methods and expression"[424] to make it capable of engaging the modern man and the

---

[421] POPE JOHN PAUL II, Apostolic Letter *Novo Millennio Inuente* (NMI) at the Close of the Great Jubilee of 2000, 6 January 2001, 40.

[422] M. BONACCI, "Evangelization before Catechesis..., *op. cit.*

[423] M. DOPP, "Relit–The Heart of Evangelization..., *op. cit.*

[424] See "The Task of Latin American Bishops," *Origins* 12, March 24, 1983, p. 661. Cited in D. NODAR, "What Are Characteristics of the New Evangelization..., *op. cit.,* p. 1; Cf. *RM* 90. Here, the pope speaks also of a new "ardor for holiness" among missionaries and throughout the Christian community.

present-day secular culture. The emphasis here is that it should be adapted to the people of our time. What this means in part is that while the message remains the same and cannot change, the manner or method of presenting it to the people of the different ages can change.

Characteristics of the New Evangelization

In *Redemptoris Missio*, Pope John Paul II enumerates some of the characteristics of the new evangelization. These will include the following: the New Evangelization is Christocentric; it is the responsibility of all; it is directed at the already baptized people in the Church; it is aimed at the transformation of culture; it involves conversion, and it is a call to holiness.

The New Evangelization Is Christocentric

In general, evangelization is Christocentric. We cannot reduce it to the dimensions of a simply temporal project or reduce the aims of salvation to a man-centred goal or material well-being as some liberation theologians are tempted to do.[425] Rather, all evangelization is centered on Jesus Christ. According to Pope John Paul II, "evangelization will always contain—as the foundation, center and at the same time the summit of its dynamism—a clear proclamation that, in Jesus Christ...salvation is offered to all people, as a gift of God's grace and mercy."[426] In fact, this explicit proclamation of the Good News of salvation in Jesus Christ is "the permanent priority of mission."[427]

The new evangelization is no different. Like all evangelization it involves much more than a mere transmission of the rich doctrines of the Church. As a matter of fact, it entails "a personal and profound meeting with the Saviour."[428] Besides, just as the Samaritan woman in John 4:27-30 and 39-42, it is about sharing with

[425] See *EN* 32.

[426] *RM* 44; Cites *EN* 27; See D. NODAR, *Characteristics of the New Evangelization..., op. cit.* p. 7.

[427] *RM* 44.

[428] See D. NODAR, *Characteristics of the New Evangelization..., op. cit.,* p. 13.

others the testimony of our personal encounter or meeting with Jesus Christ as the reason for our being Christians.

As the pope acknowledges, the Church is extremely rich with so many wonderful treasures. These include our history, apostolic succession, liturgy, theology, the Church Fathers, the saints, our art and similar. But then, the danger he sees is that we may so concentrate on these treasures and become distracted from "the pearl of great price"— Jesus Christ himself who is the centre of the universe and history.[429] Hence, he insists that this personal encounter with Jesus Christ is important to the Church's proclamation.

The New Evangelization Is the Responsibility of All

Contrary to the narrow understanding of evangelization as the responsibility of a special group within the Church with a special vocation such as priests and missionaries, the pope just as Pope Paul VI[430] before him clearly states that evangelization is the responsibility and vocation of all Christians (clergy or lay) without any exception. By virtue of our common baptism we all are called to be missionaries.[431] The new evangelization is equally the responsibility of every diocese, every parish, every institution, and every association in the Church.[432]

No doubt, this is a radical shift in emphasis as far as the mission of the Church is concerned. One of the major things that arise from it is that for the lay people to participate effectively in evangelization they need to be led to a life-changing personal encounter with Jesus Christ; they need to be trained and empowered

[429] POPE JOHN PAUL II, Encyclical Letter *Redemptor Hominis* (RH), 4 March 1979, no. 1; See also D. NODAR, *Characteristics of the New Evangelization…, op. cit.,* p. 8.

[430] Cf. *EN* 73.

[431] Cf. *RM* 1, 2, 3, 11, 23, 27, 30, 32, 37, 42.

[432] Cf. *RM* 2; See also D. NODAR, *Characteristics of the New Evangelization…, op. cit.* This represents a remarkable shift in emphasis as far as the Church's mission is concerned. But to be able to participate effectively in this new evangelization, the individual Christian needs to first encounter Jesus and experience his life-changing Gospel Message as "Good News" in a personal and intimate way and as something to be lived and shared.

for their role; and they need to be intentionally sent on mission to the marketplace. This is absolutely important because numerous and wonderful opportunities for evangelization are present within the daily environments of family life and the marketplace.[433]

The New Evangelization Is Directed at the Baptized

As we have already said, while evangelization (mission *ad gentes*) used to be directed at non-Christians, new evangelization is directed at the many baptized (and sacramentalized) people in the Church who are not living out the Christian faith fully. In *Redemptoris Missio*, the pope points out three situations in the world from the standpoint of evangelization which the Church needs to address differently. The first is mission *ad gentes* and it is directed at non-Christians and places where Christ and his Gospel are not known. The second situation is pastoral care within healthy and mature churches that are fervent in their faith. And the third, which is an intermediate situation, refers to formerly Christian countries where there are entire groups of the baptized who have lost a living sense of faith, or no longer consider themselves as members of the Church, or those who still go to church but are living anti-Christian lifestyles.

The New Evangelization Is Aimed at the Transformation of Culture

Evangelization is not merely about proclaiming the Good News of Jesus Christ to people in order to convert them and bring them into the Body of Christ. It also entails evangelizing the culture in which people live in order to transform it with the Spirit of Christ and his Gospel. Focusing on the transformation of cultures, Pope John Paul II invites us to incarnate Christian values or insert Christianity in the various human cultures to transform them from within with the goal of creating "a civilization of love."[434]

---

[433] Cf. *Ibid.*, p. 10.

[434] *RM* 51.

The New Evangelization and Conversion

Just as the whole of evangelization, the goal of the new evangelization is Christian conversion of the mind and heart of man. The reason we proclaim the Good News of Jesus Christ is not merely to pass on information about Jesus Christ or the Christian faith. Rather, it is to lead people to faith in him and to a personal conversion which entails a personal decision to accept him as our only Lord and Saviour in the sense of coming under his authority and direction in practice and becoming his committed disciples.

In the exact words of Pope John Paul II, "Conversion means accepting, by a personal decision, the saving sovereignty of Christ and becoming his disciple."[435] This conversion is not a mere intellectual thing or a mere verbal profession of faith in Jesus Christ that does not affect the life of the individual. Instead, it is a fundamental decision that brings Jesus to the centre of a person's life and marks a turning point in his life. In other words, it is something that affects the thinking and the whole life of the person and the activities in which he engages in a radical way.[436]

Thus, in evangelizing we do not just present the Good News, but we consciously and prayerfully propose it in a way that will evoke a personal response to Jesus' invitation from the recipients. Nevertheless, we should note that while we are called to collaborate with God in the work of evangelization, conversion is the initiative of the Blessed Trinity. More specifically, it is the Holy Spirit who opens the heart of a person to believe in Jesus Christ.[437] Besides, we must equally note that while there can be an initial conversion, which is crucial and the goal of kerygma, conversion is a lifelong process, which requires "a continual turning away from sin and surrendering to God."[438]

---

[435] *RM* 46.

[436] Cf. D. NODAR, *Characteristics of the New Evangelization…, op. cit.*, p. 14. The word "radical" here does mean fundamentalism.

[437] *RM* 46.

[438] D. NODAR, *Characteristics of the New Evangelization…, op. cit.*, p. 14.

The New Evangelization as a Call to Holiness

The new evangelization requires of us as missionaries a personal holiness of life, which is the basis for sharing Christ effectively with other people in order to invite them into a personal relationship with him. This does not mean that a person must wait until he achieves perfection in life before he can share the Gospel with others. However, Pope John Paul II maintains that Christian missionaries should be receptive to God and docile to the Holy Spirit. According to him, "an essential characteristic of missionary spirituality is intimate communion with Christ."[439] To transmit the Gospel of Christ to others, it should first have permeated our own lives and people should be able to see that we truly enjoy communion with God by the way we live and the fruits we exhibit.

Pope Benedict XVI on New Evangelization

Pope Benedict XVI served as pope from 2005 to 2013. He was equally passionate about the Church's mission of evangelization. Noting that Christians are Christ's disciples in our time, he maintains that we must embark on extensive evangelization all over the world. However, an extremely important point to note here is his view that the true motivation for our evangelizing mission is not to increase the size of our membership or to gain power. Rather, it is because we feel a duty to share the joy of the Gospel and to increase the numbers of people who meet Christ, enter into relationship with him, and become subjects of the kingdom of God.[440]

In September 21, 2010, Pope Benedict XVI issued an apostolic letter in form of "*Motu Proprio*" *Ubicumque et Semper*. Making reference to the Great Commission of Jesus Christ whom he called the first and supreme evangelizer, he maintains that "it is the duty of the Church to proclaim always and everywhere the Gospel of Jesus Christ."[441] Besides the Church as an institution, he considers

---

[439] *RM* 88.

[440] See Couples for Christ – Foundation for Family and Life (CFC-FFL), "Pope Benedict XVI on Evangelization," October 30, 2014.

[441] POPE BENEDICT XVI, Apostolic Letter in the Form of *Motu Proprio – Ubicumque et Semper* (US), September 21, 2010. See the Introduction.

the evangelizing mission as an urgent duty for all baptized persons, insisting that each one of us like Saint Paul should be able to say to himself, "Woe betide me, if I do not preach the Gospel" (1 Cor 9:16).

Going on to establish the Pontifical Council for Promoting the New Evangelization, as a dicastery of the Roman Curia in compliance with the Apostolic Constitution *Pastor Bonus,* he charges it to encourage reflections on topics of the new evangelization and identify and promote suitable ways and means to accomplish it as one of its important duties.[442] In particular, the Council is "to study and to encourage the use of modern forms of communication as instruments for the new evangelization."[443]

He admits the erosion of the faith in the once-established Christian countries with a strong heritage where people attempt to exclude God from their lives and exhibit a generalized indifference to the Christian faith. As a solution, he re-echoes the call of Pope John Paul II for a form of re-evangelization or new evangelization in these places in order to redirect them to their Christian roots. In recognition that the proclamation of the Gospel will be much more difficult today than before as the same Gospel Message will require renewed vigour to convince the people of the contemporary world, he calls for openness to the renewing work of the Holy Spirit who has the power to penetrate the hearts of men.

Pope Francis' Call for Evangelization

At the beginning of his pontificate in 2013, Pope Francis published his apostolic exhortation, *Evangelii Gaudium*–On the Church's Primary Mission of Evangelization in the Modern World. In the document, he re-states the teaching of the previous popes that evangelization (or the proclamation of the Good News) is the responsibility of every Christian. According to him,

> In virtue of their baptism, all the members of the people of God have become missionary disciples (cf. *Mt* 28:19).... The new evangelization calls for personal involvement on the part of each of the baptized. Every Christian is

[442] *US* Art 1, nos. 1 & 2.

[443] *US* Art 3:4.

> challenged here and now, to be actively engaged in evangelization.[444]

More specifically, his point is that all baptized Catholics whether they are bishops or priests or deacons or persons of the consecrated life or lay persons in the Church are agents of evangelization notwithstanding their level of instruction in the faith.[445] In fact, each of us is called to the saving love of the Lord in spite of our falling short of perfection[446] and as an important duty, a person who has encountered God and has truly experienced his saving love does not need much time or lengthy training before he can proclaim that love. Put in his exact words,

> Indeed, anyone who has truly experienced God's saving love does not need much time or lengthy training to go out and proclaim that love. Every Christian is a missionary to the extent that he or she has encountered the love of God in Christ Jesus: we no longer say that we are "disciples" and "missionaries," but rather that we are always "missionary disciples." If we are not convinced, let us look at those first disciples, who, immediately after encountering the gaze of Jesus, went forth to proclaim him joyfully: "We have found the Messiah!" (*Jn.* 1:41). The Samaritan woman became a missionary immediately after speaking with Jesus and many Samaritans come to believe in him "because of the woman's testimony" (*Jn.* 4:39). So too, Saint Paul, after his encounter with Jesus Christ, "immediately proclaimed Jesus" (*Acts* 9:20; cf. 22:6-21). So what are we waiting for?[447]

Acknowledging that the primary reason for evangelization is the love of Jesus Christ, he maintains that evangelization takes place in obedience to his missionary mandate, "'Go therefore and make disciples of all nations, baptizing them…teaching them to observe

[444] *EG* 120.
[445] *Ibid.*
[446] *EG* 121.
[447] *EG* 120.

all that I have commanded you' (*Mt* 28:19-20)."[448] Stressing the need for us to leave our comfort zones and go out and evangelize, he opts for a missionary pastoral ministry. According to him, "Missionary outreach is paradigmatic for all the Church's activity." And so, we "need to move from a pastoral ministry of mere conservation to a decidedly missionary pastoral ministry."[449] He states that the evangelizer must be joyful and not appear as someone who has just attended a funeral. According to him,

> Consequently, an evangelizer must never look like someone who has just come back from a funeral! Let us recover and deepen our enthusiasm, that "delightful and comforting joy of evangelizing, even when it is in tears that we must sow... And may the world of our time, which is searching, sometimes with anguish, sometimes with hope, be enabled to receive the good news not from evangelizers who are dejected, discouraged, impatient or anxious, but from ministers of the Gospel whose lives glow with fervour, who have first received the joy of Christ.[450]

Furthermore, like Pope Paul VI, he emphasizes that explicit proclamation of the Gospel, that is, the Lordship of Jesus Christ is critical to evangelization because without it, there can be no true evangelization.[451] Also, he maintains that the parish is a community of communities and in all its activities it should encourage and train its members to be evangelizers. Put differently, it should have an evangelical approach to things and be "a centre of constant missionary outreach."[452]

As a corollary to the above, he calls our attention to the centrality of kerygma (the first proclamation or announcement) and insists that it should be "the centre of all our evangelizing activity and all efforts at Church renewal."[453] This point is of utmost importance when we speak of evangelization because it is first and foremost

---

[448] *EG* 19.

[449] *EG* 15.

[450] *EG* 8; Also cites *EN* 80.

[451] *EG* 110.

[452] *EG* 28.

[453] *EG* 164.

about leading people to a life-changing encounter with Christ and relationship with him rather than catechizing or exposing them to the doctrines of the Church or the moral laws. Ordinarily, these should come afterwards, that is, they should follow the experience of an initial conversion.

To further stress the importance of kerygma today, the pope calls for a kerygmatic catechesis. In this, catechists proclaim the kerygma over and over to their catechumens.[454] This is necessary to offer them the opportunity to encounter or renew their personal encounter with Christ[455] on an ongoing basis. For Pope Francis, "all Christian formation consists of entering more deeply into the kerygma…."[456] This kerygmatic catechesis involves stressing the love of God; the life-giving sacrifice of Jesus Christ on the Cross to save us; and the fact that he walks with us side by side every day and in every situation of our lives. In fact, according to him, "On the lips of the catechist the first proclamation must ring out over and over: 'Jesus Christ loves you; he gave his life to save you; and now he is living at your side every day to enlighten, strengthen and free you.'"[457] Then, he goes on to stress the indispensability of the kerygma to catechesis and the evangelizing mission of the Church as a whole. Emphasizing its primacy in all evangelization in the qualitative sense and the need to announce it repeatedly, he maintains,

> This first proclamation [kerygma] is called "first" not because it exists at the beginning and can then be forgotten or replaced by other more important things. It is first in a qualitative sense because it is the principal proclamation, the one which we must hear again and again in different

[454] *EG* 164.

[455] The ongoing proclamation of the kerygma is a major thing that is seriously lacking in many of our churches, that is, in the catechism class, among the pious associations, and in the parish as a whole. Oftentimes, this is equally true of our catechetical schools. Indubitably, this can seriously undermine all our efforts in the area of catechesis by preventing them from bearing the required fruits in the Christian life.

[456] *EG* 165.

[457] *EG* 164.

ways, the one which we must announce one way or another throughout the process of catechesis, at every level and moment. For this reason too, "the priest–like every other member of the Church–ought to grow in awareness that he himself is continually in need of being evangelized."[458]

Oftentimes, most pastors and catechists fall into the temptation of ignoring the kerygma or relegating it during catechesis, but the pope considers this to be wrong. Stressing the importance or the centrality of the kerygma—the first proclamation or announcement—during catechetical instruction and formation as a whole, he maintains,

> We must not think that in catechesis the kerygma gives way to a supposedly more "solid" formation. Nothing is more solid, profound, secure, meaningful and wisdom-filled than that initial proclamation. All Christian formation consists of entering more deeply into the kerygma, which is reflected in and constantly illumines, the work of catechesis, thereby enabling us to understand more fully the significance of every subject which the latter treats. It is the message capable of responding to the desire for the infinite which abides in every human heart. The centrality of the kerygma calls for stressing those elements which are most needed today: it has to express God's saving love which precedes any moral and religious obligation on our part...[459]

Given the importance of the kerygma within catechesis and beyond, we should note that it is not enough to merely share a message that involves all of its components. Strictly speaking, that will not do justice to it. More importantly, it should be proclaimed in a way that truly invokes a profound response from the hearers or leads them to renew their initial response of conversion and commitment to follow Jesus and come under his Lordship and direction. This implies proclaiming it prayerfully and in the power of the Holy Spirit who alone can transform the hearts of men.

---

[458] *PDV* 26.

[459] *EG* 164.

Learning from the Infant Church

When we speak of rediscovering the culture of evangelization in the Church, it is important to note that our quest is not a question of beginning a new culture. Rather, it is more about going back to our roots to rediscover what has always been an important aspect of our history and practice as a Church and then promoting it among our faithful. More specifically, it involves going back to the infant Church of the Acts of the Apostles to see how it operated and flourished in spite of numerous obstacles and persecutions from Judaism and the pagan world.

Clearly, one of the significant characteristics of the early Church was that it was a spirit-filled Church led by spirit-filled leaders. Another is that it was a praying Church (cf. Acts 2:42; 6:2-6). Yet another is that it was an evangelizing Church. The commitment of the leader to the Great Commission of Jesus was total. The proclamation of the Good News to make new converts to Christ was considered to be a priority. This is clear in the statements of the Apostles and Saint Paul. Responding to the problem that arose between the Hellenists and the Jews in the Church with regard to the daily distribution of food, the Apostles remarked:

> It is not right that we should neglect the Word of God to serve at tables. So, friends, choose from among yourselves seven respected men full of the Spirit and wisdom, that we may appoint them to take this task. As for us, we shall give ourselves to prayer and to the ministry of the Word (Acts 6:2-4).

Similarly, those who had been converted and had joined the early Church were exposed to spiritual formation on a continuous basis. They were exposed to the teachings of the Apostles and fellowship, to the breaking of bread and the prayers (see Acts 2:42). On his own part, Saint Paul sees his primary duty as that of proclaiming the Gospel (cf. 1 Cor 1:17) and insists that he is not ashamed to proclaim it because it is Christ's power to save souls. On the basis of this conviction, he maintains:

> I cannot boast of announcing the Gospel: I am bound to do it. Woe to me, if I do not preach the Gospel! If I preached voluntarily, I could expect my reward, but I have

> been trusted with this office against my will. How can I, then, deserve a reward? In announcing the Gospel I will do it freely… So, I made myself all things to all people in order to save, by all possible means, some of them. This I do for the Gospel, so that I too have a share of it (1 Cor 9:15ff).

The point is that the early Christian Church was an evangelizing community where sharing the Gospel was a culture—a normal way of life—among her members rather than an occasional or accidental exercise. As a matter of emphasis, it was not merely an inward-looking community, but overtly an outward-looking community. Reaching the world with the Gospel of Christ in obedience to his command (cf. Mt 28:19; Acts 1:8) was a priority for them. Little wonder, under the guidance of the Holy Spirit, their evangelical mindset and outreach resulted in the Church spreading out to many parts of the world including pagan Rome within a period of about thirty years.[460] In spite of their number, they were so effective in sharing the Good News and witnessing to Christ that their impact was felt in many places in no time (cf. Acts 17:6-7).

The Christian duty to take Christ and his Gospel to the whole world is still the same today. Christ is the same today as he was in the past, and the Gospel Message as well is still the same and is as potent as ever. Even though the circumstances in the contemporary world are different and complex, God's priority for his Church and people remains "to reach out in love to a world that does not know Christ, a world that is immersed in the darkness of atheism, idolatry, modern paganism, occultism, sexual immorality and inordinate self-love, which is capable of destroying the entire mankind. While it is not the case that the Church is not proclaiming the Good News at all, the challenge is the level of commitment and how to get everyone (bishops, priests, religious and the entire laity) to commit faithfully and passionately to this responsibility which arises from our common baptism and confirmation.

[460] W. BARCLAY, *Daily Study Bible – The Acts of the Apostles…, op. cit.*, p. 4.

Forming and Re-orientating Lay People Towards Mission

It is an indubitable fact and common knowledge that the vast majority of Catholics do not share the Gospel with others and that most do not even see it as a duty or priority. In a study carried out in the United States, the members of some churches were asked if sharing the Gospel was a priority. The study showed 76% among the Protestants (including the Pentecostals) responded in the affirmative; 57% among the African churches said yes, whereas only 6% of Catholics responded in the affirmative. The situation is no different among the Catholics in Nigeria and other places. Most of the lay faithful still consider themselves as merely recipients of the priests' ministry of the Word and never see themselves as a people called to share the Gospel.

In truth, this is largely no fault of theirs as they were never sufficiently formed to see the sharing of the Gospel as a personal responsibility from the outset. Besides, the vast majority of them did not grow up in an environment (whether Church or pious associations in the Church or family setting) where the sharing of the Good News was a culture and a priority. Even now that they are being informed of this very important duty, many of them find it difficult to get involved because it has never been part and parcel of their Christian life or DNA and also because they do not even know how to go about it. Scott Hahn captures this well when he states that Catholics are not too experienced when it comes to sharing their faith with other.[461] Perhaps, the exception here will be the charismatics, Legionaries, and the members of the Catholic Biblical Movement of Nigeria. The primary role of the laity in the world in which they live and work is to fulfil their specific mission in the world.

As we have said repeatedly, the vocation and mission of lay people lie outside the Church. Their apostolate has a secular character. Since the Church's mission is to evangelize the world, and lay people who live and work in the secular world have the primary role of evangelizing it, their preparation for mission by the Church is critical. It should be such that empowers them to engage and evangelize

[461] See S. HAHN, *Evangelizing Catholics…*, *op. cit.*, p. 27.

individuals and anti-Christian cultures and structures and all strata of society.[462] As Sherry Weddell maintains, they require a thorough formation that will help them know their dignity as Christians and children of God and to become open to the guidance of the Holy Spirit. It is of great importance that they come to have a profound understanding of the mission of the Church and their own specific mission, the meaning and value of temporal things and the creative application of the teachings of the Church to specific life situations.[463]

Similar to what Pope John Paul II stipulated for the formation of future priests in *Pastores Dabo Vobis*, Weddell is of the view that the formation of lay people should cover areas such as spiritual, intellectual, relational skills, personal evangelization skills, and group and organizational leadership among other things.[464] Given the unique and personal character of the vocation of each individual, each lay person should receive personal direction and formation that will enable him to fulfil his particular mission.[465]

The whole ministry of the priests themselves revolves around the laity. More specifically, "it is to serve the mission of the laity as well as their salvation."[466] For lay people to take on and excel in their evangelizing role the priests need to adjust their thinking or mentality radically in the area of lay formation and empowerment in line with the teaching of the Second Vatican Council. Their interest should not be just to feed or nurture the lay people for their salvation and in the process turning them into mere spectators or consumers of their own ministry. On the contrary, it is absolutely important and in the best interest of the Church and her evangelizing mission to form them to the point of becoming spiritually and

---

[462] S. WEDDELL, *The Parish..., op. cit.*, p. 29.

[463] *Ibid.*, p. 30.

[464] Cf. CL 60; VATICAN COUNCIL II, *Apostolicam Actuositatem*– Decree on the Apostolate of the Laity, promulgated by Pope Paul VI on November 18, 1965, nos. 28-32; Also cited in S. WEDDELL, *The Parish..., op. cit.*, p. 34.

[465] *Ibid.*, p. 34.

[466] S. WEDDELL, *Making Disciples Equipping Apostles: The Parish as a House of Formation for Adult Catholics* (Seattle, WA: The Catherine of Siena Institute Press, 2001), p. 36.

pastorally mature Christians or missionary disciples who live out their personal vocation and, in turn, can feed and nurture other Christians to maturity and help them fulfil their own specific mission in the world.

Without doubt, this calls for a paradigm shift both at the conceptual level and at the practical level in our approach to mission. To create an enabling environment for mission in the Church that will move our parishes from present evangelical passivity to evangelical "militancy" or from *missionlessness* or occasional mission to zeal and intentionality in mission, we urgently need a shift in paradigm. As Weddell asserts, we need to domesticate the rich theology of the Church in this area to become the lived experience of every Catholic, pastors and lay faithful, to the extent that mission becomes the norm for all rather than the exception, especially for the laity. For this paradigm shift to occur in the lay people in our parishes, it must first occur in the minds and actions of the clergy as a whole.[467]

As a matter of fact, as shepherds of God's people in their dioceses, the bishops should be at the forefront of evangelization. They should be the primary promoters of mission in their dioceses as well as drive the necessary change in mindset and attitude on the part of their priests with regard to lay empowerment and active participation in the mission of the Church. They should ensure that mission receives the critical emphasis it deserves in the formation of future priests. Moreover, pastoral activities within their dioceses should aim at awakening in the minds of priests, catechists, pastoral leaders and the lay people as a whole a new consciousness of mission and driving them to massive evangelization in practice.

There is a major area where this consciousness of mission and robust preparation for it is urgently needed. That is the normal catechism class for confirmation candidates in particular. As mentioned earlier, the Church's mission of evangelization is in four stages: witness (pre-evangelization), kerygma (initial proclamation), catechesis (discipleship), and apostleship (mission). Following these processes, a man experiences the exemplary life of a

---

[467] Cf. *Ibid.*, pp. 35-37.

Christian (witness).[468] Then he hears the Good News of salvation in Jesus Christ announced to him in a way that challenges him to believe in him and be converted (i.e., kerygma). The new convert who has encountered and believed in Jesus and now wishes to be like him in character is catechized with the aim of leading him to a deeper conversion and spiritual transformation (catechesis or discipleship). Then this transformed man who has been conformed to Christ in his mindset and character intentionally commits totally to his mission (i.e., apostleship or mission).

In view of this, we can rightly assume that if this process goes well, then everyone who emerges from our catechism classes, especially the confirmation class, should necessarily be a missionary disciple who sees evangelization as a duty and a priority to which he must totally commit. But then, if confirmed Catholics who passed through catechism class for years and have been attending church from childhood still do not know that they have a duty to share the Gospel and are not doing so, it justifies the claim that we are simply "playing" with the sacrament by readily sacramentalizing people who have not been properly evangelized and catechized. Such an action, which can be compared to throwing away our "precious pearls," is clearly not in the best interest of the Church and her evangelizing mission on the one hand and the spiritual and pastoral health of the recipients of the sacraments themselves on the other.

A potential solution I see is to ensure that catechumens, especially those for confirmation and the RCIA/OCIA programme, are properly evangelized before exposing them to catechesis. There is an urgent need for a paradigm shift in our approach to preparing candidates for the sacraments. We cannot continue to put the cart before the horse and expect great results. Catechumens should be taken through the four stages of evangelization step by step. The shift in paradigm requires that we redirect them from sheer religiosity to spirituality and from "mechanical" catechizing to what Pope Francis calls kerygmatic catechesis with discipleship in mind.

---

[468] This first stage may or may not happen depending on the peculiar circumstance that evangelization takes place. But ideally, it is expected that the normal witness of Christians in their day-to-day lives should prepare the ground for the actual proclamation of the kerygma.

This task should be handled by spiritually mature Catholics who have encountered Christ personally, enjoy intimacy with him, and have been properly prepared for the task of teaching and forming people for the sacraments and the Christian life and mission involved. They should labour strenuously to lead the candidates to conviction about Christ, the Christian life and the mission of evangelization and offer them adequate practical training on the apostolate they are expected to carry out with intensity and intentionality, following the reception of the sacrament.

Those who pass through our catechism classes should leave with a clear understanding that they are not just being sacramentalized to fulfil an obligation or satisfy a Church requirement. Instead, they should be convinced that their participation in catechism has a practical (Christian life) dimension as well as a mission dimension and that their reception of the Sacrament of Confirmation in particular (or even marriage) is a form of commissioning to go into the world as missionary disciples of Jesus Christ with a mandate to witness to Christ and share the Gospel everywhere they go.

Popularizing Mission Among Lay Catholics and Lay Organizations

In his time, Jesus lamented the fact that the harvest was plentiful while the labourers were few and asked his followers to pray that the Lord will send workers into his harvest field (Mt 9:37-38). Apart from calling for prayers, he actually undertook to train some men in the task of evangelizing (cf. Lk 9:1-6; 10:1-10, 17-20). The point is that there is power in numbers[469]—in this case, in the number of spiritually mature Christians who can commit intentionally to the evangelizing mission of the Church.

In view of the above, there should be a constant and well-calculated campaign within the Church to remind Catholics that they are called to be missionaries who are expected to take the Gospel

[469] We should take this statement to mean numbers in terms of quality rather quantity. Success is more likely to be achieved and faster too where we have a good number of people who can add value to our work. Having a multitude of people who cannot add value to our work cannot help us much.

to their families, neighborhoods, workplace and similar to convert and lead people to a profound encounter with Christ and intimacy with the Holy Trinity. It is absolutely necessary to build a culture of sharing the Gospel among the entire faithful. This should be a way of life or something normal for Catholics rather than an aberration or something extraordinary.

To facilitate this and make Catholics confident to share the Good News and the Catholic faith, there are a number of things we can do in the parishes. We can promote the new evangelization by identifying and running programmes that can foster re-evangelization and a personal encounter with Jesus Christ. Such will include the Life in the Spirit Seminar, Alpha course in a Catholic context, and Kerygma courses and similar, even though none of these can take the place of intentional disciple-making in the Church. Nonetheless, once a person encounters Christ and enters into an intimate relationship with him, sharing his Gospel becomes easy.

On this note, it is advisable to organize courses on evangelization for the pious associations and other groups in the Church and the entire faithful to emphasize the importance of mission and then train them on how to evangelize or share the Gospel. The evangelization and retraining of our catechists themselves, especially in proclaiming the kerygma powerfully and prayerfully, is very critical to the re-establishment of a culture of evangelization in the Church. This is because an unevangelized catechist can never go beyond a mere transmission of the doctrines of the Church, which is largely inadequate as far as the formation of a mature Catholic Christian is concerned.

Above and beyond, since catechesis is the stage of discipleship, catechists should be discipled or at least exposed to the kerygma and practical evangelization and disciple-making programmes. They should be reconditioned to see themselves not merely as people who catechize others to pass on doctrines or just prepare them solely for the reception of the sacraments. More so, they should see themselves as people who through these authentic doctrines and the sacraments are indeed in the serious business of preparing people for a more authentic Christian life.

This will entail striving hard to lead them to conversion and an intimate communion with God through Christ in the Holy Spirit.

It should be abundantly clear to all catechists that their role is not to produce mere fans of Jesus, but to make real disciples for him who strive to replicate his lifestyle and are totally and intentionally committed to his soul-winning mission and actually prioritize it in their lives as his "militant" foot soldiers.

Parishes can plan an annual evangelization week whereby individuals and societies are sent out to do field evangelization or to fish for souls for Christ. Another way to go about raising the mission consciousness of the lay faithful and achieve success is to encourage societies in the Church to set yearly mission targets for themselves as to the number of new converts they will make as well as the number of former Catholics and non-Catholics they will bring into the Church in a year, and then work hard to accomplish it. This will surely bring intentionality about mission into their lives and their yearly programmes and activities. Besides, this is likely to transform the parish as a real centre of constant missionary outreach as Pope Francis envisages.

On a larger scale, the diocesan bishop or the provincial bishops or the National Conference of Catholic Bishops can consider creating a lay missionary group, such as the Fellowship of Catholic University Students (FOCUS) in the United States. Such a group will cater for the training and sending of young lay missionaries to university campuses and other higher institutions across the country for the purpose of evangelizing and discipling students on campus, although they can also carry out this apostolate in the parishes where necessary.

As I stated before, the lay people who constitute about 99% of the Catholic population need to be trained properly, empowered and sent, that is, unleashed at the "marketplace" for an intensive work of evangelization if we are to make significant progress in this area in today's society and world. This is the way we can wake up the sleeping giant—the Catholic Church.

The Need to Place Mission Above Method

Man is dynamic and so is society. Although the Gospel Message we are called to share is ever the same and our mission to preach it is unchanging, society is never static in people's mode of thinking and ways of acting. The challenge this places before us is that of method. To be specific, How do we present the same Gospel Message that Jesus and the Apostles preached effectively over two thousand years ago to the people of our time and age in a way that will be equally effective? This is a major concern today especially if we consider that there were many things in the past which were mysteries to us but which can now be explained thanks to ongoing scientific discoveries.

A serious mistake some Catholics continue to make is to think that our methods of propagating the Gospel must remain exactly the same in every age in spite of the new realities we have to contend with today. Still, others tend to place method over mission. But the truth is that while the Gospel and the mission to announce it cannot change, the method or approach can always change. Without necessarily implying that every method is acceptable without scrutiny, to emphasize method above mission or insist that method cannot change would be clearly a disservice to both the Gospel and our mission.

Today, if we wish to be more effective in our mission, we need to critically review and revise our methods or approach to evangelization as a whole and catechesis in particular. However, that will not be possible unless we first change how we think. This is because our thinking, to a large extent, shapes or influences our choices and actions. As Napoleon Hill observes, "more gold has been mined from the thoughts of man than has ever been taken from the earth."[470] Similarly, John Maxwell states that "a human mind with the ability to think well is like a diamond mine that never runs out. It's priceless."[471]

Ordinarily, philosophy is a discipline that improves and shapes human thinking. But while we cannot depend only on it to determine the direction to follow in pursuing the Church's mission of winning souls, we need critical thinking to navigate through the contemporary challenges to the Christian faith if we are to succeed in our evangelizing mission. And this we must do while at the same time seeking to know or discern carefully what the Spirit is saying to the Church of our time.

---

[470] See J. MAXWELL, *How Successful People Think…, op. cit.,* p. xi.
[471] *Ibid.*

No matter how intelligent human beings may be, the fact of life is that no one is limitless in knowledge. We all need to keep improving for our own good and that of our institutions or society. John Maxwell recommends an ongoing process that improves our thinking. These include exposure to good ideas or input and good thinkers.[472] Rather than shut ourselves in our own world with the belief that we know it all, we must learn to venture out to see what others are doing and critically appraise it with objectivity. We need to constantly expose ourselves to new ideas and good thinkers and other ways of doing things in a way that is open, critical, and objective.

Employing our philosophical studies to the maximum, we need to develop a progressive habit of asking very fundamental questions. These will include questions, such as: What is our mission? What is the goal of our mission? Are we achieving it today? If yes, what can we do better? And if no, what are we not doing well? What are others doing better that is working for them? Why was the early Church very effective and fruitful in her mission in spite of the many obstacles she faced in Palestine, Rome, and other places? What did the Church of the Golden Age do to be extremely fruitful in her evangelizing mission? How best can we reach and evangelize the people of our time in spite of the prevailing secular culture and seeming coldness towards God and the faith in many places?

More particularly still, we need to ask vital questions, such as: Why are people drifting away from the Catholic Church? What can we do to keep our faithful teeming and bring back those who have drifted away? Are those who come to our churches every week really getting converted and transformed? Are they spiritually fulfilled each time they come? Are they becoming spiritually fruitful or evangelical in their mindset and activities, especially in the world? How can we re-establish the healthy culture of sharing the Gospel in the Church especially among our large population of lay people? How can we Christianize the culture in our society and win our nation for Christ?

[472] Cf. *Ibid.,* xi-xii.

According to John Maxwell, "Big-picture thinkers recognize that they don't know lots of things. They frequently ask penetrating questions to enlarge their understanding and thinking."[473] Furthermore, he asserts that,

> Big-picture thinkers realize there is a world out there besides theirs and they make an effort to get outside of themselves and see other people's world through their eyes. It is hard to see the picture while inside the frame. To see how others see, you must first find out how they think. Becoming a good listener certainly helps with that; so does getting over your personal agenda and trying to take the other person's perspective.[474]

Oftentimes, the failure to step out of our own world, which may arise from fear or lack of interest or over-confidence or even arrogance, can lead to narrow-mindedness and rob us of new ideas or methods that are necessary for growth. To remain unperturbed about the drift of Catholics to other churches or to fail to ask some of these fundamental questions, which are critical to our mission of salvation, is unacceptable and certainly cannot be the mark of good shepherds who truly care about God and his Church. Just like good students aiming at excellence, we must be continually reviewing the progress of our mission, that is, where we should be, where we are, and what we should be doing now to get to where we should be. As a matter of fact, for greater effectiveness and fruitfulness in our evangelizing activities, we should always be on a continuous process of learning and growing and revising our methods, while safeguarding jealously the truth and purity of the Gospel Message we preach.

[473] *Ibid.*, p. 3.
[474] *Ibid.*, p. 4.

Chapter Ten

REDISCOVERING THE CULTURE OF DISCIPLE-MAKING IN THE CHURCH

So far, we have said a lot about stemming the drift of Catholics to Pentecostal churches and spoken extensively of the need for an explosion in the Church in the area of mission. But the truth is this explosion will never happen with the intensity we desire without intentional disciple-making at all levels in the Church. While anyone who has encountered God and experienced his love can evangelize, it is the disciple who has been transformed by Christ and has yielded himself to his Spirit who can freely commit his entire life to the service of the Gospel by way of an intentional, lifelong mission for Christ.

For such a disciple, mission is not an extraordinary or an occasional activity he carries out when he likes. Rather, he is totally committed to it as a personal vocation and a normal day-to-day activity he fulfils. As such, if the Church is serious about raising a multitude of foot soldiers for Christ who will invest in winning souls for him and bring them into the Church, our major project today should be to rediscover disciple-making as a strategy and as a culture in the Church. But before I elaborate on this or go into discipleship proper, it is important to understand the world in which we live today and the concrete situation in which we are expected to carry out our evangelizing and discipling tasks.

The Battle of the Two Opposing Kingdoms and the State of Catholics

The mission of the Church in the world is tasking. It is about establishing the kingdom of God in the world (cf. Mt 6:10-11). It involves leading people out of the kingdom of darkness or of the world into the kingdom of light. This fact presupposes the existence of two opposing kingdoms and thus the battle of two kingdoms—the kingdom of God and the kingdom of the devil, the prince of this world (cf. Jn 12:21; 14:30).

We cannot afford to lose sight of the fact that the Church is at war with the kingdom of darkness. This is not new though. Long ago, Saint Paul warned the Christians of his time about this spiritual warfare raging between the Church and the forces of darkness that are trying to gain control over the world. According to him, "Our battle is not against human forces but against the rulers and authorities and their dark powers that govern the world. We are struggling against the spirits and the supernatural forces of evil..." (Eph 6:12).

Earlier in the Gospel, Saint John the Evangelist tried to draw our attention to the same battle. In the prologue of the fourth Gospel, he writes that in the person of Jesus Christ, the Word of God took flesh and came into the world as light. Then darkness fought against this light to extinguish it but could not (cf. Jn 1:5). Jesus himself warns his disciples about the tension between these opposing kingdoms. He reminds them and indeed all Christians that, although they are in the world, they are not of this world because his choice of them has taken them out of this world. And for that reason, the rulers and people of the world will persecute them on account of their loyalty to him and the Kingdom (see Jn 15:18-21). Speaking about the same warfare in his time, Pope Saint Gregory writes:

> ...my greatest concern has been that the Holy Church, the bride of God, our lady and mother should return to her true glory and stand free, chaste and Catholic. Because this entirely displeased the ancient enemy, he has armed his members against us in order to turn everything upside down. Today, this battle still rages on and the enemy's chief weapon is no longer 'possession of souls' [as some believe] but the spread of false ideologies and ideas that corrupt the mind [and blur the truth] by way of eliminating God from people's minds, exalting man as god, exalting science as a redeemer and leading men to new paganism, secularism, vanity and self-love.[475]

[475] POPE SAINT GREGORY THE GREAT, cited in K. CUSHING,

In more recent times, Cardinal Joseph Ratzinger (later Pope Benedict XVI) acknowledged this raging battle between the forces of darkness and the Church of Christ. Among other things, he maintains that the strategy now involves "an attack on the Church from within."[476] Cardinal Robert Sarah laments the same attack from within when he speaks of false prophets within the priesthood who "do not seek the good of the flock" but who are "mercenaries who have been smuggled into the sheepfold" and are actually doing the work of Judas.[477]

Today, it is a well-documented fact, that when the continuous attempt by the enemies of the Church to destroy her from outside failed, they decided to infiltrate her and destroy it from within.[478] An essential part of their strategy was to corrupt the teachings, morals, and practices of the Church and derail her from her real mission. More precisely, they wanted to remove everything supernatural in Christianity and offer a natural explanation for everything, while at the same time seducing the youth over time "through the corruption of families, books, poems, colleges, gymnasiums, universities, and seminaries."[479]

The revelation by Timothy Marshall clearly supports a revelation by a French Catholic nurse. In the 1960s, she attended to one of the Communist agents planted in the seminary for the priesthood and, following his death, she read a set of the quasi-biographical notes she found on him. Writing about the collaboration and agenda of two professors in the seminary who belonged to the Communist network as himself, the man writes:

> This collaboration, of course, remained secret. The aim of these two men was to rid humanity of all the system

---

Reform and Papacy in the Eleventh Century: Spirituality and Social Change (Manchester and New York: Manchester University Press, 2005), p. 34.

[476] POPE BENEDICT XVI, comment on the Third Secret of Fatima during his visit to Fatima in 2010.

[477] R. SARAH and N. DIAT, *The Day Is Now Far Spent* (San Francisco: Ignatius Press, 2019), p. 17.

[478] Cf. T. MARSHALL, *Infiltration* (Manchester, NH: Crisis Publications, 2019), pp. 9-10.

[479] *Ibid.,* p. 14.

> which it had given itself through the Bible, and especially the New Testament. Thus, the virginity of Mary, the Real Presence of Christ in the Eucharist and his Resurrection, according to them, were to be set aside, in order to end up with complete suppression....All that made this ceremony [that is, the Mass] look like a sacrifice should, little by little, be suppressed. The whole ceremony should represent only a common meal, as among Protestants.[480]

The Overall Situation of the World

As a result of the activities of enemies of the Church—some modernists and the secular humanists—whose goal is to destroy her, secularism, neo-paganism, materialism, atheism, immorality and similar are multiplying by the day, especially in the West. These have led to a situation of growing coldness towards God and the Christian faith in particular.

As we all know, the work of evangelization is a partnership between the Church and the Holy Spirit. If we are not making the desired progress in our mission, it is not because the Gospel itself has become anachronistic and powerless or the Holy Spirit is no longer available or powerful to convert the hearts of men. Rather, the problem lies with some of the leaders of the Church as an institution as well as the baptized Catholics themselves (clergy and lay) who are not fulfilling their role in the evangelizing mission of the Church due to utter loss of focus, ignorance, and downright worldliness.

Perhaps, to be candid, one may dare to state that if the vast majority of baptized and confirmed lay people in the Church are largely inactive and unproductive as far as the Church's mission is concerned it is because this is the prevailing culture in the Church. We have not groomed Catholics to be missionary in their outlook and attitude. On the practical level, the Church has neither formed

[480] M. CARRE, *AA–1025: Memoirs of the Communist Infiltration into the Church* (Charlotte, NC: TAN Books, 1991), pp. 33-34. The book was originally published in May 1972 in French under the title *ES–1025* by Editions Segieb, 78 Freneuse, France.

them into evangelizing disciples nor is she actively sending them out to evangelize.

The vast majority of the laity have not received adequate information, empowerment, and encouragement to embark on intensive work of evangelization everywhere. It is not only that most of them do not know that the Church has a mission called evangelization, but they do not know what the Church has said and is still saying about it.

In fact, when one reflects on the situation among our lay faithful and sometimes many of the clergy from the standpoints of disciple-making and mission, the Scripture passage that readily comes to mind is Ezekiel 37:1-10. In the first part of this passage (that is, verses 1-6), the prophet speaks of the inspiration he received from God. He maintains,

> The hand of the LORD came upon me, and he brought me out by the spirit of the LORD and set me down in the middle of a valley; it was full of bones. He led me all around them; there were very many lying in the valley, and they were very dry. He said to me, "Mortal, can these bones live?" I answered, "O Lord GOD, you know." Then he said to me, "Prophesy to these bones, and say to them: O dry bones, hear the word of the LORD. Thus says the Lord GOD to these bones: I will cause breath to enter you, and you shall live. I will lay sinews on you, and will cause flesh to come upon you, and cover you with skin, and put breath in you, and you shall live; and you shall know that I am the LORD"[481] (Ezekiel 37:1-6).

The above passage best describes the inactive or comatose state in which the overwhelming majority of our lay people and many of the ordained ministers themselves are today as far as discipleship and mission are concerned. Continuing, the prophet writes,

> So I prophesied as I was commanded; and as I prophesied, there was a thundering noise and behold, a shaking and trembling and a rattling, and the bones came together, bone to its bone. And I looked and behold, there were

[481] See the NRSV.

> sinews upon the bones and flesh came upon them and skin covered them over, but there was no breath or spirit in them. Then said he to me, "Prophesy to the breath and spirit, son of man, and say to the breath and spirit, thus says the Lord God: Come from the four winds, O breath and spirit, and breathe upon these slain that they may live." So I prophesied as he commanded and the breath and spirit came into the bones, and they lived and stood up upon their feet, an exceedingly great army (Ezekiel 37:7-10).[482]

The key point in this passage is the transformation of dry and inactive bones to a great and immense army from their comatose state. In truth, that is simply the miracle that the Church needs today. From the mission standpoint, most of our baptized and confirmed Catholics are like the dry and inactive bones in Ezekiel's prophecy. The Sacrament of Confirmation makes us soldiers of Christ. In general, soldiers in ancient times defended their territories against every foreign invasion or attack and also conquered new territories to bring them under the rule of the emperor and the Roman Empire.

This also applies to us as soldiers of Christ even though our weapons of warfare are spiritual weapons to convert hearts. But the sad reality is that in practice most of us—clergy and laity—do not understand our identity and vocation as soldiers of Christ or appreciate our power as Christian soldiers or the mission which arises from it. We do not seem to understand that the battle for souls is raging on in the world and that there are souls to rescue. It appears that the average Catholic is oblivious of the fact that, by virtue of his baptism and confirmation, he is God's chosen instrument or a soldier of the kingdom called to join the battle to rescue or win souls for Jesus Christ or conquer new territories for him.

This has a serious negative implication for the Church and her mission in the world. Although she ought to be a giant and operate as a giant, the dearth of spiritually mature members or disciples with a strong mission consciousness who willingly embark on in-

---

[482] *Ibid.*

tensive missionary activities has reduced her to a sleeping giant or at best a shadow of herself.

The Four Components of the Great Commission of Jesus

The Great Commission of Jesus Christ in Matthew 28:19-20 favours disciple-making in the Church. The Commission has four main components, which are: Go, Make disciples, Baptize them, and Teach them. I shall explain them briefly.

Go: The first command "to go" implies going out to proclaim the Good News of salvation in Jesus Christ. The goal of this proclamation is always conversion. It is to convert people to God through Christ. The command highlights the missionary nature of the Church. It reminds us that the Church is a "sent Church" and by nature a "going Church," not a static one. The mission field is not just the four walls of our churches, but the marketplace—that is, the "whole" world. A critical thing to underline here is that we are sent to the world, and not the world to us. Hence, to wait for the world to come to us is a clear misconception of our mission as Church or disciples. It is like a fisherman waiting at home for the fish to leave the sea and come to him.

Additionally, this first command reminds us that mission is not optional for the Church or the Christian, but a command. The primary motive behind it is love—God's love for the salvation of mankind (cf. Jn 3:16). So, our own impetus for mission should be love—our love of God and our love for the salvation of souls. Just as God loved us so much and came down to save us, we too must make sacrifices and go out in search of the lost to lead them to God.

Make Disciples: The second component of the Great Commission is "make disciples." Simply put, we are not just to bring people into the Church and give them the sacraments. As Pope Paul VI states, "The role of evangelization is precisely to educate people in the faith in such a way as to lead each individual Christian to live the sacraments as true sacraments of faith–and not to receive them passively or reluctantly."[483] Normally, the sacraments

---

[483] *EN* 47.

are supposed to be a ritualisation of Christian maturity, which is why the Church has a duty to lead people to Christian maturity prior to administering some of the sacraments, such as confirmation, holy orders, and holy matrimony. In actual sense, the title of this chapter is Rediscovering the Culture of Disciple-Making in the Church. This makes this second component of the commission of Jesus our primary focus in this chapter. Hence, I shall leave it until later when I hope to give it the attention it deserves.

Baptize Them: The third component of the commission is "baptize them." This baptism is what (that is, the sacrament) incorporates the new convert into the Body of Christ—the Church. It is done in the name of the Blessed Trinity—Father, Son, and Holy Spirit. This implies that the baptized is grafted into the divine life of the Trinity and becomes an adopted son or daughter of God and an heir with Christ to the Kingdom of the Father. Interestingly too, baptism makes all the baptized sharers in the mission of Christ.

Teach Them: The last component of the Great Commission is "teach them." Just as they were taught and formed by the Master himself, the disciples must continue to teach and form the new converts and in fact the entire believing community on an ongoing basis. The contents of their teaching are not their personal views or opinions but what they themselves have been taught. The primary purpose of this teaching is not merely the acquisition of knowledge about Christ and the Kingdom, but obedience to Christ. In actual sense, it is this consistent obedience that leads to a personal transformation in the life of the individual and makes him Christlike in character.

Although all the four components of the Great Commission are very important, the command to "make disciples" can be said to be the most critical. This is because all the other three commands support the command to make disciples.[484] Perhaps, this explains why Jesus concentrated more on making disciples rather than ministering to the crowd all the time.

[484] Cf. J. PUTMAN et al., *Real-Life Discipleship Training Manual* (Colorado Springs: NavPress, 2010), p. 10.

What Is Discipleship? – Understanding Who Is a Disciple

If the command to make disciples is the most critical command in the Great Commission and is essential to the overall success of the Church's mission in the world, it is pertinent to understand the term. This is our main concern in this section and some of the questions we need to answer here include: Who is a disciple? Is there a distinction between a Christian and a disciple? And so on.

Is There a Distinction between a Christian and a Disciple?

Ordinarily, in the New Testament understanding of the word, "disciple" refers primarily to a Christian. The two terms were synonymous. As Clarence Drummond maintains, "to be a Christian is to be a disciple."[485] On this ground, one would assume that every Christian should be a disciple of Christ in practice. This was mostly the case in the early years of Christianity. In the Acts of the Apostles the people of Antioch identified the disciples of Jesus as Christians (see Acts 11:26). They were not just Christians in name, but also in deed or in their lifestyle. Listening to their proclamation and observing their way of life, the people identified them as followers of Jesus and his ways and called them Christians.

In our time, things are not exactly the same. Although in theory, many are undeniably Christians because they are baptized or still "believe" in Christ and go to church, the truth is that they may not be converted even in the most basic sense of the word and cannot be said to be true Christians from the practical standpoint.[486]

---

[485] C. DRUMMOND, in remarks given during a Georgia Baptist Convention conference, cited in D. ROGERS, "What Is Your Understanding of Biblical Discipleship?" Section 1: Focus on Your Current Discipleship Strategy, April 15, 2008, p. 1. See https://d.docecity.com/discipleship-guide-08-what-is-your-understanding-of-biblical.html.

[486] Today there are many baptized people who are "Christians" and active church-goers but are pagans in their mindset and behaviour. Still, there are others who are sacramentarians who belong to secret cults. We cannot say they are not Christians since they were validly baptized. Certainly, they are not disciples because the allegiance of the disciple is to Christ alone.

Put differently, they are Christians in name but not in their worldview or deeds.

This explains why such Christians are not changing their environments and the world, and why some writers have come to introduce a distinction between a "Christian" and a "disciple."[487] It is in this light that Putman and others maintain that, "Today, almost all our Churches are full of 'Christians' but not disciples."[488] Similarly, Chambers maintains that since "to be a disciple is to be a devoted bondservant motivated by love for the Lord Jesus," many Christians are not disciples because they are not truly devoted to him.[489] While such a distinction between a "Christian" and a "disciple" may be difficult to defend theoretically, I believe it is safer to make a distinction between a "true Christian" who is also a "true disciple" on the one hand and a "Christian in name but not in deed" who is neither a "true Christian" nor a "true disciple" in practice.[490]

Nonetheless, for those who make such a distinction, two things distinguish a disciple from the regular Christian. These are "the desire to replicate the life of Jesus" and "total commitment to his mission." What this also implies is that even a person who actually strives to live a holy (Christian) life but is not committed to the

---

[487] Perhaps one may say that the term "disciple" refers to one who can be called a "real Christian" because he strives to live the life of Jesus and is committed to his mission.

[488] Cf. J. PUTMAN, B. HARRINGTON, with R. COLEMAN, *DiscipleShift* (Grand Rapids, MI: Zondervan, 2013), p. 31.

[489] Cf. O. CHAMBERS, *My Utmost for His Highest: Selections for Every Day*, see "The Conditions of Discipleship," July 2nd. He maintains that such a passionate love and devotion to Jesus Christ is the gift of the Holy Spirit.

[490] What makes the difference here is the introduction of the word "true" to qualify a disciple as a Christian in word and in deeds, that is, one who is faithful to his Christian calling and mission. Even when we speak of true Christians or true disciples as those baptized people who are actually devoted to Christ and the Christian faith and mission, the truth remains that the level of devotedness for everyone cannot be at the same level at any given time. But then, it is still possible to talk about a basic level of devotedness to Christ and his mission that is acceptable.

mission of Christ falls short of the definition of a true disciple of Christ.[491]

What Is Discipleship or Who Is a Disciple?

In Greek, the word "disciple" means a learner or an apprentice. It implies the acceptance of the views and practices of the teacher, not only in the mind, but also in life.[492] The word "disciple" is extremely important in the Bible. For instance, while the word "Christian" occurs about three times in the entire New Testament, the word "disciple" occurs at least about 269 times, depending on the translation we are using. In general, a disciple is the follower of a particular teacher or a student or learner in the sense of an apprentice who learns from his master in order to become like him some day.

In Christianity, the term "discipleship" is mainly used in connection with Jesus Christ. It is an invitation into apprenticeship, that is, to be an apprentice of Jesus. According to Oswald Chambers, "discipleship means personal, passionate devotion to a Person—our Lord Jesus Christ."[493] A disciple primarily refers to a committed follower of Jesus Christ. A Christian disciple is one—a cleric or a lay person—who acknowledges the Lordship of Jesus Christ over his life and goes forth in the power of his Spirit to imitate his lifestyle, to imbibe his principles and vision and identify with his mission. He is not merely a fan of Jesus who professes faith in him[494] and goes to church like many Christians of today, but he is a committed or devoted follower who obeys Christ in everything and is actively engaged in his mission.

---

[491] A disciple does not merely try to replicate the life of Christ, but also, he is totally and intentionally committed to his mission as a lifelong duty.

[492] See THE ADVOCATE OF TRUTH, "Four Conditions of Discipleship," in sabbathreformation.com, November 19, 2020.

[493] O. CHAMBERS, *My Utmost for His Highest…, op. cit.*

[494] Here, I mean one who professes faith in Jesus verbally without any commitment to his principles or teachings and mission.

What Discipleship Entails and Its Purpose

To be a true disciple of Jesus Christ is to become like him. More specifically, as Bobby Harrington and Alex Absalom assert, it "is to become increasingly like Jesus in our character as we reflect the attractiveness of his personality."[495] Hence, discipleship involves changes at the different levels. These are the head-level change, the heart-level change, and the hand-level change.[496]

The first change that occurs in the disciple is the head-level change. In Matthew 4:19, Jesus invites the first disciples to follow him. According to Robby Gallaty, "[This call] 'Follow me!' was personal. It was something more than a call to study; it was a call to a person. He invited the disciples into a distinct relationship with him."[497] What this call tells us about discipleship is that it involves a head-level change. This refers to the change that occurs in the mind of the individual. As he encounters Jesus and comes under his direction, he experiences change in his mentality over time. He drops his own worldview and embraces that of Christ. In other words, his thinking or perception of life in general is influenced by Christ and the principles of his Gospel.

The second change that occurs in the disciple is the heart-level change. Jesus says, "*I will make you* fishers of men." This change refers to the transformation that takes place in the character of the individual. Dying to his own worldview and embracing only that of Christ, his attitudes and priorities in life begin to change. Jesus gradually transforms him in his character to conform him more to himself. That is to say, he begins to make him into someone different.[498] This change itself is supernatural and does not happen instantly. Rather, it takes time—a long time of consistently relating closely with Jesus with complete openness and a willingness to

---

[495] B. HARRINGTON and A. ABSALOM, *Discipleship That Fits* (Grand Rapids, MI: Zondervan, 2016), p. 27.

[496] J. PUTMAN et al., *Real-Life Discipleship Training Manual…, op.cit.*, pp. 30-37.

[497] R. GALLATY, *Rediscovering Discipleship* (Grand Rapids, MI: Zondervan, 2015), p. 79.

[498] Cf. J. PUTMAN et al., *Real-Life Discipleship…, op. cit.*, p. 33.

grow and become like him. Again, Gallaty captures the nature and process of such growth when he states,

> "Becoming" is a long process that Jesus brings about in our lives over time. It's not an instantaneous gift, but the result of an extended, intimate relationship that develops over time. Jesus is the originator of the action. We cannot grow in him on our own, but we can align ourselves with him, so that he may grow us. We can put ourselves in a position to experience the abundant, victorious life that God has envisioned for us. This is the essence of what we refer to as "discipleship."[499]

The third change that occurs in the disciple is the hand-level change. Jesus says, "I will make you *fishers of men*" (cf. Mt 4:19). This refers to the change that occurs in the individual in the area of mission. At this level, the disciple who now shares the worldview and vision of Christ for humanity becomes totally committed to his mission as a matter of intentionality and life and death. Like the Master, he develops a heart for lost souls and out of love and obedience to his command, he commits his entire life and devotes his talents, spiritual gifts, learned skills, life experiences and similar to mission.[500] In a way, Jesus made this abundantly clear to his disciples the very moment he called them (see Mt 4:19). He planted in them a spiritual multiplication agenda by clearly telling them that they will be made into fishers of men. Gallaty captures this point very well when he writes,

> From the very beginning, starting with his initial call, Jesus implanted the seed of multiplication within the hearts of his disciples. Jesus didn't call them to come [and just] sit on a pew, and listen to a pastor preach. His call was to fish, to cast for others. Jesus had it in his heart for you to go out and make disciples among the nations. Do you see the difference? It is a focus outward, toward others. It's another reminder that the Christian life is not about you or

---

[499] R. GALLATY, *Rediscovering Discipleship…, op. cit.,* p. 80; See also J. PUTMAN et al., *Real-Life Discipleship…, op. cit.,* p. 33.

[500] Cf. J. PUTMAN et al., *Real-Life Discipleship…, op. cit.,* p. 37.

> me. *The gospel has come to us because it is heading to someone else.* We are just another link in the chain, and each of us is either fumbling the handoff or passing the baton.[501]

From all we have said, it is possible to establish the real purpose of discipleship in the Church. According to Dennis Rogers, the discipleship and family-ministry specialist for the Georgia Baptist Convention, "Christian discipleship is a lifelong journey of obedience to Christ that spiritually transforms a person's values and behavior and results in ministry in one's home, Church, and the world."[502] The key words here are "becoming like Christ in character and commitment to his mission." Simply put, the goal of discipleship is to become Christlike and be zealous to see others become disciples also.[503] In other words, it is "to be conformed into the image of Christ"[504] and be totally committed to formation of spiritually mature and qualified workers for Christ who also live out the authentic Christian life.[505] Thus, the whole process of disciple-making entails leading people to Christ and then going ahead to help them grow and develop into strong, robust, mature, dedicated, and fruitful disciples who can replicate the whole process of creating other disciples.

The list by Dennis Rogers regarding what we can call the core foundations of biblical discipleship will help us understand Christian discipleship better.[506] According to him, Christian discipleship

[501] R. GALLATY, *Rediscovering Discipleship…, op. cit.,* p. 84.

[502] D. ROGERS, "What Is Your Understanding of Biblical Discipleship…, *op. cit.,* p. 1.

[503] *Ibid.*

[504] R. GALLATY, *Rediscovering Discipleship…, op. cit.,* p. 79. As Gallaty maintains, to be conformed into the image of Christ means that the individual begins to talk the way Christ talked, walk the way he walked, and respond the way he responded. This begins with an unshakeable allegiance to Jesus which implies that only a believer in Christ can be a disciple. In other words, a non-believer will need to be evangelized first before he can enter this phase of Christian growth.

[505] Cf. L. EMIS, *The Lost Art of Disciple Making* (Grand Rapids, MI: Zondervan Publishing House, 1978), pp. 12, 17.

[506] D. ROGERS, "What Is Your Understanding of Biblical Disciple-

does not happen in a day. Rather, it is a journey which is progressive in nature. It involves the ongoing transformation of a person to become Christlike in character and purpose as he grows in intimacy with Christ over time.[507] It addresses every aspect of the person's life to get him to do the right things always for the right reason. Although man's cooperation is required, the ongoing transformation that takes place in discipleship is essentially the work of grace. In other words, it is only the Holy Spirit who transforms a person and makes him fruitful.

Furthermore, Christian discipleship is both inward and outward-looking in the sense that it does not merely focus on personal holiness, but also on service to others. That is to say, it always manifests itself in service or ministry to others to make them into disciples who make other disciples. Jesus modeled it to be spiritually reproductive by its very nature. So, a Christian disciple invests his time, his experience, and his life and similar to make converts and nurture them to Christian maturity. Finally, Christian discipleship is centered in the life of a local church where the faith and fellowship of other disciples will encourage, teach, and safeguard the discipleship process of those being discipled.[508]

Discipleship is Tasking, but Rewarding

The best strategy to form the evangelized and transform them into a great army of mature Catholics who invest in evangelizing and nurturing others to Christian maturity is discipleship. Disciple-making is a tasking but rewarding venture. Following the four stages of evangelization in the Church, catechesis is the stage for discipleship. But in truth, catechists cannot disciple catechumens from the usual once-a-week catechism class of two hours.

Similarly, discipleship is not something that is accomplished through the pulpit or homilies at Mass. Priests cannot disciple their parishioners from the pulpit during Sunday Mass. Not even the best preachers in the world can achieve this feat. Perhaps, great

---

ship…, *op. cit.,* p. 1.

[507] This growth in intimacy with Christ is critical to discipleship.

[508] D. ROGERS, "What Is Your Understanding of Biblical Discipleship…, *op. cit.,* pp. 4-5.

preachers might be able to proclaim the kerygma from the pulpit and convert people, but maturing their faith and building them into intentional and committed Christians or disciples is a different thing altogether. The fact that Jesus spent about 70% of his time discipling twelve men shows that we cannot disciple a crowd. LeRoy Eims is very clear about this when he writes,

> Disciples cannot be mass produced. We cannot drop people into "programs" or material or some other thing and see disciples emerge at the end of the production line. It takes time to make disciples. It takes individual, personal attention. It takes hours of prayer for them. It takes patience and understanding to teach them how to get into the Word of God for themselves, how to feed and nourish their souls, and by the power of the Holy Spirit how to apply the word to their lives and it takes being an example to them of all of the above.[509]

Being a form of apprenticeship, disciple-making requires much time and energy. Strictly speaking, it requires presence, that is, being personally available to those in the discipleship training on a regular basis and giving them personal attention. As Robby Gallaty puts it, "Learning from a rabbi [in the past] involved more than merely sitting in a classroom and listening to his words."[510] Moreover, according to Ann Spanglar and Lois Tverberg quoted by Gallaty,

> It [discipleship or learning from the rabbi] involved a literal kind of following, in which the disciples often traveled with, lived with, and imitated their rabbis, learning not only from what they said, but from what they did—from their reactions to everyday life as well as the manner in which they lived. The task of the disciple was to become as much like the rabbi as possible.[511]

---

[509] L. EIMS, *The Lost Art of Disciple Making…, op. cit.*, pp. 45-46.

[510] R. GALLATY, *Rediscovering Discipleship…, op. cit.*, p. 36.

[511] A. SPANGLER and L. TVERBERG, *Sitting at the Feet of Rabbi Jesus: How the Jewishness of Jesus Can Transform Your Faith* (Grand Rapids, MI: Zondervan, 2009), p. 51; See also R. GALLATY, *Rediscovering Discipleship…, op. cit.*, p. 36.

The implication from the above is that discipleship involves more than words or homilies. In practice, it involves many things. One area is the Sacred Scriptures. It involves training the candidates on how to study the Word of God (the Bible) on a regular basis and get something out of their personal study through the help of the Holy Spirit. The training encompasses helping them to develop the virtue or ability to apply the fruit of their study to their day-to-day lives for their own spiritual growth. It equally includes how to memorize the Word of God and store it in their spiritual blood stream through meditation so that it is available to the Holy Spirit to remind them wherever it is needed.[512]

Further, discipleship requires training the candidates in prayer in general. This will include how to do Eucharistic adoration, how to approach worship, especially the Holy Mass, with deep faith and understanding and participate in it meaningfully in a way that will foster a personal and life-changing encounter with God, ongoing spiritual transformation, fruitfulness, and commitment to mission. Similarly, in addition to other forms of prayer, the discipler should also train them in the art of meditation, which is absolutely critical to spiritual growth.

Discipleship also entails teaching the candidates how to hear and clearly discern the voice of God and respond to it. It equally involves training them on how to go to a fruitful confession and more importantly how to overcome sin and pursue virtue. A major aspect of the training is on pursuing sainthood or holiness of life, which in itself involves forming them to become sensitive to the Holy Spirit and yielding themselves completely to him. In general, discipleship training should lead them to the discovery of their talents and spiritual gifts and equip them for service or stewardship in the Church. Importantly, discipleship training should necessarily equip them for their evangelizing mission. Among other things, it should train them to constantly hold themselves accountable as far as their own spiritual growth and commitment to mission are concerned.

---

[512] L. EIMS, *The Lost Art of Disciple Making…*, *op. cit.*, p. 21.

Although the ministry of making disciples takes time and effort as we have seen, the results are lasting and worth the investment.[513] Indeed, disciple-making is a very rewarding enterprise. It is not only rewarding for the disciple but also the disciple-maker and the Church as a whole, considering the missionary work the disciple will eventually undertake on behalf of the Church. As LeRoy Eims observes, "When you start spending individual time with another Christian for the purpose of having a ministry in his or her life—time together in the word, prayer, fellowship, systematic training—something happens in your own life as well."[514]

The Conditions for Christian Discipleship

Although a large crowd followed Jesus in the course of his ministry, he was more interested in quality than quantity as far as discipleship was concerned. Considering the enormity of the task ahead and the sacrifice involved, he outlined the requirements for becoming his disciple. We can find this in Luke 14:25-33 and Matthew 10:37-38. What is at stake in discipleship is the issue of one's ultimate loyalty. Should it be to oneself or one's family or other humans or money or possessions? In other words, becoming Jesus' disciple comes at a price. In fact, it will cost us everything, and perhaps including our lives. The conditions enumerated are summarized below.

The first is that whoever "does not hate father and mother, wife and children, brothers and sisters" cannot be his disciple (Lk 14:25). Here, Jesus is not really proposing that his followers should hate their close family members or any other person for that matter because in the first place the faith he established is rooted in love (cf. Jn 13:34-35; 15:12-13). Actually, his Word becomes clearer when we read it side by side in Matthew 10:37, where he says, "He who loves the father or mother more than me is not worthy of me...." In essence, what Jesus demands is the reordering of our priorities in life.

In the course of following him, there will always arise a clash between loyalty to him and the principles of his Gospel and loyalty

---

513 Cf. *Ibid.,* p. 46.

514 *Ibid.,* p. 26.

to other human beings—our family, friends, bosses, associations and similar. Jesus insists on the priority of a relationship with him over any other relationship.[515] As Oswald Chambers puts it, "If the closest relationship of a disciple's life conflict with the claims of Jesus Christ, then our Lord requires instant obedience to Himself."[516] The prospective disciple's love and relationship with him should surpass or must be prioritized over all other relationships.[517] He must love Jesus supremely. Jesus and no other must always come first in his life in all circumstances.

Secondly, Jesus says that his prospective disciple should be willing to die to self (see Lk 14:26; Mt 10:39). The most powerful instinct of man is self-preservation. Self-love is so strong that it can actually be said to be the real root of evil in the world. No doubt, there are people who can sacrifice their families, friends and other human relationships to attain certain goals or inordinate ambitions in life, such the acquisition of wealth, fame, and political office. But then, self-preservation will make it extremely unattractive for them to involve themselves in any venture that will cost them their lives.

On the contrary, "A disciple sees Jesus as better than life itself."[518] For this reason, Jesus insists that his prospective disciples must value following him more than life itself. He must love the Master more than his own life and place his mission above everything else—his life or any personal ambition or agenda (cf. Mt 10:39). Put differently, he must be willing to sacrifice his own life to save his relationship with Jesus. What this entails is that he should have the right intention for following Jesus. This should be to know, love, and serve God intimately and help others know him and live in right relationship with him through Christ in the Holy Spirit.

---

[515] Cf. D. ROGERS, "What Is Your Understanding of Biblical Discipleship…, *op. cit.*, p. 2.

[516] O. CHAMBERS, *My Utmost for His Highest…*, *op. cit.*

[517] See B. HARRINGTON and A. ABSALOM, *Discipleship That Fits…*, *op. cit.*, p. 36.

[518] Cf. *Ibid.*

Additionally, Jesus states that the would-be disciple should carry his cross and follow him (cf. Lk 14:27; Mt 10:38). For today's Christians, the cross is a symbol of life and victory. It reminds us of Christ's victory over Satan and death and the restoration of the divine life to mankind. But this was not the case in the time of Jesus. Then the cross was a symbol of a most degrading form of humiliation, shame, defeat, and death reserved for criminals by the Romans. Discipleship comes with its own challenges and the disciple must be ready to endure trials, persecution, loneliness, suffering and even give up his life for Christ and his mission.

Even though being a disciple of Jesus comes with a great reward, it involves openness to potential martyrdom should that become necessary or inevitable to prove one's complete loyalty to him. Moreover, it requires an ongoing sacrifice of oneself and one's interest each step of the way in favour of one's commitment to Christ. The disciple must bear all things for the sake of Christ. Just like Jesus who sought to please the Father even to the point of submitting to a shameful death on the Cross (cf. Jn 4:34; Phil 2:7-8), his ultimate desire or ambition must not be to save or please himself. Rather, he must see pleasing Jesus and the Father as the most compelling or supreme motive of his life on earth.[519]

Thirdly, the commitment of a prospective disciple must be a long-term commitment. In reference to his would-be disciples, Jesus states that anyone who puts a hand to the plow and looks back is not fit for the kingdom of God (cf. Lk 9:62). In other words, discipleship should be for the whole of life and not only when things are conducive for the individual. As Rogers asserts, "Jesus' call to follow him is never meant for an interim period of time, but it is always an invitation for one to commit the whole of life for all of life."[520] This is why he wants us to count the cost before making a decision to follow him.

Finally, Jesus says that no one can be his disciple if he does not give up all his possessions (see Lk 14:33). This does not imply that

---

[519] B. DEFFINBAUGH, "Discipleship: Its Requirement and Its Rewards," bible.org, June 2, 2004, https://bible.org/seriespage/17-discipleship-its-requirements-and-its-rewards.

[520] D. ROGERS, "What Is Your Understanding of Biblical Discipleship…, *op. cit.*, p. 3.

a prospective disciple cannot be rich, but it certainly implies that he should be free from worldly attachments. He should be totally committed to Jesus and love more than he loves money and possessions. This demand is critical because love of money or attachment to material possessions can be a serious obstacle to mission and faithfulness to the principles of the Gospel. They can condemn the individual to slavery whereby he becomes possessed by what he has or by his inordinate longing for material wealth and possessions.

Importance of Discipleship to Jesus and His Mission

The mission of Jesus was to reach all men with the Good News of salvation. He saw the key to the overall success of that mission, not only in his own ministry and his eventual death and resurrection for the salvation of mankind, but also in disciple-making. During the three and a half years he spent carrying out his ministry, he trained twelve men because they will be extremely vital to the success of his mission to the ends of the world. As Emis puts it, "The future of Christian [the faith Jesus established], humanly speaking rose or fell on the ministry of these men."[521]

He took time to train and release them into ministry through a four-step process. First, he ministered to them in private and also in public along with the crowd. They observed him closely, listened to him, and learned from him in the process. Second, he allowed them to assist him in ministry (cf. Jn 6:1-13). Third, he allowed them to do ministry themselves with his assistance (cf. Mk 9:14-29). And lastly, he sent them out to go and minister to others, thereby putting into practice what they had learnt from him (see Mt 10:5-15; Lk 9:1-6).

In actual sense, discipleship was so crucial to Jesus that he saw the making of the twelve disciples as a major achievement in his ministry. We can clearly deduce this from his priestly prayer in the Gospel according to Saint John. In the prayer, he declares, "Father, glorify me.... I have finished the work you gave me to do" (Jn 17:1-19).[522] Although he came to die to save mankind and the

---

[521] L. EMIS, *The Lost Art of Disciple Making...*, *op. cit.*, p. 38.

[522] See Jn 17:4 in particular.

Cross was central to his mission, what makes this statement quite remarkable is that he made it prior to his death and resurrection.[523] Also remarkable is the fact that he did not cite his numerous miracles but rather focused on the men he had discipled, who having received his teaching and having been equipped as disciples would now be sent into the world to disciple others.[524]

According to LeRoy Eims, "When you read the prayer [Jesus' prayer in John 17] carefully, you will notice that he did not mention miracles or multitudes, but forty times he referred to the men whom God had given him out of the world. These men were his work. His ministry touched thousands, but he trained twelve men. He gave his life on the cross for millions, but during three and half years of His ministry He gave his life uniquely to twelve men,"[525] that is, the Apostles, even though he had other disciples who had followed him from the baptism of John until the resurrection.

The Need for Intentional Discipleship in the Church

As Saint Thomas Aquinas observes, "man longs for two things above all: the knowledge of truth and the continuance of his existence."[526] Focusing on truth, the Catholic Church does not deny that other faiths and denominations possess a certain amount of truth about God. Rather, she teaches that she possesses the fullness of truth as far as what has been revealed is concerned and that the Church of Christ subsists in its fullness in the Roman Catholic communion and nowhere else.[527] There is absolutely no doubt about that. But then, this creates a huge responsibility for her to make that truth known to all.

The summary of this truth is that God loves mankind so much that he sent his only begotten Son, Jesus Christ, to die for us so

---

[523] J. PUTMAN et al., *Real-Life Discipleship Training Manual…, op. cit.*, p. 19.

[524] Cf. *Ibid.*

[525] L. EMIS, *The Lost Art of Disciple Making…, op. cit.*, p. 28.

[526] SAINT THOMAS AQUINAS, "Commentary on St. John's Gospel, Chapter 14, Reading 2." See Office of the Reading of Saturday, Week 9.

[527] See *LG* 8.

that all who believe in him will be saved (see John 3:16). Hence, the Good News is that in Jesus Christ salvation is offered to all mankind. Every individual has a right to hear this truth while the Church and Christians in general have a duty to proclaim it everywhere without bounds. This is where the words of Saint Paul are apt. In the Letter to the Romans, he writes: "And how are they to hear without someone to proclaim him? And how are they to proclaim him unless they are sent?" (Rom 10:14-15).

During the Amazon Synod held at the Vatican in 2019, one of the reasons some of the bishops from the Amazon region gave for the rapid growth of the Pentecostal churches in the region was the availability of manpower. Unlike the Catholic Church where there was a shortage of priests, the Pentecostals had enough personnel to minister to the spiritual needs of the people.

This issue of the shortage of priests is a problem in many dioceses all over the world. Indeed, the priests in many of our urban parishes in Nigeria are overworked. Even if they wish to, they cannot do everything by themselves. They too are human beings and sometimes find themselves in the same challenging situation as Moses who was overstretched by his ministry to the people of Israel (see Ex 18:1-24).

As human beings, priests need time to refresh and build themselves up spiritually both for their own spiritual health or salvation and that of the people under their care. They need help to reach their teeming parishioners and cater to their numerous spiritual and pastoral needs. They need help to build spiritually and pastorally vibrant and fruitful parishes. Moreover, they need help to reach those outside the Church and evangelize them and we cannot delude ourselves that these men who are less than 1% of our population can meet all these needs by themselves.

For them to be very effective in their work, they need spiritually qualified men and women who can evangelize the communities around them and attend to some of the spiritual and pastoral needs of other parishioners. Here, we are thinking of spiritually mature Catholics (disciples) who can commit totally to the spiritual growth of these others. Put differently, we are talking of disciples who can take great joy in leading them to Christ and nurturing them to spiritual maturity by the example of their own Christian lives and by way of regular and systematic sharing of the Gospel with them, ongoing fellowship, and a personal training in discipleship, prayer, and the spiritual life.

We should always remember that the work of evangelization which is entrusted to the Church is meant for all and not the clergy alone. It is a fact that the unevangelized cannot evangelize others while the undiscipled who are not mature in the faith cannot possibly disciple others. Besides, the areas to be covered in evangelization are so wide and the clergy and religious alone cannot reach everybody. To add to this, the success of the Church's mission lies at the "marketplace" where the lay people live and work. So, everyone and not just the clergy needs training[528] for us to have availability of spiritually mature Catholics who can collaborate with the pastors in evangelization, whether we are speaking of mission *ad gentes* or new evangelization or pastoral care. This is possible through disciple-making.

Discipleship is one thing that ties all the other recommendations in this book together. Although it is a tedious task that takes time to realize and have the desired impact, it remains the game changer and the real key to exponential growth in the Church. The Teacher and Master himself knew that, and it was his strategy for Church growth both in terms of quality and quantity. Some call it the principle of spiritual multiplication in the Church.[529] Now, if disciple-making was of utmost importance to Jesus Christ, it should be equally important to the Church that he established to further his mission on earth.

As we have already noted with emphasis, sacramentalizing the unconverted and undiscipled has not helped us much as a Church with a mission to fulfil, and it is not likely to do so now that the secular culture is taking deeper root in the hearts of the people of our generation. So, the Church needs to invest consciously in the proper discipling of the vast multitude of her lay people who form over 99% of her population. She needs to make readily available

---

[528] Cf. L. EIMS, *The Lost Art of Disciple Making…, op. cit.*, p. 24.

[529] Cf. C. MARTINS, "White Paper–Making Missionary Disciples," Fellowship of Catholic University Students (FOCUS), Denver, Colorado, 2017, p. 10.

an army of spiritually mature and zealous Catholics—an army of intentional (missionary) disciples—and send them to the secular world to win souls for Christ and nurture them to Christian maturity. Once we rediscover this winning strategy and successfully implement it in our parishes, it will not only stem the drift of Catholics to other churches, but it will also lead to a huge success in our mission as a whole.

Interestingly, the Great Commission favours disciple-making and the Catholic Church as an institution needs to reappraise her commitment and that of her members to the totality of the Great Commission, especially the command to "make disciples." Disciple-making is necessary in the Church, not only for the clergy, but also for lay people in view of their apostolate or specific mission in the world. In fact, the call to review our commitment is absolutely necessary. This is to ensure that the quality of catechesis in our parishes achieves its goal of transformation and to adequately prepare lay people to accept their vocation to be salt and light in the world (cf. Mt 5:13-16) and fulfil their mission wholeheartedly. Without intentional discipleship, it will be extremely difficult for them to witness to Christ and effectively evangelize a world that is becoming progressively more secular in its thinking, beliefs, and activities.

Investing in Programmes or Intentional Discipleship?

The transformation of a person into a disciple is the work of Jesus Christ himself through the Holy Spirit. Nevertheless, the much desired transformation we want to see in our lay people is only possible through intentional and proper disciple-making. This should be a major concern for the clergy. In actual sense, it presupposes that they themselves should understand discipleship at both the conceptual and practical levels and should have been discipled at some point in their lives.

Unfortunately, most of our priests just as the lay people have never been consciously discipled. In practice, disciple-making is not a characteristic feature of what we do in most parishes today. The point is that we hardly talk about it. In the more vibrant parishes where priests pay attention to evangelization and the spiritual growth of their members, the focus is always more on programmes and revivals.[530]

The point here is not that the different programmes and ministries that people undertake in the Church are not relevant. Without doubt, they are important and good and have the capacity to lead people to an encounter with God which can either lead to an initial conversion or a reawakening of faith in God and in the Church. Nonetheless, they cannot take the place of intentional and proper disciple-making. In fact, some commentators consider it irresponsible to lead people to an initial conversion through certain spiritual programmes without going further to disciple them.

As relevant as programmes and ministries are, they cannot transform the faithful into intentional disciples who invest time and energy in making other disciples. Hence, amidst all of this, there should be a clear strategy to invest primarily in discipleship in order to create an army of spiritually mature Catholics who are not only content that they can make heaven, but who are ready to invest in going out to make converts and forming them into disciples who can disciple others.

The Workability of Disciple-Making Today

As far as our evangelizing mission is concerned, Robert Coleman states that, "In Jesus we have a Teacher. The Scriptural accounts of his ministry constitute our best Textbook on evangelization."[531] Discipleship constitutes an indispensable aspect of his ministry. An important thing that many people would want to know is if disciple-making is possible today. No doubt, it is a conscious and deliberate step which takes place over a period of time and does not involve a crowd. But the truth remains that this evangelical strategy of the Master is possible today as we pursue the goals of evangelization—mission *ad gentes*, the new evangelization and pastoral care. On its applicability to the mission of the Church today, Leroy Eims writes:

---

[530] Although these are better than nothing, they are not enough.

[531] R. COLEMAN, *The Master Plan of Evangelism* (Grand Rapids, MI: Fleming H. Revell Company, 1993), pp. 16-17.

> It [discipleship] worked in the church in Jerusalem; it worked in the church in Antioch. This whole approach got its start in the New Testament church. It grew and flourished in these churches. *And there is no reason on earth why it cannot be applied today.*
>
> The Great Commission remains the same. The message of the gospel is the same. We minister through the power of the same Holy Spirit. We have the same Word of God. And we have the promise Jesus made after the command to make disciples, "And surely I will be with you always, to the very end of the age" (Matt. 28:20).[532]

Stressing his point further, he argues against the exaggerated emphasis on programmes at the expense of intentional disciple-making. According to him,

> What then is the problem today? Why don't we see more of this going on? Why are fruitful, dedicated, mature disciples so rare? The biggest reason is that all too often we have relied on programs or materials or some other thing to do the job. The ministry is to be carried on by people, not programs. It is to be carried out by some*one* and not by some *thing*. Disciples cannot be mass produced. We cannot drop people into a "program" and see disciples emerge at the end of the production line. It takes time to make disciples."[533]

Today, the level of superficiality of religious life is very high among Catholics just as it is with other Christian denominations. To make a very positive impact that will extend beyond our present generation, we need to review our evangelical strategy. A wise thing to do will be to understudy the strategy of the Master (Jesus Christ) himself for evangelization and use it as a model for today's evangelization. As Robert Coleman remarks, "In Jesus Christ, we have a perfect Teacher and the scriptural account of his ministry constitute our best Textbook of evangelization."[534]

---

[532] L. EIMS, *The Lost Art of Disciple Making…, op. cit.,* p. 45.

[533] L. EMIS, *The Lost Art of Disciple Making…, op. cit.,* pp. 44-46.

[534] R. COLEMAN, *The Master Plan of Evangelism…, op. cit.,* p. 16.

Furthermore, he maintains that in his method of evangelization, that is, in his disciple-making strategy, which was the principle that underpinned his ministry,[535] the Master—Jesus Christ—"disclosed God's strategy of world conquest."[536] Certainly, the crowd had their place in his missionary work, but as Coleman states, "Rather than focus primarily on the crowd, his principle was to concentrate on a few chosen men—the twelve disciples."[537] More specifically, he asserts that,

> All of this certainly impresses one with the deliberate way that Jesus proportioned his life to those he wanted to train. It also graphically illustrates a fundamental principle of teaching: that other things being equal, the more concentrated the size of the group being taught, the greater the opportunity for effective instruction. Jesus Christ devoted most of his remaining life on earth to these few disciples. He literally staked his whole ministry on them.[538]

The point is not to ignore the entire faithful and concentrate all our evangelical efforts on a few that we wish to disciple. Jesus Christ himself did not do that. He spent time and energy ministering to the multitude on a constant basis. But then the greater part of his time and ministry was devoted to the few men he chose as disciples who would have the responsibility of furthering his mission after his departure.[539]

Importance of Discipleship to Church Growth and the Success of Our Mission

Every normal church desires growth or success but how we measure success is a different thing altogether. In practice, how we measure success will most likely dictate where we place our priorities or influence the main things we invest time, energy, and resources on. We can never over-emphasize the fact that we cannot

---

[535] *Ibid.*, p. 14.

[536] *Ibid.*

[537] *Ibid.*, pp. 23-25.

[538] *Ibid.*, p. 25.

[539] *Ibid.*, p. 29.

afford to lose focus of our true identity and mission as a Church. As the universal sacrament of salvation, our mission consists primarily in saving souls.

Today, there is too much concern over the numbers of people on our pews every Sunday with little concern over their genuine conversion and spiritual transformation into disciples who reflect more and more the image and character of Christ. As Robby Gallaty rightly observes,

> Many church leaders today easily fall into the trap of gauging success in the Church by the ABCs of growth: Attendance, Buildings, and Cash. However, there is a serious problem with this score card, namely, that *Jesus never gauged effectiveness by these criteria*.... [Even though he did draw a crowd], Jesus didn't draw large crowds for the sake of counting heads or logging attendance.[540]

Seriously, we must reject the prevailing tendency to gauge Church growth and success merely or primarily by the size and splendour of our churches, the bigness of our congregations, money in the bank, our ability to erect new physical structures and our success in some social endeavours and similar. This way of measuring Church growth stands in stark contrast to Jesus' own standard.[541] Besides, it is the reason we have big churches with so many parishioners and yet only a few are truly engaged and are actively involved in mission for Christ and his Church within and outside the parish.

As a matter of fact, Jesus and his Apostles did not build any physical church. His emphasis and that of the early Church was not on money or erecting physical structures, but on converting people and building them up for the Kingdom. The people are the real Church and the people were their primary target. Their mandate was to go and make disciples everywhere, and to baptize and teach them to observe the commandments of Christ (cf. Mt 28:19), not to erect buildings primarily even though the erection of buildings is not necessarily excluded in the command.

---

540 R. GALLATY, *Rediscovering Discipleship...*, *op. cit.*, p. 19.

541 *Ibid.*

In faithfulness to the commission they received, the Apostles were more interested in mission and the raising of converted and transformed disciples. This was how they measured their success primarily, not by the number of physical structures they erected. The Church of today needs to learn a great deal from them. Although buildings (churches, parish houses, and even universities and similar) are important, they cannot be the primary measure of our success as a Church that sees herself as a sacrament of salvation.

The truth is that no matter how numerous and magnificent our churches, halls, and clergy houses are, they can neither change society nor take the place of human beings. Although these buildings or even institutions such as secondary schools, universities, hospitals and similar are very necessary, they do not in themselves fulfil the mission of the Church or guarantee the success of that mission.[542] On the contrary, they are meant to facilitate mission—the conversion and transformation of people.

Robert E. Coleman captures the present loss of focus among church leaders in general and the over-exaggerated emphasis on big churches, number and similar elements at the expense of raising interiorly transformed Christians when he states,

> .... [I]f success is measured by big meetings, big buildings and big budgets, then the Church appears to be doing quite well. But the real question has to be asked: is all this business actually fulfilling the mandate of Christ to make disciples and teaching, in turn, to do the same? That's the mission of the church. Yes, we want churches to grow, but it is becoming painfully evident that getting more people on the rolls has not resulted in a corresponding increase in

[542] For example, it is possible to build an exceptionally beautiful Catholic minor seminary and yet be raising faithless and unconverted young men there. Similarly, we can put up beautiful and gigantic churches everywhere without truly evangelizing and converting the vast majority of parishioners in these places. It is a well-known fact that some Catholic institutions abroad are not faithful to the moral teachings of the Church in its entirety.

> transformed lives. Where do we find the contagious sacrifice and all-out commitment to the Great Commission?[543]

The answer to Coleman's question lies in disciple-making. It is in the raising of spiritually mature Christians who are conformed to Christ and are totally committed to the making of other disciples and the Christianization of the cultures and structures in society. Here lies the danger! If we continue to sacramentalize people who are not properly evangelized[544] and discipled and thus can neither live the Christian life nor be missionaries to others around them, then we too will come to share the present fate of Europe and North America someday. The logic is quite simple! Any institution that is consistently losing more members than it is gaining is most likely going to end up in crisis over time.

This is why the insistence that the Church should pay attention to "evangelization and disciple-making" prior to sacramentalization (that is, before conferring Confirmation, Holy Orders, Holy Matrimony, and the Baptism of adults) ought to be treated as crucial and urgent. We must never allow our present number to blind us to a reality that is obvious to those who have perception. Perhaps, in reference to church growth or success, Rick Warren insists that our primary focus should be church health. He states that "the key issue for churches in the twenty-first century will be church *health*, not church growth. When congregations are healthy, they grow the way God intends. Healthy churches don't need gimmicks to grow – they grow naturally."[545]

For the body to function maximally, its different parts must be healthy and function very well. Once some parts are diseased and are not functioning well, it affects the overall health, efficiency, and productivity of the individual. The same is applicable to the Church. Once the vast majority of the faithful are merely consuming instead of being spiritually productive, then there is no way

---

[543] J. PUTMAN, B. HARRINGTON, with R. COLEMAN, *Disciple-Shift* (Grand Rapids, MI: Zondervan, 2013), p. 11. See Foreword by Robert Coleman.

[544] Pope John Paul II popularized the phrase "sacramentalizing people who are not properly evangelized."

[545] R. WARREN, *The Purpose Driven Church..., op. cit.*, p. 17.

she can live out her potentials, that is, grow maximally or be as fruitful as she should be. So, the challenge we need to overcome is how to get all the faithful or the vast majority of them to be fully engaged in ministry in their different communities in ways that will contribute to the overall health and growth of the Church and the success of her mission.

Sharing the secret of their survival and growth as a church at Saddleback Church, United States, Warren writes, "Our sanity and survival depended upon developing a workable process to turn seekers into saints, turn consumers into contributors, turn members into ministers, and turn an audience into any army."[546] Although he admits that it is an onerous task to move people away from "self-centred consumerism" to being "servant-head Christians," it is the narrow path to the path that can lead to success and growth.[547]

Church health which makes our churches prone to natural growth can only come through proper evangelization and discipleship. In addition to transforming the individuals into real witnesses to the life of Christ, discipleship imparts a deep sense of mission to the discipled. It creates missionary soldiers who are passionate about going out intentionally to win new converts for Jesus Christ as a lifestyle. Quite naturally, as more and more people in our churches experience conversion and become personally convinced about Christ and the mission to make him known everywhere, the Church naturally grows.

This again buttresses the need to re-direct our Church from sheer sacramentalization of her members without prior conversion and transformation to the old biblical culture of disciple-making and apostleship if we desire to see a healthy, robust, strong and effective Church that is faithful to the Great Commission of Jesus Christ. When we come to see discipleship as Christ's vision for spiritual multiplication or exponential growth of the Church, invest intentionally in it as a decisive project and actually succeed in it, our parishes will experience an unprecedented renewal and growth in numbers, authentic spiritual life and in mission.

---

[546] *Ibid.*, p. 46.

[547] *Ibid.*

Naturally, as discipleship—the process of raising healthy or spiritually mature Christians who invest in mission—is repeated on a continuous basis at all levels, our churches will be healthy and grow naturally and be successful in mission. Thus, Christian witness, conversion, discipleship and mission are the key factors in determining the health, growth, and success of a church, not buildings. The statement by Warren on this matter is quite instructive. He maintains,

> I believe that you measure the health or strength of a Church by its *sending* capacity rather than by its *seating* capacity. Churches are in the sending business. One of the questions we must ask in evaluating a church's health is, "How many people are being mobilized for the Great Commission?"[548]

According to the *General Directory for Catechesis*, "Formation for the apostolate and for mission is one of the fundamental tasks of catechesis."[549] In Michael Sweeney's view, one of the principal or fundamental tasks of the pastors is to form and equip the lay faithful and send them out to do mission.[550] Today in our parishes we have at our disposal an abundance of gifted lay people whose special talents, gifts, and potentials have remained unrecognized and untapped. The overwhelming majority of them come and go every Sunday without getting personally involved in the life of the parish and mission. Jim Putman is of the same view. According to him,

> These leaders often sit in the pews, waiting to be developed, to be released into ministry, but often they never are. Our Churches are filled with diamonds in the rough, and when pastors and Church leaders begin to take seriously our mandate to disciple our people, these leaders will emerge.[551]

[548] *Ibid.,* p. 33.

[549] *GDC*, no. 86.

[550] M. SWEENEY and S. WEDDELL, *The Parish: Mission or Maintenance..., op. cit.,* p. 16. We should always remember that equipping people involves grounding them in Scripture, doctrines, spiritual life and prayer, and morality before sending them out.

[551] J. PUTMAN et al., *Real-Life Discipleship..., op. cit.,* p. 19.

Most of the Christians we raise in our churches today are merely church-goers and spiritual dwarfs and consumers who will never be able to take over the seven models of culture we talked about for Christ. Often, they consume the spiritual nourishment their priests offer every Sunday only to return the next Sunday to consume more—they never share or nourish others spiritually. This state of spiritual unfruitfulness from the mission standpoint is the regular pattern or cycle for most Catholics and it harms the mission of the Church seriously.

There is a vital point to which we must pay strict attention here. When spiritual consumers who are not spiritually productive or who contribute little or nothing to the health and growth of a parish form the bulk or the vast majority of the members of a church, then that church is not likely to be as healthy and successful as it should be or grow to its full potentials. The challenge this poses to the church is to find a way of reaching and discipling her numerous members who are presently like spectators at a football match and then make them into active players in the church's life and mission.

No doubt, our churches are still full and we have some gifted priests (with flourishing ministries) who organize revivals in the different dioceses in Nigeria to lead people to Christ. Nevertheless, discipleship is one of the greatest needs of the Church today. Jim Putman believes that, "when done right, discipleship will produce leaders every Church needs to succeed."[552]As a matter of fact, the Church needs to invest in raising visionary and transformational leaders, priests, religious and lay people alike—who are totally committed to her mission and have a passion to take over Nigeria and the world for Christ. As Robert Coleman asserts, "without reproducing visionary leadership no great spiritual movement can endure…"[553]

---

[552] *Ibid.* The mission of the Church to take the world for Christ is an onerous task, but the truth is that only disciples who have been equipped to be transformational leaders can accomplish it at the fastest time possible with the aid of the Holy Spirit.

[553] R. COLEMAN, "Preparing Transformational Leadership the Jesus Way," a Teaching Quarterly for Discipleship of Heart and Mind," C. S. Lewis Institute, see https://www.cslewisinstitute.org/webfm_send/649c.

Thus to do things right and raise such leaders, there is a strong need for a life-transforming and highly mission-oriented catechesis in the Church at all levels (children, teens, youth, and adults) on an ongoing basis. There should be short- and long-term plans to reproduce visionary leaders with a transformational agenda who possess a multiplier mentality and what Gallaty refers to as a clear strategy of multiplication.[554]

The Need to Tailor Ministries in the Church Towards Disciple-Making

That the Church understands the importance of discipleship is not in contention. For instance, catechesis which is the third stage of her mission of evangelization is meant for discipleship, while the goal of seminary formation is also to raise missionary disciples. But the problem is that actual commitment to disciple-making in practice is extremely weak or almost non-existent. As Robby Gallaty laments,

> One of the greatest problems we face in the church today is that we have outsourced the task of disciple-makers and have depended on a handful of "full-time" ministers to do the job that Jesus gave to us. We will never carry out the Great Commission if only full-time vocational ministers are making disciples. Discipleship wasn't [just] a ministry of the first-century church. It was the ministry of the church. Shouldn't it be ours as well?[555]

Actually, he is right. Discipleship should be the business of the Church, not a few interested people. Although the present RCIA/OCIA programme[556] offers a wonderful opportunity

---

[554] R. GALLATY, *Rediscovering Discipleship…, op. cit.,* p. 21. Instead of adding new resources with the goal of achieving linear growth, the strategy of multiplication involves leveraging the talents and abilities of each of our workers, which are often not fully tapped in most organizations.

[555] *Ibid.,* p. 85.

[556] In 2021 the USCCB changed the name of the Rite of Christian Initiation of Adults (RCIA) to the Order of Christian Initiation of Adults (OCIA).

for disciple-making in the Church, it is not everyone that passes through it. Moreover, if truth be said, it will only succeed if it is handled by those who are properly evangelized and discipled themselves and are intentional about pursuing it as a goal during catechesis.

Today, we have different ministries and lay associations and groups in the Church.[557] A critical move the Church needs to make to drive mission and reach the world for Christ at the shortest time possible is to project disciple-making as a vision for the parishes and all ministries and the lay associations and groups in the Church. The existence of these ministries and groups offers a good opportunity for discipleship. Beyond gathering their members for devotion or the specific service they render in the parish, they should have as their common goal a clear plan to lead their members to conversion and spiritual maturity through a conscious process of disciple-making. To facilitate this, a well thought-out structure that is not complex should be put in place for this by the leadership.

No doubt, this will make these ministries and associations and even the parishes more spiritually healthy and fruitful. As Jim Putman maintains, "The ministries [in the Church] must all foster environments where disciples are made."[558] On the five key components that can help the ministries (and perhaps lay associations) in the Church to foster the mission of making disciples who evangelize and disciple others, he lists the following:

The first essential component is that every ministry should have "a clear goal of discipleship."[559] It should exist not merely to render a given service in the Church (such as singing or reading), but equally to help members discover Jesus Christ in a personal or

[557] The ministries include the music or singing ministry (the choir), the lectors, the welcoming or hospitality ministers, and the altar servers. The pious associations and groups include the Sacred Heart of Jesus, charismatics, Legionaries, Catholic Women Organization, Catholic Men Organization, Christian Mothers, Catholic Youth Organization and a host of others.

[558] J. PUTMAN, B. HARRINGTON, with R. COLEMAN, *Disciple-Shift…, op. cit.*, p. 177.

[559] *Ibid.*

experiential way, to love and follow him, to be transformed by him, and to join him on his mission to proclaim the Gospel and make other disciples. Everyone who is joining a ministry or association in the Church should first be led to this basic understanding of what Christianity and the Church are about. Moreover, there should be an intentional effort to create an enabling environment for conversion and spiritual growth within each ministry through ongoing kerygma and discipleship.

THE SECOND KEY COMPONENT mentioned by Putman and Harrington is *"An intentional leader who makes disciples."*[560] Leadership is important in every institution and critical to the success of its mission.[561] One of the critical problems in the Church and civil society today is that of leadership—the appointment of wrong leaders who are either ignorant or lack the vision and the will to do the right things. Visionary, strong-willed, and focused leadership matched with positive action will always yield positive fruits. Contrary to what we see in most places, the leaders of each ministry must have a clear intention and total commitment to raise spiritually mature Christian disciples who can disciple others.[562] But again, this presupposes that they themselves have been properly evangelized and discipled.

THE THIRD ESSENTIAL COMPONENT that can help the ministries and lay associations in the Church foster disciple-making is the existence of "*a biblically relational environment.*"[563] Ordinarily, the key factors that foster spiritual growth include sacramental life, studying and meditating on the Word of God, Eucharistic adoration, intimacy with the Spirit, and a sound prayer life. Each ministry or association in the Church needs to incorporate these different elements into the formation of their members with an eye on a

---

[560] *Ibid.*, p. 118.

[561] Cf. J. MALLON, *Divine Renovation Guidebook* (Toronto, Ontario: Novalis Publishing Inc., 2014), p. 11.

[562] Cf. J. PUTMAN, B. HARRINGTON, with R. COLEMAN, *DiscipleShift…*, *op. cit.*, p. 118.

[563] *Ibid.*

personal encounter with God, ongoing conversion or spiritual transformation, spiritual maturity, and mission.[564]

Focusing specifically on the Word of God, members of every ministry and society in the Church should be frequently exposed to the Sacred Scriptures. This should not be in a way that merely informs the head, but more so in a way that transforms their world view and affects the heart and all the choices and activities of the individuals.[565] According to Putman and Harrington, "Good teaching doesn't just inform the head; it also seeks to affect a person's heart and hands."[566]

The fourth key component is that the disciple-making process should be *"a reproducible process."*[567] It should not be something that is too complex to understand and reproduce. As the members of a specific ministry are being discipled, their transformation and spiritual growth should be such that manifests itself, not only in a longing for personal holiness, but also in their desire and mission to seek out and make other disciples.[568] Put in a different way, they too should become productive and fruitful in doing mission to gain new converts and to disciple new members and even others outside their ministry or association.

The final essential component that can foster disciple-making in the Church is that the Church itself must be *"a supporting organization"*[569] or institution. The disciple-making mission should not just be the vision of the ministries or associations. Rather, it must be the vision of the Church institution, which every ministry or association in the Church can adopt. As such, the Church as a whole and her leaders must continuously accentuate and communicate this vision to members to keep it alive in their minds.

In line with this, there should be a provision for ongoing formation of ministry leaders and society heads in addition to encouraging on a constant basis to strengthen them and keep their zeal

---

[564] Cf. *Ibid.*, p. 178.

[565] Cf. *Ibid.*

[566] *Ibid.*

[567] *Ibid.*

[568] Cf. *Ibid.*

[569] *Ibid.*

high. Nevertheless, it is necessary to insist on spiritual accountability to ensure that those entrusted with leadership do their jobs effectively and ensure that everyone and every ministry or association is aligned on evangelization and discipleship and are focused on realizing the common purpose of disciple-making, which is to make available spiritually mature Christians who are committed to making other disciples.[570]

In spite of everything we have said here, we must admit that disciple-making is not an easy task. It is even more difficult if it involves leading people out of their comfort zones to something that is very demanding. Change is always a difficult and painful experience for most people and in real life many people tend to resist it even before they get to understand what it is all about. Change becomes even tougher where people are entrenched in a particular tradition or ways of seeing and doing things for a long period of time, which they may or may not have appraised critically to see if it is still working.

The truth about life is that people don't see exactly the same way. Some tend to see far, while others can see only what is near. Moreover, some who have "good sight" may deliberately refuse to "see" (that is, acknowledge) that which is obvious and might require them to make some uncomfortable shifts in life. Yet, some people are just blind (ignorant) and are not likely to see at all. In reality, the extent to which a person is able to "see" depends on the lens (mental or spiritual lens) through which he views things.

A man who depends on his human ability or the physical eyes in appraising spiritual matters may see nothing or only a little. The one who depends on the lenses of the psychological eyes may see a little more than the former, but certainly not all that can be seen. But the man who wears spiritual lenses or sees with his spiritual eyes in addition to these others and is open to the inspiration and promptings of the Holy Spirit is more likely to see very far because faith and reliance on the guidance of the Holy Spirit will enable him to see or penetrate things which the human eye or mind can never reach (cf. 1 Cor 2:14-15).

---

[570] Cf. *Ibid.*

Thus bearing in mind that people see differently, we must learn to exercise wisdom, caution, and extreme patience as we try to sell this concept of disciple-making in our parishes as the main key for leading our members to spiritual maturity and stemming the current drift of Catholics to other Churches. Similarly, we need to rely more on the power of the Holy Spirit to pierce and transform the minds and hearts of our people to accept this truth and also see disciple-making as an important key to spiritual multiplication in the Church.

No matter the resistance we anticipate or actually face in this area, giving up altogether can never be an option. As the saying goes, "Rome was not built in a day." The only viable option we have is to keep pushing and to constantly review what we are doing and the challenges that arise from time to time and look for more effective ways to reach our goal. But in all, we need to rely on God and be led by the Holy Spirit who alone can convert and transform the hearts of men.

How to Raise Disciples—Transformational Leaders

In his book, *The Master Plan of Evangelism,* Coleman enumerates what he calls the eight steps or guiding principles of Jesus' discipleship training, even though we can add a ninth step. What we need to bear in mind from the outset is that Coleman himself admits that what Jesus did with his disciples did not actually follow the sequence in which they are stated below. That is to say, he did not wait for his disciples to master one step before moving to the next. Rather they were intertwined and implied each other. Now, let us look at the steps.

Selection

The first step towards raising transformational leaders or disciples in the Church is selection. It requires looking for learners. Jesus called twelve men who were not high profile people in society, but whose main qualification was that they were simple-minded, teachable in spite of their limited abilities, had a sincere yearning for God, and were looking for something more than the superficial religiosity of their time.[571] Even though he did not neglect the crowd, he concentrated his ministry on these men.

Ordinarily, we cannot disciple the unevangelized and unconverted. What this simply means is that those we admit should be people who have been evangelized and have experienced an initial conversion. They should be people whose hearts are open to Christ and are willing to follow him. Jesus himself did not admit complete strangers to his discipleship training. The evidence from Scripture is that he prayerfully selected twelve men from those to whom he had been ministering and designated them Apostles (see Lk 6:12-16). He chose men whose hearts were big and open and were willing to leave other things aside and follow him in trust.

Association

The second step in Jesus' discipleship strategy is association. Scripture says that he chose the twelve "that they might be with him" (see Mk 3:14; Lk 6:13). As we said earlier, discipleship is a form of apprenticeship. We cannot mass-produce disciples or make disciples on an assembly-line basis.[572] Just as a person learns to be a mechanic by spending quality time (about six days in a week) associating with and understudying his master, so did the disciples learn from Jesus by their close and constant association with him.

During his active ministry, Jesus spent more time with his disciples than with anybody else and offered them the opportunity to have a close fellowship with him and to connect with him.[573] He invested quality time in them. He talked with them, prayed with them, ate with them, visited people in their company, and worshipped together with them in the synagogues and in the Temple. Throughout his active ministry, he maintained a close association and a constant ministry to them by having them in his company.[574] When he ministered to the people (the poor, the sick, the heart-broken, and the crowd) they were always around him to

---

[571] R. COLEMAN, *The Master Plan of Evangelism...*, *op. cit.*, p. 23.

[572] Cf. *Ibid.*, p. 135.

[573] See J. PUTMAN et al., *Real-Life Discipleship...*, *op. cit.*, p. 62; See also R. COLEMAN, *The Master Plan of Evangelism...*, *op. cit.*, p. 37.

[574] *Ibid.*, p. 37.

observe, listen, and learn from him. He did everything in his ministry in the presence of at least some of them.

In the course of time, he opened his life to them as well as his worldview and tried to replace their old ideas of reality with the truth. They acquired knowledge and knew the mysteries of the kingdom even before he explained things to them.[575] By word and example, he mentored them to become like him in living the Kingdom and working for its establishment.[576] In view of all this, it will be absolutely correct to say that he built up his disciples by constantly staying with them.[577]

Consecration

The third step in the discipleship strategy of Jesus is consecration. The first thing he required of his disciples was obedience. Following him implies having faith in him, a willingness to surrender one's whole life to him, and conforming to the disciplines of the kingdom of God.[578] As we know, he too in his human nature was completely obedient to the will of his Father (cf. Phil 2:6-9). As Coleman puts it, "absolute obedience to the will of God, of course, was the controlling principle of the Master's own life."[579]

So, he demanded complete loyalty or obedience from them even in the most difficult times (cf. Lk 14:25-27). This was because he knew that it was the only way he could mould them to become like him in character and be totally committed to his mission.[580] According to Coleman,

> It must be remembered too, that Jesus was making men to lead his church to conquest, and no one can ever be a leader until first he has to learn to follow a leader.... No one knew better than Jesus that the satanic forces of darkness against them were well organized and equipped to make effectual any half-hearted effort of evangelism. They could

[575] *Ibid.*, p. 34.
[576] *Ibid.*
[577] *Ibid.*, pp. 34, 135.
[578] *Ibid.*
[579] *Ibid.*, p. 49.
[580] *Ibid.*, p. 50.

> not possibly outwit the devilish powers of this world unless they gave strict adherence to him who alone knew the strategy of victory. This required absolute obedience to the Master's will, even as it meant complete abandonment of their own.[581]

Actually, Jesus taught the disciples to be obedient to him and to the will of his Father (cf. Jn 14:15, 23-24; Mt 7:21-28). Such obedience involved dropping their own worldview and priorities and the ways of the world around them and coming under his direction. They were to remain faithful to his Word, to the principles of his Gospel and to his mission even in the face of trials, rejection, persecution and hardships (cf. Mt 10:37-39; Lk 14:25-27).

Impartation

The fourth step in Jesus' discipleship strategy is impartation. He gave himself away to his disciples. He gave them his peace, his joy, the keys to his kingdom and glory. "He gave them all he had—nothing was withheld, not even his own life."[582] Really, we can characterize the earthly life of Jesus as completely self-giving and life-giving. He exhibited extreme love and mercy and was completely dedicated to the mission of saving mankind.

But then, he also knew that such self-sacrificing spirit, which he demonstrated, his love for souls and total commitment to the world-evangelizing mission for which he was preparing them were clearly beyond their human power and ability and thus required the enablement of the Holy Spirit. In truth, "nothing less than a personal baptism of the Holy Spirit would suffice."[583] Coleman puts this well when he states that "[a]ny evangelistic work" without the Spirit and the life of the Spirit "is as lifeless as it is meaningless. Only as the Spirit of Christ in us exalts the Son are people drawn unto the Father."[584]

By his words and life, Jesus made it abundantly clear to his disciples that his life and work on earth were possible only through

---

[581] *Ibid.*, p. 50.

[582] *Ibid.*, pp. 53-54.

[583] *Ibid.*, p. 59.

[584] *Ibid.*, p. 60.

the Holy Spirit (cf. Lk 4:18-19). Hence, he promised them the guidance and assistance of the Holy Spirit (see Acts 1:4-5, 8; 2:1-6). On the day of Pentecost, he fulfilled his promise. He sent them the Holy Spirit to empower them to live his divine life and to effectively carry out the world evangelization he entrusted to them.[585]

Demonstration

The fifth step in Jesus' discipleship strategy is demonstration. Jesus deliberately modelled for his disciples the very life he wanted them to live (i.e. the Christian life) and the mission he wanted them to carry out. He showed them how to live with God and man and wanted them to learn from the example of his own life and work. He emphasized the importance of prayer to them; taught them some basic principles of prayer; gave them a model of prayer (cf. Mt 6:9-13); and demonstrated an exemplary life of prayer to them.[586]

In addition, Jesus' life and discourses with the disciples proved his in-depth knowledge of the Scriptures. He repeatedly quoted Old Testament Scriptures with ease and used them in his discourse with them and others. Importantly, his strong passion for preaching the Word to win souls had a great impact on them just as his example of practising what he taught them. For example, he taught them humility and service and actually demonstrated these by his own life. He demonstrated the principle of servant-leadership. His ministry was characterized by service to God and others and he tried to raise them with the same servanthood mentality.[587] A practical example of this was when he stooped low to wash their feet, thereby challenging them to wash one another's feet (see Jn 13:1-15).

Delegation

The sixth step in Jesus' discipleship strategy is delegation. In choosing twelve men to disciple, Jesus was investing heavily in

---

[585] *Ibid.*, p. 60.

[586] *Ibid.*, p. 64.

[587] R. COLEMAN, "Preparing Transformational Leadership the Jesus Way..., *op. cit.*

them to prepare them for their future world evangelizing mission. At the beginning, the disciples merely observed how he ministered and worked. As it is with every form of apprenticeship, he assigned them only minor responsibilities at first. His initial priority was to build up their relationship with God and show them how he worked. But then, he did all this with his eye on the time he will release them for world ministry.[588]

Thus, as they grew in maturity, in the knowledge of the kingdom and in the spiritual life, he began to involve them in his ministry on a gradual basis. As Putman puts it, he "gave them opportunities to put what they were learning into practice."[589] The first assignments were small, but as the disciples grew in confidence, he began to send them out to minister to others and thus reproduce what they had seen him do, following careful instructions (see Lk 9:1-6). Little by little, he led them into his vision for the kingdom and the evangelization of the world.[590]

Supervision

The seventh step in Jesus' discipleship strategy is supervision. Even after Jesus started releasing his disciples for ministry, he knew that they were still not "finished products" and so he continued to supervise their works. To keep them growing, he constantly reviewed their activities and reports from their evangelizing missions and clarified things for them on a regular basis. Similarly, he gave them on-the-job training all the way and tried to help them focus on the essentials. Indeed, he was perpetually checking on them through his constant close fellowship with them in order to teach them from his own knowledge and experiences.[591]

Although their progress was slow in some areas, he was patient in guiding them and to move them towards the goal of evangelizing

---

[588] He knew from the very beginning that his time on earth was limited and his plan was that they would take over from him when he physically left the earth to return to heaven.

[589] J. PUTMAN et al., *Real-Life Discipleship…, op. cit.,* pp. 62-63.

[590] *Ibid.,* p. 63; See also R. COLEMAN, *The Master Plan of Evangelism…, op. cit.,* pp. 72, 153. Following careful instructions, the disciples were to preach, heal, and cast out demons.

[591] *Ibid.,* p. 157.

and discipling the nations of the world.[592] Even when they eventually graduated and were ready to be released, he still did not leave them without supervision. He promised them the Holy Spirit who will empower and guide them, but at the same time supervise their work.[593]

Reproduction

The eighth step in Jesus' discipleship strategy is reproduction. In discipleship training it is extremely important to expect those being discipled to reproduce what they have learnt. It is on account of this that many commentators see discipleship as the principle of spiritual multiplication and exponential growth in the Church. As disciples reproduce, the Church grows exponentially.

Jesus understood this fact very well. When he came to save the world, he knew that his ministry in the world was going to be for a while and his strategy was to train people who will continue his mission after his departure. So, he did not just choose and invest his time, energy, and mental and spiritual resources on his disciples for nothing. On the contrary, his vision for doing that was world conquest through world evangelization.[594] As a good disciple-maker, he expected them to reproduce what they had learnt from him by words and deeds someday. As Robert Coleman puts it, it was for his disciples to reproduce his own life in themselves and through them into the lives of others. Nevertheless, though reproduction was Jesus' desire, multiplication was his ultimate end.[595]

Thus, at the appropriate time after his resurrection, he commissioned them to go to the whole world and replicate everything he

---

[592] R. COLEMAN, "Preparing Transformational Leadership the Jesus Way…, *op. cit.*

[593] R. COLEMAN, *The Master Plan of Evangelism…, op. cit.*, p. 157.

[594] Cf. *Ibid.*, p. 89.

[595] *Ibid.*, p. 161. Although Jesus considered the personal holiness of his disciples and their complete loyalty to him to be absolutely important, he demanded something more from them. It was also absolutely important that they reproduced by raising other disciples who in turn will reproduce and make other disciples. This process was critical to his ultimate plan for world conquest though evangelization.

did with them (cf. Mt 28:19).[596] Commenting on the importance of forming leaders who reproduce, Robert Coleman writes,

> Today, as then, the test of an evangelistic program is not the number of people who are being reached for the first-time decisions. The real test is: *Are those who are being reached reaching others?* Is our fruit bearing fruit? Are we only making converts – or are we building leaders who can in turn build other leaders?[597]

Prayer

The last step in Jesus' discipleship strategy which Coleman mentions in an article and not in his book, which we are considering, is prayer. Jesus prayed for his disciples. He knew the enormity of the work and the serious risks involved in the evangelizing mission he was entrusting to them. Hence, he did not merely teach them how to pray or ask them to pray, but he actually prayed for them (cf. Jn 17). However, we should not think that he prayed for them only this once. Although his prayer in John 17 was quite extensive, it is more reasonable to think that his prayer for them was a continuous exercise.

---

[596] See R. COLEMAN, "Preparing Transformational Leadership the Jesus Way…, *op. cit.;* J. PUTMAN et al., *Real-Life Discipleship…, op. cit.,* p. 157.

[597] R. COLEMAN, *The Master Plan of Evangelism…, op. cit.,* p. 161.

Chapter Eleven

LEARNING FROM THE PAST AND MAKING NECESSARY CHANGES

Man is always in the process of learning. A person or a society that stops learning stops growing as well. Fortunately, history (the study of the past) presents us with different learning curves which are useful for our personal and collective development. On the other hand, man is always generating new ideas and ways of doing things and until we learn to try things out we may never get to know what works and what does not work.

In this chapter, I wish to advocate for complete openness to both old and new ways of doing things that can best promote the proper formation and empowerment of Catholics and the realization of our mission as a Church. The recommendations here include: learning from the past to resolve present challenges, the need for change where it is necessary, grounding Catholics in four areas of formation, and promoting a purpose or mission-driven Church as opposed to the present maintenance culture in the Church.

Learning from the Past to Resolve Our Present Challenges

Every society presents its own challenges and so do institutions, families, and individuals. This is a fact of life, which is not likely to change. Interestingly, the same is applicable to the Church. Even though her origin and mission are divine and the divine element is still present, she exists and operates within human society. Besides, she is constituted at every level by human beings with different levels of faith and spirituality who see things differently, think differently, and are limited in many different ways.[598]

---

[598] Certainly, the Holy Spirit is working in the Church, meaning that the divine element is present. But then, the level of openness and docility

Due to these limitations, experiences, and the different outlook people have about life and things, they tend to approach issues and life challenges differently. In this regard we speak of the conservatives and the innovators who tend to see things differently. According to a footnote commentary on 1 Samuel 8, "while conservative elements think of re-establishing order as a return to the past, the innovators, looking for fresh structures in order to respond to present reality, forget too quickly what past experience has taught."[599]

No matter how we look at things, experience and innovation are important tools we need in life. In pursuit of our mission as a Church, there is need to critically consider both elements and strike a healthy balance between them. Just as man is rational and dynamic and capable of initiating new ideas, experience is also invaluable and always handy to remind us about what worked or failed in the past, thus equipping us to avoid the mistakes of history.

Past innovations become old in the presence of the new, but then present innovations do not necessarily render every innovation in the past useless. History is important and there is a great deal to learn from the past. In actual sense, experience from the past can have a major role to play in the resolution of present challenges. As experience has shown, the key to the resolution of serious issues in life lies in returning to the past and arming ourselves with lessons from it that will aid us in making an informed decision at present or make a calculated leap into the future.

Applying this logic to the challenges facing the Church, the priesthood and, more precisely, the drift of Catholics in Nigeria to the Pentecostal churches, there is a need to begin our search for a solution from the past. What makes this even more compelling is the fact that the mission the whole Church is carrying on today is from the past, that is, over two thousand years.

If the Gospel or the salvation Message is the same, and the mission is the same, and the Church is the same, then as a start-

---

to the promptings and guidance of the Holy Spirit is a different thing altogether.

[599] *CCB*, see footnote comment on 1 Samuel 8.

ing point, we can ask the following questions. How did the early Church perceive Christ and his claims? More precisely, How did the Apostles and early Christians receive the mission he entrusted to them? What challenges did they face at their own time, which relate to our present challenges? What mistakes or omissions did they make? How did they resolve them? Why did they succeed in spite of all the obstacles and limitations? What are the positives and the negatives we can learn from their own experiences?

Talking about the more recent past, it will also be important to know the mistakes and omissions that prepared the ground for our present situation. For example, in spite of the labour, sacrifices, and the successes of the missionaries in many areas, were there also areas they failed, such as recognizing the positive elements of our culture and incarnating the Gospel in the culture? Did they succeed in evangelizing our people properly and discipling them?

Armed with such concrete information from the past, the next step will be to critically and objectively X-ray the present time to see the opportunities it holds for us in our soul-winning mission. This is very germane. Understanding the present environment, the spirit of the post-modern world, the mindset and interests of the people of this generation, the de-Christianization agenda and campaign of the secular humanists, the opportunities for evangelization in our time in spite of all this and the tools available to us, coupled with the wealth of experience from the past years and centuries will seriously aid the success of our mission.

Being innovative and proactive can equally lead us to set clear, present and future goals, which will begin to shape and influence what we are doing now. For example, as a Church, we can strategize and draw up a pastoral plan for the Church in Nigeria as a whole and at the same time make particular provisions that can adequately address the peculiarities and challenges of the different dioceses in the country.

Such a well-thought-out pastoral plan with an overall goal of evangelizing the people of Nigeria to convert and disciple them and also Christianize the cultures will necessarily require us to ask further questions such as: Where are we now? Where do we want the Church to be in the next twenty-five or fifty years and more? What needs to change in our present mentality and approach to our mission? What should we be doing now to achieve our objectives? What methods (old and new) can we employ? What type of priests should we be raising today to enable us to reach our goals? What type of formation should we be offering our future priests, people of the consecrated life, and the lay people themselves? What level of catechesis is needed to get people to embrace the vision and commit to its realization? How can we foster unity among Catholics from the different parts of the country and collaborate effectively with other Christian denominations to achieve the Christianization of Nigeria? What are the pitfalls to avoid from our appraisal of the past?

Being proactive involves careful analysis, strategic thinking, and detailed planning and execution. No doubt, as limited human beings we cannot perfectly predict future situations and challenges, especially in the light of the rapid progress in science and technology and other fields of human endeavour. This and the dynamism of human beings and society can impact our mission either positively or negatively and cause us to adjust our projections. Nevertheless, focus is pertinent. The truth is that such projections are extremely important because they keep us alert. They constantly remind us where we are and where we should be heading.

Moreover, plans are not cast in stone. We can always review our plans and strategies in the course of time as society progresses and new realities emerge. But certainly, being nonchalant and non-proactive in our thinking and approach to the drift of Catholics to the Pentecostal churches or our failure in our overall mission can only lead to one thing—chaos or future doom for the Church and her mission as is the case of the Western world today.

To tell ourselves the simple truth, we cannot continue business as before as if Catholicism ends with us or as if we have no duty to the future generations of Catholics, that is, to hand on a flourishing faith and Church to them and to transmit the saving Gospel of Jesus Christ to non-Christians. It is here that I see the great wisdom of the Church Fathers in *Gaudium et Spes* where they assert that the Church must continually scrutinize the signs of the times and interpret them in the light of the Gospel.[600] This is needed to

[600] *GS* 4.

enable her to revise her methods or make necessary adjustments in the best interest of her mission.

No kingdom grows or falls all at once—it is always a gradual thing. Just as the rise of a kingdom is gradual and can be observed by right-thinking people over time, so also, the fall of a kingdom or an institution does not also happen suddenly. Oftentimes, it is preceded by a number of warning signs, which are often ignored. The signs we see today are always pointers to what to expect tomorrow or in the future. A stitch in time saves nine. In many cases, wise observers and leaders can turn back the hand of the clock and avert a future bad situation if they act fast enough in wise and strategic ways. Not to learn from the past is foolishness and makes us culpable in the disastrous events of the future whether or not we are alive. Again, a stitch in time saves nine.

Need for Change in Some Areas

Catholics react differently to the drift of some Catholics to the new generation churches. Some are critical of those who leave the Church for them. Others are quick to slam these churches as fake and do not see what is attracting people to them. No matter what we think, there is something we cannot completely run away from. It is either there is something those who leave the Church are not getting right or there is something we, as a Church, are not doing right, or both.

The whole effort to find a lasting solution to the problem must begin with introspection or a critical and objective self-examination on our part as a Church. Rather than sit in judgement and do nothing, a more progressive approach will be to ask ourselves a very simple and realistic question, namely, what is attracting Catholics and others to the Pentecostal churches?

Man is dynamic, not static. The way of doing things that appealed to people in the past may not appeal to a different generation. This is true about life, not only in the sphere of religion but in all areas. This obvious truth has serious implications for a Church with a mission which carries far-reaching eternal consequences for mankind and every generation. In this regard, about four main options are open to us: change the Message, but not the method; or change the method, but not the Message; or change both the Message and the method; or leave both the Message and the method.

Before we can choose any of these options, we must first determine what we have a right to do as a Church and what is possibly beyond our authority. No doubt, the Church has the authority to teach the nations. But does she have the authority to change the salvation Message (the Gospel) or water it down? Does she have the authority to change or revise the method of sharing the Gospel? Better still, does she have the authority to change both, that is the Gospel itself and the method of proclaiming it?

In practice, revising and adjusting the method of propagating the Gospel is within the confines of the authority that the Church received from her Saviour, Jesus Christ. But then, to change the mission and to change or water-down the salvific Message itself is beyond her powers and can only lead to an unjustifiable compromise, which in reality renders the action itself null and void. To put it differently, the mission of the Church is unchanging and to change the Message (the Good News of salvation in Christ Jesus) is to change or compromise the mission. This leaves us with only one option and this is to change or adapt the method if it is no longer serving the Message and the mission well.

Now, change is always difficult and most people tend to resist it even before they get to understand it. This is even much more difficult where what needs to change has become an established tradition or culture among a people in a particular society or institution.[601] Yet change—positive change—is extremely necessary for the continued health and growth of society and institutions, including the Church. Clinging to methods or particular ways of doing things as we sometimes do even when they are no longer effective as in the past can be a disservice to the Gospel and the mission of the Church and thus to the Church herself.

These problems often arise from emphasizing methods over mission, whereas our primary focus should be the mission itself and the fundamental Message around which the mission revolves. As rational beings, we need to be innovative and dynamic and

[601] Note that tradition here is spelt with a small "t" to clearly distinguish it with the Living Tradition of the Church.

come up with well-evaluated, morally sound and positive methods of propagating of the Gospel Message, bearing in mind that if the method does not attract or appeal to the audience, we may never have the audience in the first place to evangelize or share the Good News we carry.

The Church clearly understands this and teaches that we must be continuously scrutinizing things and revising our methods accordingly to make the Gospel attractive and relevant to the life and experiences of the people we are calling to faith. This is the whole point behind the teaching of Pope John Paul II that the new evangelization should be new in ardour, new in its method, and new in its expressions. A more progressive approach in this area remains the mission-oriented approach which focuses on the mission and the permanent goal, which is to convert and lead people to Christ and make them into disciples who are totally committed to his life and his mission of converting souls and making other disciples.

The point is that methods must always be at the service of the Gospel and the mission, not vice versa. Old methods can always be revised while new ones can be sought to achieve better results in our evangelizing mission. However, the reason for changing or revising a method should not be because it is old but rather because it is no longer effective.

At the other end of the spectrum, we must note that it is not every change that is positive and desirable. Even the new ways or methods we call "change" ought to be evaluated objectively to ensure that they are worthy tools that can be at the service of the Gospel and the overall mission of the Church. Although change can be desirable, we cannot embrace just anything in the name of change. In every case, we must constantly draw the line between "positive and necessary change" which clearly serves the Gospel and the mission of the Church better, and an "unjustifiable adherence" to old methods which are no longer effective as they used to be in the past. Sheer "stagnation" or "we-have-always-done-it-this-way" syndrome, which we sometimes misconstrue as stability even when it is no longer very effective or appealing to a generation, needs to be expunged from our minds.

Nonetheless, we must note that change does not mean throwing away everything that we consider to be old as if "old" is synonymous with "ineffectiveness." At times, reasonable change may involve blending what is positive in the old and the new methods to achieve the best results possible as far as mission or satisfying the legitimate spiritual yearnings of the people of God is concerned. In practice, I have seen such a beautiful blend between the "old" or the "traditional way" and the "new way" work perfectly, especially in the area of Eucharistic Adoration. Both the more conservative Catholics and the younger generation of Catholics and even some non-Catholics found it spiritually uplifting and fulfilling and always looked forward to it.

In evaluating which method we should accept or reject, the primary thing to consider should be if it serves the Gospel and the mission of the Church better. Provided that it is not morally reprehensible, some of the major questions to consider are, "Does it attract people and offer them the opportunity to hear the saving Gospel of Jesus Christ and be converted?" "Does it uplift people spiritually and satisfy their longing for God?" "Does it help them fulfil their personal mission in the world among other things?"

Formation of Catholics Along Four Major Streams

In pursuing our evangelizing mission, we can learn something from the business model. The primary goal of businessmen is to have a good market for their products and make profit even though they also try to satisfy their customers. To achieve their goal, they study their targeted consumers to understand how they think, what appeals to them, and how best to reach them and make them patronize their products.

Applied to evangelization, our primary goal is always to lead people to intimacy with God. It involves bringing Jesus Christ and his Gospel to the centre of their lives and getting them to submit to his Lordship. One of the qualities of a good evangelizer is the ability to understand the people he wishes to evangelize and the environment in which he carries out his mission. He needs to have a grasp of the prevailing culture in the place. That is to say, how the people think, their points of interests or attraction, the things that can open their hearts to the Gospel Message, and the best methods to use in evangelizing them.

Once we are armed with this information, the next step is to reach the people and get them to hear and respond to the salvific Message of Jesus Christ. This step begins with getting their attention, using what can attract them. The point is that we cannot convince a people to follow Jesus if we do not have their attention or cannot bring them out to hear the Good News we preach. Even when we succeed in reaching them, we may not be able to communicate effectively with them unless we understand where they are and what appeals to them and then meet where they are in order to lead them from there to Christ.

Observing the situation in the West, North America, and Africa, it is easy to see that the Catholic Church, the Evangelicals, and the Pentecostals enjoy large followership among Christians.[602] In reality, the different denominations have their strong points. For example, Catholics lay strong emphasis on the sacraments and sacramental life above all else, the Evangelicals emphasize the Scriptures, while the Pentecostals and the charismatics stress the Holy Spirit and the charismatic dimension of the Church.

With particular reference to Nigeria, the rapid and widespread growth that the Pentecostal churches are enjoying is largely because of their strong emphasis on Scripture, the Holy Spirit and the charismatic dimension, and music. On the other hand, the Catholic Church has remained strong because of her strong emphasis on the sacraments, especially the Holy Eucharist, even though this has not prevented a significant number of Catholics from drifting to Pentecostalism.

On the strength of this candid observation, we need to find a sure way to keep our faithful, especially the younger generation in the Church. In the same vein, we need to strive to bring back strayed Catholics and at the same time attract many others (non-Catholic Christians and non-Christians alike) to the Church. While we keep our eyes on the goal of conversion and transformation of lives and completely avoid any tendency to water down the Gospel and right practices in the Church, we must pay attention to what appeals to the people of our time and what can satisfy their

[602] While the Evangelicals are making more converts in America, the Pentecostals are making more converts in Nigeria and other parts of Africa.

legitimate spiritual yearning. In essence, we need to come up with a more vibrant and evangelical (zealous) Catholicism that is not lacking in contemplation and the solid spirituality we were known for in the past.

The Four Streams of Formation

As Scripture tells us, we are created by God and for him (cf. Col 1:15-17). Although original sin separated us from him, baptism restores us as his adopted children through Jesus Christ. By virtue of this, we are called to the divine life in imitation of Christ. Everything about our life and formation ought to revolve around divine intimacy and service to the Gospel as visible fruits of our conversion and transformation. As our model, Jesus displayed this strong intimacy with the Father and totally devoted himself to his will and service (cf. Jn 4:34). In spite of his busy ministry, he withdrew very often to be alone with his Father and sought to give him glory in all things (see Mt 14:22-23; Jn 4:34; 17:4-7).

To help today's Catholics build such intimacy with God and a devoted life of service with a strong missionary appeal, their practical formation should revolve around four main streams in addition to what we are doing now. The streams of formation in question are the Word of God (Sacred Scripture), sacramental life, the Holy Spirit, and prayer and the spiritual life.[603] These should be the spiritual pillars on which to build the Christian life of the faithful without ignoring the place of doctrine and the moral life.

No doubt, these pillars have always been in the Church. Many of the saints saw in them a necessary foundation for their spiritual development. But the reality today is that (in practice) the Christian life of the average Catholic or indeed most Catholics is not grounded in these four streams. Perhaps, an example will suffice. Even though we celebrate the sacraments, especially the Eucharist and read the Word of God regularly in the Church, the day-to-day life and choices of many Catholics are not shaped by them. On the contrary, what we often witness is a mere religiosity or a mechanical approach to the sacraments and the Christian life as a whole. The truth is that this can hardly transform the individuals

---

[603] These four streams are not listed here in any particular order.

interiorly and make them Christlike and more spiritually fruitful in the areas of witnessing, selfless service, charity, and intentional mission.

The authentic formation of Catholics along these streams should necessarily take place within the context of proper discipleship. Already, in the preceding chapters, I have said a great deal about two of them, namely, the formation of Catholics in the Scriptures and prayer. To avoid unnecessary repetition, I shall focus mainly on the sacramental life here and then the Holy Spirit in the final chapter.

However, before I proceed, it is very germane to note that formation in these four areas is not intended to be merely intellectual or theoretical. Rather, the focus is practical formation aimed at personal transformation even though it involves the former. In actual sense, it is about forming Catholics to prayerfully study and reflect on the Word of God regularly and allowing it to shape their thought and influence their practical life.[604] Similarly, it is about forming them in prayer and the spiritual life in a way that leads to intimacy with the Blessed Trinity and reflects in the way they live.

In addition, the understanding of prayer by many Catholics is inadequate even though this is also true of other Christians. In reality, most Catholics do not understand the spiritual life as a relationship, or prayer as a conversation or dialogue and often reduce it to a monologue. From early childhood days we need to lead Catholics away from sheer religiosity and expose them to the spiritual life characterized by a living relationship and intimacy with God. In the same vein, we need to teach them how to pray well and help

[604] Catholics should be grounded in the knowledge of the Word. They should be familiar with the entire Bible through regular or daily prayerful study of the Word. Since knowledge in itself is insufficient and cannot result in spiritual growth if it is not applied, we need to form today's Catholics to love the Word of God, to meditate on it, to have a practical faith in it, and apply it to their concrete life situations and to make it their guide and blueprint for life like the psalmist says in Psalm 119:105. Nevertheless, this position does not in any way ignore the authority of the Living Tradition of the Church and the Magisterium.

them build a sound prayer life that goes beyond the present dependence on the traditional prayers we say in the Church, which many often recite mechanically.

Formation in Authentic Sacramental Life

The Catholic life revolves mainly around the sacraments.[605] These are Baptism, Confirmation, Holy Eucharist, Penance, Holy Orders, Holy Matrimony, and Anointing of the Sick. The attention given to these sacraments in the Church is so strong that most parents try to ensure that their children receive the proper sacrament at the appropriate time. While this strong emphasis on the reception of the different sacraments is laudable, it is extremely important to stress the need for Catholics to live out the meaning of the sacraments in their day-to-day life.

By themselves, the sacraments bestow grace. They are wonderful gifts of Jesus Christ to the Church to be appreciated by all. Nevertheless, as the *Catechism of the Catholic Church* teaches, their fruitfulness "also depends on the disposition of the one who receives them."[606] Weddell explains that they are not magic rites, which automatically transform us and enable us to carry out the larger mission for which they anoint us or for which they are conferred on us.[607] Raniero Cantalamessa makes the point even clearer when he maintains that "sacraments are not magic rites that act mechanically, without people's knowledge or collaboration. Their efficacy is the result of synergy, or collaboration between divine

[605] A sacrament, according to a definition formulated by Saint Augustine, is an outward sign of an inward grace ordained by Christ by which grace is given to our souls. There are seven of them and they are divided into three categories, namely: the Sacraments of Initiation – Baptism, Confirmation, and the Holy Eucharist; the Sacraments of healing – Penance/Reconciliation and the Anointing of the Sick; the Sacraments of service – Holy Orders and Holy Matrimony.

[606] *CCC* 1129; Also cited by S. WEDDELL, *Making Disciples, Equipping Apostles…*, *op. cit.*, p. 9.

[607] See *Ibid.*

omnipotence (that is, the grace of Christ and of the Holy Spirit) and free will."[608]

In the area of sacramental life, it is vital to note that there is a huge difference between being a mere recipient of the sacraments (as in the case of a confirmed communicant) and living a true "sacramental life" understood in the sense of living out the actual meaning and vocation specified by each of the sacraments. It is common knowledge that many confirmed Catholics and communicants do not live an authentic Christian life that is consistent with the meaning and spirituality of the sacraments and the vocation they confer. In other words, the lives of many of them do not reflect a constant striving for personal holiness, charity, selfless service to the kingdom of God, and commitment to the mission of Christ.[609]

Too often we witness a sheer mechanical approach to the sacraments, which is devoid of a profound understanding of what they are or a proper internalization of their significance and goal. Besides, experience shows that many Catholics do not receive the sacraments with the right disposition of heart. A good number of them come to the sacraments without prior repentance or a desire to obey Christ and come under his Lordship, unlike in the early days of Christianity when Christians who came to the sacraments—for example, the Sacrament of Baptism—by way of true and genuine conversion.[610] Such a poor disposition as well as a mechanical approach to the sacraments can rob the individual and the Church as a body of the immense spiritual benefits they offer when received worthily and make it difficult for their fruits to manifest in the life of the individual.[611]

---

[608] R. CANTALAMESSA, *Sober Intoxication of the Spirit: Filled With the Fullness of God* (Cincinnati, OH: *Servant Books*, 1989), p. 42.

[609] The observation here does not apply to Catholics alone but also to other Christians, which explains why Christians in general are not changing their society.

[610] Cf. R. CANTALAMESSA, *Sober Intoxication of the Spirit…, op. cit.*, p. 45.

[611] For the sacraments to achieve their purpose, it is absolutely necessary to guard against such a mechanical approach and an unworthy reception.

Speaking in relation to the Sacrament of Baptism, Cantalamessa maintains that "for the majority of Christians, baptism is a sacrament that is still unreleased"[612] in the sense that its fruit remains bound, or unused because of the absence of certain conditions that further its efficacy.[613] Explaining further he states that although the fruit of a sacrament depends wholly on divine grace, this divine grace does not act without the "yes" or consent of the individual, which is a condition for the fruitfulness rather than the actual cause.[614] *Opus operatum* is the part done by God, while everything that depends on the free will and disposition of the recipient is called *opus operantis*, that is, the work yet to be accomplished by the individual by way of affirmation.[615]

Ordinarily, the sacraments are supposed to expose the recipients to the divine life. They offer us an opportunity for a life-changing encounter with God through Christ and in the Holy Spirit. Viewed from this angle, an ongoing participation in them, especially the Holy Eucharist and the Sacrament of Reconciliation, should not be a matter of routine, but the fruit of a conscious desire to renounce sin and to draw close to Christ. As such, regular reception of the sacraments should gradually lead the individual to an ongoing personal conversion, spiritual transformation, and fruitfulness visible in holiness, charity, service and mission for Christ, among other things.

But in practice, it is important to find out what percentage of Catholics are really getting converted and spiritually transformed by their regular attendance of Mass and the reception of the Holy Eucharist. How many Catholics are becoming holy, evangelical in their mindset and spiritually mature and fruitful as a result of having received the sacraments of Baptism, Confirmation, Holy Matrimony and even Holy Orders? It is indeed reductive to think of "sacramental life" merely in terms of receiving the sacraments without producing the necessary fruits of ongoing conversion, transfor-

---

[612] R. CANTALAMESSA, *Sober Intoxication of the Spirit…, op. cit.*, pp. 42-43.

[613] *Ibid.*, pp. 42, 44.

[614] *Ibid.*, pp. 42-43.

[615] *Ibid.*, p. 43.

mation, intimacy with God, holiness, Christian witness, charity, service and intentional mission for Christ.

To be more specific, we know that most Catholics cherish the Mass and Holy Communion in particular. But then, how many of them truly understand the Mass and approach it with the right disposition of mind—faith, reverence, strong yearning for a living encounter with God, expectations and total self-offering or surrender to God? How many Catholics even understand worship in general? Is the prevailing attitude of most Catholics towards the sacraments in general not largely mechanical or superficial other than spiritual?

With regard to the Holy Mass, the present mentality of *most* Catholics to go to church on Sunday merely to fulfil a religious obligation and often in a mechanical way needs to be looked into and transformed. Emphasis should be on a heartfelt desire for a life-transforming encounter with God. The issue should not be, "Did I fulfill my Sunday obligation?" but rather, "Did I really encounter God intimately at Mass? Is my weekly attendance of Mass transforming me to be more like Christ in my mindset, priorities, and my character? At Mass I hear the Word of God and receive the Holy Eucharist on a regular basis. Are these helping me grow in holiness, in Christian discipleship, and in the mission this most wonderful sacrament bestows on me?"

The truth is that most Catholics are not producing the expected fruits in these areas. If our goal is really to lead the faithful beyond merely receiving the sacraments to living an authentic sacramental life, their formation should take them to a level of mental and spiritual awareness. Here, the emphasis should be on a worthy reception of the Holy Eucharist and the other sacraments, the manifestation of the expected fruits in daily living, and the fulfilment of the mission they confer on them.

As I pointed out in Chapter Six, the major challenge we have in this area is with improper formation that focuses more on the actual reception of the sacraments than on conversion, concrete spiritual transformation, personal holiness, and mission. No doubt, talking about an impoverished sacramental life we can cite the tendency among many Catholics to receive the sacraments merely to fulfill an obligation or to satisfy certain requirements that will enable them to participate in the life of the Church as a major problem. Nevertheless, the most critical problem in this area is poor catechesis or formation. Consistent monumental failure in evangelization and this area are the major reasons why many confirmed Catholics or so-called soldiers of Christ are spiritually unproductive while others abandon their Catholic faith and now criticize the Church.

The result of this poor formation is that, in spite of the wonderful sacraments we are gifted with as Catholics and the graces that are open to us through them, many of us are often spiritually impoverished and thus spiritually fruitless in the area of mission, personal holiness, and charity. In actual fact, "sacramental life is impoverished and very soon turns into hollow ritualism if it is not based on serious knowledge of the meaning of the sacraments."[616] As Weddell maintains, the "serious knowledge" that empowers us to effectively live the life to which the sacraments call us, as well as carrying out the mission that the sacraments bestow upon us, is the fruit of well-articulated and goal-oriented formation.[617]

Sadly, we witness such impoverishment of sacramental life in all the sacraments, including Confirmation, Marriage and even Holy Orders. Certainly, the formation of today's Catholics is not leading most people to the goals of the different sacraments or to spiritual fruitfulness. This explains why we have many "anonymous" Catholics or "spectators" in our parishes. To buttress this emphasis on poor catechesis, the members of a Bible study class were asked who they were expecting during the time of their confirmation as they knelt down around the altar rail and the resounding response was "the bishop" instead of the Holy Spirit they were about to receive.

That was equally my experience on the day of my confirmation and it is rooted in poor formation. For example, beyond asking us to go for confession before presenting ourselves for the sacrament, nobody actual paid serious attention to our spiritual state from the standpoint of faith, conversion, and the willingness to obey Jesus Christ, to walk with the Holy Spirit and to do mission. Although sacramental confession is good, it is not enough where there is no

---

[616] *CT* 230; Also cited by S. WEDDELL, *Making Disciples Equipping Apostles…*, *op. cit.*, p. 9.

[617] *Ibid.*

true repentance and a willingness to live a righteous life. To further buttress the poor level of spiritual preparedness for the sacraments arising from poor catechesis, most Catholics were never told about the mission of the Church and their own specific mission for the Church during their catechetical formation.

Given all we have said, we need to do a lot more to ground Catholics in the sacramental life. There is need to deepen their understanding of the sacraments as a whole as an invitation into a loving, intimate, covenantal relationship with God through Christ in the Holy Spirit. This will enable them to blossom spiritually and bear authentic witness to Christ. But then, it requires us to review the present superficiality in the practice of religion among many Catholics and give critical attention to an in-depth understanding of the sacraments, their spirituality, and the vocation they confer on us. This is necessary to promote authentic Christian living among Catholics that is nourished by a regular participation in some of the sacraments.

Unfortunately, things are not likely to change as long as we have catechists and religious instructors whose primary or only focus is intellectual formation that does not upset and transform the worldview, interests, and priorities of those being formed. Formation in authentic "sacramental life" should clearly spell out the essence of the sacraments with a clear emphasis on authentic Christian living and mission.

Perhaps, in preparing the candidates for the different sacraments, our working definition of a baptized or confirmed or married or ordained Catholic should inevitably include our expectations of those who receive the different sacraments. For example, a confirmed Catholic is one who has received the Sacrament of Confirmation and strives to replicate the life of Christ and do mission for him as a matter of intentionality.[618]

---

[618] This is not an attempt to alter the Church's definition of a sacrament. In fact, this is only a "working definition" of a "confirmed person" which does not seek to change the Church's definition of a confirmed person, but merely builds into the consciousness of the candidates for Confirmation from the outset the Church's expectations or what it means to be a confirmed person in practice.

Today, the problems we have pointed out in this section are clear to the Church. This is why she is talking about the New Evangelization or how to re-evangelize already sacramentalized Catholics to convert them.[619] Unfortunately, this trend has remained so either because the pastors themselves fail to see the problem or they are simply indifferent. In practice, the idea of giving the Sacrament of Confirmation in particular to children who do not clearly understand what baptism or confirmation is or the mission they confer is difficult to justify. Giving this sacrament to even adults who have never responded to a clear proclamation of the kerygma or made a clear baptismal choice of conversion and a personal "yes" to Christ or have a personal relationship with him is counterproductive. On this vital issue, Dimitri Sala writes,

> In the early Church, the preaching of this Message [the kerygma] was clear and people knew the terms of it. That's why it stirred up so much trouble and people were even killed for it. But now we have settled for a practice of baptism in which people are welcomed to the sacraments externally without necessarily having heard a clear proclamation of the Gospel. And so many are baptized without making the baptismal choice of conversion.[620]

As a matter of fact, the inclination to give the sacraments, especially Confirmation, away so easily is an effort towards numbers rather than substance. It may give the impression that we do not value the sacraments enough or that the critical marker of the success of our ministry is the number of sacramentarians we raise whether or not they are converted and discipled. From the spiritual and the evangelical or mission standpoints, this practice is not in our best interest as a Church. In some cases, it can be a disaster.

Ordinarily, Baptism signifies repentance.[621] The reason for undergoing baptism is conversion and the willingness to live the life of

---

[619] Pope Saint John Paul II was absolutely right in identifying the sacramentalization of people who were not properly evangelized and formed as a major problem in the Church.

[620] D. SALA, *The Truth About Evangelization* (Liguori, MO: Liguori Publications, 1997), p. 18.

[621] Cf. *AG* 6.

Christ. For Dimitri, our experience of admitting to adult baptism people who are yet to make a sincere and practical baptismal choice of conversion is not different from what we do at present with the sacraments of Confirmation and Marriage and Holy Orders. Yet, no sacrament is magic, meaning that "without personal acceptance of the reality that it is supposed to celebrate, it has minimal effect in the life of the recipient.[622]

The culpable negligence in this area is partly the reason many of our poorly catechized young people and adults often drift away, while many others who remain in the Church fail to manifest in their lives the fruits of the sacraments they have received. Without necessarily advocating that we should hoard the sacraments, it is absolutely necessary to accord them greater reverence by paying attention to the quality of catechesis or formation that we offer the faithful and the quality of sacramentarians we are raising in the Church.

Growth in faithfulness to God and spiritual fruitfulness should be experienced as a necessary outcome of an authentic participation in the sacraments. As a matter of fact, growth in personal holiness is not enough. In addition to it, spiritual fruitfulness marked by a strong commitment to mission is an indisputable evidence of an authentic participation and encounter with God in the celebration of the sacraments. As we grow in divine intimacy and personal holiness, we too, like Jesus, begin to give ourselves more and more to the work of the Father and the growth of his kingdom. In other words, our sincere walk with Jesus will eventually culminate in working with him, thus making mission a critical feature of a sacramental life.

The Holy Spirit and the Charismatic Dimension

The next stream of formation to which we should expose Catholics is the Holy Spirit. The Christian life is a life lived in the Holy Spirit (cf. Rom 8:5-17; Gal 5:16-18). Although we talk about the Holy Spirit in the Church and mention him in our prayers, the truth is that we do not give him enough attention in our teaching and in practice.

---

[622] Cf. D. SALA, *The Truth About Evangelization..., op. cit.,* p. 18.

Thus, in proposing this area as a major stream we should focus on the formation of Catholics today, my emphasis is not on mere academic exercise or memorization of the doctrines on the Holy Spirit. Far from that, the more crucial thing is how we can lead our people to a living encounter with the Person of the Holy Spirit and prepare them to live their lives in the power of the Holy Spirit and manifest the different gifts he bestows on the faithful. However, since a whole chapter is devoted to the Holy Spirit and the charismatic dimension of the Church, I will save my remarks for that chapter.

Promoting a Purpose or Mission-Driven Church

All we have said in this chapter leads to an inevitable conclusion, namely, that we need to move away from the present maintenance culture in the Church and be deliberately purposeful and mission driven as a Church. We should not leave things to chance or do them merely because we are expected to do them. The Church was established for a purpose and that is the mission to convert the world to Christ. So, we must be mission driven in all we do.

Jesus was sent into the world for a purpose or with a mission (cf. Lk 4:18-19). In his lifetime on earth, he carried out a purpose-driven ministry and as Warren maintains, "What is needed today are churches that are driven by purpose instead of other forces."[623] The other forces he refers to here include finances, events, programmes, personality, fame and similar. On the contrary, what is absolutely crucial is the mission to save souls through the ongoing proclamation of the Gospel by the Church as well as the celebration of the sacraments and commitment to charity.

Today, many churches are declining or have plateaued because both leaders and the people have lost sight of their mission or the purpose of their existence as a church and busy themselves chasing other things at the expense of what is most essential.[624] This obvious misplacement of priorities does not promote effectiveness. To buttress this point, many of the lay faithful and sometimes the pastors themselves hardly comprehend the mission of the Church

[623] R. WARREN, *The Purpose Driven Church..., op. cit.*, 80.
[624] Cf. *Ibid.*, pp. 81, 89.

and the role of the parish in that mission. Sometimes, this creates confusion in the parish. Different parish priests come into a parish at short intervals and point the people to different directions thereby impoverishing them as far as mission is concerned.[625]

As Warren asserts, the starting point for every church and her leaders and people [and what we do as a church] should be the question, "Why do we exist?" That is to say, "Why does the Church exist?—What is her purpose or mission?" Until we all—the bishops, the priests, the lay faithful, and lay organizations—grasp this both conceptually and practically and make it our agenda and the primary measure of success in all we do, mission will continue to take the back seat in our churches. And if mission is not the driving force of all we do as a Church, we are not likely to have strong and healthy churches that can achieve the goals of evangelization both in its strict sense and in its broad sense of Christianizing the cultures and activities in society.

[625] For example, in one parish, some people were very critical of their new parish priest for changing the "mission" of their parish from "building a hall" to evangelization. Sadly, such ignorance is not limited to the people in that particular parish.

Chapter Twelve

REDISCOVERING THE PLACE OF THE HOLY SPIRIT AND THE CHARISMS

So much has been said in this book as far as the drift of Catholics to Pentecostalism is concerned. Following a careful reflection on this and the situation in the Church as a whole, my final word in this work will be the Holy Spirit. In practice, we need to rediscover the place of the Holy Spirit in the life, mission, and activities of the Church as a matter of necessity and urgency. In like manner, we need to help the entire faithful—priests and lay faithful alike—rediscover the Holy Spirit and the charismatic dimension of the Church in practice, not just intellectually. This will be our primary concern in this chapter.

Who Is the Holy Spirit?

Who is the Holy Spirit? Is "the Holy Spirit" a thing or a symbol or an impersonal force or a person? Experience shows that, although many Christians believe in the Holy Spirit, they have wrong notions of who he really is. Some identify him with symbols, such as wind, dove, fire, water, cloud and so on. Although these are actually symbols of the Holy Spirit, the problem is that some Christians do not go beyond the symbols themselves. Yet, there are others who see the Holy Spirit as an impersonal force with whom no one can have a personal relationship.

In reality, the Holy Spirit is neither a symbol nor an impersonal force, but a Person with whom we can have a personal relationship. Jesus himself used a *personal pronoun* "he" (not it) to describe him (cf. Jn 14:26). In actual fact, the evidence of his personhood is clear in the Scriptures. He possesses all the *characteristics* of a person, which are intelligence (1 Cor 2:10-12), emotions (Eph 4:30), and a will (1 Cor 12:11).[626] Also, he performs some *special activities* that only a person can fulfil. He speaks (1 Tim 4:1); he directs (Acts 16:6-7); he guides (Jn 16:13); he teaches (Jn 14:26); he witnesses or testifies (Jn 15:26); he comforts (Jn 14:26); he reproves (Jn 16:8); and he intercedes for us (Rom 8:26-27).[627]

Based on these facts, no one can deny the personhood of the Holy Spirit. The notion held by some Christians that he is a spiritual Being and not a person arises from ignorance. It is because some people erroneously think that only human beings are persons. The truth is that human beings are only human persons, but there are also non-human beings (that is, spiritual beings) who are equally persons. They too possess all the characteristics of a person mentioned earlier and perform actions that only a person can do. For example, God is a Supreme Being and a pure Spirit and a trinity of three divine Persons just as the angels are spiritual beings and persons. The fundamental difference is that the Holy Spirit is not merely a person like human beings and the angels. He is a divine Person—a Deity. Both Scriptures and the *Catechism of the Catholic Church* teach that, although God is One, there are three Persons in one God—the Father, the Son, and the Holy Spirit who are of the same substance.[628] So, the Holy Spirit is the third Person of the Blessed Trinity.

The Importance of the Holy Spirit in the Scriptures

The importance of the Holy Spirit is well-documented in the Scriptures. Both the Old Testament and the New Testament con-

[626] Cf. J. WALVOORD, "The Person of the Holy Spirit," in https://bible.org/seriespage/1-person-holy-spirit, published January 1, 2008; Cf. also "The Person and Nature of the Holy Spirit," in https://harvest.org/know-god-article/the-person-and-nature-of-the-holy-spirit/. The Holy Spirit knows, reveals, and teaches, and these abilities imply intelligence. The fact that he can be grieved implies emotions, while his ability to choose implies the will. The fact the Holy Spirit possesses these characteristics of a person means he is actually a person.

[627] Cf. *Ibid.*

[628] *CCC* 253.

tain passages that reveal his nature, the enormity of his power, and his work in the lives of individuals and within the community of believers. Here, we shall attempt to examine some of them and see what they tell us about his nature and works.

Creation is the sovereign act of the Triune God. Scripture tells us that the Holy Spirit was involved in the creation of life at the beginning and he is still involved in the sustenance and renewal of all natural life (cf. Gen 1:3, 2:7; Ps 33:6-7; 104:30). In the Old Testament literature, the Hebrew word for "Spirit" is frequently translated *wind* or *breath*. Thus, the act of breathing into man's nostrils at creation is one way of depicting the role of the Spirit in the creation of mankind. Again, when Job says, "By his wind (or breath in some translations) the heavens were made fair…." (Job 26:13), he was actually referring to the role of the Holy Spirit in the creation of the universe.

God is Eternal Life and it is the Holy Spirit who puts us in communion with him. Thus, the Holy Spirit is also connected with eternal life. In fact, anything of eternal value in this life and in eternity comes through his help.[629] He works in the lives of believers to transform, renew, and make them holy. Just as he raised Jesus Christ from the dead, he gives eternal life to believers in Christ.[630] As we know, man is created in the image and likeness of God. After the Fall, man continued to remain in the image of God but lost the likeness of God. According to the *Catechism of the Catholic Church*, "Disfigured by sin and death, man remains 'in the image of God'…but is deprived 'of the glory of God'…the Spirit who is 'the giver of life.'"[631]

Now, the loss of the likeness of God and consequently communion with God and eternal life was because man was deprived of the indwelling of the Spirit of God. Under this circumstance, he was separated from God who himself is Eternal Life and became spiritually dead in the sense in which Saint Paul speaks of

---

[629] See P. NOYES, "What Does the Holy Spirit Do? 10 Roles in a Christian's Life–Christianity," in https://www.christianity.com.

[630] See *Ibid.*

[631] *CCC* 705; See also B. MASON, *Kerygma, A Proclamation of the Gospel of Jesus Christ…, op. cit.*, pp. 17, 38-39.

"the natural man" who cannot understand or accept the things of the Spirit.[632] Perhaps, this critical role of the Holy Spirit explains why Jesus said that any sin against him will not be forgiven (cf. Mt 12:31-32), granted that it is he who reveals the saving truth to men and also enables them to recognize and accept it and be saved. In truth, original sin wounded man's nature, but did not completely destroy it as some hold. Nevertheless, his mind was darkened; his emotions became unruly; and his will was weakened.[633] As the Second Vatican Council Fathers state, original sin diminished man and brought him to a lower state, "forcing him away from the completeness that is his to attain."[634] Only the Holy Spirit can heal this wounded nature and help man to attain this completeness.

Furthermore, the Spirit of God regenerates or brings back to life (cf. Ez 37:1-14; Jn 3:3-6) and he has the power to transform. When he enters and dwells in any soul, he transforms the individual gradually to make him godly. As Saint Cyril of Alexandria asserts, "the Spirit changes the character of those among whom he comes to dwell, and transforms their life."[635] Following the anointing of Saul as King of Israel, Samuel told him that the Spirit of the Lord will possess him and he will be turned into a different person (see 1 Sm 10:6).

Also, the transforming power of the Spirit of God is depicted in Ezekiel's vision of the dry bones and their conversion into a living army for God. Still, on Pentecost Day, the Holy Spirit transformed the disciples of Christ and gave them courage to leave their place of hiding and go out and proclaim Christ. Similarly, he transformed their initial self-centredness and the desire to preserve their own lives and made them selfless to the point of being willing to lay down their lives for Christ and the Gospel.

---

[632] Cf. 1 Cor 2:14 in AMERICAN STANDARD VERSION; Cf. also B. MASON, *Kerygma, A Proclamation of the Gospel of Jesus Chris…, op. cit.*, p. 39.

[633] *Ibid.*, p. 39; Cf. also B. MASON, *Kerygma, A Proclamation of the Gospel of Jesus Chris…, op. cit.*, p. 39.

[634] *GS* 13.

[635] SAINT CYRIL OF ALEXANDRIA, "Commentary on St. John's Gospel," Book 10. See the Second Reading of the Office of the Reading – Eastertide: Week 7, Thursday.

Furthermore, the Holy Spirit empowers God's people with grace and equips them with the necessary gifts for their sanctification and for mission. At Pentecost, the Apostles were equipped with spiritual gifts (evangelization, teaching, healing and so on)[636] and performed great deeds they were incapable of doing as mere human beings. The truth is that the disciples did not remain the same after their encounter with the Holy Spirit. Everything changed and they were more committed to Christ and the mission he entrusted to them.

God assigned an important role to the Blessed Virgin Mary in the salvation of mankind. He chose her to be the mother of the Saviour, Jesus Christ. But then, this was made possible by the Holy Spirit. As the evangelist writes, "Mary said to the angel, 'How can this be, since I am a virgin?' The angel said to her, 'The Holy Spirit will come upon you, and the power of the Most High will overshadow you; therefore, the child to be born will be holy; he will be called Son of God'" (Lk 1:34-35). So, to fulfil her role Mary needed the infilling and the enablement of the Spirit. Besides, at the time of Mary's visit to Elizabeth, it was through the infilling and power of the same Holy Spirit that Elizabeth recognized the presence of Jesus the Lord in the womb of Mary and then went on to proclaim her blessed among women (see Lk 1:41-44).

Furthermore, Jesus himself carried out a very fruitful ministry as an adult. He was a great teacher and preacher. Those who heard him acknowledged that he taught as one who had authority, and not as their scribes (cf. Mk 1:22; Mt 7:29). In addition, he worked many signs and wonders and performed many miracles. He healed the sick, cast out demons, and even raised the dead (cf. Lk 7:11-17; Jn 11:38-44). Ordinarily, these extraordinary works would have been enough to reveal his identity to the spiritually discerning (cf. Jn 3:1-2; 9:16-17). Yet, the chief priests and most of the scribes and Pharisees still did not recognize him and even persecuted him.

But on the other hand, when Jesus was presented in the temple Simeon saw only an infant (with no signs and miracles to his credit) and immediately recognized him as God's promised Messiah. It

[636] The Protestants speak of evangelism, but the preferred term for the Catholic Church is evangelization. Hence, the gift of evangelization is used here.

is instructive to find out how this happened. Here, Scripture tells us that it was through the help of the Holy Spirit. To put it in the exact words of the evangelist, "…the Holy Spirit rested on him [Simeon]. It had been revealed to him by the Holy Spirit that he would not see death before he had seen the Lord's Messiah. Guided by the Spirit, Simeon came into the temple…." (Lk 2:25-27). So, Simeon was a Spirit-filled man who was under the influence of the Holy Spirit. Thus, the presence of the Holy Spirit in him enabled him to discern what ordinary eyes could not see.

In the Old Testament, the Spirit of God was given to the prophets, kings, and some individuals that had special assignments to carry out for God. Moses was anointed with the Spirit of God (cf. Nm 11:16-17) and so was Joshua (cf. Dt 34:9). King Saul was given the Spirit of God (1 Sm 10:6; 11:6). When the Spirit departed from him on account of his disobedience to God, the outcome was disastrous—an evil spirit tormented him (1 Sm 16:14). Also, Samson had the Spirit of God when he judged Israel. Empowered by the Spirit, he was able to accomplish some amazing deeds and overcome the Philistines. But when the Spirit departed from him he was overcome by the lords of the Philistines (cf. Jgs 16:20-21).

In Psalm 51:11, King David earnestly begs with God, saying, "Do not take your Holy Spirit from me." In actual sense, it is not difficult to understand why David pleaded with God so passionately not to take his Spirit from him. From experience, he knew the importance of the Holy Spirit in his life and in the life of a man. He equally knew that once the Spirit of God leaves a man he is doomed spiritually. For example, Adam and Eve died spiritually after the Fall because the Spirit of God left them. More specifically, David knew what happened to King Saul after the Spirit of God left him. In fact, Saul's experience was so traumatic that David never wanted anything similar to happen to him.

From all we have said here, we can summarize the works or functions of the Holy Spirit in the Sacred Scriptures as: infilling or indwelling, work of revelation, inspiration, conviction and conversion, regeneration, guidance, empowerment or enablement, intercession and the work of salvation. In addition, an important thing that stands out in Scripture is that the Holy Spirit is totally indispensable to the divine life of God.

The Importance of the Holy Spirit in the Teachings of the Catholic Church

The Church attaches serious importance to the Holy Spirit as the third Person of the Triune God. Her teaching on the Holy Spirit and his role in the life and ministry of the Church as well as the individual Christian is equally well-documented in the catechism and other writings of the Church, Fathers, and popes. Here, we hope to consider a few of them.

The Holy Spirit in the Catechism of the Catholic Church

The Holy Spirit is the one who communicates the life of God to men (cf. CCC 684). In the Nicene Creed we recite at Mass, we refer to him as the "Lord, the Giver of life." Without him, spiritual life is not possible. In fact, it is not only that a person cannot become a Christian without him, but even after baptism no one can live out the Christian life fruitfully without his help. Moreover, in the area of worship or sacramental liturgy, for example the Mass, it is the Holy Spirit who puts us in communion with Christ.[637] So, true worship of God is not possible without him.

As we saw in Chapter Four, the Bible which is the most cherished book of Christians is the product of the collaboration between the Holy Spirit and men. He inspired the human authors to write and also preserved what they wrote from error. Now, if he inspired the entire Bible, then as the Church teaches, the spiritual interpretation of the Bible is impossible without him.[638]

Furthermore, it is the Holy Spirit that bestows on believers the traditional seven gifts mentioned in Isaiah 11:1-3 and the spiritual fruits mentioned in Galatians 5:22-23, which are meant to sanctify us and help us live the Christian life fruitfully. In the same vein, he is the one who bestows the charisms or spiritual gifts mentioned in 1 Corinthians 12:4-11 and Ephesians 4:11-13 to empower us for our God-given mission or our role in the upbuilding of the Church.

---

[637] *CCC* 688.

[638] Cf. *CCC* 113.

The Holy Spirit and the Word of God and Tradition

Speaking of the role of the Holy Spirit in relation to the divine Word of God or Scripture, Pope Benedict XVI maintains that we can only have an authentic understanding of Christian revelation through the activity of the Holy Spirit. This is because "God's self-communication always involves the relationship of the Son and the Holy Spirit, whom Saint Irenaeus of Lyons refers to as 'the two Hands of the Father.'"[639] The Bible was written under the inspiration of the Holy Spirit who collaborated with the human authors to produce each book listed in the canon. He is the one who makes it possible for the Word of God to be expressed in human words.

In recognition of the importance of the Holy Spirit in the area of the Word, the Church teaches that only the Holy Spirit who inspired the Words of Scripture can give us a spiritual understanding of the Word of God.[640] While *exegetes* can arrive at the literal sense of a Biblical text through rigorous study, the spiritual meaning of the text can only be given by the Spirit. In fact, "without the efficacious working of the 'Spirit of Truth' (Jn 14:16), the words of the Lord cannot be understood."[641]

Pope Benedict XVI draws our attention to the ancient prayer (by the priest) which in the form of an *epiclesis* invokes the Holy Spirit before the readings at the liturgy are proclaimed. The prayer states, "Send your Paraclete [Spirit] into our hearts and make us understand the Scriptures which he has inspired; and grant that I may interpret them worthily, so that the faithful assembly here may profit thereby."[642] This strengthens the fact that openness to the Holy Spirit is paramount to the understanding of Sacred Scripture.

In addition, the Church recognizes the role of the Holy Spirit in making the Words of the Sacred Scriptures very effective in the hearts of believers. He opens the hearts of believers to accept the living Word of God and to produce its fruits. On this, Pope Benedict XVI maintains that, "The Word of God, constantly pro-

---

[639] Cf. *VD* 15.

[640] *CCC* 113.

[641] *VD* 15.

[642] *VD* 16.

claimed in the liturgy is always a living and effective Word through the power of the Holy Spirit."[643] Stressing this point further, he maintains that,

> The Church has always realized that in the liturgical action the Word of God is accompanied by the interior working of the Holy Spirit who makes it effective in the hearts of the faithful. Thanks to the Paraclete, the Word of God becomes the foundation of the liturgical celebration, and the rule and support of all our life. The working of the same Holy Spirit brings home to each person individually everything that in the proclamation of the Word of God is spoken for the good of the whole gathering.[644]

Equally, the Fathers of the Second Vatican Council acknowledge the role of the same Holy Spirit in relation to the Living Tradition of the Church. They claim that "Tradition of apostolic origin is living and dynamic" and that it "makes progress in the Church, with the help of the Holy Spirit."[645] Progress here does not mean that the truth of the apostolic Tradition changes, but rather that the Church experiences "a growth in insight into the realities and words that she passes on, through contemplation and study, with the understanding granted by deeper spiritual experience and by the preaching of those who, on succeeding to the office of bishop, have received the sure charism of truth." [646]

The Holy Spirit in the Mission of Christ

The Holy Spirit played a crucial role in the mission of Christ. As Pope Benedict XVI teaches, "The missions of the Son [Jesus Christ] and the Holy Spirit are inseparable and constitute a single economy of salvation."[647] According to him, "The same Spirit who acts in the incarnation of the Word in the womb of the Virgin Mary is the Spirit who guides Jesus throughout his mission and

---

[643] *VD* 52.

[644] *Ibid.*

[645] See VD 17; Citing *DV* 8.

[646] *VD* 17; Citing *DV* 8.

[647] *VD* 15.

is promised to his disciples."[648] As the *Catechism of the Catholic Church* teaches, Jesus in his humanity was anointed with the Holy Spirit for his salvific mission on earth.[649] This was evident during his baptism at the Jordan (cf. Mt 3:13-17). The fact that he was both Spirit-filled and Spirit-led is clear in his own testimony, which we refer to as his mission statement. Here, he states, "The Spirit of the Lord is upon me, because he has anointed me to bring good news to the poor. He has sent me to proclaim release to the captives and recovery of sight to the blind, to let the oppressed go free, to proclaim the year of the Lord's favor" (Lk 4:18-19).

Further, the testimony of Saint Peter in this area is quite instructive. He states that after the baptism of Jesus in Galilee that John announced, "God anointed him with the Holy Spirit and with power" and "he went about doing good and healing all who were oppressed by the devil, for God was with him" (Acts 10:38). The point from this is that Jesus operated under the powerful influence of the Holy Spirit during his life and ministry on earth. The power of the Holy Spirit worked through his humanity all the time,[650] which should be a worthy example to the Church and individual Christians.

The Holy Spirit in the Mission of the Apostles

Jesus knew the importance of the Great Commission that he entrusted to his disciples. But he was equally aware of their limitations and the fact that the mission itself was beyond every human power. So, when he entrusted his mission to his disciples, he did not intend that they should pursue it without the help of the Holy Spirit even though he had been with them for about three years. For that reason, he asked them to wait and receive the Holy Spirit and be empowered before embarking on mission (cf. Lk 24:46-49; Acts 1:4-5, 8). As a matter of fact, the Great Commission itself ends with the promise of the Holy Spirit, "I am with you always, to the end of the age" (cf. Mt 28:19-20). The way Jesus was going

---

[648] *VD 15.*

[649] *See CCC 690.*

[650] Cf. B. MASON, *Kerygma, A Proclamation of the Gospel of Jesus Christ..., op. cit.*, p. 34.

to be with them was through the Holy Spirit whom he would send to them as a Helper on Pentecost Day (cf. Jn 16:7-15).

The Holy Spirit and the Mission of the Christian and the Church

Although we are called to proclaim the Good News of salvation in Jesus Christ, we should never forget that the mission of Christ is also that of the Holy Spirit. As the Church teaches, he is the principal agent of the Church's mission of evangelization. As Pope Paul VI maintains, there can be no evangelization without the action or collaboration of the Holy Spirit. The Holy Spirit is the soul of the Church and it is only through his help that she increases or is multiplied.[651]

In the course of evangelizing a person, the Spirit is active both in the evangelizer and the one being evangelized to make evangelization succeed. As Pope Paul VI states, he places on the lips of the evangelizer words which he could not possibly find by himself and at the same time "predisposes the soul of the hearer to be open and receptive to the Good News and to the kingdom being proclaimed."[652] Thus he is able to accomplish what we cannot accomplish by our human skills even when we possess the highest intelligence and communication effectiveness. According to the pope,

> Techniques of evangelization are good, but even the most advanced ones could not replace the gentle action of the Holy Spirit. The most perfect preparation of the evangelizer has no effect without the Holy Spirit. Without the Holy Spirit the most convincing dialectic has no power over the heart of man. Without Him the most highly developed schemas resting on a sociological or psychological basis are quickly seen to be quite valueless.... Now if the Spirit of God has a preeminent place in the whole life of the Church, it is in her evangelizing mission that He is most active. It is not by chance that the great inauguration

---

[651] Cf. *EN* 75.

[652] Cf. *EN* 75.

> of evangelization took place on the morning of Pentecost, under the inspiration of the Spirit.[653]

As the principal agent of evangelization, it is the Holy Spirit "who impels each individual to proclaim the Gospel, and it is He who in the depths of consciences causes the world of salvation to be accepted and understood."[654] It can equally be said that "He is the goal of evangelization."[655] In all, conversion which is the goal of evangelization is actually the work of the Holy Spirit, not ours. According to Saint Alexandria, conversion from a sinful way of life and utter transformation can only be brought about by our sharing and participation in the Holy Spirit.[656] Although we can proclaim the Gospel in the most fascinating and appealing way, but ultimately, conversion is the work of the Holy Spirit.

The same is true of holiness. Although human effort is needed, holiness does not depend on it. No matter how hard we try, no one can attain holiness without the help of the Holy Spirit. This is because it is the Holy Spirit who "changes the character of those among whom he comes to dwell and transforms their life."[657] "He readily replaces their [worldly] desire to [make them] fix their gaze only on the things of heaven; he changes their unmanly cowardice into the spirit of courage"[658] as was the case in the experience of the disciples at Pentecost and afterwards. To desire and work to achieve holiness by our own efforts alone can only lead to frustration. Speaking on the important role of the Holy Spirit in the life and mission of the Christian and the Church, Saint Paul writes:

> There is nothing in us that allows us to claim that we are capable of doing this work. The capacity we have comes from God; it is he who made us capable of serving the new

[653] *EN* 75.

[654] *EN* 75. Here, he makes reference to *AG* 4.

[655] *EN* 75.

[656] Cf. SAINT CYRIL OF ALEXANDRIA, "Commentary on John's Gospel," Book 10, Office of the Reading, Eastertide: Week 7, Thursday.

[657] *Ibid.*

[658] *Ibid.*

> covenant, which consists not of written laws, but of Spirit. The written laws bring death, but the Spirit gives life.[659]

Now, if this is the case, then the Church, families, the lay associations and individual Christians who are called to go on mission for Christ on a constant basis cannot do without the Holy Spirit at the practical level. This calls for constant openness to the Holy Spirit and his work, intimacy with him, and total reliance on him through prayer. Although we may possess in-depth knowledge about things and even expertise in the sacred sciences, yet reliance on the Holy Spirit is absolutely necessary if we wish to be very effective in our evangelizing mission.

Here, it is pertinent to note that the same Spirit of God was at work in Jesus. At his baptism the Holy Spirit descended on him and "the voice of the Father - 'This is my beloved Son with whom I am well pleased' (Mt 3:17) - manifests in an external way the election of Jesus and His mission."[660] Although he himself was perfect God and perfect man, he was Spirit-filled and Spirit-led (cf. Lk 4:1, 14, 18). Here, we can learn a great deal from the example of his own life and his counsel to his disciples regarding the indispensability of the Holy Spirit in their life and ministry. The point is that we, as a Church or as individual Christians, can never succeed in our mission to reach and win humanity for Christ without the help of the Holy Spirit. This is because he alone can make our proclamation effective and turn the hearts of men to God.

The truth in this is that we will accomplish far more in our evangelizing mission if we are in the Spirit and are led by him than by all other human efforts expended and money spent.[661] Although, in theory, we continue to maintain that the Holy Spirit is the principal Agent of the Church's mission of evangelization, the problem is that most of us fail to see this critical point in practice and continue to rely more on our human intelligence and abilities.

If the infant Church was extremely fruitful and successful in the area of witness and mission as is evident in the Acts of the

---

[659] 2 Cor 3:5-6. See New International Version (NIV).

[660] *EN* 75.

[661] Cf. J. SKINNER, ed., *Miracles & Missions Digest,* Aug/Sept 2014, vol. 58, no. 5, p. 10.

Apostles, it was not because of the human abilities of Saint Peter and Saint Paul or any of the other Apostles. Rather, it was because the early Church was heavily Spirit-directed and her leaders were really "men of the Spirit." "The Spirit was 'a dominant reality' in her life, the 'source of all guidance' and 'the source of [its] day to day courage and power.'"[662] In practice, they allowed the Holy Spirit a free reign in their lives and missionary works. In fact, to emphasize the role of the Holy Spirit in the evangelizing mission of the infant Church and its administration covered in the Book of the Acts of the Apostles, some scholars have come to designate the Book itself as the "Gospel of the Holy Spirit."[663] The commitment to the Holy Spirit was not merely theoretical or verbal, but it was practical and total.

The Holy Spirit and Participation in the Divine Life of Christ

After the Fall of Adam and Eve in the Garden of Eden, man was disfigured by sin and death and was deprived of the Spirit of God even though God did not abandon man. The *Catechism of the Catholic Church* captures this well when it states that:

> Disfigured by sin and death, man remains "in the image of God," in the image of the Son, but is deprived "of the glory of God,"[66] of his "likeness." The promise made to Abraham inaugurates the economy of salvation, at the culmination of which the Son himself will assume that "image"[67] and restore it in the Father's "likeness" by giving it again its Glory, the Spirit who is "the giver of life."[664]

At baptism, the Spirit of God is restored to us and thus enables us to participate in the divine life once again. According to Saint Cyril of Alexandria, "God who begets us is the Holy Spirit."[665] "We

---

[662] W. BARCLAY, *Daily Study Bible…, op. cit.*, p. 19.

[663] *Ibid.*, p. 18.

[664] *CCC* 705.

[665] SAINT CYRIL OF ALEXANDRIA, "Commentary on St. John's Gospel," Book 10, 2. Cited in the Office of the Reading, Eastertide: See Week 6: Monday.

are inserted and grafted into him [Christ the Vine] so as to participate in his nature through receiving a share in the Holy Spirit; for we are made one with Christ the Saviour by his Holy Spirit."[666] It is through the Holy Spirit that we are transformed into the sons and daughters of God.[667] "Men are twice conceived, first of the body, secondly of the divine Spirit."[668] Also, it is the Holy Spirit that brings all to a spiritual unity.[669] As Saint Irenaeus asserts, "The Spirit brought the scattered races together into unity, and offered to the Father the first-fruits of all the nations."[670]

The Holy Spirit Enlightens Our Faith and Knowledge

Our human weakness cannot grasp the Father and the Son, but our faith is enlightened by the gift of the Holy Spirit. According to Saint Hilary, "Unless the human mind drinks the gift of the Spirit by faith, it will have the nature for understanding God but it will not have the light of knowledge."[671] While it is possible to "know about" God intellectually, it is impossible to "know him" spiritually without the help of the Holy Spirit. In other words, experiential knowledge of God which is life-changing is the work of the Spirit, not man or his intellect.

Similarly, Saint Hilary maintains that the unity of the Church is established by the Holy Spirit.[672] This is evident in the story of Pentecost in the Acts of the Apostles. The coming of the Holy Spirit brought unity to the children of God by allowing them to hear in their own languages what Peter spoke about God's deeds of power (cf. Acts 2:1-11). This is contrary to the incident of the Tower of

---

[666] *Ibid.,* see Week 5, Tuesday.

[667] *Ibid.,* see Week 6, Monday.

[668] *Ibid.*

[669] *Ibid.* See Eastertide: Week 6, Tuesday.

[670] SAINT IRENAEUS, *The Treatise of St. Irenaeus Against the Heresies,* Book 3,17,1-3. See the Office of the Reading–Pentecost Sunday.

[671] SAINT HILARY, *On the Trinity,* Book 2, 1, 33-35, in the Office of the Reading, Eastertide: Week 7, Friday.

[672] Cf. *Ibid.* See Eastertide: Week 7, Saturday.

Babel where the language of all the earth was confused (cf. Gen 11:1-9).

The Importance of the Holy Spirit Depicted in the Symbols of the Holy Spirit

The use of symbols in the Church has a long history. At different times, different things were used to depict certain realities about our faith. For instance, among the persecuted Christians in Rome, the symbol of a fish was used for Christianity. Similarly, different symbols are used today to denote the Holy Spirit. Although, as we said earlier, he is not any of these symbols, however, each of them has something to tell us about his person, nature, and works. Here, we shall consider some of them to see exactly what they say about the nature and works of the Holy Spirit.

The Symbol of the Dove

By far the most common symbol used to represent the Holy Spirit is the dove. This is not surprising at all. Following the baptism of Jesus in the Jordan, the four evangelists tell us that the heavens were opened and the Spirit of God descended upon him in bodily form like a dove (see Mt 3:16; Mk 1:10; Lk 3:22; Jn 1:32). Based on this information from the Gospels, the dove came to symbolize the Holy Spirit in the New Testament and in Christian iconography. The dove is perceived as a gentle and peaceful bird. When used for the Holy Spirit, it depicts his gentle and peaceful nature and his work to bring interior peace of the deepest kind to people in every circumstance of life.

The Symbol of Anointing Oil

In the Bible, the symbol of anointing oil (often olive oil) is used to portray the Holy Spirit. In the Old Testament, anointing oil was used to consecrate priests, prophets, and God's chosen kings (see Ex 30:30; 1 Sm 10:1; 16:12-13). It symbolizes the conferment of authority on them and their being set apart for special ministries. In the Gospel, Jesus himself talks about his anointing by the Spirit of the Lord for his messianic ministry (see Lk 4:18-19). Again, in the Book of Acts, Saint Peter makes reference to the anointing of

Jesus with the Holy Spirit and with power for the purpose of ministry (cf. Acts 10:38).

In Scripture, we see a link between anointing oil and the Spirit of God. It is widely used as a symbolism for the Holy Spirit. It represents the presence, infilling, and empowerment of the Holy Spirit. In addition, oil is used for medical purposes (cf. Lk 10:33-34). When applied to wounds, it is soothing—it can soothe muscle tension and help with pains. Applied to the Holy Spirit, it reveals his soothing presence and healing work in the life of God's people.

The Symbol of Fire or Flame of Fire

Fire is a powerful symbol used in the Old Testament to depict the presence of God. Moses encountered God in a flame of fire out of a burning bush (cf. Ex 3:1-6). After the Israelites left Egypt, God led them by a pillar of cloud by day and a pillar of fire by night (cf. Ex 13:21-22). Also, it was fire from the Lord that fell and consumed the burnt offering of the prophet Elijah during the contest with the prophets of Baal on Mount Carmel (cf. 1 Kgs 18:36-38).

However, the use of fire to symbolize the Holy Spirit arises from Saint Luke's account of Pentecost according to which the tongues of fire rested on each of the disciples (see Acts 2:1-4). To understand what this symbol reveals about his nature and work it is important to examine the role of fire in ordinary life.

First, fire is connected with cleansing or purification. Gold is purified by fire to get the best quality of it. This signifies the ability of the Holy Spirit to cleanse us from sin and transform us into the best version of ourselves that can glorify God. Fire has enormous power. It has the ability to penetrate anything. This symbolizes the limitless power of the Holy Spirit to penetrate or pierce any soul to reveal what lies hidden or to convert it. Additionally, at a time when there was no electricity, the ancients lighted fire as a guide to find their path at night. This emphasizes the guiding role of the Holy Spirit in our lives and in the Church. As a matter of fact, we are not supposed to be in-charge of our lives or the Church. Rather we are supposed to be Spirit-filled and Spirit-led if we and the Church are to remain faithful to Christ our Lord.

The Symbol of Water

One of the most fascinating symbols used to depict the Holy Spirit is water. In the Gospel according to Saint John, Jesus says, "Let anyone who is thirsty come to me, and let the one who believes in me drink. As the Scripture has said, 'Out of the believer's heart shall flow rivers of living water'" (Jn 7:37-38). Saint John adds that, "he said this about the Spirit, which believers in him were to receive; for as yet there was no Spirit, because Jesus was not yet glorified" (Jn 7:39).

The Holy Spirit is connected with life. In fact, he is the Spirit of life. In the Nicene Creed we profess him to be the "Lord and giver of life" with reference to divine life. Through him the Father gives divine life to men who are dead from sin.[673] This life-giving attribute of the Holy Spirit is the reason water is one of the important symbols of the Holy Spirit.

We all know the value of water to the human being. Our body is over 70% water and without water we become sick and can even die. The people of the ancient East knew that much and taught that without water there is no life.[674] Additionally, they were familiar with the desert where nothing grows for lack of water. This experience taught them that without water nothing can grow. From these two facts it can be said that water is indispensable to life and growth.

Applied to the Holy Spirit, what this tells us about his nature and work is that he is indispensable to the Christian life and our mission. In other words, there can be no spiritual life without the Holy Spirit and no one can truly experience interior conversion or grow in the divine life of God without his help. According to Saint Irenaeus, "And just as the dry soil cannot bear fruit unless it receives moisture, so we, who to begin with are dry wood, can never bear the fruit of life unless the rain from heaven [the Holy Spirit] falls upon our wills."[675]

---

[673] *LG* 4, 12.

[674] See J. CYMBALA, "When God's Spirit Moves," a DVD talk, Zondervan.com, see session 4: Water, Wind and Fire.

[675] SAINT IRENAEUS, *The Treatise of St. Irenaeus Against the Heresies...*, *op. cit.* Here, by the "rain from heaven falling upon our wills," Saint Ire-

All of the above illustrate how important the Holy Spirit is to the individual Christian and the Church as a body. Without him the Church cannot truly grow in the qualitative sense or in the spiritual life or fulfil her mission in the world effectively. Moreover, water cleanses and refreshes. When we use it as a symbol of the Holy Spirit, it signifies his power to cleanse or purify souls and the fact that he renews and refreshes us spiritually.

The Symbol of the Wind

Another exciting symbol of the Holy Spirit is the wind. Genesis 2:7 tells us how God breathed the breath of life into the nostrils of the man he formed from the dust of the earth and he became a living being. More importantly, in the Gospel according to Saint John, Jesus compares the workings or operations of the Spirit to that of the wind. He says, "The wind blows wherever it chooses, and you hear the sound of it, but you do not know where it comes from or where it goes. So it is with everyone who is born of the Spirit" (Jn 3:8).

Ordinarily, the wind is a collection of moving air or a "collection of air in its active and violent aspects."[676] Air is extremely important to our survival and the survival of life on earth. Animals require oxygen to survive. Without air there can be no life on earth. Without it no man can survive for even fifteen minutes. He will easily choke to death. Used as a symbol to depict the Holy Spirit, it seriously highlights the great importance of the Holy Spirit to the spiritual life. He is a life-giving Spirit. Without his life in us we may be alive physically, but we will be dead spiritually. This was evident in the experience of Adam and Eve. After the Fall, they were deprived of the Spirit of the Lord and died spiritually[677]—they lost their intimacy with God who is Eternal Life and thus eternal life—according to the warning God gave them (cf. Gen 2:15-17).

Again, although wind is invisible we can feel its presence and its work. This tells us that although we cannot see the Holy Spirit

---

naeus means the Holy Spirit filling us and transforming our wills.

676 See "Wind," http://www.symbolism.org/writing/books/sp/6/page2.html.

677 Cf. *CCC* 705.

with our physical eyes, we can feel him when he is present and can clearly feel his work in our lives and in other people or in any place where he is operating. The wind has immense power and those who have experienced a typhoon will easily testify to that. Similarly, the Holy Spirit is the Spirit of power and his power has no limit.[678] Actually, he has the power to transform chaos into order. He can penetrate, convict, and transform any soul and thus enable or empower people to live the Christian life. Additionally, just as the wind blows wherever it chooses, so does the Holy Spirit operate in souls in which he dwells. Moreover, he distributes his gifts freely to individuals as he chooses and thus empowers them to do great things that are well beyond their human abilities.

Promoting the Charismatic Dimension of the Church

Now that we know the importance of the Holy Spirit to the life and mission of the Church, it is important to allow him a free reign in the Church. One of the ways we can do this effectively is to promote the charismatic dimension of the Church, which we often ignore. Without neglecting the sanctifying gifts and the fruits, it entails introducing the entire faithful to practical life in the Spirit and exposing them to the charismatic or spiritual gifts of the Holy Spirit. This will be our focus in this section.

What Are Charisms?

What are charisms? The word charism is a derivative of the Greek word *charisma* meaning "favour," "gratuitous gift," "benefit."[679] According to Clark and Healy, charism is "a gift freely bestowed" and it is based on the word for "grace" – *charis*.[680] As the *Catechism of the Catholic Church* affirms, "whether [they are] extraordinary or simple and humble, charisms are graces of the Holy

---

[678] Cf. SAINT CYRIL OF ALEXANDRIA, "Commentary on St. John's Gospel…, *op. cit.*

[679] *CCC* 2003.

[680] Cf. R. CLARK and M. HEALY, *The Spiritual Gifts Handbook* (Minneapolis, MN: Chosen Books, 2018), pp. 23-24.

Spirit."[681] So, to really grasp what charisms are, we require a good understanding of grace.

The *Catechism of the Catholic Church* defines grace as "a participation in the life of God."[682] "Grace is favour, the free and undeserved help that God gives us to respond to his call to become children of God, adoptive sons, partakers of the divine nature and of eternal life."[683] Grace is the foundation of Christian life. It is "first and foremost the gift of the Spirit who justifies and sanctifies us."[684] This grace (of Christ) received in baptism is infused by the Holy Spirit into our soul to heal it of sin and to sanctify it.[685] It also includes those gifts that the Spirit bestows on us to "associate us with his work, to enable us to collaborate in the salvation of others and in the growth of the Body of Christ, the Church."[686]

Apart from the sacramental graces, which are gifts proper to the different sacraments, there are also special graces which are also known as charisms, following the Greek term used by Saint Paul.[687] "Charisms or spiritual gifts are special abilities given to Christians by the Holy Spirit to enable them to be powerful channels of God's love and redeeming presence in the world."[688] A charism can be called a "gracelet," a droplet of the vast ocean of God's grace. "It is a tangible expression of God's grace in a person's life in the form of a capacity to act in a way that surpasses human power."[689] Charisms are spiritual gifts because the Holy Spirit is their source, and they are charisms because they are freely given.[690]

More than any other biblical writer, Saint Paul has a great deal to teach us about charisms. In his letters he employs about

---

[681] *CCC* 799.

[682] *CCC* 1997, 2003.

[683] *CCC* 1996.

[684] *CCC* 2003.

[685] *CCC* 1999.

[686] *CCC* 2003.

[687] *Ibid.*

[688] See S. WEDDELL, *The Catholic Spiritual Gifts Inventory*, Third Edition (Colorado Springs, CO: The Siena Institute Press, 1997, 1998), p. 6.

[689] See R. CLARK and M. HEALY, *The Spiritual Gifts...*, *op. cit.*, p. 24.

[690] *Ibid.*, p. 24.

five different terms to denote charisms. These are "spiritual gifts," "charisms," "different kinds of service," "different kinds of working," and "manifestations of the Spirit."[691] According to Clark and Healy,

> In 1 Corinthians 12:1-7 Paul uses no less than five terms. He calls them "spiritual gifts" (*Pneumatika*, literally "spirituals") because they are given by the Holy spirit (*Pneuma*). They are "charisms" because they are given freely. They are different kinds of service "because their purpose is to serve others." They are "different kinds of working" because every time we use a gift, the Holy Spirit himself is working through us. And they are "manifestations of the Spirit" because they make the presence of the Spirit evident to others.[692]

The list of the known charisms or spiritual gifts include administration, celibacy, craftsmanship, discernment of spirits, encouragement, evangelization, faith, giving, healing, helps, hospitality, intercession, knowledge, leadership, mercy, missionary, music, pastor/shepherd, prophecy, service, teaching, voluntary poverty, wisdom, and writing. Other authors include apostleship, miracles, and speaking in tongues and the interpretation of tongues (See Ex 31:3; Rom 12:6-8; 1 Cor 12:4-11; Eph 4:11-13).

In general, charisms can be extraordinary (in the case of prophecy, healing or miracles, and speaking in tongues) and they can be simple and humble as in the case of teaching, intercession, mercy and so on. Nevertheless, what we must always bear in mind as far as they are concerned is that they are graces of Christ bestowed on the different members of the Church by the Holy Spirit to enable us to operate at a supernatural level and serve the common good in charity. So, each of the different charisms is good and useful in the Church, especially as God cannot give what is bad or useless.

---

[691] *Ibid.*

[692] *Ibid.*

Difference Between Spiritual Gifts (Charisms) and Talents

There is a huge difference between charisms or the spiritual gifts and the natural talents. Talents are natural abilities that are inborn in us or inherited from our parents at birth irrespective of whether or not we believe in God. But charisms are supernatural abilities, which the Holy Spirit bestows on believers at the time of our baptism and increases or strengthens during our confirmation to "enable us to become instruments of God's love and power to others."[693]

Our natural talents are not connected to faith. The manifestation or exercise does not depend on our relationship with God. But it is a different matter when it comes to the spiritual gifts. Although they are given to us at baptism and confirmation, their manifestation and exercise are directly dependent on our personal relationship with God. It is when we experience a level of spiritual awakening that they begin to manifest. Even then, the gifts are not fully developed at the time the individual discovers them, but tend to mature over time as he yields himself to God and exercises the gifts. Besides, the level of one's personal faith has a correlation with the degree of the manifestation of the gifts in his life.

Furthermore, talents often advance man's plans and glorify man, while the charisms serve the purpose of God for his Church and ultimately the common good of all.[694] As the *Catechism of the Catholic Church* maintains, whether they are extraordinary or simple, charisms are ordered as they are to the upbuilding of the Church, to the good of men and to the needs of the world.[695]

What makes the charismatic gifts spiritual is that their origin is God—they come from the Holy Spirit. Unlike talents, charisms are connected to the Holy Spirit and are dependent on his operations.

---

[693] S. WEDDELL, *The Catholic Spiritual Gifts Inventory…, op. cit.,* pp. 5-6; R. CLARK and M. HEALY, *The Spiritual Gifts…., op. cit.,* p. 24; Cf. *CCC* 1304.

[694] See R. CLARK and M. HEALY, *The Spiritual Gifts…., op. cit.,* p. 10; See also ST. MARY'S PARISH, Ottawa, Ontario, *Journey of Discovery: Spiritual Gifts Workshop…, op. cit.,* p. 10.

[695] *CCC* 799.

And because they are supernatural gifts their efficacy surpasses that of mere talents. The Holy Spirit either elevates the human aptitude to a supernatural level of efficacy or enables the recipient of the gifts to do what is humanly impossible,[696] that is, to produce results that are well beyond his natural abilities. In other words, it is possible for a person to have a given ability—for example, music ability—as a talent and not as a charism. But then, the Holy Spirit can transform this already existing natural talent possessed by an individual into a supernaturally empowered charism.[697]

Ordinarily, people who have particular talents can use them at will or whenever they desire. But it is not the same with the spiritual gifts or charisms. Since the Holy Spirit is their source and they are dependent on his workings, charisms are not at the disposal of the individual to use at any time and as he wishes. Again, while the exercise of the talents can excite people and bring some satisfaction (for example, emotional satisfaction), the spiritual gifts target the spirit. They work more to give glory to God and uplift the spirit of men to glorify him.

Difference Between Spiritual Gifts (Charisms) and the Traditional Seven Gifts and Fruits of the Holy Spirit

There is a difference between the "spiritual gifts of the Holy Spirit" (charisms) and the "sanctifying gifts of the Spirit" (traditional seven gifts) in Isaiah 11:1-3 and the "fruits of the Spirit" in Galatians 5:22-23. Among the gifts of the Spirit, there are some that are given to the recipient to keep and there are others that are given to him to give away.

The traditional seven gifts of the Holy Spirit (wisdom, understanding, counsel, fortitude, knowledge, piety, and fear of the Lord) and the fruits of the Spirit (love, joy, peace, kindness and similar) are given to the individual to keep for his own sanctification. They form part of our inner transformation as Christians. In

---

[696] Cf. R. CLARK and M. HEALY, *The Spiritual Gifts...., op. cit.*, pp. 23-24.

[697] See S. WEDDELL, *The Catholic Spiritual Gifts Inventory..., op. cit.*, pp. 6-7.

other words, they help us to grow and become more Christlike, which is necessary for the effective use of our charisms. But on the other hand, the charisms or spiritual gifts are for others and are meant to be given away. They help us build up the Church by serving one another with our gifts and thus revealing to them the goodness of God.[698]

A crucial thing to note is that all these gifts come from the same Spirit and are therefore connected. Growth in the traditional seven gifts of the Holy Spirit and the fruits of the Spirit translates to growth in intimacy with the Holy Trinity, and this intimacy enables the individual to be more effective in the exercise of his charisms because the charisms themselves are directly dependent on the Holy Spirit.[699]

Furthermore, a charism can be temporary or permanent. A charism is said to be temporary when it is given only for a single moment or an occasion to allow the individual to fulfil a given purpose for God at a given time. The truth is that God can elevate the abilities of a believer and use him in an unusual way to fulfil his purpose at any time if he so desires.[700] Such a temporary charism cannot be developed.[701] But the permanent ones, once discovered, can be developed further so that the individual is more effective in exercising them. In this case, faith in God, love of the Holy Trinity, intimacy with the Holy Spirit, and love of neighbour are important to its development and a more fruitful exercise.

The Controversy About the Extraordinary Charisms

At different times in her history the Church had cause to deal with controversies of diverse nature and magnitude. Today, one of such controversies within the Christian fold is with the

[698] See *CCC* 1831-1832; S. WEDDELL, *The Catholic Spiritual Gifts Inventory…, op. cit.*, p. 7; Cf. ST. MARY'S PARISH, Ottawa, Ontario, *Journey of Discovery…, op. cit.*, p. 11.

[699] See *CCC* 1830-1832.

[700] See S. WEDDELL, *The Catholic Spiritual Gifts Inventory…, op. cit.*, p. 7.

[701] See *Ibid.*, p. 7.

extraordinary charisms, namely, apostleship, prophecy, speaking and interpreting tongues, healing and miracles. The bone of contention is whether they still exist today or they have ceased. Depending on the position held by different people on this issue, we can categorize them either as cessationists or continuationists.

The cessationists are those who hold that these extraordinary gifts of the Holy Spirit have ceased. In their view, they were limited to the period between the Ascension of Jesus Christ and the end of the Apostolic age, that is, till the death of the last apostle, John the Evangelist, around AD 90. They argue that those gifts were necessary at the beginning to lay down the foundation of the Church, and after that was accomplished they were no longer necessary and ceased to exist.

Meanwhile, the continuationists vehemently disagree with that. More precisely, they argue that these gifts never ceased in the Church.[702] Although they agree that the foundation work of the Church has ended, they however contend that these gifts are still necessary in new areas where the Church needs to be planted.[703] In truth, if we consider the present unbelief or the crisis of faith in the world, one may readily agree that such gifts are needed today to stir up faith in the people of this age.

Apart from these two positions, there are some who pitch their tent in the middle. Quite frankly, they are open to the four gifts, but prefer to be cautious. Still, there are those who believe that some of these extraordinary gifts have ceased while some of them continue to exist.[704] Even the great Saint Augustine of Hippo initially defended *cessationism.* But, following a miracle involving the healing of a women with breast cancer in one of the parishes in his diocese and many other cases of healing, he retracted his earlier position.[705]

---

[702] B. GALAN, *Spiritual Gifts* (Torrance, CA: Bristol Works, Inc. & Rose Publishing, Inc., 2011), p. 5.

[703] *Ibid.,* p. 6.

[704] *Ibid.*

[705] M. HEALY, "Lectio: Evangelization and the Acts of the Apostles…, *op. cit.*

The Recipients of Charisms and the Purpose of the Gifts

As we saw in previous chapters, the mission of the Church is wide. It involves world evangelization and the Christianization of cultures and structures in all the nations of the world. Every baptized person in the Church has a specific vocation and mission to fulfil for God in and outside the Church. To enable each of us to fulfil this duty, everyone has been given specific charisms that go with his specific calling and mission.

In themselves, the spiritual gifts are charisms of service. That is to say, they are gifts that are given to individual members of the Church for the purpose of service to the community. Something to note here is that they are gifts not just because they are freely given to us by the Holy Spirit, but also in the sense that they are meant to be used for others and not ourselves. According to Clark and Healy, and in accordance with Scripture (cf. 1 Cor 12), "their very purpose is to be used for others. They are by definition and by their very nature gifts to be given away, that is, gifts to be used 'for the common good' (1 Cor 12:7)."[706] They are not something we should hoard or ignore, but something to be received with gratitude and a sense of humility and mission.

At the foundation of these gifts is God's love for each believer (i.e., Christian) and for his Church. It is a sign that God recognizes us individually and wants us to collaborate with him in the work of salvation and the upbuilding of his Church. What underpins this assertion is that the different gifts are not given to only a chosen few in the Church, but to all the faithful at the time of baptism. The fact that it is given to every Christian for service within the Body of Christ shows that every one of us is unique before God and has an irreplaceable role to play in the life and development of the Church.[707]

The charisms help us fulfil our specific mission in life. But beyond that, we must note that the particular gifts every individual has received can also give a clear insight into the specific mission

---

[706] R. CLARK and M. HEALY, *The Spiritual Gifts Handbook…, op. cit.*, p. 26.

[707] *Ibid.*

God has assigned to him in life or within the general mission of the Church.[708] On this basis, Clark and Healy maintain that since God has given every individual a role and the tool to fulfil it, "There is no unemployment in the kingdom of God"[709] as long as each person knows and exercises his gifts.

What we can also infer from this is that in God's plan no member of his Church is supposed to be anonymous or a spectator on the stands. Each individual Christian is called to be an active player in the team of Christ who uses his specific gifts and talents to play for Christ and contribute to the growth of his team—the Church. We can infer this from the writing of Jim Putman and others when they maintain that,

> If Christianity is a team sport, then the team cannot win unless everyone gets in the game.... We were chosen to be on this team and to play the role He gifted us for. We all have abilities and gifts to be used for the good of the team and the cause of Christ. Everyone is important and everyone plays.[710]

To drive the point home even more, Clark and Healy speak of a sacred responsibility as far as the gifts are concerned. They state emphatically that, "exercising our [spiritual] gifts is not optional; it is a sacred responsibility."[711] To buttress this point, they cite the words of Saint Peter who asserts, "As each has received a gift, use it to serve one another, as good stewards of God's varied grace" (1 Pet 4:10).[712]

In summary, the recipient of the spiritual gifts of the Holy Spirit is every baptized person or Christian, and the purpose is for service. God gives us the spiritual gifts to glorify him. More precisely,

---

[708] See S. WEDDELL, *The Catholic Spiritual Gifts Inventory...*, *op. cit.*, p. 8.

[709] R. CLARK and M. HEALY, *The Spiritual Gifts Handbook...*, *op. cit.*, p. 27.

[710] Cf. J. PUTMAN et al., *Real-Life Discipleship Training Manual...*, *op. cit.*, p. 21.

[711] R. CLARK and M. HEALY, *The Spiritual Gifts Handbook...*, *op. cit.*, p. 27.

[712] *Ibid.*

since the primary function of the Holy Spirit is to glorify Christ (cf. Jn 16:14), the primary function of our ministries (service) or the exercise of our charisms is to glorify Christ and also to build up the Body of Christ, that is, to develop maturity among Christians (cf. Eph 4:11-12), for the benefit of the individuals, that is, to serve one another (cf. 1 Cor 12:7) and to bring about unity in his Church.[713]

Because the gifts are not meant for ourselves but for the glory of God and the good of others and the Church, we cannot choose the particular gifts we desire. Rather, it is God who chooses what he wishes to give to every individual based on the specific assignment he wants each person to carry out for him. Nonetheless, a person can pray for particular gifts and allow God to choose whether or not to give him the gifts. But once given, we cannot lose our spiritual gifts although they can be suppressed as a result of a mortal sin and restored if we later repent. Once received at baptism, the gifts may lie dormant in an individual until there is a spiritual awakening which enables him to develop a living relationship with God.

Ignorance of the Charisms Among Catholics

Every baptized Catholic has at least one or more charisms, but the truth is that about ninety percent (90%) of Catholics, even the confirmed ones, are ignorant of the spiritual gifts they possess by virtue of their baptism and confirmation. When asked about their specific charisms, the vast majority of them appear confused or lost and many actually confess that they neither know what charisms are nor their specific gifts and mission in the Church. As a matter of fact, many Catholics have gone to their graves not knowing anything about their specific gifts and mission in the Church.

Even today, the ignorance of many Catholics in this area is monumental. The main reason is that the vast majority of them were never told about these gifts or helped to discover and use them. This is also because a majority of the priests themselves were never exposed to them and their manner of manifestations during

[713] See Eph 4:13; See B. GALAN, *Spiritual Gifts…, op. cit.,* p. 3; Cf. ST. MARY'S PARISH, Ottawa, Ontario, *Journey of Discovery: Spiritual Gifts Workshop…, op. cit.,* p. 8.

their formation. As a result, they too are ignorant of the gifts and do not intentionally teach or foster them in practice. In fact, some consider them the business of the charismatic renewal, which is a notion that is deplorable and grossly harmful to our common good.

On the other hand, most Catholics are familiar with the traditional seven gifts or the sanctifying gifts of the Holy Spirit because of the emphasis we place on them. Actually as Mary Healy rightly observes, for most Catholics, the phrase "gift of the Holy Spirit" is often viewed from the standpoint of the sanctifying gifts of the Spirit, such as wisdom, understanding and similar.[714] The simple explanation is that, in the Catholic Church, there is a strong emphasis on the sanctifying gifts of the Holy Spirit listed in Isaiah 11:1-3. These are wisdom, understanding, counsel, fortitude, knowledge, piety, and fear of the Lord.

According to the Catholic Tradition, individual Christians receive these sanctifying gifts through the sacraments of baptism and confirmation.[715] But, as Mary Healy maintains, the Church has never limited the gifts of the Spirit to these alone. In fact, Saint Thomas Aquinas wrote about these gifts, including prophesy, tongues and miracles, and stressed their immense value for the soul-winning mission of the Church.[716] Even some Catholics who acknowledge the existence of these gifts tend to view them as rare gifts found only among some great saints.

Healy explains that this unfortunate situation arose because the charisms were neglected in the Church for a very long time in both theology and practice. Theologians erroneously thought that many of the gifts (including the word of knowledge, prophecy, and healing) were for the benefit of the individual and did not have any value for the Church and her mission.[717] Healy considers this view

---

[714] R. CLARKE and M. HEALY, *The Spiritual Gifts Handbook…, op. cit.,* 29.

[715] *Ibid.; CCC* 1831.

[716] See R. CLARK and M. HEALY, *The Spiritual Gifts Handbook…, op. cit.,* p. 30; Citing SAINT THOMAS AQUINAS, *Summa Theologica* II-II, q. 171-178, especially q. 178, a. 1.

[717] *Ibid.,* p. 30.

or practice to be a "category mistake" because charisms, by their very nature, are not given for personal spiritual enrichment of the individual, but for others, the community, the common good of the whole.[718]

Growing Awareness of the Spiritual Gifts and the Obstacles

In more recent times, the spread of Pentecostalism has made it possible for many Christians to read the Bible and become aware of the spiritual gifts and their immense value. More specifically, some Catholics who witness the exercise of the gifts in Pentecostal churches and by some of their peers have come to believe in their authenticity. Some others who are aware of these gifts actually exercise them and know from experience that they are authentic and efficacious. Still, some who have merely witnessed the exercise of these charisms and strong manifestations of the Spirit desire them. Oftentimes, these wonder why they were never told about the gifts in the Church and why we do not promote them among the faithful.

Sadly, instead of promoting these gifts in the Church, some criticize, discourage, and even persecute Catholics who exercise some of the extraordinary charisms in different ways. Out of sheer ignorance of the teaching of the Bible and the Church in this area, some priests are quick to condemn without proper discernment what they do not understand. Others are suspicious of some of the charisms, while some completely deny their existence.

Still, some who see them as a contamination of the Catholic faith fueled by Pentecostalism busy themselves trying to extinguish the fire of the Spirit by discouraging their use even when they are authentic. Ironically, they believe that they are doing Christ and his Church a great favour when, in fact, their actions actually impoverish our Catholic life, our parish communities, and our mission.[719] The sad thing about this is that some Catholics interpret their deplorable actions as representing the official position of the

---

[718] *Ibid.*

[719] Indeed, their actions have grossly harmed the Church and her mission for too many years.

Church, which then causes some of them to have doubts about the Church.

Ordinarily, the exercise of charisms brings a great sense of value and excitement and joy to the one who exercises them and to the beneficiaries of their service and the whole community. Indeed, the charisms reveal God's love and his presence among his people. Thus, when highly-gifted lay people are prevented from exercising their gifts, some become disillusioned and question the level of spiritual awareness of their priests. In fact, when they can no longer bear this situation, some leave for the Pentecostal churches which offer them an enabling environment to develop and use their gifts instead of being reduced to complete recipients of the ministry of their priests.[720]

Negative Impact of Ignorance of the Charisms on the Mission of the Church

The present situation whereby most of the ordained ministers and lay people do not know or exercise their charisms does not serve the best interest of the Church. On the contrary, it has far-reaching implications for the success of our mission whether we are talking about the individual Catholic or the parish community or the institutional Church as a whole. This is because the specific type of *charisms* we have may indicate the specific mission God has for an individual or the specific direction he is leading each of us to serve him in his Church. According to Benjamin Galan,

> God empowers his people to carry on their ministries in the Church. Spiritual gifts aren't only about the abilities one may have, but about what God is doing in and through the Church and how we fit in. God is always active inside and outside the Church. We must discern how he is active and ask him to empower us to be part of those activities.[721]

[720] Although some gifted Catholics leave the Church out of frustration, there are also others who, on discovering their extraordinary gifts, become selfish and seek to establish their own churches or go to places where they can use them to make money and become famous.

[721] B. GALAN, *Spiritual Gifts…, op. cit.*, p. 7.

Another way the mission of the Church suffers is when people who actually serve in the Church operate outside the areas of mission that God designed for them by virtue of their gifting or charisms. This can happen when people are attracted to particular ministries in the Church they are not wired for or are driven by personal interest or a sheer desire to be active in one thing or the other. It is a common phenomenon in most parishes to see people serve in the "wrong" ministries just because they like them. The truth is that this does not lead to fruitfulness and excellence in these ministries. A good example is the author himself who discovered his own charisms with certainty after forty years of age. Also, there are a few other Catholics who are discovering theirs in their sixties and seventies with deep regret. Yet, the vast majority of Catholics are yet to discover their specific charisms and mission within the Church.

Such a collateral damage to the effectiveness of the Church and the success of her mission is something we cannot allow to continue unabated in this age and time, especially with the drift of some Catholics to other churches. If the familiar slogan that the Catholic Church is a sleeping giant is true, then a major source of that problem lies here in part, given that lay people who are more affected by this reality constitute over 99% of the Catholic population, while the clergy make up less than 1%. The logic behind this assertion is that the work and fruitfulness of each individual member of the Body of Christ is critical to the overall success of the mission of the Church.

Viewed from another perspective, the ignorance and the consequent inaction of Catholics in exercising their charisms explain why the vast majority of them are not engaged Catholics or have remained spiritual "infants" or "babies" or "consumers" who are almost completely dependent on the clergy for everything. In other words, spiritually they are unproductive and tend to remain at a passive level where they do not participate in mission or begin to feed others.[722]

[722] Although we all need to be fed consistently on a regular basis to remain spiritually healthy, we do not have to be mere consumers who are completely dependent on the priests and are not sharing what we are receiving with others.

Although we receive our charisms during baptism, they can remain latent in us and only begin to manifest as we experience a rebirth and begin to personalize our faith and engage in the service of God. Knowing and using one's charism is such a beautiful thing. Experience shows that as individuals come to know, develop, and use their charisms, they are fired up to collaborate with God and other believers in the work of salvation. They serve him and their brethren better and with greater enthusiasm and satisfaction. Thus, growing in the sanctifying gifts and knowing and developing their charisms will empower the faithful for a more fruitful and effective work of evangelization, and make the parish community and the Church as a whole more alive and vibrant and successful in her mission.

Charisms in the Sacred Scriptures and the Teachings of the Church

Is the idea of charisms Catholic or foreign? Is it scriptural? Against the position of some Catholics that this whole thing about charisms is a Pentecostal phenomenon brought into the Catholic Church by the charismatics, it is necessary to point out here that they are totally wrong. This is because the notion of charisms is well-grounded in both the Sacred Scriptures and the teachings of the Catholic Church.

Charisms in the Sacred Scriptures

The idea of spiritual gifts is not strange to the Bible. The Sacred Scriptures teach about the immense value of the spiritual gifts to the building up of the kingdom of God or the Church. Both the New and the Old Testaments contain a number of passages that involve the exercise of these gifts. In the Old Testament, Bezalel was gifted with the charism of craftsmanship, which is a special ability to be creative and skilful by using one's mind and hands creatively to design things that further God's kingdom. According to Exodus 31:11,

> The Lord spoke to Moses: See, I have called by name Bezalel son of U'ri son of Hur, of the tribe of Judah: and I have filled him with divine spirit, with ability, intelligence, and

> knowledge in every kind of craft, to devise artistic designs, to work in gold, silver, and bronze, in cutting stones for setting, and in carving wood, in every kind of craft.[723]

Furthermore, King David, King Solomon, and some of the Old Testament prophets like Elijah, Elisha and similar exercised a variety of charisms. In the New Testament the exercise of the spiritual gifts is more glaring. Jesus himself exercised different charisms in the course of his earthly ministry. He exercised the gift of teaching—he taught in a supernatural way, unlike the scribes (cf. Mk 1:22). He exercised the gift of knowledge (cf. Jn 4:16-19). He exhibited the gift of evangelization and was actually the greatest evangelist that ever lived. Also, he healed the sick, cast out demons, and performed all sorts of miraculous deeds, including stilling the storm and raising the dead (see Mt 8:1-4, 23-27; Mk 1:21-28; Lk 7:11-17; Jn 11:38-44).

Saint Peter also touched on the spiritual gifts and encouraged believers to exercise them in love for the good of one another and more so for the glory of God who is the author of the gifts. More specifically, in his first letter he writes,

> Above all, maintain constant love for one another, for love covers a multitude of sins. Be hospitable to one another without complaining. Like good stewards of the manifold grace of God, serve one another with whatever gift each of you has received. Whoever speaks must do so as one speaking the very words of God; whoever serves must do so with the strength that God supplies, so that God may be glorified in all things through Jesus Christ. To him be glory and the power forever and ever. Amen.[724]

Nevertheless, we owe the concrete discourse on the charisms of the Holy Spirit to the work of Saint Paul, especially in his letters to the Corinthians and the Ephesians. He used the analogy of the human body and the functioning of its different parts for the overall good of the human individual to illustrate the importance of the charisms in the Church.

---

[723] Ex 31:1-5 in NRSV.

[724] 1 Pt 4:8-11 in NRSV.

First, he notes that the human organism needs each member or all the different parts of the body (the eyes, the ears, the nose, the hands, and similar) to function well for the good of the whole person. Applying this to the Church and the charisms, he maintains that, in a similar way, God has given different charisms to each member of the Church for different ministries (services) in the Church to enable the Church, the Body of Christ, to grow and function well and maximally, and thus fulfil her mission on earth. According to him in his First Letter to the Corinthians,

> Now there are varieties of gifts, but the same Spirit; and there are varieties of services, but the same Lord; and there are varieties of activities, but it is the same God who activates all of them in everyone. To each is given the manifestation of the Spirit for the common good. To one is given through the Spirit the utterance of wisdom, and to another the utterance of knowledge according to the same Spirit, to another faith by the same Spirit, to another gifts of healing by the one Spirit, to another the working of miracles, to another prophecy, to another the discernment of spirits, to another various kinds of tongues, to another the interpretation of tongues. All these are activated by one and the same Spirit, who allots to each one individually just as the Spirit chooses (1 Cor 12:4-11).[725]

Again, in his Letter to the Ephesians, he writes,

> The gifts he gave were that some would be apostles, some prophets, some evangelists, some pastors and teachers, to equip the saints for the work of ministry, for building up the body of Christ, until all of us come to the unity of the faith and of the knowledge of the Son of God, to maturity, to the measure of the full stature of Christ (Eph 4:11-13).[726]

If we read these passages against the backdrop of the missionary mandate of Christ in Matthew 28:19-20 and his promise in Acts 1:4-5 and 8, there are some critical points we should not allow

[725] 1 Cor 12:4-11 in NRSV.

[726] Eph 4:11-13 in NRSV.

to escape our attention. These include the source and the purpose of the spiritual gifts or charisms themselves. The different charisms represent the different ministries or services to be rendered in the Church. They are God's gifts through the Holy Spirit to every member of the Church for ministry or service to one another, for the upbuilding of the Church and for the common good. Thus, in his wisdom, God empowers every individual to carry out one or more ministries in the Church and we can infer from this that he recognizes every believer and desires that everyone should be an active collaborator with him in the mission of his Church.

This all-wise God who desires the success of his mission knows that even the most intelligent and talented human beings do not have the capacity to succeed in this mission unaided. To put it differently, the evangelizing mission that Jesus entrusted to the Church is first and foremost spiritual in nature—it is about eternal life. Conscious that its demands and those of the different ministries involved are beyond the human capacity, God bestows the charismatic gifts of the Holy Spirit on each member of the Church to empower him for his specific role in that mission. So, his proactive solution was to give supernatural assistance or enablement to his Church in the form of bestowing a variety of charisms to her members.

That being the case, the exercise of the *charisms* is critical to the success of the mission of the Church. If they are not necessary, the wise God will not bestow them on us in the first place. Bearing in mind that none of us can merit these gifts, we must respect the will of the Giver and use them for the purpose for which he gave them to us. In other words, we are meant to use them graciously and generously and not hoard them.[727] In fact, the more we use them the better we get, and the more the Church and her mission flourish.

Charisms in the Teachings of the Catholic Church

It is not only the Sacred Scriptures that speak favourably of the spiritual gifts. Also, the teaching of the Church in this area is

[727] Cf. B. GALAN, *Spiritual Gifts…, op. cit.,* p. 2.

positive. In clear terms, the Catholic Church recognises the charismatic gifts of the Holy Spirit and encourages her members to exercise them. In a document of the Second Vatican Council, *Lumen Gentium*, the Council Fathers state categorically that,

> It is not only through the sacraments and the ministries of the Church that the Holy Spirit sanctifies and leads the people of God and enriches it with virtues, but, "allotting his gifts to everyone according as He wills, [1 Cor 12, 11] He distributes special graces among the faithful of every rank. By these gifts He makes them fit and ready to undertake the various tasks and offices which contribute toward the renewal and building up of the Church, according to the words of the Apostle: "The manifestation of the Spirit is given to everyone for profit" [cf. 1 Thes 5, 12, 19-21].[728]

In a similar way, the *Catechism of the Catholic Church* speaks favourably about the charisms. It teaches that they "are a wonderfully rich grace for the apostolic vitality and for the holiness of the entire Body of Christ, provided they really are genuine gifts of the Holy Spirit and are used in full conformity with authentic promptings of the same Spirit, that is, in keeping with charity, the true measure of all charisms."[729]

But some questions that may arise at this point are, "Who are the recipients of these charisms? Do they have any right and obligation to exercise them in the Church?" Already, we have stated that the recipients of the gifts are all the baptized. Re-emphasizing this, the purpose of the gifts and the rights of those who possess them, Benjamin writes that,

> The church teaches that every baptized person has received a spiritual gift or more from God to use for the upbuilding of the church and each has a right and a duty to exercise those gifts (Decree on the Apostolate of the Laity). Our response to those gifts is to be open and welcome them

---

[728] *LG* 12.

[729] *CCC* 800. Here, the document cites 1 Cor 13.

> with gratitude and use them for the good of one another and the upbuilding of the church.[730]

Indeed, the Church affirms that these charisms, whether they be the more outstanding (that is, extraordinary) or the more simple and widely diffused, are graces of the Holy Spirit and they directly or indirectly benefit the Church.[731] As such, they are to be readily accepted with gratitude and consolation by the persons to whom they are bestowed and by all the members of the Church because they are perfectly suited to and useful for the renewal and building up of the Church, for the good of men, and for the needs of the world.[732]

Furthermore, the Church teaches that the faithful should not seek after the extraordinary charisms or look for profit in their use. Additionally, she maintains that "discernment of the charisms" is extremely necessary at all times. They ought to be referred and submitted to the shepherds or the leadership of the Church. But then, the role of these leaders is not to extinguish the fire of the Holy Spirit by preventing the use of the spiritual gifts. Rather, they are to test the Spirit behind them to establish their authenticity and then promote what is good in the best interest of the Church and the common good.[733]

Specifically, for Pope Paul VI, it was unthinkable to attempt to extinguish the Spirit. Instead, he wanted believers to use their talents for God. On this he maintains, "Do not refuse to put your talents at the service of divine truth. Do not close your mind to the breath of the Holy Spirit."[734] More so, he emphasized the importance of the Holy Spirit in relation to the charisms. He was very much aware that these spiritual gifts were not activated and have remained dormant in the lives of many Catholics. He believed that they have potent energy that can renew the Church in the modern

[730] B. GALAN, *Spiritual Gifts…, op. cit.,* p. 2.

[731] Cf. *CCC* 799.

[732] Cf. *LG* 12; *CCC* 799-800.

[733] Cf. *LG* 12; *CCC* 801.

[734] POPE PAUL VI, "Address to Artists at the Closing of the Second Vatican Ecumenical Council," 8 December 1965.

world and make her come alive. But then, only the Holy Spirit can activate them in the faithful. According to him,

> The free breath of the Spirit, too, has come to awaken latent energies within the Church, to stir up dormant charisms and to infuse the sense of vitality and joy. It is the sense of vitality and joy that makes the Church youthful and relevant in every age and prompts her to proclaim joyously her external message to each new epoch.[735]

The Responsibility to Discover and Use Our Charisms

Saint Paul sees the charisms as something every Christian should desire. Advising the Christians in Corinth, he maintains, "Pursue love and strive [eagerly] for the spiritual gifts, and especially that you may prophesy" (1 Cor 14:1). Now, desiring or possessing the spiritual gifts is not enough. We have a responsibility to use them. As Benjamin puts it, "Spiritual gifts are not meant to be stored or publicized. They are meant to be used for the service of the body."[736]

Sadly, today it is normal to find Catholics who neither know their specific gifts nor desire to know and use them. The gifts are for others, the Body of Christ, the world, and the glory of God. Thus, the nonchalance of most Catholics or Christians not to desire or seek to discover and use them mirrors selfishness and ingratitude to God who generously bestows the gifts on us. When we fail to use these gifts, we do not only fail to glorify God but also we short-change others and rob the Church of her vitality and, thereby, impede the success of her mission. This is why it is very crucial to re-emphasize here that when God gives gifts to us, it is because

---

[735] POPE PAUL VI, International Conference on the Catholic Charismatic Renewal in Rome on the Feast of Pentecost, 1973. Cited in L. SUENENS, *A New Pentecost?* Translated by Francis Martin (New York, NY: The Seabury Press, Inc., 1971), p. 88. Leon Joseph Suenens is a cardinal in the Catholic Church. See also M. MALLETT, *The Now Word: Reflections on our Times,* "Charismatic? Part VI" in https://www.markmallett.com/blog/charismatic-part-iv/.

[736] B. GALAN, *Spiritual Gifts…, op. cit.,* p. 2.

they are essential to what he wants us to accomplish for him, that is, to promote the good of others and further his purpose for the Church and the world.

As a matter of fact, Scripture makes it abundantly clear in the Parable of the Talents that we all are responsible for the different talents and gifts we have received from God and will account for our stewardship someday (see Mt 25:14-30; Lk 19:11-27). So, we all have a sacred duty or responsibility to discover, develop, and use our specific charisms to fulfil the purpose or specific mission for which God gave them to us. We must always remember that the spiritual gifts we have received are both a right and a sacred duty for which we are accountable to him.

Helping Lay People Discover the Charisms

If lay people are expected to exercise their charisms in the Church and the world, then they must first know them.[737] Thus, as a significant part of lay formation, Church leaders should not merely teach lay people about the charismatic dimension of the Church. More so, they need to help them become more aware and open to the divine moves of the Spirit in their lives. They need to help them discover the natural talents and the charisms (i.e., spiritual gifts) they have received from God for the building up of the Church and for the common good. Additionally, they should help them develop these gifts and empower, encourage, and intentionally send them out to use them in their specific mission in the world.

As a matter of fact, Weddell believes that the principal task of the Church and her pastors in the area of lay formation is one of discernment.[738] She maintains that any preparation of the lay people that measures up to what can be called adequate and acceptable

---

[737] Also, the priests themselves need to be helped to discover, develop, and use their own charisms. If they are ignorant in this area, then they are not likely to be in a position to assist the lay faithful. This is a major area diocesan bishops, directors of vocations, and those involved with seminary formation need to look into seriously. Proper formation in this area will not only enhance the fruitfulness of priests in their pastoral work, but also, it will help to reduce abuses in the ministry.

[738] Cf. M. SWEENEY and S. WEDDELL, *The Parish: Mission or Maintenance…*, *op. cit.*, pp. 30, 33.

must necessarily include the "calling forth" of their spiritual gifts in order to be used for mission. According to her, "the mission of the Church and the needs of our world demand a new generation of pastoral leaders who do not only care for lay men and women, but also equip them for their mission"[739] and actually send them forth intentionally to do mission.

In light of this, the Church needs to create an enabling environment within the parishes that will challenge lay people to discover their talents and spiritual gifts and find excitement and fulfilment in using them under the guidance and supervision of their pastors and leaders. We need to motivate and lead everyone to make the critical paradigm shift from being a mere spiritual observer or spectator in the Church to being an active and fruitful spiritual player in the team of Christ—the Church.[740] In practice, this will make the Church more fully alive and healthy and extremely successful in her soul-winning mission.

The Holy Spirit, Church Authority, and the Charismatic Dimension of the Church

An inspiration I received in Arizona, United States, in 2016 was that, for the Church to keep her faithful from drifting away and also to build them up into a formidable force that can stand their ground anywhere and even educate other Christians and evangelize effectively, there is need for "a healthy marriage" between the Opus Dei and the charismatic renewal models of formation. Even though some people think that such a "marriage" is impracticable, I am strongly convinced that it is possible.

From my observation, the two models of formation have something significant to offer us in the formation of a well-informed, committed, and vibrant faithful. To be candid, they both have their strengths and, more so, each has something to offer the other. Based on my critical appraisal of Christianity in the world of today,

---

[739] S. WEDDELL, *Making Disciples, Equipping Apostles: The Parish as a House of Formation for Adult Catholics* (Colorado Springs, CO: The Catherine of Siena Institute, 2001), p. 35.

[740] The description of the Church as "the team of Christ" is borrowed from Jim Putman and others.

especially in Africa, I consider bringing together the positive elements in these two models to create a new model of formation for the faithful as a wonderful path to explore.

Among other things, the Opus Dei model will help ground Catholics in the teachings of the Church and the sacraments, while the charismatic model will expose them to regular Bible study as a culture, greater openness to the Holy Spirit, and will help them to discover, develop, and use their God-given charismatic gifts. In a nutshell, arming the lay faithful in particular in this way will mean that no other Christian group or non-Christian groups will be able to intimidate them and lead them out of the Church since they will most likely not have anything new to tell them. More importantly, leading our people to an experiential knowledge of God through Christ and in the Holy Spirit and thus to intimacy with the Godhead will move them away from a "sheer religiosity"[741] to something more—authentic spiritual life. In all, this new experience of the faith will add to their excitement and commitment to Christ and bring more vitality to the Church in the area of mission and holiness. This brings us to the two channels of grace in the Church.

Actually, the Catholic Church has two dimensions, namely, the hierarchic or institutional dimension and the charismatic dimension. According to the Constitution on the Church from the Second Vatican Council, the Holy Spirit dwells in the Church and in the hearts of the faithful as in a temple.[742] "Guiding her [the Church] into all truth and uniting her in communion and service, he bestows upon her various gifts, both hierarchic and charismatic, and adorns her with the fruit of her grace."[743] Speaking further, the Constitution declares that,

> It is not only through the sacraments and the ministries of the Church that the Holy Spirit sanctifies and leads the people of God and enriches it with his virtues, but,

---

[741] By "sheer religiosity" we mean a situation whereby an individual observes all the externals of religion while indeed he has no "personal relationship or communion with God" or his heart is far from God as Jesus told some of the Jews in Mark 7:6.

[742] *LG* 4.

[743] *Ibid.*

> allotting his gifts to everyone according as He wills, [1 Cor 12:11] He distributes special graces among the faithful of every rank. By these gifts he makes them fit and ready to undertake various tasks and offices which contribute toward the renewal and building up of the Church....[744]

In his book, *Sober Intoxication of the Spirit*, Raniero Cantalamessa cites the redemptive sacrifice of Christ on the Cross as the main centre of grace.[745] Then he talks about the two channels or directions of grace in the Church which flow from this centre and through which God waters and nourishes his Church.[746] The first, which comes from the top downward, is the hierarchic dimension and the second, which moves from the bottom upward, is the hierarchic dimension.

The first dimension focuses on the sacraments, while the second focuses on the charisms or spiritual gifts of the Holy Spirit by which he gives grace to every member of the Church for the good and sanctification of all.[747] Speaking of these two channels, Pope Saint John Paul II maintains that both are co-essential. To put it in his exact words,

> Both are co-essential to the divine constitution of the Church founded by Jesus, because they both help to make the mystery of Christ and his saving work present in the world. Together they aim at renewing in their own ways the self-awareness of the Church, which in a certain sense can be called a "movement" herself, since she is the realization in time and space of the Father's sending of his Son in the power of the Holy Spirit.[748]

---

[744] *LG* 12.

[745] R. CANTALAMESSA, *Sober Intoxication of the Spirit..., op. cit.,* p. 61. Father Raniero Cantalamessa is the preacher to the papal household, beginning with Pope Saint John Paul II to Pope Francis.

[746] *Ibid.,* pp. 61-63.

[747] *Ibid.,* p. 62.

[748] POPE JOHN PAUL II, *Message to the Participants of the World Congress of Ecclesial Movements Promoted by the Pontifical Council for the Laity,* (27 May 1998, no. 5: *Insegnamenti* 21/1 (1998), 1065; See also CONGREGATION FOR THE DOCTRINE OF THE FAITH, Letter

Thus, Cantalamessa asserts that "If the sacraments are the established outlets of grace," we can say that, "the charisms are the surprise outlets of grace and of the Holy Spirit."[749] On the basis of all this, Father Cantalamessa asserts that, if we are to have the "complete Church," then these two channels of grace must be present, that is, accessible to all. According to him,

> The complete Church—the living organism that is watered and given life by the Holy Spirit—is the combination of these two channels or the result of these two directions of grace. Sacraments are the gifts given to all for each one's use, while the charisms are gifts to each one for the use of all. The sacraments are gifts given to the Church as a whole to sanctify the individuals; charisms are gifts given to individuals to sanctify the whole Church.[750]

Even many years after the Second Vatican Council, experience still shows that most Catholics are only familiar with one dimension of the Church, that is, the hierarchic dimension which the sacraments represent. The vast majority of Catholics, including priests, are not conversant with the teaching of the Council regarding the charismatic dimension.[751] No doubt, this has a very serious implication for the Church and her mission in the sense that most lay people today continue to act as mere consumers of the ministry of the priests without realizing their own giftedness and special calling to participate actively in the mission of the Church. Commenting on the negative implication of this reality to the missionary Church, Cantalamessa laments,

---

Iuvenescit Ecclesia to the Bishops of the Catholic Church Regarding the Relationship Between Hierarchical and Charismatic Gifts in the Life and the Mission of the Church, no. II, 10.

[749] R. CANTALAMESSA, *Sober Intoxication of the Spirit…, op. cit.,* p. 62.

[750] *Ibid.*

[751] Most people, including priests themselves, are often lost each time we bring up this topic and many do not appear to be too interested because they think that the whole idea is foreign to Catholic teaching and practice.

> It is easy to see, then, what a loss it would be for the Church if, at a certain point, it decided to do without one or the other of the two channels—to forego either the sacraments or the charisms, that is, either the Spirit who descends from on high or the Spirit who is diffused throughout the Church. Unfortunately, this has happened in the Church, at least on the practical level if not in principle.[752]

The critical point in this statement which we must not skim over is that the Church stands to lose if she sacrifices any particular one of these channels of grace. Ignorance is always bad, while knowledge is good because it can transform our mindsets or worldviews. Put differently, contact with truth changes our perception if we maintain an open disposition.

If the Dogmatic Constitution on the Church, *Lumen Gentium,* teaches that the Church has two dimensions and Pope Saint John Paul II maintains that they are co-essential, then we need to pay attention to them. In fact, one of the ways we can reverse the drift of Catholics from the Church and at the same time build a very vibrant, mission conscious, and more progressive Church is to re-educate both the clergy and the entire lay people in this area and intentionally promote the charismatic dimension of the Church with great intensity and zeal. This way, we will be able to transform the teeming population of lay people in the Church into a vibrant, passionate, and committed army for Christ who can engage in active evangelization or ministry everywhere as a matter of intentionality.[753]

---

[752] R. CANTALAMESSA, *Sober Intoxication of the Spirit..., op. cit.,* p. 62.

[753] The point here is not that the charisms alone will do the magic, but that we need to bring both the sacraments and charisms together to achieve our goal. Our mission involves both proclamation and witness, but it also includes the demonstration of the presence, mercy, and power of God as the Holy Spirit permits or uses us as his instruments. In a nutshell, powerful evangelism is still needed in today's secular and faithless world to demonstrate the presence of God and lead people to a life-changing encounter with Christ.

My Final Word: The Holy Spirit

In the light of all we have said so far, my final word in this book is the Holy Spirit. More precisely, it is that we all—the hierarchy, the clergy, and lay people—need to step down from being in-charge of the affairs of the Church and yield control to the Holy Spirit. In practice, we need to, as a matter of absolute urgency, handover the Church back to the Holy Spirit and at the same time intentionally promote the charismatic dimension of the Church in addition to the hierarchic dimension. This is necessary so as to have what Cantalamessa rightly describes as "the complete Church." Claiming that the Holy Spirit is in-charge of the Church and her mission, when in actual fact this is only true in principle but not in practice all the time, is tantamount to a serious deceit in those who do not make effort to have it so.

Although Christ appointed human leaders for his Church, Christ is the head and the Holy Spirit is the source of the Church's life, without whom we, our human leaders inclusive, cannot do much if anything at all. Jesus knew exactly what he was doing when he told his Apostles that he will give them another Advocate or Helper like himself (see Jn 14:16; 16:7-8; cf. Mt 28:20).[754] He equally knew what he was doing when he told them to wait in Jerusalem until they receive the Holy Spirit (see Lk 24:45-49; Acts 1:4-5, 8). He knew that, on their own, they were not equal to the missionary task he entrusted to them.

On our own, we too, no matter how knowledgeable and talented we are, can never be equal to the same task or even the demands of the Christian life. The Holy Spirit, and not any human person, is the principal agent of the Church's mission of evangelization. He alone can convert and transform the hearts of men and make our evangelical works fruitful. We need to be Spirit-filled and Spirit-led and this entails yielding control of our lives to the Holy Spirit and allowing him to be in-charge of the Church both in principle and

[754] The way Jesus fulfilled the promise in Matthew 28:20 to be with his disciples after his ascension into heaven was through the Holy Spirit. It is in the same way that he is with us today. So, to cut off the Holy Spirit in practice is to cut off our communion with Christ in which case we put ourselves in-charge of the Church in practice.

in practice. Like the infant Church of Jerusalem, we all (especially the leaders of the Church) must rediscover the place of the Holy Spirit in practice and give him a chance to lead the Church and do his work.

Commenting on this very critical issue, Father Cantalamessa maintains, the whole Church in its human dimension needs to undergo a real Copernican revolution in order to experience a genuine spiritual renewal.[755] For this to happen, he maintains that God is man's satellite and we need to give power back to him. To put in his exact words,

> However, the Word of God declares, "We need to give the power back to God" (see Psalm 68:35) because the "power belongs to God" (Psalm 62:11). That is the trumpet call! For too long we have usurped God's power, managing it as though it were ours, acting as though it were up to us to govern the power of God. Instead, we need to revolve around the sun. That's the Copernican revolution I'm talking about. Through that kind of revolution, we recognize simply, that without the Holy Spirit we can do nothing. We cannot even say [in all sincerity and by our lives], "Jesus is Lord" (see 1 Corinthians 12:3).[756]

Still, on the importance of the Holy Spirit, a major point we need to note with critical emphasis is that he is indispensable in the life of the Church and the Christian in all ramifications. He is indispensable as far as true worship of God is concerned. Jesus reminds us that God is Spirit and the true worshippers worship him in spirit and truth (cf. Jn 4:23-24). Now, it is the Spirit who connects us to Christ. So, without him, our worship may appear "robust" and enjoyable, but it certainly cannot go beyond mere mechanical "worship" that can neither glorify nor please God nor transform our lives as worshippers. Similarly, we may receive all the sacraments in the Church and continue to attend Mass regularly, but without the Holy Spirit we cannot experience the inner transformation that true worship brings or be fruitful in the Christian life and mission.

---

[755] R. CANTALAMESSA, *Sober Intoxication of the Spirit...,op. cit.,* p. 40.

[756] *Ibid.,* pp. 40-41. The emphasis here is mine.

Again, our deep and beautiful theology, our wonderful doctrines and even the richest catechism we have may cause people to marvel, but without the action of the Holy Spirit all will end in sheer religiosity, not practical Christianity or authentic spirituality. Again, without the Holy Spirit, we can only know about the Father and Jesus intellectually, but we can never know them experientially in a life-transforming way or enjoy an intimate loving relationship with them.[757] Speaking on this from his own personal experience, Cantalamessa states that,

> He [Jesus Christ] is no longer just a set of theses and dogmas....no longer just an object of worship and remembrance but a living reality in the Spirit. The Holy Spirit not only brings Jesus to life in believers, but also (as confirmed by the *Catechism of the Catholic Church*) gives them charisms (gratuitous gifts) for the building up of the Church.[758]

To buttress what he is saying we only need to look at the life of the disciples before and after they received the Holy Spirit at Pentecost. As we pointed out earlier in this chapter, their perception of Jesus changed most significantly after this life-transforming spiritual experience. The Holy Spirit gave them a deeper understanding of the person of Jesus and his mission. Pope Paul VI understood all this and when he was asked the greatest need of the Church in the modern world, he simply declared, "the Holy Spirit." According to him,

> More than once we have asked ourselves what the greatest needs of the Church are...what is the primary and ultimate need of our beloved and holy Church? We must say it with holy fear because as you know, this concerns the mystery of the Church, her life: this need is the Spirit...

---

[757] Cf. *CCC* 684 and 688. The Catechism states that it is the Holy Spirit who first awakens faith in us and communicates the life of God to men, a new life which involves knowing God and Jesus Christ whom he sent.

[758] R. CANTALAMESSA, in "The Catholic Charismatic Renewal: A Current of Grace for the Whole Church." See https://en./m.wikipedia.org. Retrieved 21-12-2019. Here, he also quotes *CCC* 2003.

> the Church needs her eternal Pentecost; she needs fire in her heart, words on her lips, a glance that is prophetic.[759]

Stressing this further he maintains that, "The Church needs the Spirit, the Holy Spirit. He it is who animates and sanctifies the Church. He is her divine breath, the wind in her sails, the principle of her unity, the inner source of her light and strength.... This is what the Church needs; she needs the Holy Spirit.... So let all of us ever say to him, 'Come.'"[760] Before him, Pope John XXIII knew this secret to renewal and vitality in the Church and world and was open to the Holy Spirit. Asking God for a new Pentecost, he prayed, "Renew your wonders in our day, as by a new Pentecost...."[761] It was clear to him that only the Spirit of God can truly renew humanity and the Church and make our life on earth more meaningful, peaceful, and fulfilling.

Even today, the Holy Spirit remains the greatest need of our Church and a world immersed in the crisis of neo-atheism and secular humanism on a scale never known before.[762] In reference to this tsunami of secular influence sweeping across the cultural landscape, Cardinal Donald Wuerl once remarked that, "It's almost as if a tsunami of secularism washed across Western Europe and, when it receded, it took with it all of those foundational concepts: family, marriage, right and wrong, common good, objective order...."[763] To resolve this crisis in the world and the Church we

---

[759] POPE SAINT PAUL VI, General Audience, November 29, 1972; See also CHRIST THE KING PARISH, "Parish Mission – A New Pentecost for a New Evangelization: Activating the Laity," March 21, 2014.

[760] POPE PAUL VI, General Audience, November 29, 1972.

[761] POPE JOHN XXIII, Apostolic Constitution *Humanae Salutis* (HS), December 25, 1961. It was with this Apostolic Constitution, *Humanae Salutis,* that Pope John XXIII solemnly convoked the Second Vatican Ecumenical Council on Christmas Day, 25 December 1961. See also CHRIST THE KING PARISH, "Parish Mission..., *op. cit.*

[762] Cf. M. HEALY, "Lectio: Evangelization and the Acts of the Apostles..., *op. cit.*

[763] CARDINAL WUERL, "Synod strives to turn back 'tsunami of secularism.'" Cited in F. ROCCA, *Catholic News Service* (CNS) of 10/04/2012; Also cited in M. HEALY, "Lectio: Evangelization and the Acts of the

need a tsunami of the Holy Spirit for any meaningful spiritual renewal or rebirth to occur.

Thus, if there is one thing we cannot overemphasize in this work, it is the fact that, as a Church and as individual Christians, we need the Holy Spirit more than anything else in the whole world. So, as a matter of necessity and urgency, let us step down in humility and give power back to God by yielding control of our lives and the Church to the Holy Spirit.

PRAYER: COME HOLY SPIRIT

Come Holy Spirit, fill the hearts of your faithful and kindle in them the fire of your love. Send forth your Spirit and they shall be created. And You shall renew the face of the earth. (*Let us pray*): O, God, who by the light of the Holy Spirit, did instruct the hearts of the faithful, grant that by the same Holy Spirit we may be truly wise and ever enjoy His consolations. Through Christ Our Lord, Amen.

Apostles…, *op. cit.*

About the Author

Paschal John Chibuzo Nwaezeapu is a priest of the Catholic Archdiocese of Lagos, Nigeria. He studied Philosophy and Theology, and specialised in Bioethics at *Universita Regina Apostolorum* in Rome. Although not a trained missiologist, Msgr. Nwaezeapu worked in seven parishes and acquired enormous pastoral experience during this time. He is the author of *Bioethics: Childlessness and Artificial Reproductive Technologies?!* (2005) as well as an enlarged edition in 2011, *When Does the Human Person Begin?* (2007), *When Salt Loses Its Saltiness* (2012), and *Novena for Difficult Temporal and Spiritual Cases* (2018).

About Leonine Publishers

Leonine Publishers LLC makes fine Catholic literature available to Catholics throughout the English-speaking world. Leonine Publishers offers an innovative "hybrid" approach to book publication that helps authors as well as readers. Please visit our web site at www.leoninepublishers.com to learn more about us. Browse our online bookstore to find more solid Catholic titles to uplift, challenge, and inspire.

Our patron and namesake is Pope Leo XIII, a prudent, yet uncompromising pope during the stormy years at the close of the 19th century. Please join us as we ask his intercession for our family of readers and authors.

www.ingramcontent.com/pod-product-compliance
Lightning Source LLC
LaVergne TN
LVHW010050110826
845155LV00028B/273

* 9 7 8 1 9 4 2 1 9 0 7 4 5 *